Neoliberalism and Unlawful Governance

Neoliberalism and Unlawful Governance

The Crisis of Democratic Rights

Guillermina Seri

UNIVERSITY OF MICHIGAN PRESS

Ann Arbor

Published in the United States of America by the
University of Michigan Press
First published February 2026

A CIP catalog record for this book is available from the British Library.

Library of Congress Cataloging-in-Publication data has been applied for.

ISBN 978-0-472-07793-9 (hardcover : alk. paper)
ISBN 978-0-472-05793-1 (paper : alk. paper)
ISBN 978-0-472-90571-3 (open access ebook)

DOI: https://doi.org/10.3998/mpub.14493839

The University of Michigan Press's open access publishing program is made possible thanks to additional funding from the University of Michigan Office of the Provost and the generous support of contributing libraries.

The authorized representative in the EU for product safety and compliance is Easy Access System Europe, Mustamäe tee 50, 10621 Tallinn, Estonia, gpsr.requests@easproject.com

Cover image: Photo courtesy iStock.com/Fernando Podolski.

To Maite, Martín, Manuel, and María

Contents

Digital materials related to this title can be found on
the Fulcrum platform via the following citable URL:
https://doi.org/10.3998/mpub.14493839

List of Figures

Acknowledgments

This book has been in the making for a long time. The idea started taking shape as I found myself puzzled by overlaps and parallels between the forms of state power into which those studying the police, security, and emergency politics kept running. While it seemed as if different literatures—and those cultivating them—didn't connect, some of the most provocative and productive political theorists—from Michel Foucault to Giorgio Agamben—kept raising questions that bring exceptional powers, on display in governing us, together.

As a native of Argentina, marked by the darkest legacies of the 1976–83 military dictatorship and connected hope about democratic life, the normalization of state abuses and exclusions continues to shock me. Their persistence led me to study the police, policies of (in)security, and related emergency practices in view of the extraordinary faculties that those in charge exercise in selecting between deserving and underserving lives.

Another central piece in this puzzle is the rise of a form of governmental rationality presided over by the logic of unrestricted markets. First imposed through a bloody military coup in Chile in 1973, the unhinged form of capitalism known as neoliberalism has taken over our world. Neoliberal reason of state, the book argues, has colonized institutions and spaces that should serve the people instead.

What can neoliberal reason and its governmental apparatuses tell us about the ongoing crisis of democracy? This is the main question I tackle here, with chapters mapping what I see as the main pieces of this puzzle.

After exploring the expansion of neoliberalism and its unlawful governmentalities as well as the spectacular resources normalizing them, I revisit people's ways of reaffirming and advancing democracy, rights, and life. As I progress, the meaning of democratic rights and their foundation gain prominence, to occupy the center toward the end. Along these lines, this book makes an intervention in critical conversations on neoliberalism and the persistence of state abuses alongside an expanded concept of emergency politics. Moreover, I am puzzled by the crisis of democracy and its simultaneous vibrancy in the streets in ways that seem to point toward the commons—including as a potential foundation for rights.

For over a decade, I presented versions of chapters and sections at various conferences. Sharing my work at meetings of the American Political Science Association, the Western Political Science Association, and the Latin American Studies Associations was key. So was attending the International Political Studies Association and the Association for Political Theory annual meetings. Other meaningful venues included panels at the Law & Society Association, the Sociedad Argentina de Análisis Político, and the Asociación Latinoamericana de Análisis Político. Smaller, focused meetings such as the Insecurity Conference in Milwaukee, the Security, Accumulation, Pacification conference in Salento, a Police Science in the 21st Century and an Anti-Security conference at Carleton University. Finally, an invited talk at the Center for Latin American Studies at the University of Florida offered an exceptional opportunity to receive comments early in this project. I am most grateful and indebted to the discussants at those conference panels, as well as to this book's anonymous reviewers and to all who shared criticisms and suggestions.

Along this journey, I have a number of people to thank, starting with friends and coauthors, including Jinee Lokaneeta, Mary Rose Kubal, Michelle Bonner, Dave Siegel, Paulo Ravecca, and Diego Rossello. But I would not be here without the most generous friendship and support of colleagues like Lori Marso or Çiğdem Çıdam. I have also been gifted to work with an exceptional group of colleagues in the Department of Political Science at Union College. Our department runs a colloquium, and I benefited from generous and challenging comments and criticisms on earlier versions of the introduction and chapter 2. I appreciate my colleagues' attentive feedback and their support and collegiality, every day.

Beyond the department, I need to thank my institution, Union College, for the sustained support for research, including mini-sabbaticals, conference travel, and research funds as well as research assistant support. Thanks to these institutional channels, spending a semester at NYU with a Faculty Resource Network fellowship was key to jump-start this book and a second fellowship to advance with revisions.

I also have Paulo Ravecca and Marcela Schenck, with whom we worked together at LASA Culture, Power, and Politics section to thank, as well as the Anti-Security Collective, with whom I have had some of the most challenging and stimulating exchanges. And to Karin, for support.

The research supporting this study benefited from the assistance of several students, all of whom I want to thank. Special gratitude goes to Bridgit, Ty, Marina, and Jenna, whose fantastic contributions were decisive to the progress of this book.

Teaching has been a great inspiration, as it has been an ongoing dialogue with my students. Whether in a seminar on the Lives of Sovereigns or neoliberalism, as when exploring populism or the politics of extraction, working together in the classroom or on their senior thesis has offered inspiration and incredible opportunities to keep asking questions and learn.

Finally, I want to thank Madison Allums, the editor from the University of Michigan Press who trusted this project, for her work, insight, enthusiasm, and generous support, as well as Haley Winkle, Delilah McCrea, Marcia LaBrenz, John Raymond, and Danielle Coty-Fattal, from the press, for the brilliant editorial work and dedication.

In closing, my gratitude goes to Manu and María, and to our expanding family.

1 | Introduction

Neoliberal Reason and Democracy's Crises

"I do not know about human rights. What is that?," General Augusto Pinochet sarcastically quipped in 1995. By then the army's chief in democratic Chile, Pinochet earned iconic dictator status after his September 11, 1973, coup and air bombing of La Moneda government palace. The coup ended the life of President Salvador Allende, seven decades of democracy, and the first democratically elected socialist government. In the following days, reports of torture accompanied images of Santiago's Nacional soccer stadium turned into an open-air death camp. The Pinochet-led military Junta suspended the Constitution, ordered the burning of books, banned unions, political parties, and elections, and installed military officials to head universities. "A complex hierarchy of states of exception" was imposed, Peter Winn notes, as the military in power suspended constitutional guarantees and declared a domestic war.[1]

Besides these measures, the Chilean coup started a governing experiment, the first of its kind. It did so by subjecting the entirety of life to market principles "with the blessing and support of the military junta headed by General Pinochet," as acknowledged by Milton Friedman. It was the full launching of neoliberalism, based on the belief in the superiority of "market mechanisms to solve most of society's problems and needs," as Sebastian Edwards put it. Still, in scholarly discussions, it is almost customary by now to refer to neoliberalism's multiple meanings and debates surrounding the concept.[2]

Over the years, the end of neoliberalism has been repeatedly proclaimed. In the Global South, since the 1990s, and in the Global North, following the 2008 financial crisis, mass protests and political movements brought to power governments—such as those of Latin America's "Pink Tide"—that pledged to leave neoliberalism behind.

Edwards argues that the agreement to reform the Chilean constitution following the 2019 mass protests "marked the beginning of the end of the neoliberal experiment." A few months later, the COVID-19 pandemic disrupted global supply chains and exposed the hollowed-out state institutions left by decades of neoliberal policies, with deadly consequences. At the time, policies such as free, mandated vaccinations, subsidies to businesses, and expanded health and social programs led many to declare the end of the neoliberal era.[3]

"The sun has set on neoliberalism," Louis Menand wrote in 2023 in the *New Yorker*, describing the neomercantilist approach of "Bidenomics" and its "immense" government spending. In the United States, he argued, "the language of the market has lost its magic." As in this case, when describing the end of neoliberalism, voices including Nobel laureate Joseph Stiglitz point to the US rise of trade tariffs and the delinking of once fully globalized industries as signs of "free market" decline. In a video, Robert Reich endorsed the notion that a forty-five-year-old "Neoliberal Consensus" was reaching an end, as he asserted "Joe Biden is changing it." Once again, claims that "neoliberalism itself is definitely and finally dying"[4] resurfaced as President Trump introduced trade tariffs in April 2025.

Reports of neoliberalism's demise have been greatly exaggerated. Decades of deregulation, privatization, debt, and concessions to foreign corporations have deeply reshaped societies, labor conditions, markets, and ecosystems in ways that are not easy to reverse. These conditions enabled INV Metals, a Canadian mining company, to threaten Ecuador with legal action and challenge the people's sovereignty after citizens in Cuenca voted to ban mining near their water supplies. Moreover, the belief that to improve people's well-being and resources "the neoliberal formula" of drawing on "incentives and competition in the private sector . . . remains the best one that humanity has so far devised," as Anne Krueger, the former head of the World Bank put it, still has many fans.[5]

Reducing neoliberalism to lower trade tariffs suggests how ingrained and taken for granted its main components are in our common sense. The term "neoliberalism" was introduced at the 1938 Walter Lippman colloquium, in Paris, and discussed by Milton Friedman in 1951. It resurfaced decades later in the study of Latin America's authoritarian experiments with a critical tone. In the words of Friedman, neoliberalism shares the classical liberal focus on the individual but replaces laissez-faire with "the goal of the competitive order." Market competition, he claims, is crucial to guaranteeing freedom, and markets are always most effective at addressing every kind of problem. Housing, schools, healthcare, pensions, roads, safety, water, seeds, personal communication, and even governing, Friedman believes, can be best managed through markets. Under Pinochet, Chile was "the first country in the world" to fully embrace such radical market policies, Hoover Institution professors Robert Packenham and William Ratliff acknowledge. The Chileans paid a hefty price for all that pioneering, though.[6]

Neoliberalism—at once a set of policies, a capitalist phase, and a form of political reason—is based on the belief that for every conceivable problem a market solution is always best. Understanding neoliberalism as the current shape capital has taken, I treat it as a form of rationality that sees markets as the highest type of human institution and promotes dealing with all our main problems, individual and collective, through them. Once this rationality gains a governmental quality, it reaches out everywhere and transforms our lives—and planet—in particularly insidious ways. As the most distilled expression of the logic of capital, neoliberalism manifests in plural modalities and adapts and coexists with a variety of actors, conditions, and scenarios.

It is puzzling to hear proclamations about the end of neoliberalism when the commodification of additional layers and dimensions of life—human and nonhuman—and their subjection to markets keeps expanding.

In the following chapters, I show how neoliberal reason intensifies many preexistent problems and generates new ones—which I approach with a focus on democracy, rights, and fundamental disputes about our shared horizon. This book examines the ways in which the expansion of neoliberal governmental rationality impacts democratic politics, people's rights, and life while exploring an alternative foundation for rights and democratic politics beyond neoliberalism. Radically privileging markets, neoliberal reason not only disregards rights and democratic politics but also endangers life on Earth through a politics of extinction. This is the scenario against which the explorations in this book take place.[7]

But first we need to understand how we got here.[8] The Pinochet dictatorship introduced market-driven reforms "on the point of a bayonet," threatening even the lives of those spared repression, Andre Gunder Frank, his former student, writes in a letter to Friedman. Addressing the dark side of what his former mentor deemed "a miracle," Frank describes how the regime's brute force helped subject workers to conditions of "super-exploitation." Half of small farmers, Frank continues, were stripped of their properties. As the price of bread increased twentyfold, many lost access to essential services that privatizations turned into commodities. Telecommunications, education, utilities, social security, and health services were privatized, as the dictatorship gave the private ownership and commodification of water constitutional status. Notably, the dictatorship privatized the pension system, which President George W. Bush called to emulate in the US. By 1979, Pinochet's "seven modernizations" program ended collective bargaining and labor protections. In creating new markets, the dictatorship subsidized private investors' buying of undervalued public assets while forcing the public to assume the burden of the nationalized corporate debt.[9]

The dictatorship's violence and exceptional measures "profoundly transformed" Chilean society. In 1976, in an article in the *Nation*, Orlando Letelier, Salvador Allende's former minister, questioned those who praised the military dictatorship's "free market" policies while "pretending to reject the system of terror it requires to succeed." Three weeks later, Letelier was murdered in Washington, DC, along with his American driver, on the Chilean military's orders and with local support. If with varying degrees of "success," the Chilean and other neoliberal experiments from the 1970s could not "have been applied in any other way" than with support of state terror including torture and disappearances, Federico Glodowsky observes. Under the military's state of exception, market values infused all facets of life, first exposing its links to state violence and emergency rule.[10]

By 1977, not just Chileans but two-thirds of Latin Americans, 110 million people, lived under some form of a state of siege while the other 112 million were in similar conditions under their military's "institutional acts" in Brazil. "We did not have any rights, and if any theoretically was left to us, we did not have anyone before whom to make it count," Guillermo O'Donnell recalls, writing in 1979 from Buenos Aires. Militarized zones, curfews, road controls, and soldiers pointing machine guns at family members for car and ID checks became routine. Step by step, so did the most unusual reports of people going missing in classrooms, cafes, or holiday resorts. With the oddest stories circulating, South American cities brought the darkest twists of magical realism to life.[11]

Meanwhile, in Santiago, Pinochet entrusted policies to the "Chicago Boys," University of Chicago Chilean alumni trained in neoclassical economics under a program that stood as "an integral part" of US anticommunist initiatives. Their report *El ladrillo*, "the brick," called for radical market-driven reforms. Privatizing services and deregulating finances were among the trademark neoliberal policies imposed through "shock treatment," the method Friedman urged Pinochet to adopt. Friedrich Hayek went further in justifying Chile's dictatorship. "At times it is necessary for a country to have, for a time, some form or other of dictatorial power. As you will understand, it is possible for a dictator to govern in a liberal way," he observed during his second trip to Chile in 1981.[12]

Hayek's open defense of Pinochet and his and Friedman's meetings with the Chilean dictator still make many uncomfortable. As much as his fans try to prove that there is a misunderstanding, Hayek's sympathy for Pinochet seems consistent with his ideas about markets, emergency politics, and reason of state. Only within capitalism "is democracy possible," Hayek asserts. Democracy, he adds, is "essentially a means, a utilitarian device" to keep peace and freedom, a mere instrument he believes often fails. In Hayek's view, competitive markets are the engine of freedom, and he makes it clear that markets must be protected at any cost. Exposing the "unacknowledged relationship" between violence and capital and the "marriage" between state terror and neoliberalism, to borrow from Corey Robin, Hayek and Friedman's words betray the neoliberal authoritarian core.[13]

In Chile, under military rule, "market reason metamorphosed into reason of state," as Arnol Kremer puts it. Protecting and expanding markets redefined state priorities. As it progresses, neoliberal reason, to borrow from John Bellamy Foster, "embed[s] the state in capitalist market relations" as it shrinks its role in social reproduction into promoting capital alone. In its attempt to make capitalism "absolute," neoliberalism unleashes the "extreme human and ecological destructiveness" distinctive of our times.[14]

While the Chilean military is long gone, the neoliberal takeover of governments and life is not. Our subjection to markets makes us taste what the Chileans first experienced. Since 1980, the world's GDP has grown from $11.4 trillion to $106 trillion, transforming the planet. Amid what Isabel Ortiz and Matthew Cummins characterize as "staggering" global income inequality, cuts to healthcare, social programs, and schools affected three-quarters of the world's population and are expected to reach at least 130 countries in 2024. Countries from Belgium, France, and Italy to Ecuador continue to embrace—by now, normalized—austerity agendas, often imposing unpopular measures by executive decree, as in France in 2024.[15]

By 1990, the Chilean neoliberal "miracle" was celebrated internationally. "Most countries of Latin America; North America; Western, Central, and Eastern Europe; China; India; Russia and its former republics; much of Africa; and many other places around the world ha[d] followed the Chilean lead," Packenham and Ratliff approvingly reported. Indeed, as a response to the crisis of Keynesian, regulated capitalism, neoliberalism gained global currency.[16]

The Pinochet era experiment left about 40,000 victims of torture, 200,000 exiles, and 3,000 killed and "disappeared," all justified in the name of fighting communism. With state terror in the background, the Chilean dictatorship forced the market into the entirety of people's lives, as over 40 percent of the population fell into poverty. Moreover, Pinochet's 1980 Constitution inscribed neoliberalism at the heart of the Chilean legal system, transforming life into what Víctor Orellana Calderón describes as "a series of market choices." Uniquely, the Constitution made Chile the only country to fully privatize water, while the principle of subsidiarity of the state made healthcare or education accessible through private companies. Only when the provision of public goods is not profitable may the state provide them. The democratic transition did not challenge these rules, as the Concertación coalition further opened Chile to global capital and conducted more privatizations.[17]

As in Chile, by the early 2000s, the "reasonably democratic" conditions that political scientist Guillermo O'Donnell longed for when describing life under military rule in 1970s Buenos Aires were becoming the norm. Around the world, millions of people regained political voice and recognition and sought to build or rebuild democracies. Political scientists showed that democratic governments surpassed nondemocracies for the first time in history, and their numbers continued to rise. Elected governments pierced through Cold War authoritarianism in waves, first in Latin America and Eastern Europe. From thirty-six electoral democracies in 1974, the world went to ninety-four in 2011. Yet by that time, the early Chilean neoliberal shift that Jessica Whyte describes as one of "endless austerity" also reigned over the globe.[18]

Austerity policies pivot on reducing public deficits and expenditure through privatizations and cuts to public works and services. Deregulations, or eliminating labor, environmental, and safety standards, let capital move freely, as privatizations make essential goods into commodities. Austerity does not necessarily involve a lack of resources, which are "actively shifted away from the working people in favor of shareholders, the saving, investing elite," as Clara Mattei explains.[19]

By destroying jobs and social programs, austerity makes essential goods unavailable to many. First brutally imposed under military rule through state terror and emergency provisos in Chile, neoliberal austerity became normalized since the late 1970s after being adopted by the UK and the US. From there, through the alchemy of political and academic discourse, neoliberalism became treated as a defining facet of liberal democracies. Across countries, most notably in Chile, austerity came to stay.[20]

Aligning policies with the demands of markets and investors, neoliberalism came with shocks, emergency measures, authoritarian rulers, and abusive governmentalities. The neoliberal exceptions that Aihwa Ong describes as an "extraordinary departure in policy" and legal standards in response to market needs took roots beyond dictatorships. Democracy's neoliberal takeover hurts people, perhaps in less spectacular but no less consequential ways than the military dictatorships of the 1970s, including by abandoning too many into the most precarious conditions. Precarity, Judith Butler notes, defines a "politically induced" exposure to "injury, violence, and death" that leaves entire groups on their own to confront "disease, poverty, starvation, displacement, and vulnerability to violence" and state abuses. In so doing, precarity erodes living conditions and rights.[21]

On October 18, 2019, demonstrations placed Chile at the heart of a "year of global protests," when people in unprecedented numbers went into the streets across sixty-three countries demanding democratic rights and rejecting austerity. In the South American nation, a mass of protesters joined in after the repression of high school students who opposed rising subway fares. "We are at war against a powerful enemy, who is willing to use violence without any limits," President Sebastián Piñera stated in response to the protesters, as he declared a state of emergency in Santiago de Chile and sent 20,000 military personnel into the streets.[22]

The popular response was massive. "Chile woke up" and "We are not in a war" were written on a giant Chilean flag displayed during a 1.2 million people protest on October 25, the largest in Chilean history. A myriad of demands and slogans combined with street art as citizens continued mobilizing across the country. "It is not [the] 30 pesos [of the fare rise]; it is [the] 30 years [of austerity in democracy]," or "Until dignity becomes a habit," the slogans acknowledged deep-seated demands. The messages, displayed on placards as on Santiago's walls, inspired protesters' chants, graphics, and street art. These signs and voices expressed the "fundamental contradiction all over the world, between neoliberalism and democracy," Alexis Cortés writes, which excludes citizens into "sacrificial areas." Chilean protesters demanded dignity.[23]

Repression was brutal, with the killing of over 20 protesters, 5,500 arrests, and 2,000 wounded—including over 300 people deliberately hurt in their eyes by the police—plus cases of torture and sexual abuse. With graffiti and artwork reminding everyone that "violence is dying in a [hospital] waiting room," protesters denounced neoliberalism's violent face. Their struggles would continue until "living is worth it," they announced.[24]

Protesters demanded replacing the Constitution imposed by Pinochet's dictatorship with one in which "rights are above the free market." They questioned neoliberal policies and institutions that served "the same interests that nurture that shameful inequality," as Alia Trabucco writes.[25]

Neoliberalism did not die in Chile in 2019. But the Chilean protests exposed the dark truths behind the country's "miracle." As popular demands were muffled, political scientists introduced a new term, "autocratization," and mapped its rapid spread. In early 2020, a global pandemic entered people's lives and changed our world, infusing a sense of living in "a state of exception, in which normal rules, expectations, and social routines are altered," writes Paolo Gerbaudo. Worldwide, lockdowns and harsh policing made the number of protests shrink. By early 2025, eighty-eight countries were considered democratic, with democracies being outnumbered for the first time in two decades by nondemocracies. At the time, most people lived under authoritarian rule, and forty-five countries were moving toward autocracy, with consistent losses in media and academic freedoms, freedom of expression, assembly, movement, and free and fair elections or clear laws. Only nineteen countries were becoming more democratic—with Brazil accounting for roughly half the people involved. For the average person, the quality of democracy experienced in 2024 was back to 1985 levels.[26]

While we may be still mostly spared the spectacular military coups of the past, the erosion of democracy described by scholars such as Anna Lindberg and Staffan Lührmann is a cause for concern. Especially so as officials "gradually, but substantially" weaken norms and institutions "under a legal façade." Consider the US. Questioned for the persistent violence against African Americans and other groups, the country was ranked as a "flawed democracy" in 2016 and labeled a "non-democracy" in 2020. Reasons for the drop included weak legislative checks on the executive, the president's dismissal of "disloyal" officials and the "vilifying" of critics, added to the police's excessive use of force in protests, weakened citizen trust, and the January 6, 2021 insurrection.[27]

It is not just in the US. "A third wave of autocratization is here," Lührmann et al. note. With rights breaches and abuses typical of authoritarian regimes, experts and surveys converge in addressing democracy's ongoing "decay," "rupture," and even eventual "death." And as more countries turn authoritarian, and democracies are "no longer the majority," rights and freedoms dwindle in what Amnesty International characterized as a global human rights "rollback."[28]

Censorship, arbitrary arrests, brutal policing, forced displacements, torture, and killings, but also denying people access to schools or healthcare, or failing to protect those in danger during crises are all forms in which governments abuse, mistreat, or abandon their citizens. These practices may or may not technically violate the law, but in all cases they undermine fundamental rights and constitutional provisos, freedom, and life. As Johan Galtung showed, they involve violence, whether in direct forms—physical or psychological—or in structural and cultural variants, such as spreading through narratives that naturalize abuses. In their distinct ways, these forms of violence make migrants, minorities, the Indigenous, people with disabilities, or those experiencing poverty invisible, in such a way that excluding them seems compatible with liberal democracy.[29]

Whereas abusive, violent governmentalities are central to authoritarian regimes, the neoliberal subjection of collective life to markets has pushed narrow meanings of key political concepts. Milton Friedman, for example, assimilated human rights to property rights, and defined property as "the most basic of human rights and an essential foundation for other human rights." Alongside the assimilation of rights to property, neoliberalism hijacked the rule of law, democracy, and human rights to serve the expansion of markets.[30]

Thus wars advancing corporate agendas have been disguised as "democracy promotion" campaigns—as Wendy Brown discusses regarding the "Bremer Orders" brutally imposed in US-occupied Iraq. But neoliberal "wars" continue to be waged as well against the poor under the guise of fighting drugs or illegal immigration. Following multiple examples where we see the law used as an instrument "for disseminating neoliberal rationality," as Brown puts it, terms such as democracy or rights may sound bland, even empty. Disputing such distortions and their concealing of persistent breaches of law and state abuses, as well as the ongoing (neo)liberal enclosure of rights, is part of the purpose of this book.[31]

The persistence of state abuses at the clash of liberal democracy and neoliberalism guides my study. My focus developed from the shocking realization that police abuses and extrajudicial killings could plague democracies, from my native Argentina to neighboring Brazil and beyond. Their persistence led me to study the police, policies of (in)security, and emergency regimes. Besides destroying lives, abuses and exclusions undermine people's access to rights and democratic life. Worse, in targeting grassroots resistance to austerity, inequality, or policy neglect, unlawful governmentalities block alternatives and deprive us of the knowledge and resources to confront the major challenges of our times. As the neoliberal reason first taking over in Chile became widespread, the expansion of profits threatens social reproduction and lives.

Ultimately, the rationale behind persistent abuses and exclusions speaks of the (self)destructive turn linked to making the subordination of life to capital near absolute. This book expands on these questions. In a dialogue with political theory and interpretive epistemologies, drawing on news records and datasets, chapters tackle state abuses in democracies, resistance to abuses, and the struggle for rights—which I treat as a form of commons—in scenarios of neoliberal governmentality.

Michel Foucault defines governmentality as the "conduct of conduct," an art or craft made of techniques, knowledge, practices, and institutions to keep the population orderly. States, from this perspective, have no essence, nor can their existence be taken for granted outside the governmental configurations that make them a reality. The state, Foucault writes, results from a myriad governmental practices, "nothing else but the mobile effect of a regime of multiple governmentalities."

With this concept, he describes governing practices and the knowledge supporting them—in particular, political economy and security. In his 1979 *Birth of Biopolitics* lectures, the French thinker offers an original, insightful analysis of the neoliberal art of government. Neoliberalism, he notes, models the entire "exercise of political power . . . on the principles of a market economy." An economic rationale thus guides policies and the everyday governance of individuals. To effectively subject people to markets, this economicism takeover ultimately leads (back) to the idea that "total despotism is necessary," Foucault concludes. Like other points in his lectures, from reason of state's embracing market principles to a distinct neoliberal art of government, they were all visibly at play in Chile under Pinochet.[32]

By solely focusing on countries in the North Atlantic, however, Foucault did not acknowledge the rise of neoliberal reason in 1970s Chile. Had he done so, the "explicit link between the use and support of state terrorism and efforts to entrench neoliberalism" described by Ruth Blakeley would have been clear in his work—and likely influence political theory more broadly. An opportunity was lost to expose the salience of mass repression, torture chambers, and forced disappearances accompanying "really existing" neoliberal experiments. Violence is central, however, to the project of "creating society as an economic game and for policing the transgression of its rules," as Johanna Oksala puts it.[33]

Foucault's silence regarding Pinochet seems puzzling. By the time of his 1979 lectures, the Chilean military dictatorship's state terror and neoliberal policies had received plenty of international media coverage, including details about torture, forced disappearances, and Chile's murderous police state. In addition, Foucault was involved with human rights groups supporting political exiles. Why does he not mention Chile? Was his omission of the brutal South American neoliberal experiment somehow linked to being himself "enamored" with neoliberalism, as Daniel Zamora proposes? Or does it at least suggest Foucault's "strategic endorsement" of these ideas, as suggested by Michael Behrent?[34] Truly, in his lectures, Foucault somehow seems to buy into the mythical neoliberal trope of market competition. He might well have fallen for some enticing plural possibilities that later revealed their "trafficking in the naturalization of capitalism under the cover of difference," as Paulo Ravecca puts it. While not a neoliberal, as João Ferreira-Neto argues, Foucault may have found some potentially productive insights in revisiting the tradition as he developed a "critical ethos" committed to "the right of the governed."[35]

Definitively proving Foucault's allegiances may be difficult. Ultimately, what remains crucial are his seminal contributions to making the neoliberal "rationality intelligible," as Zamora observes, and his theorizing of neoliberalism as a form of governmental rationality. Still, several decades later, Foucault stands as "the critical figure who best captured the essence of neoliberalism almost the moment it rose to dominance," as Foster acknowledges.[36]

That the 1979 lectures earned praise from figures like Gary Becker and critics of neoliberalism alike speaks to Foucault's merits. A rigorous representation of the subject at hand is essential for a critique, which also demands revisiting the "assumptions, what kinds of familiar, unchallenged, unconsidered modes of thought," as Foucault puts it. This is exactly what his 1979 lectures do in his original and prescient analysis of neoliberal rationality. For the purpose of the present project, Foucault's insightful characterization of neoliberal reason as a governmental matrix and his quest for forms of rights that let us escape the traps of sovereignty, discipline, or biopolitical exclusions is what matters the most.

In this regard, if in his pioneer theorizing Foucault may not have noticed neoliberalism's links to the Chilean dictatorship, decades later, most of the literature in English still omits or only marginally mentions them. Only recently has this piece of the puzzle been acknowledged. Within this literature, Jessica Whyte's work stands alone in its engagement with the Chilean case. This matters, as the abusive governmentalities first on full display under Pinochet offer insight into the current erosion of rights, democracy, and life.

If my understanding is correct, unearthing the roots of current patterns of rights breaches and state abuses requires mapping the neoliberal project and its state. It was Foucault who set the basis for a critique of neoliberalism as a "contemporary economic orthodoxy guiding the particular 'raison d'état,'" as Adam Davidson-Harden writes. Indeed, behind state violence and exclusions lies a governmental rationale that, drawing on Foucault, I characterize as neoliberal reason of state. Addressing such abuses and exclusions pushes us to stare at "the other side of the looking glass" of politics, to borrow from John Bew, or to venture into the governmental "dark arts" of—a neoliberal—reason of state. This neoliberal reason and the state it produces, I contend, lie at the roots of the current democratic "decay," although this is just part of its all-encompassing destructiveness.[37]

This book has two parts. In the first half, chapters map institutional mechanisms and the governmental reason grounding emergency rule, securitization, and state abuses and exclusions in democracies. Examining these legitimizing practices is part of this inquiry. In the second part, chapters scrutinize instances under which people reclaim rights to then revisit the foundation of democratic rights, their limits, and potential. Roughly, the first three chapters focus on the conditions of life under the reign of (a neoliberal) reason of state, whereas the last two chapters venture into taking a glimpse at what may lie beyond. In engaging these questions, the book intervenes in connected debates on the crisis of democracy, violent neoliberal governmentalities, the role of security, police, and emergency regimes in perpetuating abuses and violence, and the possibilities of grassroots democratic initiatives to reclaim expansive rights. These possibilities are, of course, not a given, as the progress of neoliberal reason threatens us with collapse. In what follows, sections revisit neoliberal reason's conceptual and governmental underpinnings and their impact on— and tension with—rights and democracy.

Democracy and Neoliberal Reason

In his *Funeral Oration*, Pericles celebrates democracy alongside Athenian splendor. When power is in the hands of the "whole people," he observes, citizen voices shape life in common. The ancient ideal of rule by ordinary people, or by "anyone and everyone," as Jacques Rancière puts it, embraces a plurality of voices in constant renewal. Led by ordinary people from streets and squares, politics involves imagining and advancing new worlds. In this endeavor, democracy, to borrow from Ernesto Laclau and

Chantal Mouffe, strives to eliminate "relations of subordination and of inequalities." Governments "can give democracy more or less room," Rancière reminds us, according to how they address people's demands, equal voice, and rights. Still, democracy, as the ultimate expression of politics, consists of a series of moments ultimately irreducible to institutions, he contends.[38]

Rights are central to democratic life as they are to our lives. In the way of "social barriers," Karl Marx writes in *Capital*, rights protect people. In this sense, universal rights are the ultimate "rights of the demos," as Rancière notes. Allowing us to care for ourselves, our families, and communities, rights define the currency and lifeblood of democracy.[39]

"Neoliberals believe the entire world can be a market," Adam Kotsko observes. This belief system, often likened to a true faith, makes neoliberalism "an exemplary form of political theology." At its core lies an unshakable belief in markets' ability to advance wealth, well-being, and freedom. Yet market freedom often proves not to leave much room for rights and demands for rights.[40]

In a perspective that portrays competitive markets as the source of freedom and freedom as strictly individual, neoliberal governance brings "market logics into all areas of life," as Orellana Calderón puts it. In so doing, it replaces the deliberating demos with market experts and technocratic rule. All relationships are presented as economic, and good government as transforming additional areas of life into competitive markets while promoting private profit. In this perspective, not only are rights linked to property, as Friedman claims, but democracy is possible only in a "competitive system based on free disposal over private property," as Hayek puts it.[41]

With market-driven responses to all public matters, the state redefines subjectivities and politics in economic terms. Inequalities and exclusions multiply, and neoliberal policies condition—and corrode—the basis of democratic life. To borrow from Foucault, we can infer that, pivoting on the market, the (neo)liberal state intensifies and refines reason of state.[42]

The claim may seem counterintuitive. Linking freedom-loving neoliberals to reason of state principles may sound odd. After all, liberal demands for individual rights and freedoms fueled revolutions against absolutism and its political reason. And yet, in his extensive study Thomas Poole shows that the doctrine, if it is anachronistic in evoking bygone images of intrigue and palatial splendor, it has persisted by incorporating ideas, principles, and techniques found the most efficient in preserving and strengthening the state. Reason of state has stayed strong.

Developed out of Italian Renaissance cities in a waning feudal world, the doctrine of reason of state offered the "knowledge of the means" to maximize state power without regard for legal or moral concerns. The doctrine advised the "business of ruling" by inviting the "most ready and swift," even "repugnant" methods. With the concept of reason of state, Giovanni Botero synthesized two distinct trends. On the one hand, there was a shift to move away from the Aristotelian view of politics as synonymous with reason, justice, and good government. On the other hand, an art of state supported the preservation of the private dominions—*stato*, or state—of the powerful at any cost. Ultimately, the doctrine affirmed the need for the state's existence as a separate, autonomous entity, "only for itself and in relation to itself," as Foucault puts it.[43]

Making the state wealthy and resourceful, "sturdy and permanent," is reason of state's main goal. In the competition between states, rulers are expected to "respect" principles, institutions, and entities—from law to religion to nature—while simultaneously avoiding subjecting themselves to them. Reason of state rejects any limits, including those imposed by law. Any action, regardless of morality or legality, even behavior deemed "disgusting," can be justified if it is deemed necessary to protect the state. "At once that which exists, but which does not yet exist enough," the state, Foucault observes, is always in (re)construction, a process that relies heavily on the knowledge and tools of reason of state. In the end, the doctrine protects and perpetuates a state that it treats as preexisting but that it is actually its own product and creation.[44]

Its means, including deception, cruelty, and force, were all associated with tyranny. Thus, Maurizio Viroli explains, this art of the state was to be kept confidential, as there was no moral justification for their use. By bringing reason and state together, Botero legitimized "derogations from civil and moral law" to increase state power.[45]

Varied and eclectic, reason of state's principles and practices came together into a prolific "art of governing," Foucault observes, that offered everything rulers needed to perpetuate themselves. The doctrine's repertoire included diplomacy, warfare, coups d'état, police, economic and administrative measures, statistics, and distinct "dark arts" of secrecy, propaganda, and state crimes that still give reason of state its bad rap. Most of the time, it was acknowledged, reason of state could proceed by assimilating policies and laws to "its own game," as Foucault notes. Still, the "suspension of, a temporary departure from, laws and legality," he adds, was key to the doctrine's success. Suspending norms, an expression and instrument of reason of state, would gain prominence in modern times through various modalities of the emergency—as I discuss in chapter 2.[46]

Not everybody agrees about the origins of reason of state. Scholars like Friedrich Meinecke, for example, trace the doctrine back to ancient Greek mythological accounts. Reason of state, he claims, merely gained visibility once the state became strong enough to impose its "unqualified right to existence." Taking distance from these positions, Foucault points out the novelty of the doctrine when it first appeared in Renaissance Italy. Scholars from Foucault to Viroli to Poole agree: The rise of reason of state, with its focus on "measures required for political survival," as Nancy Rosenblum notes, and "preservation," as Botero puts it, stood as a revolutionary event, comparable to scientific and technological breakthroughs such as Galileo's theories or the invention of telescopes.[47]

With its set of practical principles, reason of state helped build modern states. Foucault acknowledges the doctrine's formative impact on institutions. At its core, reason of state involves practices that develop in "between a state presented as given and a state presented as having to be constructed and built," he notes. In all cases, the need for the existence of the state is presupposed. Pointing to reason of state's productivity both as a blueprint and a set of practices, Foucault presents the state as "nothing more than a type of governmentality." From his account, the state arises as a bundle of governing practices targeting a population through security apparatuses springing out of reason of state.[48]

As Foucault's analysis reveals, the art of government has drawn on distinct sources, from the wisdom of kings to the rational knowledge and apparatuses of the modern state, to the market and the economy, to the perspective of the governed. These alternative frameworks, and contention over them, continue to shape politics. As both Poole's and Foucault's work suggests, reason of state has proven able to adapt to and incorporate all of them. Foucault's genealogy of state reason, spanning from the early sixteenth century to twentieth-century German and US-based neoliberals, highlights reason of state's shifts and continuities.[49]

Throughout these phases, reason of state, in its quest to strengthen the state and ensure its survival, underwent changes following "epochal shifts in state form," as Poole notes. The doctrine, adopted by France's absolutist monarchies, gradually consolidated around the state as an autonomous, sovereign agent. Strategic in this shift was Thomas Hobbes's portrayal of the Leviathan as a "mortal god" and an "artificial person." Despite its character of "something like an optical illusion," as Giorgio Agamben puts it, it helped normalize treating the state as possessing a "personality" and an identifiable interest separate from monarchs. Both reason of state and state personality claims portray the state as "an entity in its own right with a will of its own," as Mark Neocleous observes. With profound impact, primarily concerned with the survival of this imaginary, these arguments treat the state as above legal responsibility. Claims about state personality persist. Its fictional status has not prevented scholars from asserting that the state must be treated as a person reclaiming the use of all means toward its preservation, as Hent Kalmo and Quentin Skinner put it.[50]

Another step to detach reason of state from the person of the monarch came with the entrance of the concept of prerogative during the English Revolution of 1688. Claims of prerogative authority, whether "a special right or privilege" as Poole describes it, a form of "legally unregulated" authority, as Martin Loughlin notes, or of "legitimate arbitrary state action," as Brown writes, make it possible to bypass the law on behalf of the common good.[51]

Judith Butler once characterized prerogative as "an anachronism that refuses to die." Indeed, its roots go back to ancient Roman patriarchal privileges that reemerged in the twelfth century among European kings. As an "amalgam of feudal and regal rights" with an additional "vague reserve of power" eventually evolving into an arcane imperii or "mystery of state," Loughlin describes the king's prerogative as an unlimited form of authority at the foundation of the legal order. It helped centralize power and make it personal by treating the kingdom as the monarch's personal property. And when monarchies turned absolutist, the sovereign prerogative stood as the king's "autonomous power . . . to govern . . . according to 'reason of state.'" While antiabsolutists and early liberals opposed reason of state and the monarch's prerogative as symbols of despotism, liberalism— Poole observes—appropriated and transformed both.[52]

One decisive move in this direction came in seventeenth-century England, and John Locke helped with this shift. After proclaiming that authority can be based on consent and the law only, his *Second Treatise* presents one of the strongest arguments supporting extralegal measures that echoes the language of reason of state. Locke defines prerogative as the power of doing good without a rule, even against the law, in response to unforeseen "accidents and necessities." Prerogative in the *Second Treatise* appears as a natural power, a sediment of archaic forms of government that exceeds and cannot be subsumed by the law of which it serves as a foundation. In the end, Locke explains, it all comes down to *Salus populi*, or prioritizing the health or well-being of the people or the common good. On this ground, lawmaking, which Locke judges the highest power, can be legitimately displaced by expedient executive discretionary decisions, as the ultimate end of government is the people's well-being. Accordingly, Locke proposes to entrust the executive power with discretionary authority over both domestic and foreign affairs, thus "obliterating" the gap between politics and war—as Neocleous observes.[53]

Prerogative "depersonalized reason of state" while echoing its rationale, Poole notes. It helped consolidate state interest and the state's survival as ends in themselves. Expanding bureaucratic apparatuses brought a "dissemination" of prerogative among officials in the exercise of "ordinary" lawmaking and judicial roles. Step by step, reason of state became embedded in support of market mechanisms. In *Wealth of Nations*, Adam Smith claimed that an "invisible hand" guides humans so that "by pursuing his own interest," individuals can help advance the common good. Smith justified reason of state arguments as he favored "security and well-being" and "national self-interest." In fact, the economic rationale grounding liberalism expanded "from inside the field of debates on reason of state," Roberto Nigro explains, as he points out to Botero's considerations of economic interest. Authority thus transmuted from the monarch to the state, only for the latter to become increasingly subjected to the market. A "liberal reason of state tradition" then developed, Poole acknowledges, in a dialogue with economic thought.[54]

New forms of state rationality developed under the dominance of political economy. The idea that governments could increase their power and the people's well-being by protecting the "invisible hand" through trade, private property, and markets gained traction. Leaving the market to itself, through laissez-faire, would favor state "enrichment, growth and therefore power," Foucault refers to eighteenth-century beliefs that strong markets would strengthen the state. The rule of law may have been superior to personal rule by a monarch, but markets looked more effective than both. The market promised to advance order and discipline, wealth, and even make the state stronger. Supported by a myriad of state resources, including laws, police, and prerogative authority, a liberal art of government developed that pivoted on economic mechanisms. Rather than simply governing less, as liberal images of "frugal state" claim, the challenge became how to help the market produce—and preserve—its distinct form of social order. And as the market became adopted as a criterion of governmental validation, states focused on optimizing their positioning in the play of competition and interests. Moreover, with its radical "irreducibility to the sphere of right," as Foucault puts it, the *homo œconomicus* and its market-driven rationale eventually defined a distinct strain of reason of state.[55]

Liberal thinkers had opposed reason of state. But they did so without questioning its bases, Foucault writes. Capable of absorbing disparate traditions, reason of state returned with a vengeance. In its liberal iteration, it brought capitalist markets to the heart of state interest. Thus, accompanying the spread of capitalism, since the early nineteenth century, liberal reason of state expanded across modern republics together with emergency regimes and governmentalities.[56]

Through what Foucault describes as "the intensification or internal refinement of raison d'état," liberalism, its earlier enemy, perfected the paradigm it was supposed to leave behind. And as economic emphases reshaped a (neo)liberal art of government, its unlawful practices started to look acceptable or necessary—again.[57]

Some of this ambiguity transpires in Hannah Arendt's matter-of-fact reference to the doctrine when writings about the trial of Adolf Eichmann. Reason of state, Arendt notes, invoking necessity and Realpolitik, treats "the state crimes committed in its name (which are fully criminal in terms of the dominant legal system of the country where they occur)" as emergency measures. The latter seek to preserve the continuity of power, the state, and the legal order. In a "normal political and legal system," these types of crimes are committed exceptionally when the "existence of the state itself is at stake."[58]

This passage captures the liberal tradition's complicated relation to rights, the law, and reason of state. The problem, in Arendt's analysis—which on this matter seems standard—seems not to be state crimes but their frequency. The term "exception" is critical to the argument. Thus, whereas in a "normal" system state crimes only "occur as an exception," under Nazi rule, she argues, they were the norm. The gap between the world of freedom and what Arendt labeled "totalitarianism" is then one of proportions—of how much state crime and *raison d'état* it is tolerable to accept. The liberal answer captured in Arendt's words: only exceptionally.

That the logic of the exception has been shown to expand toward colonizing politics and life is one of the lessons of recent history that I revisit in chapter 2. In the meantime, the premise that the promise and wonders of political life and freedom ultimately rely on a few state crimes is strangely not put into question even by Arendt in the above passage. Exceptional crimes do not count when the state's existence is supposed to be "at stake," as reason of state gets simply accepted as a fact.

Twentieth-century neoliberalism is both a continuation and a break with these traditions. On the one hand, it merely intensified preexistent legal views and market principles and practices. As Friedman wrote in 1951, "neo-liberalism would accept the nineteenth century liberal emphasis on the fundamental importance of the individual." In this sense, it was a continuation. Likewise, states' adoption of neoliberal principles as central to their survival in increasingly competitive global markets came as a contingent yet still consistent step. "Neoliberal governmental reason posits 'competition' as its code of conduct, and aims to govern the social in a decentralised manner by manipulating incentive structures," Yahya M. Madra and Fikret Adamen observe.[59]

At the same time, however, as Friedman notes, for neoliberals competition became the central principle that replaced the old laissez-faire. Indeed, on full display in Chile, neoliberal state reason embraced a market-driven rationale expanded through ideals of competition. If now with a focus on the market, competition was already a central element of reason of state. As the paradigm spread, states brought market rules to all life's domains. Friedrich Hayek was a key ideologue of this shift. Even when arguing in ways that Carl Friedrich finds "imprecise and historically questionable," Hayek eloquently advocates for putting the state in the service of markets and private property.[60]

Freedom, or liberty, ranks highest in Hayek's writings as "the source and condition of most moral values." He makes clear, however, that his focus is on individual liberty, which he defines as a "state in which a man is not subject to coercion by the arbitrary will of another or others." In a free world, competition lets individuals assess and select the most appropriate information, skills, and tools. Competition, it follows, offers the best form of organizing life in common, Hayek argues. Competitive rules promote individual freedom—the true basis of society, he notes—while the alternative—planning—is based on coercion and risks leading societies into totalitarian rule.[61]

The defense of freedom thus requires that "competition be left to function unobstructed," Hayek contends. He sees competition at the heart of all freedoms and markets and the rule of law as essential to secure its conditions. Hayek portrays the rule of law and markets as developing out of customary traditions. As a set of rules that are "fixed and announced beforehand," the rule of law lets individuals know how the state will use its (coercive) power and plan accordingly, Hayek notes. In this regard, state force can prevent interpersonal coercion and support enforcing laws in such a way as "assisting the individuals in the pursuit of their own ends," he adds.[62]

If defining his philosophy, freedom does not stand as absolute for Hayek. While individual freedom is essential to support the "normal running of society," during crises, freedom and other "fundamental principles" may have to be "temporarily sacrificed . . . [to preserve] liberty in the long run." This is the place for emergency powers and other mechanisms for suspending rights in the argument. Not just in his political writings was Hayek "not afraid to use reason of state type arguments," as Poole notes. The passage above comes from *The Constitution of Liberty*, where he also interprets the *Salus populi suprema lex esto* as meaning that "the end of the law ought to be the welfare of the people." Contradicting his declared anti-authoritarian commitments, Hayek repeated these arguments, accompanied with dismissive treatment of democracy and justification of dictatorship.[63]

Friedman agrees. Economic freedom and a "free private enterprise exchange economy," he argues, lie at the foundation of all forms of freedom. Friedman describes competitive capitalism as arising out of households exchanging with one another in the way of "a collection of Robinson Crusoes." Despite these "Robinsonades" making markets and competition look innate, neoliberal thinkers are clear that a market-driven social order is neither spontaneous nor natural. Market competition brings freedom, Friedman argues, but its principles must be imposed. Far from the classical, older "invisible hand" arguments, Friedman describes competitive rules as a "formal game" that must be made compulsory. In a significant departure from his liberal precursors, he acknowledges the contingent character of social organizations and that market principles must be imposed. The state's role then becomes redefined as protecting, expanding, and creating markets, even by subsidizing and imposing them.[64]

Indeed, if markets are the source of our freedoms, the state must secure both. Thus the need to enforce the "rules of the game," an essential task that Friedman argues the market "cannot do for itself." Both Hayek and Friedman compare market-driven societies with a game. For Friedman, the role of government involves securing "law and order . . . property rights . . . [the] rules of the economic game," and a stable currency while establishing how to interpret norms, enforcing contracts and market rules, and supporting "private charity and the private family" to protect the "irresponsible."[65]

A shared concern for Hayek and Friedman is the distortion of competitive markets, as with laws and policies protecting specific individuals or groups of people with stipends or other benefits. Inability to sustain oneself, Friedman observes, indicates immaturity, disability, or mental health problems. Only "the irresponsible, whether madman or child," should receive the assistance of families or charities. Attentive to "not distort the market" and undermine freedom, other than in those cases, individuals must make plans for contingencies including illness, aging, or job losses, and provide for themselves, Hayek contends—and Friedman agrees.[66]

Hayek objects to any substantive uses of the law to address the needs of a particular group (let us say women, the elderly, or Indigenous groups), which he finds arbitrary and unjust. By involving a forced redistribution of resources, social programs and benefits distort markets and undermine freedom, he thinks, just as they bypass the universal character of the law. In his view, anything that constrains markets appears to be an arbitrary attack on freedom, as with Social Security recipients "whose income is entirely dependent on coercing the young."[67]

Such threats to freedom may at times include democracy. Hayek warns readers against falling into "a fetishism of democracy." As a tool in the quest to advance individual freedom, democracy is "by no means infallible or certain," he explains. More so, democracy can be "as oppressive as the worst dictatorship," Hayek contends. For him, the opposite is also true. "An authoritarian government may act on liberal principles," he argues, observing that there can be more freedom "under an autocratic rule than under some democracies."[68]

As a corollary, Hayek calls for governments to protect a private-property-centered rule of law and (market) freedom from unruly democratic initiatives and the demands of popular sovereignty. Forcing people to be free in neoliberal terms involves using policies and state force to push individuals into market competition. But freedom also requires preventing and punishing those resisting the market whether by unionizing or going on strike. Hayek sees group protections (e.g., for women, the Indigenous) as invalid entitlements, as he stresses that the law can only contain universal principles—such as securing private property. The goal, he makes clear, must be protecting what he sees as individual freedom. Since the market stands as the ultimate source of freedom, anything that undermines the full reign of the market, whether it is labor rights or social programs, must be eliminated. To this end, he sees all forms of political regimes as instrumental. Passages like these help understand how and why Hayek—and Friedman—supported Pinochet.

While Hayek's and Friedman's emphases on freedom make it difficult to see links to reason of state, the trick lies in their definitions. For example, while the importance of protecting individuals from coercion and abuse seems unquestionable, they oddly treat workers' unionizing, demands for social programs, or policies addressing inequality as forms of interpersonal coercion. Their rather narrow, individual, market-driven views of freedom thus can lead to justifying institutional breaches, emergency rule, or even overthrowing democracy.

All means seem acceptable in enforcing competitive rules. Centered on the protection of a "free" economy and markets, the neoliberal art of government can support state violence and full-fledged dictatorship. It is in these terms that Hayek declared a dictator—Augusto Pinochet—preferable to a democratic government to protect the rule of law, which he conflated with the defense of private property. And this is why, when asked about the Spanish courts' attempt to extradite Pinochet for his crimes against humanity, an unfazed Milton Friedman replied that the "really remarkable thing about Chile" was the military's adoption of free-market policies.

As with their defense of Pinochet, praise of the market can turn into a neoliberal argument for raw state force. From coups d'état to constitutional and legal breaches to various forms of emergency measures, all instruments of reason of state can be deemed acceptable in the defense of markets and, allegedly, of freedom through them.

With unprecedented speed and reach, neoliberal policies have extended market rules to all of life's domains. "Competitive" markets, should we say? For all this discursive emphasis, competition is enforced mostly to introduce new enclosures by commodifying goods and services previously accessible to all. Job seekers, workers, and small capitalists are thrown indeed to compete against each other. Corporations, for their part, can be conveniently sheltered from competition and heavily subsidized—and their debts taken on by the public—under "too big to fail" claims in the name of the common good. In all cases, bringing markets forward requires constant state intervention, articulated by capitalist modalities of reason of state.[69]

While Hayek's and Friedman's support for Pinochet should not come as shocking, considering their claims, what seems surprising is that neoliberal ideas and policies continue to be treated as synonymous with liberal democracy. The neoliberal recasting of life in market-driven terms conflicts with the conditions of democratic and political life. People's demands for expanded rights can be deemed a threat to markets. So can demands for the right to education or healthcare be cast as threatening freedom as that the neoliberal understanding of freedom ends opposing rights. Javier Milei, the president of Argentina whose significance I discuss in the conclusion, conveys this perspective: "The idea that where there is a need, there's a right is a problem. Because there can be infinite needs, but someone always has to pay for those rights." Assimilating freedom to market freedom, Milei seems determined to defund and dismantle educational, cultural, human rights, and social programs developed over four decades of democracy.[70]

As the totalizing market logic expands, liberal democracy risks "evisceration," to borrow from Brown. Narrated in terms of economic freedom, claiming to lift unfair restrictions to individual initiative, trade, and markets while protecting private property and enforcing contracts, the neoliberal story creates an epic of sorts.[71]

The doctrine of reason of state may be only seldom invoked, but it continues at play, summoned through what Neocleous calls its "sister concepts" like national security or state interest. Such concepts and scholarly and media discourses help produce the state threats they claim merely to describe, as they naturalize state-imposed market dominance over rights and lives. From the start eclectic, reason of state considerations and defining principles turn neoliberal.[72]

Neoliberal Reason Goes Democratic

By the time of Foucault's lectures, with links to military coups and state terror elided, the policies "pioneered" by the Chilean "Chicago Boys" went north. The crisis of import substitution in Latin America and the broader crisis of Fordism had provided the opportunities, and Margaret Thatcher in the UK and Ronald Reagan in the US gave the neoliberal agenda liberal democratic credentials. From that moment, at the cry of "there is no alternative," which Thatcher recited in her speeches, no ultimate truth other than the market's has presided over policymaking, even after repeated failure.

The neoliberal "revolution" launched "a dizzying rise in inequality within countries that continues to this day," as Abhijit Banerjee and Esther Duflo write. Marie-Laure Djelic and Reza Mousavi reconstruct some of the ways in which, over the last five decades, neoliberal reason remade the world, powered by an expansive constellation of NGOs through Atlas and other networks, plus donors, politicians, and developing an expansive academic base.[73]

"Stabilize, privatize, and liberalize"—the neoliberal mantra called for deregulating interest rates, privatizing and outsourcing public services, relying on regressive taxation, and expanding and subsidizing markets. Entrepreneurial self-reliance, individual responsibility, and freedom understood as consumer choice were celebrated while cuts to pensions, social programs, and labor protections advanced.[74]

Thatcher's government carried out privatizations and budget cuts while halving wealth taxes from 83 to 40 percent. On the other side of the Atlantic, the Reagan administration followed suit by lowering wealth taxes from 70 to 28 percent. Gains, people were told, would eventually "trickle-down" and benefit all. It never happened. Income inequality has been rising around the world. Worldwide, fourteen individuals own nearly $2,000 billion. In the US, the top 1 percent of the population makes 26.3 times more than the lower 99 percent as the world's wealth inequalities doubled over the last two decades. Meanwhile, market-driven policies undermined social programs that Hayek described as "a hodgepodge."[75]

The International Monetary Fund, the World Bank, and other financial institutions and think tanks helped expand the neoliberal agenda. Training in neoclassical economics became mainstream and defining of the field of economics. Capital moved freely, helped by loose financial rules. To lure global investors, governments lifted regulations as "nations, firms, and workers" found themselves in fierce competition to attract capital, buyers, and employers. Across dozens of newly (re)gained democracies, people celebrated their rights and political freedoms while neoliberal austerity—often accompanied by emergency measures—undermined the resources needed to effectively access them.[76]

Neoliberal capitalism showed itself to be unstable and crisis prone. In 1982, as an international crisis followed Mexico's default on its debt, the IMF added austerity policies as a condition attached to loans. Deregulating markets and privatizing public goods and services while cutting social and welfare programs to reduce deficits soon became standard. Weathering crises and thirsty for funding, newly democratized governments embraced neoliberal restructuring and policy shifts.[77]

Crises deepened, with countries in the Global South serving again as neoliberal laboratories. In 1985, Bolivians woke up to the closure of 120 factories and the layoff of 23,000 miners. "Shock therapy" entered daily parlance. A lengthy state of siege followed, with curfews, tanks in the streets, mass arrests, and preemptive detentions to crush protests. Stripping people of rights and access to food, schools, or hospitals, from neighborhoods to continents, supported by the repression of protesters in the streets while invoking the rule of law, neoliberal reforms exposed unlawful—often deadly—grounds.[78]

With its push to deregulate, privatize, and privilege indirect (rather than wealth) taxes, the 1989 "Washington Consensus" gave the neoliberal agenda global reach. While eventually a few neoliberal populists won elections, in most cases, conditionalities attached to loans overrode constituents' voices. Neoliberal policies were imposed even against citizens' mandates through overnight policy switches, shock therapy, emergency regimes, and traditional and new forms of coup d'état and state violence. Market reforms, as Naomi Klein observes, kept being "written in shocks."[79]

In 1989, in a radical departure from his former policies, Venezuelan president Carlos Andrés Pérez shocked voters with new taxes, while privatizing state companies and ending subsidies to public transportation and fuel prices, which were imposed overnight. As desperate people took to the streets in the protests known as the Caracazo, the government declared a state of emergency and martial law. Repression was brutal, with an estimate of 4,000 protesters killed.[80]

Shock therapy became the norm, traveling from Bolivia to Argentina, Brazil, Eastern Europe, and the former Soviet Union. As in Venezuela, governments imposed neoliberal reforms against their mandates, supported by emergency measures and repression in the streets. In Perú, in 1990, Alberto Fujimori reversed his electoral promises with "sweeping" neoliberal reforms. Gasoline prices increased 3,000 percent, and the price of bread tripled in a country with a $15 monthly minimum wage. A nationwide state of emergency followed, including killings of protesters and hundreds of arrests. Eventually, through an *autogolpe*, Fujimori shut down Congress and took on dictatorial prerogatives. Even without coups, Presidents Carlos Menem, Fernando Collor de Mello, and Cesar Gaviria introduced austerity packages "by surprise," as Susan Stokes reconstructs, supported by emergency measures soon after taking office in Argentina, Brazil, and Colombia, respectively. Neoliberal policies extended to Poland and Russia, as dismantled social protections brought sudden misery to millions. This way, across regions, people mobilizing for democracy soon got caught in storms of high inflation, recession, and lost jobs, wages, and access to healthcare or retirement. Massive layoffs, unemployment, and poverty left 2.5–3 million excess deaths of middle aged people between 1992 and 2001 in Russia alone.[81]

Oblivious to these market tragedies, with the fall of the Berlin Wall, political scientist Francis Fukuyama celebrated capitalism and democracy for having finally "found a way of . . . reinforcing one another," as he wrote. Fukuyama proclaimed liberalism's "unabashed victory" as the final system in human history. His "end of history" claim became an instant hit. Associated with markets and serving "the public interest," liberal democracy received praise as the most potent vehicle for expanding wealth, rights, and freedom. US-led "democracy promotion" campaigns, supported by NGOs and financial organizations, assimilated democracy, human rights, and the rule of law to markets. Finally, the "reasonably democratic" conditions evoked by Guillermo O'Donnell were with us. But this democracy was neoliberal. Stripped of its radical egalitarian promises, democracy was sanitized "from the revolutionary fantasies of the collective body," as Rancière puts it.[82]

Nowhere did the neoliberal agenda become as mainstream as in the US. The lure of conspicuous consumption, celebrity culture, and rag-to-riches media and social media stories helped spread market-driven ideas of freedom, the law, the human condition, or democracy. Cheered on by Reagan and consolidated during the President Bill Clinton years, an odd coalition of Chicago economists and cultural progressives helped shape a new neoliberal hegemony, Nancy Fraser observes.[83]

In the US, a "progressive" recoding of neoliberalism followed, as market policies were linked to feminism, ethnic and cultural diversity, and other forms of "non-economic emancipatory aspirations." Under the neoliberal spell, feminism and antiracism became individualistic and entrepreneurial, diversifying (rather than eradicating) social hierarchies. Environmentalism, in turn, led to carbon trading, Josefina Martinez notes.

Thus the political and cultural spectrum in the US became dominated by neoliberalism's reactionary and "progressive" wings.[84]

The latter's "neoliberal fantasy of progress" remains pervasive. "Girl power, inclusion, diversity, and happiness are on display, but as hollowed out pageantry: it's enjoyable, and witty, but also empty, all spectacle"—the lines that Lori Marso writes about the movie *Barbie* work also outside the screen. The at once artificial and hyperreal "bright colors, clichéd gestures, and shallow, surface emotions" from Barbie Land's Instagrammable "pastels and plastic" could be those from a cruise ship or upscale shopping mall.[85]

Thus, from popular culture to the media to academic circles to political science textbooks, pro-market ideas have become common sense. Helped by the Schumpeterian reduction of political life to market competition, markets and democratic politics were treated as interchangeable as political science naturalized capitalism as "the uncontested (back)ground for democracy," as Paulo Ravecca notes.[86]

Views of humans as inherently individualistic, self-centered, and competitive, and of economics as the discipline best suited to understand society accompanied such beliefs. They found support in the ideas of scholars like Gary Becker, Foucault shows. Claiming that all human behavior is economically motivated, Becker proposed to treat "any conduct whatsoever" as the product of cost-benefit analysis.[87]

Making all of us into capitalists, he universalizes the logic of cost-benefit analysis and an all-encompassing notion of human capital. Becker treats everyone as a capitalist, entrepreneurial being who offers goods in some markets to obtain profits and satisfy (our and others') needs. Individual interest and a quest for material gain preside over every choice. Even mere consumption, wages, or childcare are portrayed as investments—in human capital in the case of motherhood. Plus, a mother's decision to give birth and raise a child is seen as providing her with "psychic" forms of profit. This way, neoliberal reason recasts citizens as agents driven by economic goals "by perpetually calculating and systematically responding to incentives," as Madra and Adaman note.[88]

This imagined individual, a *homo oeconomicus* maximizer, resembles the Hobbesian man—lonely, distrustful, forced into competition, and under permanent threat. Assimilating these traits as human "nature," this view grounds not just mainstream economics or political science but also psychology, biology, or criminology. As if by magic, neoliberal storytelling makes entire dimensions of reality vanish from view. Labor, for example, does not seem to make sense when everyone is defined as capitalists in possession of (human) capital. Likewise, the critical role of reproductive labor—often unpaid—in supporting and subsidizing the accumulation of capital, as well as the exploitative appropriation of habitats (reduced to "natural resources"), are simply omitted or dismissed. In this way, the neoliberal lens pushes entire dimensions of life out of sight and obscures the realities of labor, exploitation, and enclosure that the Marxian critique brought to the fore, no less than the environmental destruction underway.

Making the market the driver of people's lives turns societies into "an economic game" with no opting out, Johanna Oksala explains. By subjecting habitats and populations to cost-benefit analysis, their worth and the likelihood to "be invested in or divested" may be determined by their contribution to (human) capital and GDP growth, as Brown points out. Moreover, to the extent that corporate profits and economic growth are assumed to be defining of state interest, anything challenging them, whether environmental or labor movements, can be securitized as a threat.[89]

If internalized discipline and compliance can make violence invisible, "widespread state-violence is inherent to the rationality of neoliberal governing," she concludes. Free to sell and consume, individuals find themselves prevented, neutralized, or repressed from exercising freedom alongside "non-economic rationalities," as Fraser observes.[90]

Among those objecting to this critique stands Byung-Chul Han. Neoliberalism, Han contends, is neither driven by shocks nor imposed through discipline or coercion. The neoliberal lure, he claims, works through "positivity" and "psychopolitics" alone. Psychopolitics is all about seducing "the soul . . . wishes, needs, and desires" through consumption and sensory enjoyment so individuals choose markets and turn themselves into human capital.[91]

No question that the glitz of consumerism is central to neoliberal charm, just as the old commodity fetishism kept serving capital. Han's lack of acknowledgment of the violence involved in neoliberalism's history seems surprising, however. Shock therapy, discipline, and even open, deadly violence have been significant in advancing market reforms. By forcing people to approach life as a competition and to see themselves as human capital, the neoliberal "noble lie" makes us internalize values and lifestyles. Still today, state violence accompanies austerity policies and crises—whenever consensus fails.[92]

A dark face of neoliberalism turned visible in Bolivia in 2000 when Cochabamba's water prices tripled following the privatization of water services. Privatization was a World Bank condition to extend a loan for improving infrastructure, and a US company, Bechtel, became the provider. Indigenous water rights were disregarded as water was turned into a commodity. "Even rainwater was privatized," Oscar Olivera, a leading figure in the struggle over water in the city recalls. The cost of water amounted to a fifth of the income of poor families, and the outlawing of the possibility of obtaining water from streams or the rain pushed a mass of poor citizens to the edge. To the ensuing massive "water wars" protests, the government responded with a state of emergency, curfews, and the deployment of the military in the streets. "A 17-year-old boy named Victor Hugo Daza was killed along with four indigenous Aymara in El Alto," Olivera notes.[93]

Still, neoliberal reforms continued to rely on emergency measures, exposing what Hiroyuki Tosa theorizes as their "complementary" character. Between 2000 and 2010, Claire Wright documented over 300 states of emergency, often linked to budget cuts or to imposing big mining projects, in Bolivia, Ecuador, and Perú.[94]

At the epicenter of austerity crises, Latin Americans were not alone. By 2000, about 20 percent of the world's population had experienced declining life expectancy caused by neoliberal reforms. Shock therapy and emergency regimes were pivotal to imposing austerity, as were conditionality loans, foreign incursions, and violent repression.[95]

By 2008, the global financial crisis exposed the cracks of the neoliberal order to the wider world. Extraordinary profits channeled into speculative financial "asset bubbles" burst amid some of the highest levels of income inequality to date. This "triple crisis of food, fuel, and finance" took a toll on rights, living standards, and life expectancy. As previously in Russia, deaths ensued. By 2010, Greece saw hundreds of excess deaths every month, as evictions led to 13,300 suicides in Spain. Across Europe and North America, the crisis left over 10,000 "economic suicides," which displaced car accidents as a leading cause of death in the US.[96]

The response included massive subsidies to corporations. In the US, the government's 2008 bailout was conservatively estimated at $498 billion. It was almost ten times more, if we factor in the $1.3–$1.4 trillion yearly deficits between 2009 and 2011—the highest deficit outside wartime up to that point. If we include the Federal Reserve's support for financial markets in 2009–12, state subsidies of capital totaled $12.2 trillion or 20 percent of US GDP. This is without counting the subsidies to General Motors, Chrysler, Goldman Sachs, and AIG.[97]

Similar bailouts were implemented in Europe, as the European Central Bank brought interest rates down almost to zero to supply "unlimited" cash—the director acknowledged—to support the banks' recovery. Not much other than the size of the subsidies seemed new. Corporate and bank bailouts, plus massive tax breaks and state subsidies, have been delivered "with clockwork regularity" to keep neoliberal capitalism afloat. Starting in the Reagan years in 1983, bailouts in 1987, 1990, 1997–98, 2001, 2008, and 2020 tried to avoid a 1930s-like "meltdown." Free-marked advocates, starting with Milton Friedman, have consistently supported such giant subsidies to capital even when they flagrantly contradict their own critiques of "big government."[98]

The Unreason of Neoliberal Reason and the Destruction of Life

In a 2016 article, IMF experts acknowledged the failure of the Washington Consensus's "market fundamentalism." Despite this recognition, international financial organizations continued to promote the same orthodoxy, encouraging governments to embrace austerity as "the new norm," as Isabel Ortiz and Matthew Cummins show. In the UK, university budgets were slashed by 80 percent as neoliberal policies became even "more deeply entrenched" than in the 1980s. "Alarming" fiscal and macroeconomic policies continued imposing severe cuts across countries to schools, health services, and social programs. Austerity conditions were attached to 85 percent of new IMF loans during the early times of the COVID-19 pandemic, and over 150 governments embraced the agenda in 2021.[99]

Decades of neoliberal austerity combined with low-paying temporary jobs have taken a severe toll. Successive budget cuts have "hollowed out" services and communities, leaving people impoverished, disempowered, and isolated. Marked by stagnant wages and dismantled social safety nets, austerity has given rise to what Guy Standing describes as a swelling precariat. As a growing class of precarious workers with "no secure occupational identity," they find themselves exploited within and beyond the workplace.

In 2020, before the start of the pandemic, the International Labor Organization identified 630 million of the working poor as unable to meet their families' basic needs. By 2023, hopes of improving labor conditions had been "shattered." At the bottom of the income stiff pyramid, a mass of the excluded remains confined to what Hiroyuki Tosa describes as a "global slum."[100]

Among them, too many poor citizens, over 281 million migrants, and 120 million refugees and internally displaced live in a de facto state of emergency. Aihwa Ong describes them as being reduced to "the status of nonbeings," while Agamben characterizes their condition as "bare life." Judged "devoid of value," they are given no legal or political recognition and exposed to being destroyed without any repercussions, left at the sheer mercy of discretionary authority.[101]

Under those conditions, the excluded face extreme difficulties in making institutions work for them as in seeking redress for state abuses. While Agamben traces the ancient roots of biopolitical hierarchies underlying these exclusions, Marx showed the extent to which labor exploitation lies behind social hierarchies. Surviving as *vogelfrei*, or as isolated, rightless, and "entirely unprotected," Marx's portrayal of workers' exclusions in *Capital*, as Arne de Boever observes, overlaps with Agamben's definition of bare life.[102]

For centuries, capitalism has relied on structural exclusions, justified through slavery, colonial regimes, apartheid, or other forms of racist subjugation, to deny members of excluded groups access to rights. Capital separates people from their means of living and transforms societies into massive "collections of commodities," Marx writes. All of life's necessities, from food to shelter to clothing, become accessible only through money. Starting with enclosures, disregard for common law rights, and the brutal expulsion of peasants from the land in fourteenth- and fifteenth-century England, a massive wave of expropriations often referred to as "primitive accumulation" launched modern capitalism. Endless commodification and successive separations—these two capitalist traits stand out. Colonial, imperial, and elite regimes helped further dispossess people and outlaw communal property and rights over centuries as capital dominated globally. Turning goods into commodities exchanged for profit and counting with cheap labor has been central to the spread of capital.[103]

Capital, Jason Moore observes, involves a "world-ecology" and a distinct understanding of life. Ideologically diminishing and dehumanizing others made it possible to treat entire groups, from enslaved people to women, as part of what Moore describes as "cheap nature." Thus capital appropriated food, energy, raw materials, and unpaid labor by treating beings and materials as part of "nature," in ways that deeply transformed social order and habitats. Over half a century, driven by unleashed markets, neoliberalism intensified these trends.[104]

Neoliberal reforms accelerated new cycles of fossil fuel, mineral, and biomass extraction. Deregulation was key. Since the 1980s, at least 110 countries changed their mining codes under IMF and World Bank pressure to weaken environmental or safety standards. Reorganizing "natural resource governance in favor of extractive interests," to borrow from Alejandro Artiga-Purcell et al., helped expand mining frontiers. The move involved privatizing public land and easing conditions for foreign ownership, leasing, or having dubious property titles recognized. It also involved "suspending already fragile spaces of democracy, dialogue, and dissent." From Colombia to Greece to the US, governments let corporations bypass environmental and safety norms. Commodity territories were thus extended, supported by exceptions, emergency, and securitization.[105]

By the early 2000s, what Maristella Svampa described as a new "Commodities Consensus" brought major actors together to remake entire economies, habitats, and lives. High international prices, the use of fracking or genetically modified seeds (GMOs), corporate tax benefits and lowering tariffs, flexible labor conditions, and allowing foreign land ownership and profit remittances helped.[106]

In Argentina, soybean crops introduced in the 1970s covered 63 percent of the harvested land by the 2000s. Worldwide, metals, nonmetallic minerals, fossil fuels, and biomass extraction expanded by 244 percent between 1973 and 2024. Not even the oceans or protected areas are spared by neoliberal enclosures in the effort to "release . . . a set of assets" as cheaply as possible to maximize profits and value for shareholders, as Harvey points out.[107]

By the turn of the century, driven by mass protests against austerity, a series of center-left governments won elections in Latin America. Beyond "pink tide" proclamations of anti- and post-neoliberalism, the neoliberal matrix persisted, however, anchored in exports of primary goods focused on large-scale extractive and agricultural operations. Public appeals to the common good, progress, and development, only half veiledly justifying "sacrificial zones," as Gabriela Valdivia calls them, proliferated among conservative and progressive governments alike. By declaring emergency regimes, governments "deemed mining, oil, and gas extraction 'essential' activities and community resistance a 'security threat,'" Artiga-Purcell et al. note.[108]

The process continues. To the demands of the $33 trillion in global trade in 2024, there is now a pressing need to ramp up "green energy." For all the promises, solar or wind technologies are more mineral intensive than fossil fuels, and the production of lithium and rare minerals will have to increase five times by 2050 to address energy storage needs. Embracing the "transition," the World Bank and other international financial organizations promote a "global commons" discourse. Resources from water to rare minerals are "for all of humanity," we are told, and that "we are in this together," only to more or less openly suggest that some "difficult decisions" may have to be made for the greater good. This discourse, Digno Montalván Zambrano and Isabel Wences note, is part of a capitalist strategy of appropriation of resources. Along these lines, the energy transition and its "critical natural resources," including lithium or rare minerals, are increasingly framed as foreign policy and national security matters. A "Wall Street Consensus" intends to support extractive operations while shielding them and finance from "environmental justice and Green New Deal initiatives." Facing the need to speed up the "energetic transition," neoliberal reason turns "green."[109]

Renewable energy operations, from biofuels to solar, "can be as conflictive" as those linked to fossil fuels, Arnim Scheidel et al. reminds us. With 1,016 ongoing land conflicts in mid- 2025 recorded by the Global Atlas of Environmental Justice, the extractive takeover continues. "A global land grab unprecedented since colonial times" has been unfolding in recent years as investors take over "millions of hectares," Farshad Araghi and Marina Karides write.[110]

More farmers and Indigenous communities become displaced, protesters criminalized, and natural preserves or national parks threatened to make room for extractive industries from fossil fuel extraction, industrial agriculture, logging, and the mining of "rare minerals." As banks and investors buy or lease large swaps of land, including blocks of housing, around the world, enclosures intensify in urban settings as well. Gentrification is "economic displacement" that uproots communities due to rising real estate prices, rent, and property taxes.[111]

Enclosures and the exclusion of local populations advance just as rights and protections weaken, leading to the erasure or "'disappearance' of the crimes of capital," as Philomena Mariani observes. Labor precarity, weakened health and environmental regulations, and suppression of citizen input and consultation contribute to the erosion of democracy and human rights as neoliberalism's "spillover effects."[112]

In Colombia, for decades, extractivism and neoliberal reforms expanded alongside the armed conflict, as paramilitary squads forced farmers to leave their lands while the state recognized usurpers' property rights. Until 2014, the land grabbed or abandoned due to forced displacement was estimated at 7,073,897 hectares. While the 2016 Peace Accord and several laws mandate reparations and land restitutions, implementation is slow, and the links between forced displacement and extractive, often illegal, economies still need to be addressed.[113]

The neoliberal grabbing of nature is messy. In its extracting and accumulating unprecedented wealth, capital generates violence and (dis)order. Subjected to displacements and migrations, terrorized and left without access to land and resources, often also criminalized, people treated as rightless serve as cheap labor. Others simply die.

"Gaza's waterfront property could be very valuable," Jared Kushner, Donald Trump's son-in-law and former policy advisor for the Middle East, declared in a February 2024 interview at Harvard University, as he suggested moving Gazans into the Negev Desert and perhaps to Egypt. Less than three months later, the office of Israeli prime minister Benjamin Netanyahu announced its Gaza 2035 Plan to rebuild the strip "from nothing." With a futuristic, Dubai-looking AI rendering featuring high-rise buildings surrounded by greenery, gardens, water desalination plants, and cropland alongside the beach, the plan seeks to "revitalize the Gazan economy." The rendering includes a crystal-clear canal with bridges, train lines, and the view of sailboats, ships, and oil-pumping floating stations. Supported by investments, we learn, Gaza 2035 would reposition the area as a communication hub in the Middle East and take advantage of recently discovered oil reserves. The plan, to unfold over a decade, is expected to start with humanitarian aid, followed by the creation of "safe zones" with no Hamas control, governed by "deradicalized" Gazans overseen by a coalition of Arab governments. Eventually, Gazans could gain full "self-governance," though Israel would reserve the right to intervene to protect its security.[114]

Except perhaps for Kushner's reference to moving people out of Gaza, nothing in the previous paragraph about waterfront properties and zoning would help the reader figure out that the International Criminal Court had launched arrest orders for individuals including the Israeli prime minister, under charges of "war crimes and crimes against humanity." Or that South Africa initiated a case for genocide against Israel for its actions in Gaza with the International Court of Justice.

By early February 2025, a couple of weeks after his inauguration, President Trump had doubled down. "You're talking about a million and a half people, and we just clean out that whole thing," Trump enthusiastically endorsed the prospect of turning Gaza into the "Riviera of the Middle East" after forcefully moving Gazans into Egypt and Jordan.

When not massacred, as the 68,875 Gazans estimated to had been killed by November 2025, entire groups of people continue to be expelled from their land, abandoned, and subject to violence—with the number of the displaced reaching 120 million in 2024, according to the UN High Commissioner for Refugees. Criminalization and violence often also await protesters reclaiming rights for the displaced, or exposing the destruction of forests, pollution of rivers, or effects of glyphosate.[115]

In the meantime, an unprecedented financialization of nature is in the making. "Green" securities—such as bonds, indices, and funds tied to "natural assets"—assign monetary value to mountains, lakes, and forests, often partly to support carbon offsetting. "While the asset value of the world economy is $512 trillion, the asset value of the earth's natural capital is estimated at $4 quadrillion ($4,000 trillion), all potentially for the taking," John Bellamy Foster notes. Ironically, in the name of conservation, corporate "green" charities are expelling Indigenous groups from their lands as neoliberal enclosures reach everywhere.[116]

Intensive extraction levels favor economic growth and help accelerate the environmental and climate crises. Extractive industries linked to fossil fuel, gas, minerals, logging, and agriculture have led to unprecedented deforestation, air, water, soil pollution, desertification, and a 90.86 percent increase in CO_2 emissions since 1979. In their commodifying of life, neoliberal policies favor the rise of new, even virtual extractive social territories. Data mining and other technologies help create new markets by digitizing entire social domains. Housing, financial markets, and even our very selves are targeted by countless apps, while corporations like Google or Facebook, often in breach of privacy, market our digital profiles.[117]

From a world-ecology perspective, Moore sees the crises of neoliberalism as a sign of the exhaustion of cheap nature and unlimited economic growth. In their 2023 report, the Intergovernmental Panel on Climate Change (IPCC) concludes that global warming of 2°C will be reached in the next decades. World temperatures have "increased faster since 1970 than in any other 50-year period over at least the last 2000 years," the report notes, whereas comparable global surface warming goes back 125,000 years. The climate is changing faster than expected, and many places across the planet may be unlivable sooner than previously imagined. "This is code red for humanity," UN Secretary-General António Guterres declared, adding that he had never seen anything this dire in previous reports. In the meantime, favored by neoliberal deregulations of environmental, industry, financial, health, or labor standards, greenhouse gas emissions and warming appear to be accelerating as food and water threaten to become scarce, more people migrate for climate-related reasons, and new diseases develop. These changes coincide with more democratic governments turning authoritarian while inequality and poverty keep increasing. Under what Foster describes as "absolute capitalism," the epistemic and institutional colonizing of neoliberal reason sees no limits as market principles "engulf the state itself."[118]

Trapped in Self-Destructing Loops

Neither reason of state nor the forms of authority it produces are well suited to the people's body politic. Even when "constitutionally secured," reason of state "paves the way for inhumanity as soon as a certain threshold of social and political tensions is crossed," according to Ernest Mandel, in reflecting on twentieth-century massacres. In what follows, I delineate the main traits of neoliberal reason of state as a canvas to illuminate persistent and concerning state abuses and the current decay of democratic rights and life. First imposed under a brutal military dictatorship half a century ago in Chile, then made to coexist with liberal democracy, neoliberal reason has unleashed the "inhumanity" Mandel refers to with such an intensity that it is threatening our world.[119]

Through massive deregulation, privatizations, and austerity policies, significant dimensions of life—from access to schools and healthcare, to roads and retirement—became commodified as part of new enclosures. States, in turn, increased subsidies to companies while progressively abandoning the role of securing social reproduction. As protecting capital turned into "the ultimate reason of state" as Dardot and Laval put it, labor productivity, GDP, energy, extraction levels, and financial markets skyrocketed. Societies, however, became drastically more unequal and jobs insecure while isolation and precarity swelled.[120]

Neoliberal reason's victory looks Pyrrhic. In assimilating market principles to state interest, it promotes policies that endanger people, habitats, and life on Earth. By exhausting key resources and accelerating environmental and climate collapse, an "unparalleled and historic conflict between humanity and neoliberal capitalism" determines "the future of the species," as Orellana Calderón writes from Chile.[121]

Against Fukuyama's early celebration of the encounter between markets and liberal democracy, Mike Davis reminds us that their association remains "tenuous at best." Throughout history, "capitalism more often than not is associated with dictatorship and oligarchical rule, not with democracy," Davis notes, as the Chilean authoritarian experiment and the current spread of austerity and autocratization bring into view. No matter the decades of liberal democratic normalizing, with the imposition of austerity policies neoliberalism can turn full-fledged authoritarian in a snap. As unlawful, violent interventions and emergency measures expand what Agamben describes as a "technique of government," democracy and rights are undermined and differences between forms of regime wane.[122]

Suspending the law and legal guarantees defines one of reason of state's main resources. Emergency regimes are distinctive modern mechanisms to bypass norms in response to threats to the state. Declarations of the state of exception by presidents, prime ministers, and other leaders, as well as martial law, curfews, and legal loopholes are some of its forms. This is the subject of chapter 2, which surveys the recent spread of state abuse-prone emergency regimes. Mapping trends, modalities, and the impact of what I describe as governmentalities of emergency, the chapter argues for the need to acknowledge links between emergency politics, security, and police. Driven by the same exceptional logic, emergency measures, security, and police work as part of a broader multilayered matrix. They connect through policies, rules, and discretionary uses of authority into a multifaceted emergency apparatus with special regimes that tend to become normalized. Drawing on a range of examples, in a dialogue with debates on the state of exception, security, and the police, the chapter reviews key empirical trends alongside insights from Agamben, Foucault, and other scholars, including Kim Scheppele, Hiroyuki Tosa, Judith Butler, Leonard Feldman, and Mark Neocleous.

The circumstances and modalities under which neoliberal governmentality gains legitimacy even when violent or abusive define the theme of chapter 3, "For the Common Good." Grand displays and ceremonies seemed strategic to theorists of reason of state to project strength and impress citizens and foreign powers. Along these lines, for centuries, reason of state and connected concepts of state interest, national security, and political realism have inspired variants of the political extraordinary, at once terrifying and enchanting in their grandiose reaffirming of state might.

These days, state performances are supported by electronic media and social media (with the increasing role of artificial intelligence) in spectacular forms first theorized by Guy Debord. At a point where states and corporations turn indistinguishable, presided over by a neoliberal reason of state, mesmerizing entertainment and marketing fuse with police and military apparatuses in their tracking and targeting of individuals. Engaging with insights from Agamben, Alex Murray, and Mitchell Dean, among others, the chapter revisits reason of state's semiotic alchemy by showing mechanisms that keep state violence opaque or that legitimize it as authority.

The conditions in which citizens contest abusive governmentalities define the subject of chapter 4. While the repertoire of resistance is ample, people in the streets define one of its ultimate political forms. Building on the "movement of the squares," including the Occupy Movement and the Arab Spring, millions gained the streets to join protests at unprecedented levels in half of the world since 2019. With unique, local demands, people came together to reject precarity, challenge legal, political, and socioeconomic exclusions, and demand more or "true" democracy. Protests proved resilient, extending through 2020 despite the pandemic and police repression in countries including the US, Chile, and France. At the peak of this wave, in summer 2020, twenty-six million Black Lives Matter protesters flooded the streets in the US.

Chapter 4 revisits popular protests, their dynamics, and trends while acknowledging people in the streets as an embodiment of the democratic extraordinary and the ultimate line of defense of rights and democracy. Sections draw on media archival research to map popular demonstrations in light of critical theories of protests' democratic role. Relying on established frameworks (e.g., Charles Tilly's), I primarily engage Jacques Rancière's approach to politics and democracy and Andreas Kalyvas's concept of the democratic politics of the extraordinary to illuminate the struggle for rights and "real" democracy.

Theory-focused, chapter 5 revisits rights as fundamental forms of social and political empowerment and protection. Whereas an individualistic, legal, market-driven rationale prevails in their treatment, rights admit alternative groundings. After reviewing established views, the chapter revisits the ancient principle of Isonomia and traditions of rights as commons. The Marxian critique of capital, law, and the state, as well as

Massimo De Angelis's and others' work on rights as forms of social commons, offer a robust framework for a democratic language of rights. In exploring alternative democratic rights traditions, the chapter engages with voices including Marx, De Angelis, Jessica Whyte, Jacques Rancière, Bonnie Honig, Eugeny Pashukanis, Nasser Hussain, and Bhikhu Parekh.

The concluding chapter examines the resurgence of radical neoliberal experiments against a backdrop of rising authoritarianism and emergency regimes, as it explores their impact on democratic politics, rights, and daily life. Revisiting Javier Milei's government in Argentina, which is serving as a "world's social laboratory" for a revitalized neoliberal wave, I scrutinize this program in light of neoliberal reason and its politics of extinction.

Will more substantial, vibrant forms of democracy and rights develop out of our multifaceted crises, including the threat of climate collapse? In some light, what looks like an inexorable decay may contain reinvigorating possibilities. Another world—or at least another end of this world—is possible. Fueled by people's direct action, radical demands for rights and voice delineate possibilities for a move toward a more solid grounding for democracy. In the conclusion, I identify alternative scenarios and possibilities in resisting what, at this point, amounts to a neoliberal politics of extinction.

2 | Emergency, Security, Police

> *Raison d'etat* appeals . . . to *necessity*, and the state crimes
> committed in its name . . . are considered emergency measures,
> concessions made to the stringencies of *Realpolitik*, in order to
> preserve power and thus assure the continuance of the existing
> legal order as a whole.
> —Hannah Arendt, *Eichmann in Jerusalem*

In a lapse of twenty minutes, on the night of November 13, 2015, a rampage of shootings and blasts shook neighborhoods across Paris. In some locations, attackers opened fire. Others detonated suicide vests as they ravaged packed cafés, bars, and restaurants, a soccer stadium, and Le Bataclan theater, leaving 130 dead and scores of people injured. The attacks shocked the French public. It had been just months since the killing of twelve people at the *Charlie Hebdo* magazine headquarters, and "significantly heightened security" measures were in place. "It is horror," President François Hollande said in his speech to the nation, as he described the "unprecedented" nature of the violence. Wearing a black suit, with the French flag in the background, Hollande linked the "barbaric act" to a "terrorist army." After characterizing the attacks as an "act of war," the president declared a national state of emergency—the first such declaration since 1961.[1]

Emergency situations are exceptionally hazardous events, ranging from earthquakes or hurricanes to epidemics, invasions, military attacks, or the outbursts of civil war that call for an immediate, often unusual response. As of mid- 2025, the Emergency and Disaster dataset recorded 16,250 disasters worldwide since 2000, including those of natural (e.g., droughts, floods) and technological (e.g., industrial accidents, infrastructure collapse) origin. Still, only a fraction of them led to declared emergencies. It is the explicit recognition by the state, usually through a formal declaration, that turns such occurrences into an emergency. As political and legal constructs, emergency regimes let the authorities qualify and suspend laws to protect the state and its people from catastrophic threats. In so doing, officials can bypass standard procedures, suspend fundamental guarantees, and grant themselves special powers. "All domestic legal systems establish rules and procedures for governments to respond to such crises," Laurence Heifer notes, most often involving rights restrictions, derogations, and increased executive prerogatives. Alleging no time for deliberation, governments react through formal declarations, executive orders or decrees, ad hoc initiatives, or more subdued procedures to introduce special temporary regimes of "emergency, exception, urgency, discretion," as Claire Wright explains. Over the last century, these regimes have become more frequent and have gained in intensity.[2]

Whereas an extensive literature addresses formal emergency regimes and executive powers, actual measures involve a number of actors and extended governmental chains. At the juncture of policies, discourse, and scholarship, emergency mechanisms are at play at various levels, from the state of exception through small emergencies to security to embedded in policing, guided by claims of necessity and state "interest." Thousands of agents intervene every day, directly regulating people's behavior across all corners of society, loosely coordinated in response to problems perceived as urgent, whether formally or at the discretion of agents themselves. Supporting the expansion of neoliberal reason, a multilayered system of governmentalities of emergency is in place. Different agents exercise prerogatives in implementing emergency regimes, security policies, and police routines at once distinct, overlapping, and coordinated. Ultimately, as captured by Arendt's words and yet bypassed in most studies, emergency politics forms part of the antiquated sounding but very present repertoire of reason of state.

Emergency narratives bolster a governing apparatus that helps the state extend its domain. The same state from which people should expect protection often hurts them and the conditions of democratic life. Through claims of an urgent need of addressing threats through exceptional measures, known emergency narratives that Jennifer Rubenstein labels "canonical," from the "Ticking Bomb" to the "House on Fire," help bypass laws and justify rights violations.[3]

Under the umbrella of emergency, security, and police, a myriad of interventions disregarding rights get treated as de facto exercises of prerogative authority. And as emergency regimes, security, and police receive differential, separate treatment in the literature, studying them in isolation leaves the links between them in the dark. This chapter addresses these practices in their continuities as governmentalities that intensify and normalize the reach of emergency regimes. Interrogating these mechanisms and their links should help illuminate the persistence of state abuses and rights breaches in democracies.

Discussing trends in a dialogue with arguments and examples, in particular Agamben's and Foucault's insights, while engaging the contributions of emergency politics scholars like Kim Scheppele and political theorists like Leonard Feldman or Mark Neocleous, among others, sections revisit perspectives, practices, and trends connecting distinct facets—governmentalities—of the emergency. The chapter presents police, security, and the state of exception as part of a three-faceted emergency governmental apparatus rooted in, and ultimately uncovering, modalities of reason of state.

In what follows, the first section identifies emergency regimes' main forms, tools, and trends. As there is no definitive official record, I rely on media archival research, database coverage—including Varieties of Democracy—and documents to identify trends. Next, I discuss the global expansion of emergency regimes alongside democracy. After revisiting some of the most productive perspectives on the emergency, the following section discusses the role of the security and police forces in extending and normalizing emergency regimes. Securitization, police discretionary powers, and emergency regimes form part of the same governmental apparatus. Together, its practices restrict access to fundamental rights and constitutional protections in ways that the chapter brings to light.

Emergencies

In France, the November 2015 state of emergency authorized the government to close borders and mobilize the armed forces—including the military—to patrol Paris. The authorities set security zones to regulate people's movements. Raids looking for "jihadists" expanded into Belgium, as the French government allowed local authorities to set curfews, conduct searches, and make arrests.[4]

During a visit to the site of the deadly attacks, announcing a "pitiless" war, President Hollande asserted that terrorists targeted France because of "who we are, a free country which speaks to the whole planet." While some objected to Hollande's "act of war" definition, he found ample support from leaders including former president Nicolas Sarkozy's call to "annihilate the enemies of the Republic" through a "total" war. Meanwhile, Hollande's approval ratings, which had plummeted amid unpopular austerity measures, rose to 50 percent in the polls.

In Articles 16 and 36, the French Constitution gave the president full authority under a state of emergency, including the option to deploy the military. Still, President Hollande found the articles insufficient, claiming that "this war of a different type requires a new constitutional regime." Weeks later, speaking to lawmakers at Versailles, the president shared his intention to extend the state of emergency as thousands more police agents patrolled the streets. Hollande used a language that Sylvain Cypel describes as "unknown to international law" by assimilating individuals to military enemies. Moreover, Hollande claimed that the Constitution should allow antiterrorism measures, including stripping the citizenship of those involved, without having to declare an emergency.[5]

Why reform the constitution when emergency provisos were already established in France? By constitutionalizing emergency measures in response to a "terrorism of war," a hybrid of criminal acts and warfare, the French government sought to introduce a new exceptional regime of "civilian rule in crisis mode." With new emergency powers made permanent and vaguely defined targets, the police would gain authority over judges, among other things. Critics worried that the Constitution could shift from a charter guaranteeing fundamental rights into one threatening citizens with denationalization. In any case, the move aligned France's policies with the US global war on terror, Jean-Claude Paye writes. And it helped the French president's image, too.[6]

While Hollande's attempt to add a new form of emergency and a supplementary constitutional article failed, the push continued. Renewed six times between 2015 and 2017, the state of emergency became the longest one in France since first being introduced in 1955. The authorities imposed over 4,600 warrantless searches, closed religious sites, and set limits to the rights of assembly, alleging "threats to public order." At least 155 decrees restricted demonstrations and prevented over 600 individuals from joining rallies. Police powers, securitized border areas, and special zones were significantly expanded under the emergency.[7]

Soon, in 2016, local authorities across France banned half of the planned rallies, including protests against labor precarization. "I have been mobilizing on many issues for the past 20 years, and I don't remember any instance in which authorities prohibited a protest," a journalist from Nantes declared to Amnesty International. "It has never happened in the past," an activist placed under personalized restrictions in Rennes noted. In Paris, the police attacked protesters with tear gas and made arrests on false charges. At least on one occasion, protesters were ambushed on a bridge by the police for hours when protesting neoliberal labor reforms. The police hurt at least 1,000 protesters in 2016 in Paris alone.[8]

Meant as short-term restrictions, emergency provisos often "become part and parcel of the ordinary law, chipping steadily away at human rights," John Dalhuisen, Amnesty International's director for Europe, observes. It took two years and President Emmanuel Macron's signature of a "sweeping" counterterrorism law for the state of emergency to end. The new law authorized "protection perimeters" with expanded search powers around sites judged at risk of terrorist attacks. Its provisos let authorities monitor individuals considered dangerous. Suspects could be confined to predefined zones while having to report to a police station every day. Restrictions on protests and broadened search and arrest powers allowed the closure of mosques perceived as promoting "terrorism, hatred, or discrimination." Likewise, investigating public officials judged at risk of "becoming radicalized" was made permanent by the 2017 internal security law. The French, Amnesty International found, had fallen into "a near-permanent state of securitization" amid exceptional measures and austerity.[9]

"By experience, each time we've had a state of emergency, we've never returned to the state of 'before,'" Anne-Sophie Simpere said of France. Pressure to normalize exceptional conditions continued. In 2019, an anti-riot law authorized preventing individuals from taking part in demonstrations and deploying the military to repress protests. In 2020, "health emergency" laws came in response to the pandemic in a scenario of heightened security. The electronic tracing of cases, using thermal scanners, drones, and additional security cameras to monitor lockdowns, raised privacy concerns. As Macron used decrees to impose labor and pension reforms amid protests, a bill sought to increase surveillance, criminalize student protests, and ban posting pictures or videos of the police. By mid-2021, the National Assembly introduced provisos from the 2015 state of emergency in two antiterrorist bills. They included setting up security zones, the closure of religious sites, keeping those who completed prison sentences for terrorism under surveillance, and expanding police faculties to enter homes. While repeatedly struck down by the courts, similar bills were sponsored by the government, which also sought to expand closed-circuit television cameras and the drone recording of citizens while repression of protests continued. The state of emergency returned with sticking power in France.[10]

Exceptional measures offer fertile ground for abuses. Imposed on claims of state survival that assimilate people's fate to the state's, agents from executive authorities to the police can suspend rights and constitutional protections just as restrictions to their authority are lifted. By derogating rights, emergency regimes weaken standards and erode legal protections, making it more likely for government officials to abuse citizens while shielding themselves from accountability. Concerned with potential abuses, human rights treaties include derogation clauses stipulating which rights can and cannot be suspended under emergencies.[11]

The 1966 International Covenant for Civil and Political Rights, for example, recognizes national security, public order, and public health as legitimate reasons to temporarily restrict the freedom to express one's ideas, assemble, associate, or unionize. Still, Article 4 of the Covenant mandates governments to make public the reasons for an emergency. It also prescribes time limits and effective oversight. Fundamental rights to life, equality before the law, freedom of thought, or the ban on torture, cruel treatment, or arbitrary criminalization cannot be suspended under any circumstances—the Covenant is clear on this. Rights derogation clauses are also included in the European Convention on Human Rights and the American Convention on Human Rights, which refer specific tribunals for monitoring and accountability. Despite such efforts to accommodate states' exceptional measures, most governments do not follow the protocols. And even when they do, as in France, it is unclear whether reporting prevents abuses, the successive renewal of the state of emergency, or including its main provisos into regular laws. Those in charge can disregard laws for various reasons, from invoking security threats to "popular unrest," natural disasters, or health crises, even in contradictory ways.[12]

In 2020, following the World Health Organization's declaration of the COVID-19 pandemic on March 11, hundreds of declarations of national, regional, and local emergencies were set in place. Massive restrictions were imposed across countries as the initial response. Three months into the pandemic, thirty-two countries and a number of regional and local governments were under states of emergency mandating social distancing, quarantines, and border closures. Often, enforcement undermined the measures' stated purpose of protecting public health. Newspapers reported geo-tracking individuals; censoring media or social media; militarized security agents abusing people and leaving them stranded far from their homes, or detaining individuals in unsanitary conditions, deprived of medical care, running water or sanitation, sometimes leading to deaths, with those responsible protected under exceptional regimes. Killings of individuals transgressing curfews made media headlines in countries including from India to Nigeria, Kenya, and the Philippines to Colombia and Argentina.

Often, victims found themselves forced to transgress social distancing rules to get food or medicine or to care for a loved one. Even in countries that did not formally introduce emergency measures, ordinary powers were expanded in ways amounting to an "unofficial" state of emergency, Neus Torbisco Casals explains. By June 2021, under sanitary emergencies, over 144 governments had committed abuses, imposed censorship, and ignored time limits for health emergency regimes. The pandemic thus was treated as a threat to the state—at least until travel, real estate, and entertainment corporations and electoral campaigns demanded a quick "return to normal" and the lifting of most health measures.[13]

Two decades ago, Giorgio Agamben's claim that the state of exception was reaching "its maximum worldwide deployment" was highly debated. By now, big and small emergencies have evolved from potentially scandalous to part of routine governmental "scripts," as both Mark Neocleous and Thomas Poole put it. Both concepts and policies of emergency have expanded to comprise scenarios that would not have been considered emergencies in the past. Indeed, scholars increasingly acknowledge their complexity and nuance. Thus Sergei Prozorov describes "a plurality of empirical states of emergency," while Conor Bean highlights their "compounding and intertwining" character. With differential legal standing and changing character, emergencies are defined and administered by a myriad agent, Bean notes, ultimately subjected to "essential contestability" through institutional mechanisms and popular resistance. Furthermore, as governments apply exceptional measures without formally acknowledging them, undeclared "de facto emergencies" spread out, further weakening rights and democratic politics. Meanwhile, emergency measures spread and, as I discuss later, may have also shifted from a trait of authoritarian regimes to prevailing in democracies.[14]

The available evidence supports Agamben's claim. Varieties of Democracy country experts assess the type and intensity of states of emergency due to natural disasters, terrorist attacks, armed conflict/war, mass protest/popular uprising, and others. The graph below, figure 1, represents the average use of declared emergency measures—adding all categories—across countries between 1900 and 2023. The graph shows a steady, significant rising trend in the use of emergency measures across all countries, which gives empirical support to Giorgio Agamben's claim about the expansion of the state of exception.

Among the highest-ranked democracies, the case of France is telling.

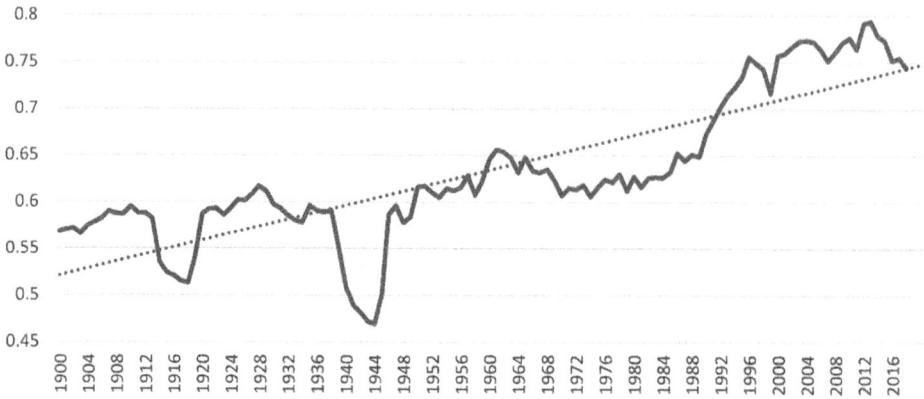

Figure 1: Emergency measures, world average use, 1900–2023 (Source: V-Dem)

For years, emergency measures in response to terrorist threats led the French authorities to silence protests against neoliberal austerity and regressive labor and pension reforms. As in France, an expansive policy repertoire—ranging from the state of emergency to security laws to the police micromanaging citizens' lives—lets governments get away with criminalizing and brutally repressing citizens, even for reasons unrelated to the emergency. And as the joint rationales of emergency and securitization gain ground, room for democratic politics shrinks.

The study of emergency regimes has developed into a profuse literature. The established scholarship illuminates its spectacular top surface, however, while keeping other modalities of emergency opaque. Emergency regimes are often imposed by invoking security reasons, expanding room for police intervention. Emergency regimes also expand room for discretionary authority; even local, less visible protocols can lead to highly consequential outcomes.

The Exception and Its Repertoire

In 1987, when asked about the prospects of lifting Paraguay's thirty-three-year-old state of siege, citizens in Asunción expressed anxiety as they wondered how *not* living under a state of exception would affect their lives. At the time, 70 percent of Paraguayans had been born under General Alfredo Stroessner's dictatorship, where individuals deemed "security risks" could simply vanish. Paraguayans were far from a rarity. Generations of Latin Americans grew up under emergency rule. Violent military coups and dictators like Augusto Pinochet or Jorge Rafael Videla drew on states of exception that lasted many years. Emergency regimes made it easier for these dictatorships to carry out massive human rights violations, including forced disappearances and extrajudicial executions supported by a network of clandestine camps.[15]

First developed in the aftermath of the French Revolution to safeguard nascent republican institutions during crises, emergency regimes spread over the nineteenth century as most new republics across continents adopted some of their mechanisms. Embedded in the constitution and the law, like the French state of siege or the German state of exception, or under norms regulating local and nationwide states of emergency, they can define "alternative forms of legality" with executive approval. Emergency measures may come as "rushed" legislation or packed as part of policies, executive orders, or decree laws with parliamentary support, Oren Gross notes. They also take the form of special "need and urgency" decrees bypassing legislatures and administrative rules. Emergency regimes may remain "dormant or implicit," as John Ferejohn and Pasquale Pasquino explain, not formally acknowledged but effectively imposed. Even presumably "innocuous" routine administrative rules or regular laws may channel exceptional conditions. They can be adopted without formal acknowledgment and hide unannounced, in plain sight. While it is by now clear that declared emergency regimes have been rising since the start of the twentieth century, as the above graph shows, the data does not capture the volume of undeclared measures or their cumulative effects.[16]

Despite their legal—often even legalistic—framework, emergency regimes presuppose that, as Nasser Hussain points out, "the law knows that it will not be sufficient." Thus exceptional measures introduce a "legal void," as Agamben explains, or hybrid conditions in which rights are suspended and state agents claim de facto authority. Through a variety of mechanisms, emergency measures can suspend rights, laws, or constitutional provisos, introducing a legally opaque zone where the fate of thousands may be decided outside formal channels as the state disregards its own laws.[17]

Key emergency institutions are rooted in colonialism and war and were imported from the battlefield, Neocleous observes. Martial law, for example, evolved as a military institution used in the British colonies that was later extended to the metropolis. It was part of the "feedback effects of colonial lawmaking," Thomas Poole notes, which normalized institutions initially designed for subjecting others through force. Likewise, the French state of siege initially described the special powers granted to military commanders when taking over an enemy position. By 1800, however, the state of siege allowed for temporary intervention by the military and military courts in domestic matters in France.[18]

On the other side of the Atlantic, the US Supreme Court recognized martial law by the late 1840s. Since then, the state of siege and martial law have become equivalent emergency regimes subjecting the population to expanded executive prerogatives, military powers, and suspended rights and liberties. They represent a move toward direct "regulation *by* the military of the whole social order on behalf of the state," as Neocleous puts it.[19]

If the "prerogative emergency power" defined the standard for treating colonial populations, as Tina Dafnos observes, emergency rule eventually entered legal systems back in the metropolis. The extralegal resources used to govern people considered "lesser" shaped the very "development of Western legality" and its institutionalized repertoires, as Hussain notes. Over time, emergency provisos became part of "liberal order-building," Neocleous adds, also used to suppress domestic "others," starting with workers' protests. Thus, from war scenarios and the treatment of colonial subjects, key emergency institutions became mainstream.[20]

With World War I, as emergency regimes were adopted across Europe, the US Congress gave President Woodrow Wilson "sweeping powers" to declare emergencies and bypass laws in ways that defined the country's distinctive "piecemeal" emergency style, Scheppele writes. During these years, in both the UK and the US, special legislation authorized the selective suspension of rights and liberties, the domestic deployment of the military, martial law, and summary executions.[21]

No wonder that fears about the "liquidation' of democracy" by the state of exception were recurrent. Concerns grew larger in Germany in the 1920s, when the Weimar Constitution, in its Article 48, authorized the president to introduce emergency measures without parliamentary approval. When the crisis worsened, extraordinary measures were normalized as a governing tool in response to hyperinflation, labor activism, or undisciplined regional authorities. Eventually, President Paul von Hindenburg used emergency decrees to bypass—and then dissolve—the parliament, which led to the rise of Hitler to power. After the staging of the Reichstag fire, through new emergency measures Hindenburg suspended fundamental rights and liberties for "the protection of the people and State." At that point, Hitler assumed unrestricted power, and the entire Nazi regime unfolded under a twelve-year state of exception that was instrumental to his expansionist war and the extermination of millions across Europe.

Following the end of World War II, after Germany committed to never again resort to emergency rule, the belief developed that these institutions would not lead to abuses in liberal democracies. Measures to suspend rights, Pasquino and Ferejohn write in 2006, "are almost never equally employed in the advanced or 'stable democracies,'" where, the authors claim, emergency powers tend to "die out." If this account does not quite match the records, it became part of political science's commonsense.[22]

Emergency institutions turned into a staple of the Cold War. The US "so-called 'national security doctrine' and its variants," as Leandro Despouy, the United Nations rapporteur on states of emergency, put it, led to paramilitary state-terror-driven crusades. Satellite wars followed, as a flurry of US-sponsored coups d'état supported by emergency regimes— like the ones referred to in Chile, Argentina, and Paraguay. National security claims legitimized exceptional conditions, abuses, and atrocities. Operation Condor, the 1970s South American state terror network initially headquartered in Chile and with participation of Argentina, Bolivia, Chile, Uruguay, and Paraguay, was one of them. Supported on the international collaboration of police and military personnel, US intelligence, and clandestine torture camps, teams were dispatched to kidnap and assassinate dissidents across countries. Overall, state terror in South America led to about 80,000 killings, over 30,000 forced disappearances, and 400,000 detainees, whereas paramilitary violence in Central America left a conservative estimate of "160,000 people killed and two million displaced" in the 1980s alone.[23]

The end of the Cold War saw only a partial decrease in exceptional measures, which continued to gain ground by invoking new threats. Widespread democratization since the 1980s only initially lowered their use. Concerned with these trends, in the mid-1990s, the UN Rapporteur for States of Emergency Leandro Despouy denounced the language of emergency for "clothing in legal apparel what was in fact nothing more than arbitrary rule." Showing that emergency regimes had tripled over the previous decade, Despouy documented patterns of government abuses.

Since then, the trends described by the UN rapporteur intensified. Varying circumstances, from the threat of (loosely defined) terrorism to environmental disasters to protests and health crises, have been met with emergency measures. Even prior to the pandemic, the number and intensity of emergency regimes were on the rise. Between sixty to eighty countries declare emergencies every year, including a number of democracies. In managing emergencies, governments, including established liberal democracies, undermine fundamental rights and guarantees with "pervasive and insidious effects" on democracy, as Oren Gross and Fionnuala Ni Aoláin note. Both the crises leading to the adoption of emergency measures and the abuses allowed by the measures themselves hurt the most vulnerable the worst, from migrants to members of racial, ethnic, or religious minorities, protesters, and the poor.[24]

Amid accelerating climate change, emergency measures declared in response to natural disasters have gained center stage. Insurance records show that the number of disasters generating losses quadrupled since 1980 to reach 820 in 2019. Somehow, legal scholars seem to assume that disasters are difficult to manipulate politically, as Kim Scheppele explains: "The emergency is declared, the problems are fixed (or managed), and then the emergency is clearly over, so everything goes back to normal." In reality, emergency protocols are rarely so neatly defined. Land and rights defenders have documented how frequently emergency measures declared for environmental reasons lead to abuses, as when governments use clauses out of context to target protesters denouncing the extractive operations behind disasters. Local states of emergency are often declared to protect extractive operations deemed of national security interest, which immediately criminalizes those protesting them. Disaster-related emergencies and protocols leading to abuses became more concerning as the number of environmental emergencies skyrocketed in recent years, from ten emergencies linked to natural disasters declared every year in the 1980s to seventy-three in 2020. Adding to these concerns, one-third of rights violations targeted "environmental, land and indigenous peoples' rights defenders" in the Americas.[25]

V-Dem experts assign scores for every variable to every country. Figure 2 represents the average scores assigned by V-Dem experts for emergency measures responding to natural disasters for all countries, every year since 1900.

Confirming different studies, the graph shows a steady rise in governments' use of emergency measures in response to natural disasters since the 1980s. It jumps up in the 2000s to then significantly peak in 2010, 2016, 2019 and—dramatically—in 2020. The ramifications of emergency regimes are considerable, including supposedly benign measures addressing environmental causes. The conditions opened by states of emergency invite the state's "ability to act extralegally" in ways leading to systematic police abuses of poorer citizens and those from immigrant and minority groups. In the summer of 2014, as the video of the killing of eighteen-year-old Michael Brown by the Ferguson, Missouri police became viral, massive Black Lives Matter protests followed in major cities across the US. The

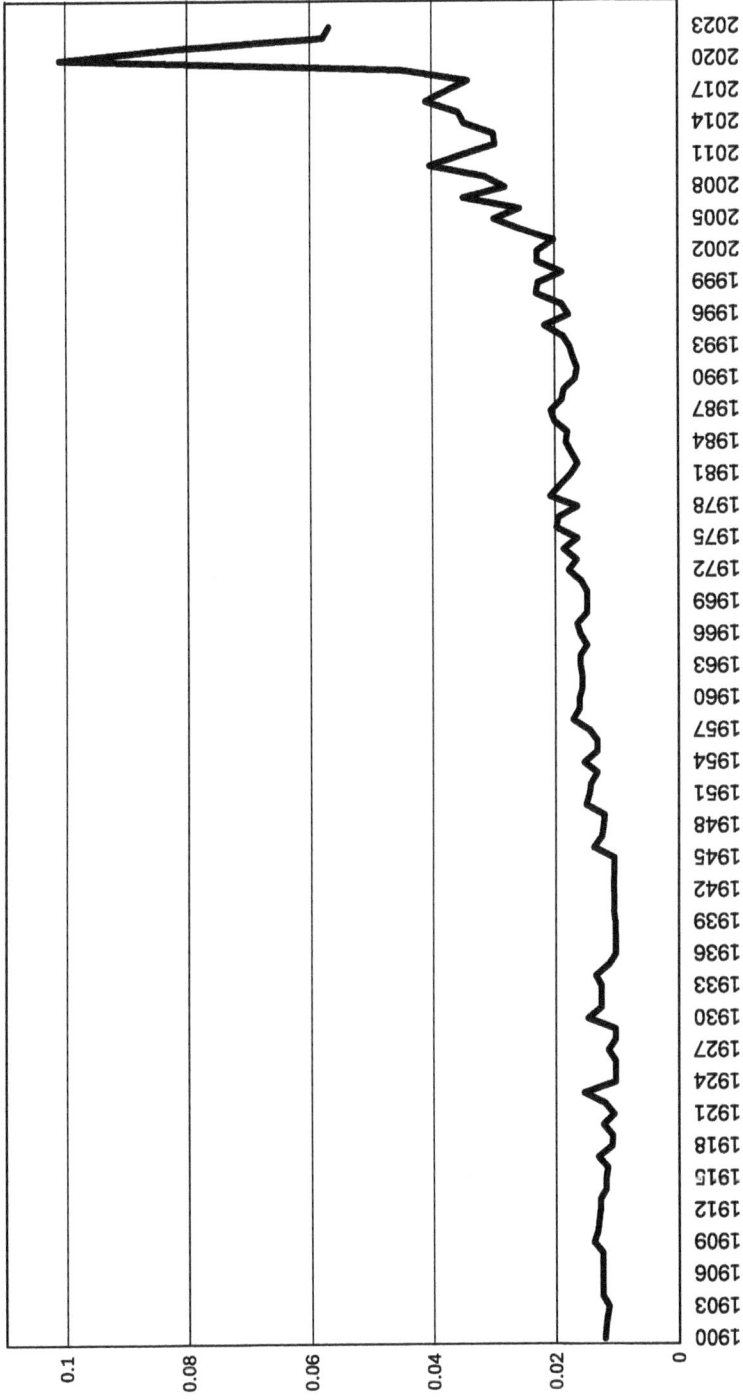

Figure 2: Average worldwide use of emergency measures for natural disasters, 1900–2023 (Source: V-Dem)

head of St. Louis County in Missouri invoked the 2013 Natural Disaster Emergency Operations Plan to declare a state of emergency and treated the protests as "civil disorders" under the Emergency Operations Plan. The state of emergency protocols gave the county's head authority to impose curfews and expand police prerogatives across sixty local police departments in ways that bypassed Ferguson's authorities. Even seemingly uncontroversial emergency provisos addressing natural disasters can be used against citizens to repress protesters—Black Lives Matter protesters in this case.[26]

Such administrative or local, "small emergencies," judged as in need of "exceptional solutions" and yet "too minor" to justify declaring an emergency, Scheppele argues, can proliferate without media coverage underneath the surface of the division of powers and the law. These local regimes, also referred as "creeping emergencies," include partial measures in response to crises that may seem "too minor" to warrant constitutional or public debate. While their authorization under administrative protocols helps officials avoid scrutiny, the example of Ferguson shows how consequential these "small" emergencies can be.[27]

Beliefs that emergency measures can be easily subjected to judicial review persist, however, despite systematic court deference to the authorities. While legally challenging the violent repression of protests in court takes time, judges often concede that local executive authorities have discretion to define "what counts as a civil disorder" in their jurisdictions. In turn, even when available, "ex-post" forms of control come too late, making it impossible to reverse the consequences of emergency measures and their effects.[28]

The emergency repertoire brings together an extended map of governing practices that greatly exceeds the dominant constitutional law focus of the scholarship on emergency regimes. Often, as Ferejohn and Pasquino acknowledge, crises that used to lead to declarations of emergency can be confronted with "more or less ordinary policing techniques, beefed up with a few extra powers permitting the detention of suspects without charges, and perhaps suspending their access to lawyers." Rather than a mere simplification of procedures, this speaks of the links between extraordinary proclamations by executive leaders and the routine discretionary administration of emergency conditions by low-ranking public officials, especially the police. Despite this rare recognition, the dominant constitutional lens in the emergency politics literature continues to dismiss the police-emergency link.[29]

Life in the State of Exception: From National Security to the War on Terror and Beyond

Decades-long emergency regimes are not exclusive of authoritarian governments. With elected authorities, Colombians spent over three decades under a state of emergency between 1949 and 1991, while citizens in Northern Ireland were subjected to an "exemplary instance of emergency legality" from 1922 until 2004. In turn, Israel has been under uninterrupted emergency regimes since the country's founding in 1948. Renewing what Adam Mizock describes as a "perpetual" state of emergency is an annual Knesset ritual, Glenn Frankel writes, amid a permanent crisis in which powerful parties "thrive."[30]

A country without a constitution, perhaps with one closer to the British style, or rather with a constitution in the making, Israel counts with fourteen Basic Laws with quasi-constitutional status intended to become part of a constitution. The country's emergency regime is no less unique, with various mechanisms loosely overlapping and complementing one another in what Yoav Mehozay characterizes as "a legal patchwork of sorts."

On the books, Israel has three types of emergency powers: First, mandatory emergency defense regulations, with origins in British colonial powers; second, administrative emergency orders granting exceptional authority to ministers (for a maximum of three months, with the possibility to delegate authority); and, third, primary—or formal—emergency laws passed by the Knesset. Neither mandatory defense regulations nor administrative orders require further authorization, whereas the Knesset's emergency legislation needs prior declaration of a state of emergency.

This enumeration makes things look simpler than they are. Just one of these categories, formal emergency laws, comprises distinct "clusters" including renewed administrative emergency orders, laws dependent on a declared state of emergency, and independent (emergency) laws. Some regulations depend on the formal declaration of an emergency, whereas others do not. In turn, mandatory regulations specify the prerogatives granted to officials, while others authorize discretionary lawmaking powers, and secondary orders can be transformed into primary laws.[31]

In a way reminiscent of France, the trend has been for matters that used to be the subject of executive emergency declarations to be turned into laws, accompanied by an active judiciary checking on the use of state authority, as Gideon Sapir explains. Still, Mehozay argues that a fourth source of emergency measures exists in Israel, specifically targeting the occupied Palestinian territories, which may invoke international law.

Israel's emergency regime epitomizes the fluid and flexible framework of the emergency that allows the state differential treatment of groups while still invoking democratic legitimacy. The "immense complexity and ambiguity" of the emergency system, Mehozay observes, allows greater flexibility in the treatment of citizens and noncitizens within Israel and in the occupied territories.[32]

Both in Israel and Colombia, decades-long emergency regimes have been justified on the grounds of conflict. Colombians learned a hard lesson following decades of violence, militarization, and abuses under and a state of siege. Still facing challenges to fully implementing the conditions of the 2016 Peace Accord, in 2022, the official report was released documenting 450,666 homicides, 121,768 forced disappearances, and tens of thousands of cases of torture, kidnappings, child recruitment, and a staggering eight million internally displaced people.[33]

Earlier, in 1991, with the armed conflict still unfolding, Colombians significantly restricted emergency powers through a constitutional reform. In chapter 6, the Constitution establishes emergency measures for a declared war or "a serious disruption of the public order." The president, supported by their ministers, can declare a "state of foreign war" in response to foreign aggression or a "state of internal disturbance" for ninety days, renewable twice—in the last case requiring a vote by the Senate. Finally, in case of a "grave public calamity" involving ecological, social, or economic disturbances, the president and ministers can declare a thirty-day state of emergency, renewable up to ninety days in a year.

At no time "may civilians be questioned or tried by the penal military system," the Colombian constitution states. Restrictions require exceptional measures to be related and proportionate to the emergency, as well as a ban on suspending human rights, fundamental freedoms, social rights, or checks and rights protections, including judges' assessment of the constitutionality of the measures. Furthermore, the emergency must end as soon as the cause is no longer there, and the president and ministers are responsible for abuses committed under the emergency regime.

As in Colombia, residents of Perú's mining corridor in the Huallaga Valley have endured for decades what Richard Kernaghan described as "a zone and time of legal exception" under a permanent state of siege. The "emergency zones" discussed by Kernaghan make Perú's 115 presidential declarations of states of emergency between 2000 and 2010 recorded by Wright more significant. Emergency zones and regimes can place populations in extreme conditions of vulnerability, as with the 324 documented cases of land and rights defenders killed around the world in 2024 alone, 233 of them in the Americas.[34]

A rise of emergency measures has been documented also in the "stable democracies" referred to by Pasquino and Ferejohn, from Italy to France to the US. With at least forty-four ongoing national emergencies as of June 2025, US presidents have declared ninety national emergencies under the National Emergencies Act since 1979, with over thirty of them routinely renewed. In June 2020, President Trump made for the first time an official international organization into a national security threat. The measure came in response to the International Criminal Court's intention to investigate possible war crimes committed in Afghanistan. Rather than collaborating with the investigation, Trump's executive order characterized any ICC attempt "to investigate, arrest, detain, or prosecute" US or US-allied officials as an "unusual and extraordinary threat" to the nation. Soon after, two top ICC officials and their families had their assets frozen and could not enter the US, while US nationals were forbidden from engaging in transactions with them. President Biden ended the emergency only after the ICC dropped the case in April 2021. Again, in February 2025, by Executive Order 14203 President Trump declared an emergency against the ICC, for engaging in "illegitimate and baseless actions targeting America and our close ally Israel." For years, the US has refused to accept the jurisdiction of the ICC, claiming that its military personnel can only be brought before US courts. Yet, except for a few low-ranking personnel, prosecutions for war crimes have either been lenient or not held at all, as when, after the Department of Justice's report on the Bush-era torture program, President Barack Obama chose not to bring prosecutions and called for "reflection" instead. Considering the "poor record" of the US in prosecuting its citizens for war crimes, "immunity from local laws usually means impunity," Linda Pearson concludes.[35]

Drawing on media and archival research, figure 3 shows formal declarations of the state of emergency or equivalent emergency measures in democracies and nondemocracies (according to Polity V scores) since the 1970s.[36]

While earlier in the series, mostly nondemocracies adopted emergency regimes, by the mid-2000s, democratic governments appeared to start resorting to emergency measures more than nondemocracies, in contradiction with the belief that associates the use of emergency rule to authoritarian regimes. These records delineate clear trends and put into question claims that democracies "almost never" resort to measures suspending rights. Considering that this data does not capture undeclared emergen-

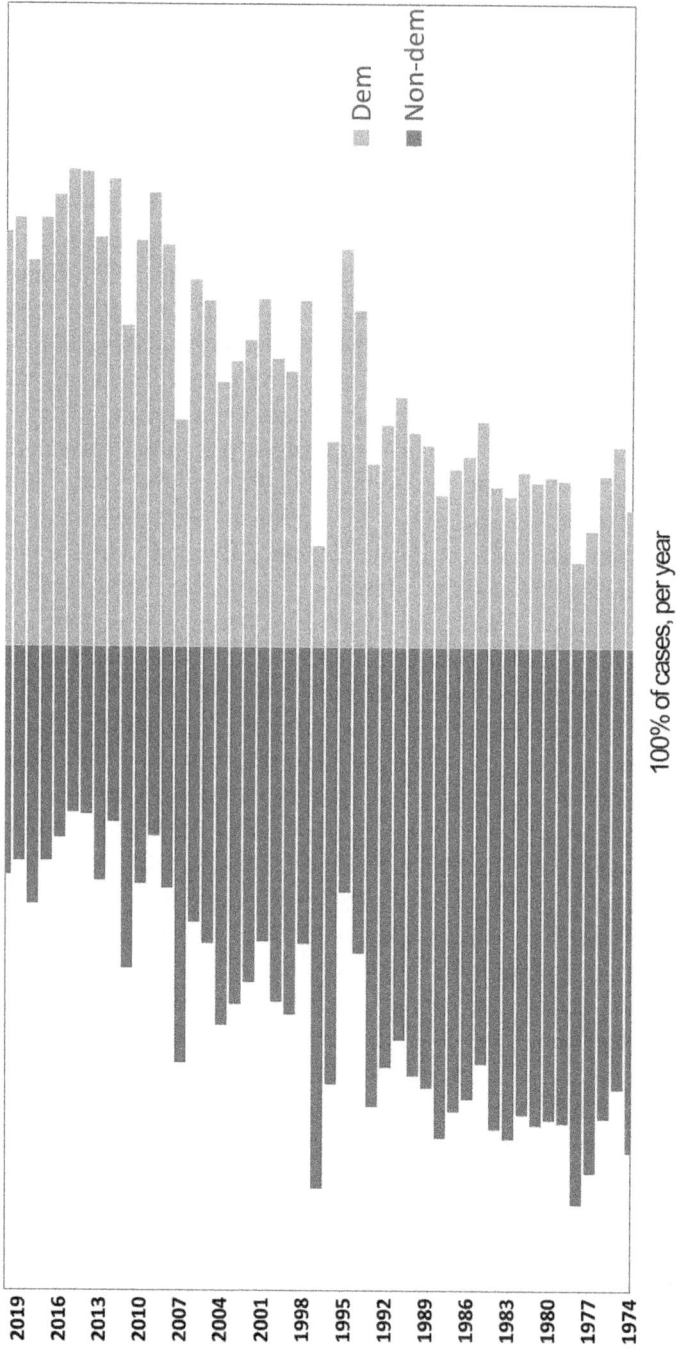

Figure 3: States of emergency and emergency measures, 1974–2019, democracies vs. nondemocracies (% share) (Source: Newspaper records, Polity IV, and V-Dem)

cies, their normalization as part of regular laws, or small emergencies, the actual picture should be more significant.

These trends are not surprising, considering that emergency measures "tend to perpetuate themselves," absorbed by laws and policies, as Gross explains, even with different purposes than those stated initially. Returning to the original conditions is exceedingly rare, if not impossible. Often renewed, emergency provisos are made part of regular laws and governance, as in France. As in that case, far from a return to prior standards after emergencies are lifted, emergency conditions tend to become normalized and the standards altered, with cumulative effects.

In Italy, parliamentary decree-laws from the 1970s allowed detaining individuals without a charge for more extended periods as well as "preventive" police shootings. Such old provisos were used in post-9/11 antiterrorism and anti-immigration campaigns, Francesca Menichelli shows. The old decree-laws expanded police prerogatives to restrict rights, extended preventive detention for terrorist suspects, introduced harsher prison conditions, and excluded immigrants from effective access to legal protections.[37]

Difficulties in restoring prior conditions seem apparent when emergency measures are supported by widespread technologies. Warrantless wiretapping may still be illegal (except for provisos such as FISA's Section 702), but surveillance technologies fall into a gray area that both states and corporations tap. Thus, even when involving illegal surveillance and harvesting of our own personal data from emails, cloud servers, and social media, or through heightened airport screenings or biometric controls, they have become routinized thanks to widely available devices from cell phones to security cameras. Likewise, bringing the military into routine policing, as in France, or empowering forces or offices such as ICE or Homeland Security in the US are steps that are challenging to reverse. As extraordinary measures, institutions, and technologies define the normalized starting point for new generations, historical standards and protections may be gone with minimal debate.[38]

"Borderless threats," impossible to identify and delimit in time, should not be the object of emergency measures, Bernard Manin reminds us. Such threats, as well as manufactured or staged emergencies, can damage—even kill—constitutions, as Scheppele observes. Yet governments do invoke fuzzy threats to declare emergencies. Examples can be puzzling. In 2011, a year after the new prime minister ironically defined "rain" as his only concern, the government of Trinidad declared a state of emergency in response to an undisclosed threat of a "magnitude [that] can never be eliminated," with no further justification.[39]

Undefined threats, as Manin warns, lead to indefinite emergencies. This is the kind of emergency the US presented to the world. On September 14, 2001, at the National Cathedral in Washington, President George W. Bush defined the September 11 attacks as an act of war while expressing his "steadfast resolve" to confront an enemy that he characterized as "terror," as he pledged to "win the war against terrorism." Since then, the US embarked on, and pushed much of the world into, a "global war on terror" that, as Jinee Lokaneeta notes, brought its own "'state of exception' . . . in which laws applicable under ordinary times are suspended." The US-led global war on terror's elusive goals and purview made conditions of emergency permanent. Both citizen and foreign suspects were denied legal protections. It then became clear that, as Agamben had predicted, exceptional measures were becoming "the norm." Over the decades, the US has become "saturated with emergency rule," as Elaine Scarry notes.[40]

Outside wartime, the nation has been under multiple emergency regimes since the 1930s, starting with responses to the Great Depression, intensifying during the Cold War, followed by dozens of national emergencies—a number of them continually renewed since the 1970s. With emergency measures on the rise prior to 2001, the global war on terror added to the US's spreading of the paradigm of national security. Even though their violent, lawless traits were openly visible overseas—as in Latin America's terror campaigns referred to in the previous chapter—national security ideas still shape US common sense.[41]

In the escalation of emergencies, however, the development of a nuclear arsenal has been defined as a point of no return. Nuclear weapons have made the risk of their unintended use into an actual permanent threat, Scarry observes, thus raising the need for exceptional security measures. Far from Cold War spy movies, the danger of the use of nuclear weapons has never been higher. Or so say the scientists at the *Bulletin of Atomic Scientists*, whose Doomsday Clock was introduced in 1947. For 2025, the group has set the clock at "9 seconds to midnight—the closest to global catastrophe it has ever been." The rationale of the emergency finds ways to perpetuate itself.[42]

"This is the kind of fight we're in for the rest of our lives and probably our kids' lives," General David Petraeus, later head of the CIA, declared about the war on terror. In September 2001, Congress authorized the US president "to use all necessary and appropriate force against those nations, organizations, or persons" found to be linked to the World Trade Center attack, then to enact its own emergency regime through the Patriot Act. Expanding the definition of terrorism in vague terms, the law defined

individuals and nonstate actors as enemies and legalized indefinite detention without an arrest warrant in blatant defiance of domestic and international laws.[43]

President Bush followed up with a military order authorizing the
indefinite detention of foreign terrorist suspects under the military's
"exclusive jurisdiction." The order nullified the detainees' legal standing
and protections by not recognizing them either as criminal suspects or
prisoners of war. Treating detainees as vague "entities that could be neither named nor classified by the Law," as Agamben writes, they were
banned from accessing courts in the US, other countries, or internationally. Driven by classical emergency tropes, with appeals to imaginary
"ticking bomb" scenarios and the need to strike a "balance" between liberty and security, the war on terror and its supporting experts helped normalize unlawful practices.[44]

Discussing the post-9/11 world, Judith Butler notes how states of emergency affirm the state's "right to suspend rights" and treat the law as a mere
set of rules that can be tactically bent through "fully discretionary, even
arbitrary" decisions. All the more so, these regimes of indefinite detention
displayed "state power in its lawlessness" under a state of emergency that
became potentially indefinite as well. What was new was not the state's
tactical treatment of the law, which sixteenth-century reason of state theorists had already identified, but the extension and intensity of unlawful
governmentalities that the war on terror coordinated globally.[45]

Confined in spatial and legal limbo, individuals denied protection
under the Geneva Conventions or other international or domestic laws
found themselves subjected to torture. As the intentional administration
of "severe pain or suffering . . . physical or mental . . . by or at the instiga-
tion of or with the consent or acquiescence of a public official or other
person acting in an official capacity," torture is "strictly illegal in any circumstances" and a crime in both international and US law.[46]

Attempts to give criminal state actions a semblance of legality supported these initiatives, as politicians, media figures, and experts, including psychologists, defended "waterboarding," "enhanced interrogation,"
and other euphemistic labels for torture practices. Academics, journalists,
and popular culture figures helped give such unlawful practices a semblance of legitimacy. Unprecedented, often blatantly illegal conditions
became normalized as the additive expansion of exceptional conditions
turned the Patriot Act into a "new normality and benchmark," Gross
notes. Yet legalizing purely discretionary "legal grey holes," as Leonard
Feldman adds, can be worse than sheer state lawlessness.[47]

While torture never stopped being used in liberal democracies with purposes of "confession, information, or intimidation," as Darius Rejali's comprehensive study shows, governments publicly dismissed torture as uncivilized and as held by lesser, authoritarian others, Lokaneeta observes. All of this changed with the launching of the "global war on terror" when, for the first time in centuries, torture became openly defended and banalized. At the time, legal scholar Alan Dershowitz claimed authority for US officials to produce "excruciating" pain as he called for "torture warrants" to authorize its use in interrogations.[48]

A decade into its global "war," the US claimed the prerogative to detain suspects "without trial until the end of the hostilities," a euphemistic claim for a military mission with no clear end and potentially affecting anyone on earth. Laws, courts (like the Foreign Intelligence Surveillance Act, or FISA, court), executive orders, prisons, arrests, criminal charges, evidence, legal doctrine, and even legal cases were classified as secret by US authorities. A secret law makes no sense. And yet secret laws and courts expanded under the US exceptional regime, making it possible to use state secrets to criminalize citizens for requesting information about policies whose secret status they ignore.[49]

By 2021, the war on terror had cost over $8 trillion. It had killed over 900,000 people, displaced over thirty-eight million people, and caused 3.6–3.8 million additional deaths by the destruction of infrastructure and services by US-driven or supported military campaigns.[50]

Like its national security doctrine predecessor, the US antiterrorist agenda gained international dominance. It was pushed onto countries through diplomatic and military channels with the support of international organizations, including the IMF, and it helped normalize emergency measures and unlawful governance globally. Thousands of people have gotten caught up in emergency-driven irregular "wars" and their unlawful maze. The US war on terror relied on dozens of torture camps in undisclosed locations around the world, evasively called detention centers or facilities. In these camps, or sites "placed outside the normal juridical order," to borrow from Agamben, both foreign suspects and US citizens underwent detention and torture, and at least 100 people were killed. Introduced in the late nineteenth century to round up people resisting colonial subjection, the use of camps by liberal democracies expanded with emergency rule. "The United States is running concentration camps on our southern border, and that is exactly what they are—they are concentration camps," said Representative Alexandria Ocasio-Cortés objecting to the mass detention of migrants, only to be criticized for her words.

Still, as the site of torture, extrajudicial killings, and death, camps from Guantanamo Bay to the Chicago Police Department's Homan Square or -twenty-first-century refugee and immigrant detention centers, now also increasingly outsourced to third countries—all are supported by the emergency rationale.[51]

Stories of Exception

"You have no rights," seventeen-year-old Francisco Erwin Galicia heard after being detained at a border checkpoint in Falfurrias, Texas. Galicia, a US citizen, was sent to an ICE center in July 2019, where he stayed incommunicado for weeks. A federal emergency at the Mexico-US border had been declared by President Donald Trump earlier that year. As "Build the wall!" chants spread, the US authorities made asylum applicants wait for weeks in Mexican territory, in the most precarious conditions, and then denied most applications while forcefully separating migrant families and detaining children and their parents. Among detained migrants and residents, cramped in a cell with sixty men, with little food, in unsanitary, dangerous conditions, during his twenty-three-day detention, Galicia lost twenty-six pounds. "It was inhumane how they treated us. It got to the point where I was ready to sign a deportation paper just to not be suffering there anymore," Galicia declared. He described seeing sick detainees afraid to ask for medical attention following guards' threats.[52]

Galicia's refusal to sign deportation papers and his mother's and lawyer's efforts to prove that he was a US citizen eventually led to his release. Most migrants and asylum applicants do not get a chance. When not abandoned to their deaths in the desert—with 80,000 estimated disappearances on the US-Mexico border since the 1990s—they get thrown into so-called detention centers, estimated in 200 in the US. Between 2015 and 2020, the Immigration and Customs Enforcement (ICE) deported seventy US citizens, and by 2025, with expanded raids following President Trump's order to protect US citizens against the "invasion" of "illegal aliens," cases like Galicia's have become more frequent. Since 2018, ICE has reported seventy-seven deaths in custody, most of which the American Civil Liberties Union concluded were preventable. [53]

What amounts to a true emergency and how to define it remains the subject of a politico-discursive dispute. Since the early nineteenth century, the French differentiated between a siege imposed by military commanders and the "fictitious, or political" state of siege as a special legal regime responding to an "aggravation of the systems of police" under a national threat. Indeed, in the way of a "juridical fiction," emergency regimes justify suspending laws while state agents demand exclusive authority over the "empty" alegal space thus created, Agamben explains.[54]

A vast literature assesses emergency declarations, decrees, and informal responses, as well as the role of the executive and lawmakers in emergency regimes. Most arguments highlight emergency regimes' rights suspension or derogation and the state's de facto exclusive claims of authority. Allusions to the past abound. Scholars of public law, constitutional studies, and legal and political theory trace the roots of emergency institutions in history to figures like the dictator in ancient Rome, principles of *salus populi*, or the Comité de Salut Public in revolutionary France.

While nearly unanimously accepting the need for emergency institutions, scholars differ. Some argue that emergency regimes must be separate institutions stipulating a clear purpose, procedures, time limits, and the identification of agents and organs authorized to make decisions in an emergency. Constitutional emergency institutions recognize roots in the Roman dictator. In ancient Rome, during severe crises, the Senate appointed a well-respected citizen as a dictator invested with unwarranted authority for six months. At the end of the period, the citizen in the role of dictator returned to private life. The Roman tradition is hailed as an illustrious antecedent and model for current crises.[55]

Others contend that emergencies should be governable through regular institutions and laws. When well designed, they argue, laws and policies should suffice to respond to both exceptional circumstances and everyday life just as well. Still others argue for non-institutionalized, informal emergency regimes and extralegal action as the most fitting response to unusual challenges. The law, they argue, should not be tainted by the rationale of the emergency, as when legalizing extralegal measures. Nor should responses to emergencies be constrained in ways that make the law an obstacle to the state's survival.[56]

The idea of preserving the institutional order through routine extralegal actions echoes the tradition of extraconstitutional prerogative. Officials, the argument goes, need to be granted ample discretionary authority, and their actions should be assessed only after the end of the emergency. In all cases, the need to make room for emergencies by adapting rules and institutions appears self-evident. While positions differ, the factual character of threats and need for special measures and faculties seem to be accepted as reasonable and common sense.[57]

Identifying an exceptional situation, the German legal theorist Carl Schmitt argues, is the task of an individual with authority to suspend the law. Indeed, he adds, responding to an actual emergency may require suspending "the entire existing juridical order." In his view, addressing emergencies cannot be limited by law since no norm can contain or regulate its own suspension, the same way that the law cannot ground itself.[58]

The most the law may do is to anticipate who should make such decisions. Aside from that, it is always ultimately a person "who decides on the exception," Schmitt adds, both on the existence of a threat to the state and how to respond to it. This decision—which Schmitt treats as sovereign—can suspend the constitution in an emergency for the sake of its protection.

Schmitt claims that true emergencies demand suspending the constitution. By so doing, he delineates a space that is both external and internal to the law. Even in its suspension, the constitutional framework makes otherwise contingent decisions legally binding and gives exceptional measures "juridical meaning." And if extralegal, the decision forms part of the legal order that citizens are bound to obey. Other than that, the law's legitimacy "emanates from nothingness," Schmitt writes. The sovereign decision that serves as the foundation for the legal system simply grounds itself. In a consistent, compelling way, Schmitt's theory helps normalize zones of suspended law and state unlawfulness.[59]

The authority to suspend laws goes back to old sovereign claims portraying the king as the ultimate lawmaker not subjected to law. In this tradition, the law exposes its extralegal foundation, while emergency measures result from sovereignty, whether "monarchical, dictatorial or republican," as Michael Lowy reminds us. In all cases, when confronting an emergency, the state alone has authority, even during the time when the law is suspended. In this regard, Schmitt claims that in the exception "an order still exists," which makes the lawless and legally indeterminate the object of exclusive de facto state governance. Whereas state agents can disregard laws, citizens remain subject to them, however, and must continue obeying and showing loyalty to the state. Neither under the law—which at least in part emergency measures suspend—nor entirely outside the legal order, the state still enforces laws and claims authority over the people. A Möbius strip serves Agamben to describe such scenarios of "anomie" where inside and outside are impossible to separate. And yet, by tying the suspension of the law to the juridical order, the state reasserts control over both the regular order and the legal void that it creates, Agamben explains.[60]

For all its original points, Schmitt's approach to the state of exception looks surprisingly narrow. "Not every extraordinary measure, not every police emergency measure or emergency decree, is necessarily an exception," he contends. Only the suspension of "the entire existing juridical order" constitutes a true exception in his view. Schmitt's dismissal of smaller, grassroots emergency practices seems unwarranted. In turn, by assuming a normality to go back to, Schmitt's argument loses ground. Under our present conditions, as Alex Murray observes, laws get suspended so frequently "that one cannot treat the state as a solid, impervious concept." It is as if the idea of normalcy to which we are supposed to return vanishes altogether.[61]

Indeed, as William Scheuerman points out, Schmitt's "vivid" theorizing of the emergency brings into view the dangers of expanding emergencies and their role in the "ongoing democratic decay," which has only worsened since the time of his writing. And yet Schmitt's theory conceals as much as it reveals. Portraying sovereignty as a contingent but ever-present, quasi-natural form of power, distilling its practices down to a single individual decision at the top, his theory helps normalize exceptional conditions while leaving much of their dynamics in the dark. This is the case as he defines the state of exception narrowly—as suspending the constitution. Not only are the constitutional order and its suspension portrayed as distinct, clearly identifiable moments, but the perspective makes invisible what this chapter tries to bring into view—the emergency's networked governing structures and discretionary practices sustaining the scaffolding of the state and beyond. Schmitt's binary theorizing of the exception as a momentary disruption and his refusal to acknowledge other forms of emergency or the links between them seems limiting. The theory only illuminates the state's most spectacular top surface while keeping other forms and levels of the emergency out of sight.[62]

Despite critically distancing themselves from Schmitt, most theorists either support the need for exceptional regimes or take them for granted—even legendary liberal or libertarian figures. Friedrich Hayek, for example, famously distrusted state intervention but did not see a problem with an "occasional necessity of withdrawing some of the civil liberties by a suspension of habeas corpus or the proclamation of a state of siege." Suspending rights and restricting the freedom of the press or forcing land sales on grounds of public domain only had to be truly exceptional and legally justified, Hayek noted. In turn, impacted individuals should be "fully indemnified for any damage they suffer as a result of such action," he concluded.[63]

Emergency narratives help neutralize competing actors and foreclose possibilities opened by the suspension of the law. They presuppose a sovereign right for the state to govern even the spaces and beings it abandons. Specifically, the state's claim of exclusive authority over the legally indeterminate that recognizes legal force to otherwise illegal acts tends to be treated as unquestionable. But why? Why, when the law and legal protections are suspended, should we still obey the state? Agamben helps unpack the mechanisms behind this. Legitimizing unlawful governance under conditions of exception, he shows, draws on recognizing legal status to the anomic scenario introduced by the emergency. This is where sovereignty plays a role by serving the "historical function of producing anomie," Daniel Loughlin notes, discussing Agamben and of reclaiming the governance of the anomic situation for the state.[64]

The sovereign's ability to reclaim authority over people and territories even through its own suspension is key to its effectiveness. Schmitt's justification of state legitimacy rooted in "sovereign emergency power" stands out, as it turns conditions where state power is most challenged into "arguments in its favor," as Adam Kotsko observes. Such claims seek to eliminate a true outside where people could move beyond sovereignty.[65]

Indeed, by asserting exclusive authority over the exception, the state criminalizes "insurrection and the right to resist," Agamben observes. Through what Jef Huyssman describes as a "jargon of exception," state storytellers redefine normalcy and carve out room for unlawful governance despite and through the law. Under such conditions, neither clearly within or outside the law, "a liminal creature" is both "produced and entrapped," Diego Rossello notes. In what Agamben describes as "*inclusive exclusion*," the exception captures those it proclaims to leave out in conditions of rightlessness. Citizens remain bound to the law even if at the mercy of state agents acting extralegally, where disobedience to either amounts to a criminal act. In the spaces thus created, a gray area where the institutions of liberal democracy coexist with unlawful abandonment and violence, people can be killed with impunity.[66]

In the hellish social territories of the exception, driven by a rationale that ascribes worth alongside biopolitical hierarchies that sort out the deserving, the worthless, and enemies, emergency conditions intensify the differential treatment of individuals and groups. At times, exceptions may let software engineers brought to Silicon Valley or Singapore, who are discussed by Aihwa Ong, get recognized rights. Most of the time, the unlucky ones find themselves thrown outside the law, treated as merely living entities with no rights attached, a condition that Agamben describes as bare life. Labeled criminals or terrorists, they find themselves detained or punished. Or simply deemed worthless and abandoned—often to death, as the 29,731 migrants who died crossing the Mediterranean Sea since 2014 or the tens of thousands dead and missing in the US-Mexico border. Only sometimes have the excluded the choice to leave—at least in ways that leaving means something else than death. More often, disenfranchised and securitized, deprived of legal recognition and protections, they remain trapped in the legal limbos of the exception where they can be treated "like animals."[67]

It is the exception, rather than "nature" or "natural" conditions—as Thomas Hobbes had claimed—that produces bare life through the "animalization" of humans. While Diego Rossello rightly points out the need of exploring the indistinction between human and animal as a "productive zone" of encounter and exchange, its negative connotations still dominate considering the absolute vulnerability—and real chances of annihilation—that the status of "animal" still brings with it. One need look no further than the conditions of a twenty-first-century abattoir to understand the grim reality of being treated or killed "like animals."[68]

As formal, informal, global, national, local, and individualized emergency measures reinforce one another, the legal and extralegal domains get blurred as a main governing tool. Thus the framework of the state of exception appears to be "not entirely adequate" as a heuristic device anymore, Agamben observes. Or at least not alone. Rather than a neat constitutional order to which we return following extraordinary moments, "an unprecedented generalization of the paradigm of security" with its rationale of administering and governing threats diffuses cumulative unlawful standards in ways crucial to understanding the rise of permanent emergencies. Indeed, emergency institutions "created the platform for security to become the central category of liberal order-building in the twentieth century," as Neocleous writes. And if traditional emergency measures still require formal acknowledgment and time limits, security reasons find no such restrictions. Emergency mechanisms introduce and normalize major rights breaches, while the security rationale diffuses them and makes the need for emergency measures permanent.[69]

Security

> "BEWARE
> Suspicious light bulbs
> Soft drink bottles
> Aerosol cans
> Fire extinguishers
> Briefcases
> Mayonnaise jars

Men with shaving cuts
THINGS TO BUY
Three days of food and water, duct tape and plastic sheeting to seal
your house."

In early 2003, the US Homeland Security threat color code system was raised to the top "orange alert" level for the first time since 2001. Both American and British police and security forces blocked parking spaces and intensified patrolling around critical buildings such as the House of Commons and train stations. Checkpoints were set up from Heathrow Airport to the Holland and Lincoln tunnels in New York City. Police agents at Heathrow Airport were tripled as Prime Minister Tony Blair mobilized 450 soldiers in London.[70]

"The threat is real. The threat is real," Tom Ridge, the head of Homeland Security, warned. "The threat is very real and very possible," confirmed a British security expert. "I don't want people to panic. People should not be alarmed, they should be alert," declared Scotland Yard Commissioner Sir John Stevens, adding that the measures were "necessary for the safety of Londoners and visitors to the city." While rumors circulated about missile launchers, sarin gas, and cyanide attacks, officials offered no reports about the threats. Meanwhile, US authorities warned citizens about the possible release of poisonous substances in subways and other public areas. They instructed them to get tape and other materials to protect their homes from attacks.

To date, those mysterious threats remain undisclosed. The color-coded Homeland Security threat system was phased out in 2011 and replaced with the National Terrorism Advisory System. Security alerts continue to persuade people to accept extraordinary measures from time to time. From its early modern spread as states and markets reshaped social bonds with elusive promises of sheltering from danger, security's appeal continues to lure individuals, groups, and nations.[71]

The basic mechanism is rather simple. "By uttering 'security,'" as Ole Waever writes in his famous essay, invoking a sense of imminent threat, agents authorized by the state claim the prerogative "to use whatever means are necessary" to neutralize an object characterized as a threat. Security discourse thus defines existential threats and calls for mobilizing "all necessary means" against them. Its ubiquity speaks to ever-increasing budgets, as with the $21 trillion the US spent between 2001 and 2021 "on militarization, surveillance, and repression—all in the name of security," as Lindsay Koshgarian, Ashik Siddique, and Lorah Steichen note. In addition, developing in close relation with governments, private security is a $132 billion annual industry worldwide. Finally, after leaving behind its darker, authoritarian national-security-supporting state terror campaigns through which "large sections of the population were exterminated in various parts of Latin America," like neoliberalism, security has gained democratic credentials. And popularity. Asked to choose between security and liberty, 68.1 percent of 100,000 World Values Survey respondents across sixty-six countries choose security. No wonder security remains central, confirming its place as what Agamben characterizes as the state's "only task and source of legitimacy."[72]

Nowhere does the security rationale remain as entirely on display as in Thomas Hobbes's *Leviathan*. Hobbes built a radical body of political theory by drawing on the desire for protection. In a world he describes as an inhospitable, hypothetical warlike state of nature, isolated individuals must compete for resources, often violently. Imagining natural life as lonely, "nasty, brutish, and short," facing permanent dangers of violent death, Hobbes theorized fear and the desire for security as universal. To secure "life, and . . . the means of so preserving life," the Hobbesian solution involves instituting a sovereign power by renouncing natural equality and rights and subjecting ourselves to the sovereign. Entering the covenant on these terms appears as our only chance to gain "perpetual security against enemies and want," Hobbes writes. While the sovereign demands absolute loyalty and is himself not bound by laws or the covenant, hoping for his protection is better than having none, one learns from reading *Leviathan*. Even under an abusive ruler life should be less miserable than the prospect of returning to Hobbes's imagined natural state of permanent war. And as no security can be found outside subjection to a sovereign, the arrangement seems both desirable and rational.[73]

These arguments gained currency as a system of sovereign states consolidated following the 1648 Treaty of Westphalia. Since then, security has defined what Agamben describes as "the basic principle of state politics," its ultimate promise. Still, the expansion of security took time. Only after the mid-eighteenth century did security become a matter of policy in France, Foucault observes. The security rationale rapidly outgrew its early mercantilist ties to become a critical link bringing state and capital together in governing risk. Whether to keep disease under control or to distribute food, security measures assess risks and seek to contain them while "let[ting] things happen" within tolerable levels. With the rapid spread of travel and trade, security interventions protect the movement of commodities while monitoring the poor, crime, disasters, disruptions, and disease.[74]

Ever gaining in speed and intensity, security initiatives, laws, policies, offices, experts, academic programs, publications, and scholarship—ranging from conservative to liberal—have expanded to become "a permanent technology of government," as Agamben writes. At its core, Neocleous reminds us, the security rationale instills governmental techniques that work by "modelling the whole of human society," including our inner selves, after standards of state authority. Among its enduring effects, security tends to "neutralise political action" and it pushes us—as Hobbes suggested—to look for protection from (state) authorities.[75]

The Hobbesian view that dominates security narratives tends to be presented as primordial or "natural." For critics, starting with Jean-Jacques Rousseau, it instead describes "numberless passions which are the work of society." There is nothing natural about Hobbes's world. Adding to this critique, Georg Wilhelm Friedrich Hegel wrote that, far from natural, the scenario portrayed by Hobbes of "the contest of the private interests of all against all" defines the specific "field of conflict" of modern civil, bourgeois society. The aggressive, competitive Hobbesian state of nature speaks of the conditions of capitalist societies, Marx concludes, which—as privileged by Friedman, Becker, and other neoliberal thinkers—are presented as "natural" to us.[76]

Truly, the Hobbesian subject forms part of our immediate daily experience. As more dimensions of life become commodified, individuals find themselves increasingly isolated and subjected to uncertain market conditions. At risk of losing jobs and falling into poverty, the subject of the market is forced into the position of the Hobbesian individual seeking protection. In a world where market relations make and remake our lives, security—as Marx puts it—becomes the "supreme social concept" of bourgeois society for the have and the have-nots alike.[77]

In this regard, security's appeal to protect communities and address people's care needs reveals traces of the communities that security itself helped expropriate—reflecting its distorted projection. Coming a long way from ancient Roman pleas to the goddess Securitas to live a life free of worries, security constitutes "a mode of governing, a political technology through which individuals, groups, classes, and, ultimately, modern capital is reshaped and reordered," as Neocleous puts it. Security practices saturate our lives with worries as they subordinate the protection of rights, laws, and liberty to the needs and flows of capital. In so doing, security measures re-create core emergency traits and extend exceptional conditions in everyday life.[78]

The governance of (in)security pivots on swelling threats as governmental apparatuses make crises permanent. In the private sector, global industries offer risk assessment and solutions. Their products fuse with governments' conjuring of dangers, which opens to "the exercise of emergency powers in the name of security," as Neocleous writes. Helping normalize emergency measures, security claims support government "calls for exceptional powers, and atypical legal frameworks," Poole observes. Security makes the logic of the emergency populate the "script" of politics. Both a commodity and part of state apparatuses, security mechanisms continue to define new threats.[79]

The adoption of emergency provisos by the 2017 Security Law in France discussed earlier illustrates these trends. Laws allowing special "protection perimeters," the closure of religious sites, constant searches and harassment of Muslims, all while preventively searching buildings and monitoring terrorist suspects, exemplify ways in which legal instruments and policies can make initially exceptional measures routine. Add this to the increasing criminalization of protests and dissent, including "the folding of emergency anti-terrorist regulations into statutory law and a new security law that allows drones to film the population," Sudhir Hazareesingh writes.[80]

In perspective, the 2003 US and UK security warnings referred to earlier look unsophisticated today. Governments and corporations know significantly more about us now, thanks to loose standards allowing what Shoshana Zuboff calls "surveillance exceptionalism." Evolving informational technologies make it possible to collect immense amounts of data in real time, as corporations like Google or social media apps demand "freedom from law." After 9/11, a major initiative of Homeland Security in their quest to "preempt" threats was linking "the entirety of domestic intelligence—from municipal police departments to the federal intelligence community" through a series of fusion centers, Brendan McQuade explains. Massive data gathering and cutting-edge technologies have been deployed to collect and analyze data, from automatic license plate readers to software that extracts patterns from social media and communications to Stingrays. Like government intelligence agencies, and with their support, corporations gather our data even in disregard of the law, which makes us increasingly vulnerable, including to new forms of extraction.[81]

Thus, security blends with surveillance by monitoring urban, national, and global threats and risks while tapping into our individualized personal communications, social media, homes, and even our biomarkers and genetic information, all enhanced by artificial intelligence. Threat finding and security measures are increasingly embedded in our daily lives, often imperceptibly, bypassing traditional liberal standards of privacy. The more information gets collected, the more the risks and threats unveiled. In a self-perpetuating loop, new threats make the prospects of some dangerous events call for more preemptive monitoring and security measures.

For all this securitization, risk assessment, and preparedness, natural disasters and disease outbreaks have found most governments unprepared. Presciently, in October 2019, the first 195-country assessment of health preparedness found all systems "fundamentally weak around the world"—even in the wealthiest nations. Confirming the worst fears, despite the US's trillion-dollar security expenditure and topping the preparedness ranking, security mechanisms failed to prevent or halt the spread of the COVID-19 virus. The contrast, early in the pandemic, between Robocop-clad police officers and health care professionals wearing trash bags to protect themselves when assisting patients even in wealthy New York City offered a telling vignette of security's inadequacies.[82]

By 2025, COVID had "left an estimated 20 million people dead," Tedros Adhanom Ghebreyesus, the head of the WHO, reported. Public health emergencies have long since ended, and most monitoring and preventive measures were abandoned as governments actively promote a "return to normal." Tourism, cruises, restaurants, and shopping centers, as well as commercial real estate, actively reclaimed consumers and employers and states ended remote work, just as people were encouraged to travel, go to restaurants, and shop. On the ground, the pandemic was far from over. "The actual circulation [of COVID-19] is somewhere between two and twenty times higher than what's actually being reported by countries. The virus is rampant. We're still in a pandemic," Maria Van Kerkhove, a leading World Health Organization official, explained in 2024. "We cannot talk about COVID-19 in the past tense," Tedros reminded the audience in June 2025. However, comprehensive preventative policies are largely absent, and, in likely a first for a pandemic caused by a virus for which there is no cure, risk has been privatized at the cry of "you do you." The belief that only "the vulnerable" are at risk, and we all need to "learn to live with COVID" by getting repeatedly infected seems to have been accepted. Those dealing with disabling Long Covid—estimated in about 400 million worldwide—have been, for the most part, dismissed. To complete the 180-degree reversal from 2020, following pro-Palestinian student protests and occupations across US campuses in 2024, the same authorities who securitized COVID-19 and mask and vaccine mandates have made strides to ban face masks.[83]

These contradictory measures attest to how, in times of crisis, security shows cracks. More so, it reveals itself as a "dangerous illusion," as George

Rigakos and Mark Neocleous write, as when people assume that they are protected from diseases, disasters, and enemies, when—as the pandemic showed—they are not. Security narratives conflate the population's well-being with the state's just as neoliberal state reason turns anything that may seem threatening to markets into state threats and enemies—often starting with the victims of enclosures. As states securitize and embrace business agendas as their own, neoliberal reason of state thrives.[84]

Absent formal emergency regimes, security measures can keep "a stable state of creeping and fictitious emergency," as Agamben observes. No ultimate Schmittian decision is needed as security apparatuses' continuum identification of risks and threats routinize the emergency rationale. Guided by an autonomous logic, self-perpetuating, security mechanisms bypass state institutions in ways that threaten to make Schmittian sovereigns irrelevant.[85]

Not that the powers discussed by Schmitt are gone. The routine governance of risks and threats drives us into a renewed "age of prerogative," as Thomas Poole observes, by making emergency measures permanent. While distinct, the security and emergency rationales complement each other, from large to small-scale emergencies to the routine governance of (in)security, both of which call for expanded police powers. Looking closely at policing in the next section, new facets and surfaces of a triadic structure of unlawful governance come into view.[86]

Routine, Street Emergencies, and the (Sovereign) Police

"I am the law. If I feel like it right now, I can fuck you up, and no one will say anything about it," Sergeant Bosque told a Florida teenager. Despite misconduct charges, including three arrests, forty investigations, and getting fired six times for sexual assault, stealing drugs, using counterfeit money, and abusing citizens, Bosque was reinstated to his job in 2018 by a judge. Both the police officer's misbehavior and the court's leniency toward the police were remarkable. If extreme, this case brings established patterns and routines into view.[87]

The "I am the law" line above captures the distinct status of the police. Two centuries after London first introduced modern uniformed police forces, police agents patrol societies in vast numbers, from a million in the US to half a million in Brazil and a total of seventeen million police officers worldwide. Traditionally portrayed as law enforcers thought to prevent and stop crimes, police agents share unique faculties. Across countries and districts, despite specific institutional arrangements and cultural differences, police agents stand out for their authority to make arrests, use force, and take lives—a traditional prerogative deemed a sovereign mark.

Police regulations were first developed in fifteenth-century Europe as feudal social bonds disintegrated and the need to restore order became patent. A myriad of initiatives spread to first reestablish, then "fabricate" new forms of social order. Neocleous reconstructs the process—including by enforcing enclosures and increasingly repressing nonmercantile lifestyles in ways that accompanied the rise of modern states and capital. In this regard, in *Discipline and Punish* Foucault notes the role of police methods, bodies, and practices in managing "the accumulation of men" that paralleled the accumulation of capital. As part of a governmental "take-off," Foucault shows, police techniques were capable of governing both entire populations and particular individuals through "a subtle, calculated technology of subjection" supported by expanding technologies and, ultimately, by deadly force. This approach proved superior in helping assemble the disciplined and docile masses of subjects and waged workers within capitalist societies and their colonial offshoots. A salient example is the London police, which Robert Peel modeled after the colonial force deployed in Ireland, as Alex Vitale and Daniel Gascon et al. discuss. Drawing on technologies developed to subject the poor or colonial populations—which often "rebound back" to the metropoles, as Gascon et al. put it—distinct forms of police intervention helped capital accumulation, as Marx observes, including by forcing people into wage labor and containing the poor.[88]

By the seventeenth century, a "police science" developed that distilled principles and an art of government into hundreds of treatises. With the ultimate goal of strengthening state power, the police science stressed the importance of a healthy, ordered, productive, and happy population, as it organized a myriad of norms and standards to govern people's daily lives. The police science, with a focus on government, approached the population as a key resource, as it devised technologies to improve good order and general well-being while also identifying individuals and groups considered dangerous through a series of biopolitical hierarchies. In turn, police technologies helped connect governing territories, from "self-government, the government of others, and the government of the state," as Mitchell Dean puts it.[89]

Taking care of the population thus involved being able "to act quickly and expediently," as William Novak notes, to dispose of threats and nuisances, including by physically eliminating them. In his police treatise revisited by Foucault, Nicolas Delamare discusses monitoring the health of the population, public safety, production, trade, factories, and the flow of supplies, just as the state of roads and buildings while protecting arts and science, good manners, and taking care of the poor. But the goal of police and its magistrates, Delamare explains, was achieving people's happiness to guarantee a collective life properly lived. An orderly, healthy, productive, and happy people, Delamare thought, should strengthen the state.[90]

These police treatises, Foucault notes, highlighted the police effort as "vital" to the state in conditions where helping shape people's morality and lifestyles seemed as essential as keeping a tax system, an army, or a judiciary. By the nineteenth century, the police science progressively lost visibility. Its body of knowledge split between several disciplines just as bureaucracies delegated roles into specialized offices, including the creation of the modern professionalized police. But if uniformed officers got to monopolize the label, the police effort continued to involve the entire state. Moreover, the roots of the modern police, as David Bayley writes, "antedate most other institutions" and their authority, "essentially unlimited," captures the nature of state power like no other institution. And there is more, for far from what the label of "law enforcement" suggests, the uniformed police constitute just a visible face of an extended governing network including from local authorities to higher-level offices and policies that ultimately extend through the global domain.[91]

Police traditions vary, just as training and organizational standards keep changing, and new technologies, now drones and robots, challenge logistics and practices. Likewise, emphases on who or what counts as worth protecting as to what threatens order may shift according to the circumstances, dominant assessments of worth affecting different groups of people, and the prevailing governing rationale—in this case, neoliberal. The police rationale of searching for things "out of place" and intervening to restore order, however, remains the same.[92]

Discretionary powers are integral to policing. Identifying threats, preventing disorder, and determining whether and how to intervene, the police's discretionary prerogatives include selectively enforcing laws and ordinances, making arrests on "reasonable" and "probable" grounds, or taking life even through summary executions. Through these interventions, police agents craft a hegemonic understanding of social order and administer a one-on-one, personalized micro-politics of security. In this endeavor, "guidelines, rather than legal codes and principles, are the medium of police," Markus Dubber reminds us. Police edicts, misdemeanor codes, and administrative rules routinely assist agents in criminalizing the lifestyles of the poor and other socially vulnerable groups. In so doing, police practices push the limits of what is considered "'legal' behavior," as Neocleous points out, in ways that courts and legislators tend to accommodate and legalize.[93]

Under the conditions described above, the gap between sound discretionary judgment and extralegal violence gets blurrier. The study of police authority, including the power to take lives, has made scholars like Lennie Feldman wonder whether we should consider the police as agents of "'princely' prerogative power in a liberal order," or even as performing sovereign roles "more nakedly and clearly" than other state officials, as Agamben writes.[94]

In the US, as Feldman notes, "a 'legal grey hole'" is being created by the judiciary to immunize police violence. Both courts and legislation strengthen police prerogatives by giving the police protected status, including warrantless search powers and various forms of qualified immunity. The doctrine protects "all but 'the plainly incompetent or those who knowingly violate the law," as per *Malley v. Briggs*, having for its limit a police officer's intentional violation of a person's known and established constitutional rights. Furthermore, claims about the need to protect state secrets have led judges to dismiss cases of police abuse while secret laws and "evidentiary problems" can make the use of specific witnesses or evidence illegal.[95]

"Federal law-enforcement officials are privileged to do what would otherwise be unlawful if done by a private citizen," US Solicitor General Seth Waxman argued in a 1992 case to justify absolving an FBI agent accused of murder. Indeed, police agents can authorize and even commit crimes. In 2021, it was reported that US federal agencies, including the FBI and the Drug Enforcement Administration, had paid $548 million to informants in the years prior, just as a number of them were authorized to commit at least 22,800 crimes between 2011 and 2014, and over 40 government agencies had reported resorting to some form of undercover policing.[96]

Officer Bosque's "I am the law" declaration, or the admission of a few of my police interviewees that they actually were "little sovereigns," are among those moments when police agents glimpse the true scope of their power. Undifferentiated, virtually unlimited, and alien to law, police faculties let agents subject, reshape, protect, and destroy lives. In light of these faculties, those in charge of policing us exercise forms of subordinate, semiautonomous, delegated sovereign authority.[97]

"He gave his life because he stepped in to protect other people," Thomas Strobl, the German state minister of interior, acknowledged a twenty-nine-year-old policeman killed while stepping in to protect people during an anti-Muslim stabbing attack in July 2024. Stories of altruism by police officers abound. Still, a Brazilian police officer observes, "If a police officer says he puts his life at risk for any citizen, he is lying. . . . In my view, cops are willing to put their lives at risk to protect some types of people and to kill others." In other words, the police have in their hands the power to qualify and either protect or dispose of life. Governing individuals directly by selectively suspending and bypassing laws, police agents decide "when and where to suspend constitutionally protected rights, that is, to suspend the Constitution and the rule of law," as Judith Butler observes. In fact, suspending rights and protections on an individualized basis describes ordinary police prerogatives.[98]

In patrolling and searching for (dis)order, the police categorize individuals along hierarchies of worth that often include ethnicity, gender, class, or religion, just as those left out by the market, perceived as "expendable" once they "no longer assist[s] in the circulation of value," as Joshua Barkan puts it. Through this biopolitical labeling, police agents construct groups as suspect while suppressing workers and keeping a "tight surveillance and micromanagement of black and brown lives," as Alex Vitale writes. In their selective labeling, protecting, and disposing of life, the police preside over people's access to and exercise of citizenship even through what with Jinee Lokaneeta we call "violent exclusions" as they administer—and suspend—the law on the ground.[99]

No wonder police abuses are frequent. Dismissed by political scientists for years as a problem of dictatorships or newer democracies, neglected by representations of policing as law enforcement, police violence has been gaining visibility. In England and Wales, between 2011 and early 2020, citizens filed 325,000 complaints against the police for sexual and other forms of assault, harassment, unlawful detention, mishandling evidence, corruption, and discrimination. The police are responsible for most of the 20,000 yearly "legal intervention" killings around the world. Yet most governments offer no data on killings by their police and security forces, and even cases of torture, arbitrary detentions, and extrajudicial killings, when carried out by the police, tend to be "simply not investigated as potential crimes." Between 2006 and 2016, the London Metropolitan Police received 22,944 assault complaints—including sexual assault. Only 133 cases were judged worth investigating, and only 10 police officers were dismissed. This leaves grassroots activists, human rights organizations, and journalists with the challenge of gathering information from survivors, families, and communities.[100]

Considering examples from the Americas, the police kill about 6,000 people every year in Brazil alone. Most cases take place in big cities like Sao Paulo or Rio de Janeiro, with horrific episodes such as the May 2021 Jacarezinho favela massacre where the police killed 28 people. In Argentina, CORREPI documents 9,672 extrajudicial killings since the restoration of democracy in 1983. In the US, drawing on media reports, the police killed at least 1,165 people in 2024, at an average of +1,100 people every year. The pervasive racist profiling, abuses, and killings by agents across the 18,000 US police departments led the UN to send a 2016 special committee. Following the investigation, the report declared a "human rights crisis" in the nation due to the police's "impunity for state violence" and the number of killings.[101]

Over the decades, US scandals of police abuse, including the videotaped beating of Rodney King in Los Angeles or the killing of Amadou Diallo in New York City, led to mass protests, public awareness campaigns, and—mostly performative—promises of reform. Following earlier initiatives from survivors, victims' relatives, and activists such as Stolen Lives, in recent years the Black Lives Matter movement gained international notoriety. The disproportionate number of arrests, criminalization, and murders of mostly young men identified as Black, Latino, and Native American were brought into full view. Massive protests followed the killings of Trayvon Martin, Michael Brown, and other African American citizens by the police. "Say their names" accompanied reports of police killings, even if the thousands of deaths listed on databases make it impossible to name them all. By 2019, "officer-involved deaths" stood as the sixth leading cause of death among men between the ages of twenty-five and twenty-nine, disproportionally victimizing nonwhites. Against this background, in the summer of 2020, the release of the videotaped murder of George Floyd by a police officer in Minneapolis brought tens of millions of people into the streets to demand justice and police defunding and abolition.[102]

Despite repeated government promises of reform, police officers continue to enjoy heightened discretion and qualified immunity, making it difficult for victims to sue as courts increasingly treat the police as a legally protected group. Only rarely do those responsible for killings undergo prosecution. And when they do, most times they walk free. Meanwhile, civil lawsuits have cost Chicago, New York, and other US cities hundreds of millions of dollars of taxpayer funds in settlements.

Both under and outside formally declared emergencies, police agents routinely replicate extraordinary exercises by top authorities. Under emergency regimes and heightened securitization, their prerogatives get a boost. In France, in 2015, the authorities preemptively banned citizens from attending demonstrations. The police subjected people to arbitrary arrests, often on false charges, prevented them from joining protests, tear-gassed, beat, and hurt them. "I wasn't prepared to demonstrate and then get arrested and beaten up," one student recalled. In 2020, under the health emergency declarations set early in the COVID-19 pandemic, researchers documented police abuses in 79 countries while enforcing social distancing.[103]

Locally or transnationally, with organizations such as INTERPOL as with less visible networks, police agents are entrusted with impressive combinations of discretionary authority, advanced technologies, and qualified legal immunity. Linking local and transnational networks, conditions of "greater surveillance, scrutiny, and power" spread under US-led "wars" on drugs and terror, as Keeanga-Yamahtta Taylor puts it. Indeed, as Stuart Schrader describes in great detail, a true system of global policing has been assembled with a preeminent US role that fuses policing and counterinsurgency techniques into "a single repertoire," presiding over emergency conditions that put police agents brandishing military-grade weapons, including drones, robots, and artificial intelligence at the forefront.[104]

Whether exercised by the state or by individual uniformed officers, the police power contains the rationale of the emergency where discretionary decisions lead to applying laws or disregarding them in view of the circumstances. And just as Schmitt dismissed police emergencies, they somehow remain excluded from the literature on states of exception or emergency regimes.

So far, scholars only episodically refer to policing, which they continue to treat as "law enforcement," a lesser power in a subordinate, instrumental, auxiliary role. Though "nothing formally" distinguishes them, as Poole notes, the spectacular displays of prerogative by top officials coexist with prerogative exercises disseminated in routine governing practices such as those performed by the police. Independent from the law, synonymous with discretionary authority, police prerogatives seem fitting to the concept of emergency. With their unique discretionary powers and ample legal immunity, the police assess threats and act on them directly without the need for formal emergency recognition. Ultimately, a broad governmental matrix articulates emergency, security, and policing mechanisms. The same emergency rationale is at play in allowing for and legitimizing discretionary exercises on the ground.[105]

Governmentalities of Emergency

"When the president does it, that means that it is not illegal"—Richard Nixon's definition during a 1977 interview with David Frost captures the gist of prerogative authority in liberal democracies. On occasion, out of concern for "national security or . . . a threat to internal peace and order," a presidential order may require those carrying it out to do things typically considered illegal, but "without violating a law," Nixon argues. In other words, he explains, "what would otherwise be technically illegal does not subject those who engage in such activity to criminal prosecution." US presidents are not above the law, Nixon adds, but the Constitution has invested them with "extraordinary powers" to be used when appropriate.[106]

Following up on the controversial interview, in a letter to the *Washington Post*, Nixon offered some clarification. While no president is above the law, he insisted, those in the office may have to "go beyond the strict letter of existing law" to fulfill their duties under exceptional circumstances. This is not abusing power, Nixon emphasizes, even if some "technical breach of statutory limits" may be involved. The ultimate question, he adds, "is what is the law" and how it applies to the president's office, considering the need for "some degree of latitude in the use by presidents of emergency situations," which he judges "vital."[107]

Nixon's words capture the unlawful, undefined core of state power. Daniel Ross's statement that "whether it is crime or miracle is always undecidable" captures unlawful governance's ambiguous status in between crime and prerogative authority. Which one we are dealing with depends on a political, symbolic, and legal dispute on the character of these actions. Considered in their "structural and organizational nature," officials' abuses may amount to state crimes, as Barak observes. And yet, most times, they are treated as legitimate exercises of prerogative authority.[108]

Not just presidents but also lesser officials including police and security agents invoke exceptional circumstances to justify bypassing laws and shielding themselves from accountability. These unlawful exercises do not solely take place when officials follow orders, as in Nixon's example, but also through discretionary interventions of their own. Even deadly transgressions by government agents are regularly treated as prerogative exercises immune to judicial review. Emergency, security, and policing are ultimately driven by the same rationale.

Emergencies, security, and police may define distinct fields—both epistemic and governmental—but they are part of the same matrix. Intertwining through different channels and mechanisms, they all open room for prerogative exercises and fuel one another's exceptional ways. Emergency regimes introduce drastic changes, which undeclared "small" emergency measures and security policies and policing spread on the ground. Rooted in reason of state, pivotal to the advancement of (neoliberal) capital, these governmentalities of emergency help expand a sovereign "domain . . . immune from law," as Butler notes, where individuals can find themselves treated as bare life. Made voiceless and rightless, these people—whether migrants detained in camps or poor teenagers at the mercy of the police—find it extremely difficult, often impossible, to pull themselves out of those conditions, even in established liberal democracies.[109]

Besides affecting specific individuals, emergency, security, and police mechanisms block political action and people's collective chances to address real emergencies. Under these conditions, protesting the consequences of austerity, precarity, and police violence, but also of global warming, pollution, and pandemics linked to the extractivist "rampant land-use change, lightning-fast global commodity chains, social dislocation, and ecological destruction" can get brutally suppressed.[110]

This chapter revisited these governmentalities of emergency, in their scope, links, and rationale, as main mechanisms or formations of the governing reason of capital; the next chapter interrogates the ways in which they gain legitimacy. Creating a sense of awe for the state by impressing citizens through ceremonies and signs of splendor and strength stood as a main dimension of reason of state from the start. Linking aesthetics with public discourse, including concepts such as sovereignty or state interest, variants of a state-centered political extraordinary developed that helped turn state violence into authority. These legitimizing discursive practices seem poignant under twenty-first-century electronic production of a neoliberal spectacular. Accompanying those trends, tropes circulating through the media, social media, popular culture, and legal and political theory help legitimize emergency measures and turn the unlawful into a source of authority. They materialize the storytelling roots of the state's epistemic and practical productivity.

Glimpses of a different life can be hinted at in the "revolts and uprisings that interrupt, if only for a brief moment, the triumphal procession of the powerful," as Michael Lowy writes. Radical moments such as the "Chile despertó" in 2019, or the 15-M Indignados in Spain, Istanbul's Gezi Park, the French Nuit Debout, or the 2001 Argentine "¡Que se vayan todos!"—all part of the "movement of the squares" that I discuss in chapter 4—or the unprecedented numbers joining Black Lives Matter protests in 2020, express the democratic extraordinary against the dominance of reason of state.

Such moments and gestures are neutralized under the rationale of the emergency. Its critique should contribute to developing "an alternative political language" that tackles the emergency, security, and police governmental apparatus. Beyond this universe, as I explore in chapters 4 and 5, are a series of practices and ideas open to people-centered, rights-affirming forms of politics and law.[111]

3 | For the Common Good

For too long, a small group in our nation's capital has reaped the
rewards of government while the people have borne the cost.
Washington flourished but the people did not share in its wealth.
Politicians prospered but the jobs left and the factories closed. The
establishment protected itself but not the citizens of our country.
Their victories have not been your victories. Their triumphs have not
been your triumphs. And while they celebrated in our nation's
capital, there was little to celebrate for struggling families all across
our land. That all changes starting right here and right now because
this moment is your moment, it belongs to you.[1]
—President Donald Trump, Inauguration speech, 2017

Flanked by military commanders, family members, former presidents,
legislators, and magistrates, on Friday, January 20, 2017, Donald Trump
uttered these words as part of his inaugural speech, after taking the oath of
office while his wife Melania held the Bible. The ceremony included a
prayer service at the Washington National Cathedral, a march on Pennsylvania Avenue, and three gala balls, which the Trumps visited, after dancing to Frank Sinatra's "My Way" to launch the Liberty Ball.

"Everyone is listening to you now," Trump addressed the "forgotten"
Americans in his 2017 inauguration. Proclaiming "We are transferring
power from Washington, D.C., and giving it back to you, the people,"
Trump pledged to restore common citizens as "the rulers of this nation."
He described destitute children, closed factories, collapsing infrastructure, and vanishing wealth, to then promise "this American carnage stops
right here and stops right now." His oath of allegiance "to all Americans,"
Trump noted, came with a "new vision" inspired by the motto "America
first." From that moment, he promised, all decisions would prioritize US
citizens' well-being. In his concise sixteen-minute speech, the president

criticized countries for "stealing our companies and destroying our jobs." Portraying his movement as unprecedented, he pledged to "fight for you with every breath" and "never, ever let you down." Trump assured the audience: "You will never be ignored again." Expanding on his campaign motto, he promised to make America "proud," "safe," and "great" again.

Imagined futures and communities are key to political life, "both in creating revolution and in maintaining order," as Keally McBride notes. The MAGA "Make America Great Again" motto turned out to be a powerful signifier. Like other politicians, but stressing his position as an outsider, Trump claimed to know Americans. After invoking gloomy images, including that of "American carnage" to describe a crisis, he promised to return the nation's lost greatness, thus stepping in the traditional political role of making promises and offering the audience both a framework and a horizon. And he committed himself to defend Americans' well-being, which he described as threatened by hostile, predatory outsiders.[2]

Trump's portrayal of the US in his 2017 Inauguration speech was characterized by critics as "darkly pessimistic." Eight years later, a seasoned, powerful Trump—no longer an outsider—returned to power to announce the beginning of a "Golden Age." Trump's vision for the flourishing of the nation, in prosperity and harmony, or for rebuilding state capacity to attend to children's health or disasters seemed part of what he proclaimed a "revolution of common sense." Bold, nationalist dreams included that of sending astronauts to plant the US flag in Mars. Ending "the Green New Deal," enforcing "only two genders, male and female," and "returning millions and millions of criminal aliens" to their countries followed. With his references to God and religion, (nuclear, heterosexual) families, law and order, and emphases on (two-gendered) patriots, manufacturing, cars, and the space race, Trump's retrofuturistic tone seemed complete when he mentioned oil. "We will be a rich nation again and it is that liquid gold under our feet that will help to do it," he asserted. "We will drill, baby, drill"—this could be the most consequential part of his 2025 inauguration speech. Dreams and promises, whether enchanting or terrifying—or both—anchor our lives.

Authority, Hannah Arendt notes, infuses our world with "permanence and durability." It makes people obey, just as they "retain their freedom," which Arendt likens to following good advice. Authority also involves the ability of naming and describing the world and producing some shared common sense. Ceremonies and regalia, rituals, metaphors, and performances are key. They coat those in power with a mystique that separates them from everyday life. They help leaders earn people's respect and remain authoritative. Under the influence of Max Weber, legitimacy has been recast pragmatically as the study of legitimating processes. Power, Beetham notes, is deemed legitimate when it is accessed through accepted rules and its exercise justified with appropriate claims regarding the source and purpose of authority, accompanied by public recognition. In other words, legitimacy speaks of the "capacity to stay in power," as Russell Hardin puts it.[3]

All politics involves performances, Benjamin Moffitt and Simon Tormey argue, with "actors, audiences, stages, scripts, *mise en scène*." Since ancient times, political performances, speeches, ceremonies, symbols, and regalia have been pivotal to producing and preserving authority. They stand as "signatures," as Agamben calls them, or glorifying marks that project power and law as legitimate and compelling. The symbolic and ceremonial, he notes, are at play "where the gestures become words, [and] the words become facts" as they blend with each other through performative uses of language. Political performances appeal to us personally. They carve a special time distinct from everyday routines just as they may advance entire worlds. Charming and striking, they reshape our perspectives while inscribing our selves into what Eric Santner describes as the "normative social space" of sovereignty.[4]

The political performative ranks as a main element of reason of state, as part of what Giovanni Botero describes as "the arts which win for a ruler the love and admiration of his people." Impressing citizens and enemies alike involved mastering the art of war and being a prudent, just ruler, while taking care of providing appropriate forms of "public gratification," enjoyable and educational. A political theatrics of reason of state would then develop, Foucault notes, to reach full display in Louis XIV's court, with magnificent displays and ceremonies where what was represented was "the state itself." Such displays, they believed, were strategic in projecting state strength. Centuries later, spectacular political performances keep bringing variants of the politically extraordinary, at once charming and frightening in its reaffirmation of state might. The focus of this chapter is to delve into the charming arm of reason of state, into its semiotic and affective alchemy of turning state power, even lawlessness, into authority. Embedded with media and social media-infused discursive and performative mechanisms, it makes things such as glimpses of state terror entertaining and helps keep unlawful governance out of sight.[5]

Extending through the media and social media, state power relies on the "control of appearance (of doxa)," as Agamben notes. Controlling appearance is as much about what people see as about what we do not. It is about defining the limits of the public sphere, which determines what people perceive, the field of visibility that "will count as reality," as Judith Butler observes. Politically infused, discursive, and semiotic, loaded with emotional and moral claims, the public sphere delineates the arena of the "sayable and the thinkable" and the parameters through which we represent political reality. Some things have changed, however, with the historically recent development of a digital world.[6]

Access to the internet remains uneven, ranging from 97.4 percent of the population in North America to 78.4 percent in Central America to 26.8 percent in eastern Africa. Still, in 2025 Internet users were estimated in 5.6 billion, 5.24 billion people used social media, and there were over seven billion mobile subscriptions. Whereas in ancient times the ceremonial of power was formally ritualized, this dimension gains new contours in our "networked public sphere" on the expanding electronic and social media. Setting a giant, 24/7 performing scenario, the electronic media and social media not only shape public opinion, but—as suggested by Agamben—thrive on their liturgical, performative ability to celebrate and legitimize the authorities. Learning about and interacting with events though screens and audio gives us a sense of immediacy that brings together the personal and the public in lively, direct, and intense ways.[7]

"Within an hour of anything major happening almost anywhere in the world, YouTube expects to see footage uploaded," Tufekci notes. News videos on Facebook, YouTube, and other platforms reach hundreds of millions of adult viewers while a quarter of social media users post their own news videos or submit content through news organizations or blogs. By 2024, Facebook had over 3 billion users, YouTube 2.1 billion, TikTok 1.7 billion, and X, the former Twitter, reached 429 million people. In turn, in terms of revenue, in 2023, Google made $305 billion and Meta $135 billion. Overall, the global social media adds $251.45 billion to the $2.5 trillion media and entertainment global market, including newspapers, TV, magazines, radio, film, books, and music. In this privatized media and social media ecosystem controlled by a few corporations and billionaires that happens to define our public sphere, technologies keep renewing and redefining modalities of content creation, sharing, and consumption. The arts that will make people love their ruler referred to by Botero are available to us mostly in the form of entertainment.[8]

"Wealth and splendor" are, in the end, the things with which power "clothes itself." Mechanisms of splendor fill up power's cracks and contradictions, enchant people, and promote and impose consensus. In their production, which Agamben calls glorification, "ceremonies, acclamations, and protocols" all play a key role.[9]

While the ceremonies of power may go back to times immemorial, distinctively, reason of state introduced a "modern kind of theater," as Foucault notes, led by the sovereign. The royal court, with its intrigue, was turned into the space where the "theatrical practice of raison d'état" went on display. It was there that "the state itself" was represented and consolidated its presence. These days, the royal court has expanded over electronic surfaces. There, as in those traditional sites, politics revolves around imagination and meaning-making, and politicians stand as privileged interpreters that re-create the world while helping us to make sense of our lives. Politics, in the end, is about generating "simulacra by manipulating a blend of natural and artificial signs," Jens Bartelson notes.[10]

"To every parent who dreams for their child and every child who dreams for their future, I am with you. I will fight for you and I will win for you," Trump observed in his 2025 Inauguration speech. He reminded the audience of his successful election and stressed his unique historical position as a leader "saved by God to make America great again"—as he put it, referring to the attacks against his life during his presidential campaign. He described a people betrayed by politicians and at the mercy of foreign gangs and criminals.[11]

Trump's characterization of a People united against common enemies seems rather classical populist. Populism's distinctive traits include an "appeal to 'the people'; crisis, breakdown, threat; and 'bad manners,'" Moffitt and Tormey observe. With a rhetoric and a style that defy social conventions, populist politics appropriates the language of the common people while claiming to speak on their behalf. Strong and direct, populist speech brings multitudes together through the discursive aggregation of their demands, Ernesto Laclau explains. Demands regarding poverty, unemployment, crime, democracy, are made equivalent, and so a multitude becomes unified. Rather than simply describing preexisting publics, political discourse helps produce them. It brings the people it describes into existence just as the speaker excludes others, ranging from the stranger to enemies, in a play of identification, good and evil, love and hate. While these traits are identified with populism, in the end, Laclau argues that they characterize politics itself.[12] Mediated by the logic of entertainment and the spectacular, that is.[13]

Trump's first administration did not go exactly as promised. His early dismissal of the "Chinese virus" led to inaction that helped COVID-19 turn into a global pandemic. Asylum seekers were denied rights and thousands of them placed in detention sites while children were illegally taken away from their families. Trump was impeached, twice. Furthermore, claiming fraud in the 2020 presidential election, on January 6, 2021, at the cry of "Stop the steal!" he gave an inflammatory speech to a crowd that then violently stormed the Capitol to prevent Congress from certifying the people's vote.

Eventually, an eighteen-month bipartisan congressional investigation including over 1,000 witness interviews, ten hearings, and a million pages of documents concluded that Trump led a "multi-part conspiracy" to overturn Biden's election. Among other recommendations, the committee recommended that Trump be banned from running again.

While not banned, Trump did not escape criminal prosecution. He was found guilty of thirty-four felony charges for falsifying business records to influence the 2016 presidential election. He was also charged in an "election subversion case" for obstructing the certification of Biden's 2020 election, and for taking national security documents when he left office. Despite the scandals, Trump easily won the support of Republican voters to become their presidential nominee in 2024. In view of Trump's November election victory, later that month special counsel Jack Smith dropped the two pending cases considering his newly regained presidential immunity.

Trump claimed "I have an Article 2, where I have the right to do whatever I want as president" and repeatedly claimed to be "absolutely immune from state judicial process." In July 2020, the Supreme Court unanimously rejected Trump's interpretation of the Constitution. In the summer of 2024, however, on a 6–3 vote, the Court acknowledged that Trump—and therefore all US presidents—are endowed with broad immunity in the exercise of executive "core" powers, and with "presumptive" immunity from prosecution for other actions. Furthermore, the Court recognized that the president has virtually unlimited pardon authority, which on January 20, Trump put to work by extending "a full, complete and unconditional pardon" to 1,500 participants in the January 6, 2021, assault of the Capitol. Considering his many transgressions and expanded powers of immunity, by the turn of events Trump's interpretation of presidential authority may have prevailed—for now.[14]

How are unlawful governing practices, including taking lives, made invisible, normalized, and justified in democracies that praise themselves of being governed by law? The US remains a democracy, if a flawed one. A "zombie" democracy, as David Runciman puts it, that reduces citizens to "watching a performance in which their role is to give or withhold applause at the appropriate moments." Amid a weakened civic life, politics degrades into a continuously running media show, with a myriad little dramas calling for our attention. While the political success of film, media, and TV personalities from Ronald Reagan to Silvio Berlusconi to Donald Trump attests to these trends, the spectacle first theorized by Guy Debord helps address the blend of media and social media entertainment under (political, economic, environmental) emergency conditions characteristic of our times. Coined in 1970, Debord's concept of the spectacle captures the charming, even amusing face of public life under ongoing neoliberal enclosures supported on law as on the unlawful logic of emergency.[15]

This chapter explores the alchemy of turning lawlessness into authority, reason of state's glamourous face. Drawing on examples and theories, sections scrutinize the spectacular, legitimizing mechanisms that normalize state abuses, exclusions, and rights breaches in democracies, as they enchant and capture us all. I draw on Debord's insights on spectacular democracies as "a moment in the mode of production," as well as on Agamben and Mitchell Dean to illuminate the neoliberal spectacle's reason of state rationale. Both Eric Santner's and León Rozitchner's arguments support my discussion of the spectacular interlocking with state violence. To put it in the broadest terms, borrowing from Foucault, I am set to explore the "knowledge apparatus" of our neoliberal governmentalities—and some of its connected practices.[16]

In what follows, I start by characterizing traditional and spectacular modalities of state splendor through which sovereign power charms us. Next, the chapter describes some vital mechanisms, at times hidden, to finally move into discussing the ways in which discourse and the spectacular prepare for and interlock with state violence and terror. Sections alternatively focus on mechanisms that transform lawlessness into prerogative along modalities of charm, silence, and crush. All discursive and performative mechanisms (e.g., acclamation, silencing, constructing enemies) contribute to legitimize unlawful state acts in democracies with a view of their dissemination.

Charm 1: Sovereign Splendor

"We princes are always on a stage"; royal courts may be gone, but Elizabeth I's words remind us that their spirit, play of appearances, and "stories, ceremonies, insignia, formalities, and appurtenances" still thrive among us. Magnificent locations like the Élysée and Westminster palaces, the White House, the Palácio do Planalto, or luxurious summit settings like Borgo Egnazia still frame major political events, but a number of them have moved to electronic platforms. From both the screen and the palace, political events and performances continue to turn gestures into words and words into facts and new realities. They, and the stories behind them, let us learn about "our own inner lives, fantasies, moral commitments, [and] political passions," Santner observes. Thanks to their meaning-making character, they may contain "more reality" than our daily lives. When enacted by those in power, ideas and stories spread to the point of appearing as natural.[17]

One preeminent such story, sovereignty, developed out of its theological roots in medieval Europe to be first adopted "as a domestic term in a domestic context" to describe the relations between monarchs and their subjects. Since the twelfth century, with the expanding power of kings and emperors, the idea of sovereignty gained juridical standing, helping consolidate monarchical prerogatives as the early institutions of the modern state.[18]

Kings across Europe became known for their magnificent, ornate ceremonies. Among them, Henry VIII in England set royal courts as a scenario for "theatrical judicial ceremonies" and "conscious cultivation of royal magnificence" that impressed nobles and foreign diplomats, Greg Walker explains. Palace courts grew in splendor with the commissioning of artwork.[19]

On the political and legal front, the sovereign's "indefinable" prerogative stood above all laws, Ernst Kantorowicz notes. As "the living image of Justice," the king was seen as the source of the law, from which he was exempted. Alongside holding sovereignty, kings were made sacred first drawing on religious traditions, later by taking inspiration on the law, and eventually—more modernly—by pivoting on the nation and its peoples as a source of legitimacy.[20]

One belief that accompanied the consolidation of monarchical sovereignty and its (e)state was the doctrine of the king's two bodies. Believed incapable of thinking or doing wrong, the king was also legally ubiquitous—his soul was assumed to be present across institutions. Moreover, he was in possession of two bodies, one natural, one "politic," which formed a unity. The king's body politic—angelical, immortal, free of defects—overpowered and minimized his human condition. It was believed, Kantorowicz explains, that the body politic "never died." When the king died or was removed from power, the two bodies were believed to separate so that the body politic migrated into his successor. Sovereignty, absolute, continual, and perpetual, belonged with the body politic and incarnated in the sacred body of the king. Meanwhile, the king's human body functioned as a general equivalent for authority that gave the monarchical state its unity.[21]

The doctrine had practical implications. The belief that the king's flaw-less body politic was always present in courts across the kingdom made it possible for judges to decide on cases by themselves. The doctrine also eased the transmission of power and stability. Notoriously in France and England, royal funerals focused on an effigy or replica of the deceased monarch adorned with crown insignia. The effigy represented the king's body politic, which was treated as an actual living monarch. As the king's body politic migrated into the new human, his passing was referred to as "demise." Symbolizing a power that "never dies," the effigy brought sover-eignty into full view. Both effigies and the doctrine were pivotal in gener-ating the notion of an absolute, continual, and perpetual power. As odd as it sounds, this belief somehow still has currency among us.[22]

Sovereign liturgy also involved ordinary people through festive rituals going back to ancient times. Through the masses' "cry of approval," cere-monies bolstered the renewal of authority. Whether celebrating victories, expressing praise or disapproval, or conveying wishes, acclamations, Agamben explains, were "yelled by a crowd," often accompanied with applause. In his earlier work, Carl Schmitt deems acclamations "an eternal phenomenon" in political life, concluding that peoples come into exis-tence by taking part in them. In medieval times in Europe, acclamations accompanied the crowning of kings. An archbishop asked people for their "consent to the consecration of the prince," followed by the cry "Fiat!" or singing the *Te Deum*. While absolutism stripped the common people from such a powerful role, festivals and rituals continued to include them.[23]

As the modern state consolidated, symbols and ceremonies helped (re) generate the sovereign's legitimacy and his prerogative as "the autonomous power of the king to govern . . . in accordance to 'reason of state.'" Courts and royal festivals offered the splendor that reason of state called for.[24]

Henry II was one who regularly "joined with his people." Besides invit-ing his subjects to the opulent festivities of his Marseille marriage with dancing and gift giving, Henry had them attend his crowning at Notre Dame. During the summer, he joined them in celebrating "midsummer night's eve" with a bonfire that impressed the crowd with a performance of the artillery. Henry also attended religious processions and banquets, administered justice in public, and staged naval battles on the Seine. Louis XIV, in turn, touched as many of the sick as Henry did for scrofula, honor-ing the popular belief that the king's sacred touch could cure disease. But Louis was masterful in enchanting "his subjects through spectacle and sovereignty." It was through such rituals and performances that sover-eignty was made to look natural.[25]

Modern revolutions displaced and overthrew traditional monarchs and their prerogatives, but the symbolism, rituals, and traditions surrounding kings and princes did "not simply disappear." They just changed forms. The first national anthem was introduced in 1740 in Britain, Eric Hobsbawm notes, and the French national flag took inspiration on the tricolor emblem of the French Revolution. Nations were represented as women like Marianne and Germania, or informally with "cartoon stereotypes of John Bull, the lean Yankee Uncle Sam and the 'German Michel.'"[26]

With declarations of independence, revolutions, and pivotal "We the People" moments, new symbols, monuments, and festivities marked the establishment of popular sovereignty. Diego Rossello reminds us that investitures "are not just royal affairs." Sovereignty migrates into the body of the people. A "'horizontal or democratic dissemination of the dynamics of the King's Two Bodies into the domain of 'popular sovereignty' and so into everyman" has taken place, Santner explains. Yet what he describes as the elusive "semiotic and somatic" matter of sovereignty, unstable and unresolved, is still today finding its ways into its new collective body. The real promise of "aristocracy for all," the popular biocracy that comes with sovereign investiture, brings also the tensions in the past experienced by kings, Rossello reminds us.[27]

One problem with popular sovereignty is that people are not suited to the sovereign logic, Rancière observes. While political performances continued to produce authority, the demos has "no constant body" and no one can embody the sovereign regalia the way kings did. In fact, as discussed in chapter 5, the organic form of what we call popular sovereignty seems to be the commons. Still, over the last centuries, people were turned into members of nations, rooted in blood, soil, and language. A frantic circulation of sovereignty in search of a new body ensued, giving rise to always temporary, incomplete, and exclusionary sovereign embodiments. For as people were mediated through the idea of the nation, only those recognized as members could claim rights and protections. Like the priests and officials attending to the effigy of the deceased king in sovereign funerals, Santner notes, nineteenth-century scientists and doctors sought "to isolate and protect" the sovereign matter now incarnated in the people, which they did through the idea of race.

Modern democracies declared individuals to be free and equal and the people the sole sovereign. And yet as state claims of popular sovereignty expanded, racist, gender, class, and other biopolitical hierarchies and markers led to exclusionary definitions of a people that keep pushing many out of citizenship. As discussed in the previous chapter, people—

sovereign or not—are constantly surveilled and fractured, and groups of the "lesser" continue to be singled out and securitized. The ones judged unfit, like the so-called "illegals" in US politicians' speeches, can be oppressed and excluded on the People's own behalf. These are just a few ways in which the story of sovereignty keeps us trapped in its play of exception(s).[28]

In the meantime, while invoking the people, sovereignty actually moved from the king's body to "the abstract body of the state." Since the times of absolutism, kings delegated the exercise of their "ordinary" prerogatives to officials, consolidating the power of earlier bureaucracies. As those apparatuses continued expanding, with the king gone and an evanescent popular sovereign, the prerogatives associated with this power became linked to nonpersons like governments and states. Yet, as sovereignty favors to be personified, fetishes kick in.[29]

The doctrine of the state's "personality" treats the state as an individual struggling for survival. It equates protecting the "person of the state" with the common good or public interest. This story has major implications. Protecting the life of the state justifies any type of action, even those bypassing legal and constitutional norms, on democratic grounds. It lets state agents qualify, suspend, and disregard people's rights, laws, and constitutional guarantees to protect the state, treated as a person, whose well-being is deemed essential for the fate of the actual people thus abused.

While Hent Kalmo and Quentin Skinner acknowledge the doctrine's "mystical" or "mythical" character, this does not necessarily lead them to its critique. Rather, the authors judge the fiction of "the sovereign state as a distinct *persona ficta*," a necessary construct to provide unity and continuity essential to our lives. This "sovereignty speech" invests its creations with impressive power, as it turns its fetish's survival into the absolute priority. Recognized authority in such terms, just like those old funeral effigies, the state apparatus and its officials get treated as the true sovereign.[30]

State agents thus take for granted their "right to embrace lawlessness," as Henry Giroux puts it, in determining who may live and who must die. In turn, the "mantra of sovereignty" and its connected tropes treat rights as optional for states, to honor according to their discretion. Thus the unresolved incarnation of sovereignty in the changing body of the people resolves as a fetish—and as a lawless, deadly one.[31]

"Tenaciously repeated," through ceremonies and speeches, claims like "necessity has no law," *salus populi*, or security, or that preserving the state comes prior to legal or ethical considerations, often suffice to justify exceptional measures. Identifying an object as a threat allows state agents to exercise any means judged needed to neutralize it. Appeals to necessity, state interest, reason of state, and national security—the modern equivalent of the *salus populi*, as Kathleen Arnold points out—help justify emergency measures, crush dissent, and exclude groups from legal protections.[32]

Invoking security reasons, at all levels, works in the way of "a password" to impose conditions that "people have no reason to accept," Agamben observes. "Knowing that no act undertaken in the name of American 'safety' and 'security' will ever be prosecuted," politicians and bureaucrats may learn not to care much about laws, as Tom Engelhardt notes. Indeed, besides immunity regimes for higher ranking officials, discretionary prerogatives have expanded also for street-level police. In recent years, as Leonard Feldman describes, "Blue Lives Matter" campaigns supported passing laws that give police enhanced immunity and status as a protected group.[33]

By 2025, things got worse. On Tuesday, May 6, neighbors in downtown Great Barrington, Massachusetts, witnessed heavily armed men in unmarked cars, their faces covered, taking two people with them. Customers came out of a café to videotape the scene and asked the armed men for identification and warrants. Other than eventually being told they were ICE, Immigration and Customs Enforcement agents, no explanations were given. A few days later, while voicing concerns about "excessive" measures, 55% of respondents in a national poll expressed support for deportations of so-called "illegal" immigrants, and 33% agreed with deporting people to "any country that will take them." The Great Barrington scene was replicated hundreds of times across the US, as it became customary for ICE agents to operate without identification and detain people without warrants. The mainstreaming of unlawful state actions can be effective, as reflected in polls showing acceptance for censorship, torture, as for, in this case, treating refugees and immigrants as threats. Securitization, as a discursive framing that stresses an existential threat, indeed demands an immediate response. Mounted on the structure of prerogative discussed in chapter 2, securitization carves out room for expanding exceptional measures. And as the media helps make objects into threats, securitizing narratives become part of the state itself.[34]

Tropes and legal and political concepts "enable people to do the state," as Bob Jessop puts it. In fact, the story of state personality involves a myriad images, stories, theories, and laws. Political fictions such as emergency and sovereignty make it possible for state agents to enjoy immunity while subjecting the rest of us both to the law and their unlawful routines. Imagery stemming out of *Leviathan*'s iconic book cover support beliefs on a state whose body incorporates us, but that keeps looking at us from above.

Countless routine governing interventions over bodies, cities, and territories by a loose network of agents and practices rely on this image. Carried out with prerogative authority, these governing practices generate the semblance of the state they invoke. As essential mechanisms of power, such fictions and narratives are a constitutive part of the state itself.[35]

If anything, they show that "the raw material of political power," the old royal regalia "did not disappear from the modern vocabulary of power," as Denis Baranger points out, but that got "rearranged." Ceremonies, often supported by popular acclamations, include carefully curated media portrayals of politicians that highlight gestures celebrating and committing to the People through speeches, making promises, and shaking hands. Myths and ceremonies can bring "together a populace that otherwise is divided and heterogeneous," as commemorating past events together adds new meanings, helping legitimize power and helping become a people.[36]

Popular acclamations are still with us. Enacted across multiple surfaces, from social media platforms to the streets, popular acclamations can be festive. In May 2010, over six million people took part in Argentina's bicentennial, with events, exhibits, iconography, and theatrical performances featuring the nation's history, including the celebration of the Mothers and Grandmothers of Plaza de Mayo as a living symbol of human rights. One attendee, in view of the inclusion of memorials to the *desaparecidos* (disappeared) under the last military dictatorship, suggested that "the 30,000 [disappeared] turned into thousands and thousands of kids from the Bicentenario," in ways that helped bring together past, present, and future, the people and the government.

Popular acclamations can also be mournful. In Paris, following deadly attacks against the *Charlie Hebdo* magazine and a Jewish kosher supermarket, about 3.7 million people joined in a rally in January 2015 to honor the dead while celebrating "Western values of democratic liberty and freedom." French president François Hollande spoke, praising the nation's culture and lifestyle while stressing that "terrorism will never destroy the Republic. The Republic will destroy terrorism." The image of world leaders heading the march, with French president Hollande interlocking arms with Israeli prime minister Benjamin Netanyahu, German chancellor Angela Merkel, Malian president Ibrahim Boubacar Keita, EU Council president Donald Tusk, and Palestinian Authority president Mahmoud Abbas, went around the world. Leaks about the staging of the photo and the digital addition of the crowd were met with outrage. Still, Hollande saw his approval ratings go up over 20 points after the attack, eventually reaching 50 percent of support, in another expression of acclamation.

Democracy's colonizing by the rationale of the emergency in the name of protecting the people betrays a political imagination antagonistic to the democratic and yet nested within it. Through emergency and security practices, imagery, and ceremonies, sovereignty is kept "alive and kicking," as Mark Neocleous observes. Of course, the life of fetishes can only mimic real life. As in the funeral rituals of kings, supported by their effigies, as much as by appeals to the sacred trying to reach the immortal, they may just produce some form of the undead. The logic of the spectacle makes this dynamic look charming, however. And entertaining.[37]

Charm 2: Spectacular Democracies

In his 1967 book, *Society of the Spectacle*, Debord characterized modern societies as "an immense accumulation of spectacles." A century after Marx defined capital as a social relation that we experience as a "fantastic form of a relation between things," Debord redescribed capital as a social relation "mediated by images." At a time when television was central, he captured the rationale of media technologies targeting the most intimate aspects of our selves. Blandly and smoothly, through entertainment and advertisement, the spectacle colonizes social territories and subjectivities while shrinking experiences into "gazing" and spectatorship. Debord describes the spectacle in its unlimited capacity to absorb and commodify identities, conflicts, violence, resistance, contestation, and even its own critique. Douglas Kellner expands on this by characterizing various forms of the spectacular, from recurrent events such as the Oscars or the World Cup, or political spectacles such as elections, to catastrophic spectacles surrounding disasters and well as spectacles of terror such as 9/11. In all cases, they condense dominant values and "enculturate individuals into its way of life," Kellner notes. Overall, as Debord reminds us, the spectacle is an expression of capital, "accumulated to the point where it becomes image." It is also "the extreme form of the expropriation of the Common," of the human ability to communicate, Agamben adds.[38]

At a time when Wall Street stocks fluctuate along social media "moods" over the "real" economy, Debord's insights on spectacular capitalism seem timely. In particular, his claim that "all that once was directly lived has become mere representation" and his description of the spectacle as the "autonomous movement of the non-living" speak to our increasingly AI, artificial intelligence–driven virtual and social media worlds.[39]

For over five billion people on the planet, social media and the digital world have become a second skin, just as two-thirds regularly use AI. With the internet, electronic media, and social media the possibilities of communication reach new heights. Favoring an explosion of channels and democratizing access to information, the electronic media has diversified outlets and voices. Platforms offer seemingly unlimited possibilities of expression, sharing sources and grassroots organizing, including with instant translation support. These channels help disseminate ways of perceiving, judging, feeling, and expressing ourselves while "engender[ing] experiences"—increasingly through "augmented reality." They also promise bringing us closer to making government officials accountable. In addition to emailing or calling our representatives, we can attend and organize social media live forums and even engage in an exchange with presidents on X, and then take a break on Instagram, watch films or attend festivals virtually, or perhaps chat with an AI bot, all exhilarating possibilities.[40]

While social media lets ordinary citizens participate and even report by themselves, the multiplication of outlets and voices can amplify unsettling prospects. Through emotional appeals and bizarre claims, drawing on the illusion of "an eternal present," the corporate-driven spectacular can impair our sense of reality. Information wars, astroturfing, propaganda campaigns, and the dissemination of false information that claims to be combating "fake news" are a few common experiences that may turn an initial sense of freedom into feeling overwhelmed by total surveillance and trolls. Of course, years of reality TV shows taught millions of people to feel "at home in Panopticon," not to worry much about privacy as "life on the screen" can feel natural, as Nancy Rosenblum notes.

Perhaps the worst part is that we may believe we are engaging with the world whereas the information we access is being carefully—if automatically—curated to meet our demographics, preferences, and interests. "Recommender systems," including software and machine learning algorithms, personalize content with the sole purpose to increase "user" engagement that helps advertisers reach us qua consumers. As similar filtering gets applied to all the contents we access, opaque proprietary algorithms curate our digital selves into what Ermelinda Rodilosso calls "epistemic isolation." Moreover, by presenting us with contents that smooth our exposure and make it pleasant, we are herded into "filter bubbles" that reconfirm our preexisting beliefs and hurt our chances to think critically, learn, and adapt to changing environments. This electronic herding introduces new ways of framing discourse and visibility, delimiting public space, shaping politics and subjectivities, and further commodifying life. The one thing these algorithms take away from us is a chance to encounter the unexpected.[41]

Designed with commercial purposes, proprietary algorithms "perfectly" match "users" preferences and habits. They select contents to make our experience pleasant to keep us engaged "for as long as possible." Likeminded communities connecting through shared views about the same celebrities or products converge in dense small networks and self-referential bubbles that act as echo chambers on social media sites. Personalized predictive advertising and content delivery reinforce those bubbles.[42]

Meanwhile, corporations promise us "a bright future" starting with "replacing our current reality." No wonder social media is addicting! Opportunities keep opening for new markets, with digital media revenue projected at $560 billion for 2024, up from $360 billion in 2022. As the electronics revolution makes images, video, data, or video games key commodities shaping our daily lives, Debord's description of the spectacular as "gazing" gains new relevance.[43]

Like liberal democracies, corporations celebrate diversity alongside the "spectacularisation of legal and political categories" including human rights and the value of life, as Alex Murray and Thanos Zartaloudis put it. Media and social media outlets and platforms shape the public's views through political marketing that appeals to individuals in intense and emotional ways. The figure of the "influencer," including celebrities, is key in this regard, as are brands like Apple. Or logarithms, which already determine "more than 70 percent of what people watch on YouTube."[44]

Far from their egalitarian patina, broadcast networks and social media ownership have grown centralized and concentrated, in the hands of a few individuals who also rank among the world's wealthiest—Rupert Murdoch, Elon Musk, and Mark Zuckerberg among them. They serve as the "storm troopers" of spectacular commodification, as the media shepherds public opinion close to the status quo that Agamben discusses. More so, they are transforming our world into a place where "nothing is true and all is spectacle," as Jonathan Taplin notes.[45]

In the meantime, we users contribute to corporate profits as consumers, unpaid content creators, and by becoming ourselves a source of massive data extraction. Reaching us from our phones, through "microspectacles" described by Samir Gandesha and Johan Hartle, the extractive mechanisms of spectacular capitalism appropriate our labor as well.

Digital mining draws on algorithms that capture value from "the labor and life of populations," Verónica Gago and Sandro Mezzadra note. As we participate "in global capitalism's tight chains of enjoyment, production, and surveillance," as Jodi Dean puts it, our demographics, personal views, preferences, and affect are turned into the raw material for "various marketing, actuarial, security circuits", Gandesha and Hartle add. While the contents we create may well serve our purposes, our personal data is turned into a commodity, as David Hesmondhalgh notes. Targeted marketing lets corporations amass unheard amounts of information in record times. Dissecting the exploitative mechanisms of "communicative capitalism," Jodi Dean reminds us that corporations like Facebook claim property over the content we produce. They also appropriate and exploit our metadata links, connections, and search patterns and make users compete for rewards and opportunities through things such as "Likes" or retweets. Multiple sites, contents, messages, and demands compete for our attention in ways that exhaust our energies and force us to speed up, in what ultimately turns into a boundless, 24/7 production line. Furthermore, the unpaid labor of billions feeds increasingly autonomous AI systems that now even mimic our subjectivities.[46]

This way, the capitalist spectacle, as Agamben observes, expropriates not just labor but also language and communication to turn them into value "accumulated in images and in the media"—a superlative theft of the commons materializing in the ways in which AI systems displace humans from jobs. Moreover, the spectacle advances to take over the very experience of human communicability, the thing that unites us. Hence its violence, Agamben concludes.[47]

On their part, governments expand their reign into electronic arenas, including the entire repertoire of reason of state. They take advantage of media coverage of regular "live, ceremonial, and pre-planned events," such as the US Super Bowl, to reinforce tropes and narratives. Patriotic holidays enter entertainment and consumption, as with Presidents' Day or Veterans Day tourism and retail sales. Profuse coverage of national celebrations, sports, and celebrity culture and entertainment can help keep people away from debating issues that affect their lives.

Keeping consumption going can be branded as patriotic. After 9/11 George W. Bush encouraged citizens to "Get on board" and "Fly and enjoy America's great destination spots. Get down to Disney World in Florida. Take your families and enjoy life, the way we want it to be enjoyed." On his part, Boris Johnson saw no problems with his "Eat Out to Help Out" campaign subsidizing restaurant prizes to encourage people to go out in August 2020, despite likely contributing to spreading COVID-19 infections.[48]

Often, curated popular culture naturalizes state lawlessness and makes it even look glamorous. Since the aftermath of 9/11, the "truly bizarre" idea that enemies can only be defeated in "the domain of illegality, that is, in places where no law applies," has gained currency, as Stephen Holmes observes. A common sense linked to characters and stories continues to reinforce these views. Lawless patriotic warriors—increasingly diversified in terms of gender and ethnicity—are permanent features of Hollywood films, TV shows, and video games. The media has fully embraced the Hobbesian premise that "might is right," that "due process is a luxury," as Holmes notes, and beliefs that only lawbreakers can truly protect communities, countries, and even civilization. Thus law breaches and state violence can be made to look acceptable, even charming, as the spectacular governmentalities of emergency feed its entertainment department.[49]

To some extent, these themes and tropes owes to the role of agencies like the Central Intelligence Agency in advising playwriters and curating scripts for Hollywood—now also Netflix, a long way since the CIA's first appointed an agent to help improve the image of American spies back in the 1990s. In publicly available guidelines, the agency states its goal to collaborate with writers to get "a balanced and informed portrayal of the hard work done by Agency officers." Likewise, over 2,500 Hollywood films have been made with Pentagon assistance, Tanner Mirrlees reports, and even unsuspected cooking or travel TV shows include military-friendly messaging to help recruit youths.[50]

Not just for entertainment, our thoughts and personal experiences feed marketing as much as state intelligence apparatuses, which can turn against individuals potentially any time. The tools of neoliberal reason of state to monitor the population in search of targets and threats draw on the same networks of communication and entertainment. By 2025, the US State Department requires applicants for student and exchange visas to share their social media usernames of the last five years and make those accounts public to identify potential threats. In the age of "surveillance capitalism," an extraordinary wealth of personal information is unlawfully farmed, collected, monetized, and used by both corporations and states.

If distortive, the spectacle addresses our need for stories. Whether truthful or manufactured, events and storytelling help us make sense of our world, with plots of heroes and villains, lessons, punishments, and rewards. This may in part explain the rise of media or celebrity figures into spectacular politics, whether it is Silvio Berlusconi in Italy, Volodymyr Zelensky in Ukraine, or Ronald Reagan or Donald Trump in the US.

Like Berlusconi, Trump made his fortune through real estate speculation. Both Berlusconi and Trump showed exceptional ability to master the new media of their time—cable TV in Italy in the 1990s, TV and social media since the 2000s in the US. While Berlusconi ran his own "media empire," Trump became popular playing himself, a millionaire celebrity, in a TV show, *The Apprentice*. But it was the former Twitter that gave Trump a unique, decisive political platform since he joined it in 2009, one that grew into a collection of 56,571 tweets until being banned in January 2021.[51]

As epitomized in political figures like these, extending to all, thanks to the electronic media and social media, the old forms of popular acclamation of approval to princes and emperors break traditional boundaries to reach "every area of social life," Agamben notes. Indeed, if street protests and public opinion are modern forms of acclamation, "social media gives [it a] new form," Mitchell Dean observes. Even the simple "liking," "following," or reacting to posts with emojis mimic gestures with a history, as with the "*pollice verso* (turned thumb)" of Roman gladiator fights. To the traditional cry of the assembled multitude in the public square, followed with the public opinion of the modern mass media, the "Likes" of social media add acclamation as public mood. Just like public opinion, acclamatory events can be staged, as with the expert curating of social media that has become the norm. And as acclamation develops new facets, so do the mechanisms for its "capture and regulation," Dean notes, to generate legitimacy and consensus. Thus, the glorious production of splendor makes the extraordinary routine, expanding 24/7 through the electronic media into our lives.[52]

With the addition of social media and countless apps, the digisphere brings together and fuses the entire productive cycle under capital and state governance. Distinct moments of production, distribution, exchange, and consumption are enacted electronically. Seamlessly integrating news, entertainment, communication, socializing, networking, advertising, consumption, surveillance, governing, and propaganda, entering our domestic life through the Internet of Things, spectacular capitalism goes full circle. Information, at the stage where AI systems take over, feeds both capital and states.

In the background, a "computational" logic seeks to replace politics with "smooth operations" of a "data-driven instrumentation society," Shoshana Zuboff notes. New technologies make available "total knowledge" in "continuous streams," with predictive capabilities. Politics can be replaced, technocrats promise, with more efficient computational systems that anticipate and organize traffic, trade, investment, or health needs in such a way to prevent or minimize financial crashes, crime, or epidemics "for the greater good."

"It is possible that Big Data can even read desires we do not know we harbour," Byung-Chul Han notes in acknowledging our "digital unconscious." If so, as he suggests, control of the population could reach new heights. Knowledge of the state's resources, the population, and threats lies at the very definition of reason of state. As new subjective, epistemic, and political territories develop alongside electronic communications and social media, forms of "algorithmic governmentality" follow, Mitchell Dean observes. Favored by joint state and corporate strategies, drawing on Big Data's behavioral predictive analytics, governing interventions are tailored to individuals according to their "digital traces" by recommendation systems, Dean observes. Impervious to ideas of law, rights (other than those of property), or democracy, algorithmic, and computational governmentalities enter reason of state.[53]

As if an extension of its fictional lawless warriors, in its terror-centered variants the spectacular advances a politics "increasingly constituted outside of the law and the boundaries of democracy itself." When sovereignty's violent storytelling gets reenacted, "subjection is legitimated by clothing the body politic in a mysterious veil." As referred to earlier, the narrative-driven, fictional apparatus of our spectacular democracies opens room for violent state interventions. Glorifying those performances legitimizes governmental practices and the underlying sovereign claims.

Perpetuating the state involves charming its people, silencing dissenters, and crushing enemies and threats. The intensity of these moves feels stronger these days, as digital networks embed extraction, surveillance, and governance in the same channels that serve as legitimizing mechanisms. No wonder the same state that enchants us also often terrifies us. The complement of controlled appearances is controlling silence and invisibility, since there is no need to legitimize acts that nobody knows about. The sovereign ceremonies and splendor heightened by the spectacular find their complement in the governance of visibility and threat.

Silence 1: Secrecy

"We are psychologically damaged; it is like being raped by the state," declared Jacqui, a British woman who maintained a romantic relationship and had a child in 1985, ignoring that her partner was an undercover police agent. At the time, Jacqui was an animal rights activist, and agent Bob Lambert, from the Metropolitan Police Special Demonstration Squad, used the relationship to infiltrate the group. Between four and eight agents fathered children and at least twenty entered romantic relations with women under false identities in the UK between the late 1960s and 2010, an inquiry revealed. They used women to spy on activist groups on the left. Leaks and scandals offer a glimpse into the governmental "penumbra of secrecy."[54]

Secrecy defines a main component of reason of state. Under its guidance, secrets were thought necessary to avoid the "disgust" that knowledge of certain government actions would trigger among the people. Only those "initiated" in the *arcana imperii* (the secrets of power, originally referring to the secrets of Roman emperors) could see what most others could not, Martin Loughlin notes. Secrecy seemed needed also to protect "the knowledge that the state must develop of itself," Foucault explains, including the governmental art and technologies to crush sedition and revolution.[55]

Invoking the publicity of the acts of government, modern revolutions consecrated freedoms of thought, speech, and association that put into question the *arcana imperii*. As a result, in modern democratic republics secrecy is "strictly regulated by law," Marjan Brezovšek and Demir Črnčec observe. Or it should be. Easy access to information over the internet may distract us from how zealously governments keep secrets. Whether as classified information, executive privileges, or covering for surveillance or detentions, secrecy persists as governments' "constant companion."[56]

"The national defense has required that certain information be maintained in confidence in order to protect our citizens, our democratic institutions, our homeland security, and our interactions with foreign nations." This quotation comes from President Barack Obama's 2009 announcement of a three-tiered framework for classification, expressing a "commitment to open Government" by making criteria for classification and declassification more transparent. In the US, the executive branch controls the classification system through decisions that only the president can reverse. For every issue the government defines as secret, hundreds of thousands of documents are classified. The US classifies fifty million documents every year. Not only is the overclassification of government documents "rampant," as a former head of the classifying office acknowledged in 2016, with a labyrinthic 3,000 guides for classification, but the harsher treatment of media disclosures threatens journalism.[57]

While batches of documents get declassified from time to time, and citizens can file declassification requests—under the Freedom of Information Act in the US—the process is slow, selective, and often undergoes reversals. In contrast, classification works by default. Even the US president can meet resistance. In 1998, after the Clinton administration announced the release of 24,000 documents on the US role in the 1973 coup in Chile, the CIA alleged not to be "legally obliged" to release records of operations "never . . . officially acknowledged" by the government. Eventually the National Security Agency joined in, and declassification required a presidential order. Then, following 9/11, massive reclassification took place, with secrecy expanding into new arenas. Under the new regime, secrecy became treated as a necessary part of normal governance, invoking "vital" state interests, necessity, security, and people's protection.

Every year, "government agencies create petabytes—or millions of gigabytes—of classified information," Bryan Bender reports. Made possible by the electronics revolution, for years governments and corporations collect "all forms of human communication," with little to no citizen control or accountability. Even the 1.7 million documents released by Edward Snowden stand as a fraction of the NSA secret files, in turn just one of several US intelligence agencies that routinely classify millions of documents besides Homeland Security and the Pentagon.[58]

US officials treat individuals responsible for media "leaks" by sharing government secrets with journalists as more dangerous than foreign spies. By releasing classified information on the internet, "leakers" are said to "amplify the potential damage to the national security." Accordingly, individuals sharing classified information with journalists are treated with severe criminal sentences.[59]

"Our budgets are classified as they could provide insight for foreign intelligence services," declared James Clapper, the Director of National Intelligence, in an interview in 2013. Using the same arguments, hundreds of billions of dollars in state corporate contracts remain "secret or hidden." Intelligence agencies such as the CIA administer discretionary budgets big enough to even run "private wars" around the world. In turn, the government keeps a wide, loose net of contractors and domestic informers and infiltrators, about whom we learn only on rare occasions, when some scandal or odd report outs them—as discussed in the previous chapter. As "secrecy about secrecy" becomes established, laws, courts, executive orders, prisons, arrests, criminal evidence, legal doctrine, policies, and even legal cases have been classified as secret by US authorities. The FISA (Foreign Intelligence Surveillance) Court, characterized as "a judiciary for the secret world," produces secret jurisprudence.[60]

The very notion of a secret law is absurd. Yet in the US laws, courts, and institutions (and laws?) can exist in secrecy. Their secret status can lead to the criminalization of citizens, as of those who demand information about policies or request classified materials. Often, the charges remain secret as the indicted are brought before secret courts. In so doing, the US government has invoked the state secrets privilege. This British common law allows the Crown, and now also US authorities, to refuse evidence to courts or lawmakers purportedly because the information "would harm national security or foreign relation interests if disclosed." Initially used to avoid releasing evidence, the principle has been invoked to ask courts not to hear lawsuits, alleging that "to even answer the complaint by confirming or denying its allegations" would endanger national security.[61]

The defense of the "greater good" supports the state secrets privilege. Other than guidelines, no report on the use of the doctrine has been submitted by the US Department of Justice, and lawmakers' requests have been denied with the argument that acknowledging the use of the privilege would require revealing information that "may be too sensitive to acknowledge or disclose," the attorney general responded in 2012. In 2021, the US Supreme Court heard two cases related to the doctrine, and restated that a legal case may not proceed when the classified evidence is central to the litigation. A congressional report, in turn, recommended further revision, considering courts' leniency toward the executive power and that, even if "invocations of the state secrets privilege are relatively rare, they may have stark results for civil litigants."[62]

Keeping citizens in the dark regarding what governments do on their behalf, state secrecy impairs "public debate about serious matters" and can put citizens at risk when governments neglect informing about the actual scope of crises or natural disasters. Secrecy undermines officials' and lawmakers' ability to make sound policy decisions. It shields policies from review, hides mistakes, abuses, and corruption, and makes a small group into "privileged interpreters of necessity" in ways contrary to democratic principles.

While nobody in a democracy can deny the publicity principle, governments often devalue their duty to inform the public into a vague right to access information "of a public character." Limited to what the authorities choose to make public, this right goes in circles, by letting people know what the government allows the public to know, with no appeal. In some cases, misappropriating citizens' language by imagining the state as a person, governments frame secrecy as their own "right to privacy."[63]

Besides concealing government acts, secrecy stands as a security performance asserting that enemies can be anywhere and that only a selected few can be trusted with knowledge. As a performance, it reinforces mechanisms of security and emergency while leaving lives, voices, instances of abuse, and deaths in the dark. By 2015, in the US alone, over 2,000 "original classification" officials had power to restrict access to documents, and over 4.5 million people had security clearances.

Secrecy consolidates "a state within the state" in conditions that let officials escape accountability. Pyramidal views of the state help maintain opaqueness, with Leviathan-like metaphors illuminating only the top and outer surfaces of the state apparatus. Not exclusive of elite agencies, however, these prerogatives extend more broadly to the police. With their traditional "Move along, there is nothing to see here" routine orders, masters in the play of (in)visibility, at the bottom of the state apparatus layers of secrecy protect police agents responsible for abuses from disciplining and prosecution.

"Torturers have benefited mightily from censorship," James Bovard observes, which is favored by officials who, whichever their intentions, censor documents alleging classified information concerns. As the dark underbelly of the state gained in extension, with only bouts of visibility offered by leaks and investigative reports, with their commitment to secrecy a number of US officials contribute to the unlawful parallel world of torture, clandestine camps, laws, and courts. But when the veil of secrecy gets cracked, the actions of state agents are called into question, silence turns into silencing with state attempts to dismiss criticism through indictments and prosecutions. Political discourse thus moves to the center, as rhetoric and symbolism gain in intensity with officials invoking "mitigating circumstances" that made their choices inevitable while diluting their individual responsibility.[64]

Silence 2: Silencing

"We tortured some folks," US President Barack Obama declared in an August 2014 televised news conference at the White House. The use of torture, Obama claimed, was due to the "pressure" experienced by those in charge of national security in their quest to prevent terrorist attacks. Concluding that "we did some things that were contrary to our values," Obama asked citizens "not be too 'sanctimonious'" in judging those actions from their current, safer perspective.[65]

Obama's "folksy" reference and declarations trivialized his government's human rights violations in an almost humorous way that shut down debate. Torture is a major crime under both international and domestic US law. Unlike warfare, torture cannot claim any accidental victims, as "the torture of a single individual is strictly illegal in any circumstances." Of course, President Obama, a law professor, knew all this. During his 2008 electoral campaign, he had promised to investigate human rights violations by members of the Bush administration. Years later, with no need for such niceties, in his first interview as a president, doubling down on the defense of torture, Trump expressed declared "absolutely I feel it works."

Human rights violations and law breaches, bypassing international law, or embracing "secrecy as security" are described as necessary responses to a formless, omnipresent enemy. Claiming exceptional circumstances under which laws do not apply, appealing to necessity, urgency, security, or the common good, agents along the governmental chain demand to be exempted from any form of accountability. State contractors, in turn, make the same argument as higher authorities. This way, for all practical purposes, entire networks are exempted from the laws, domestic and international, as from constitutional norms. As with the police, they may not have formal authority to suspend the legal order, but their practices re-create emergency governance at local points across the state apparatus. And when not even put into question, or made visible, unlawful governance is treated as a legitimate prerogative exercise.[66]

Faced with the deadly outcome of their policies, politicians often allege the impossibility of having foreseen the ultimate consequences of their chosen course of action and still assert it as the only possible one. They may blame their victims for their own fate, as the Trump administration did with the forced separations of immigrant families and their (deadlier) abandonment in camps. Or as the Italian Matteo Salvini, who made immigration into a major threat and an emergency while severely criminalizing those rescuing refugees from drowning in the Mediterranean Sea. Not only blamed for their fate, victims are also turned into enemies.

Manipulative discourse, Teun Van Dijk observes, draws on "persuasion, information, education and other legitimate forms of communication" combined with the appeal to fear and to traumatic events such as memories of war, as well as deceit.

To make the audience accept the unacceptable, manipulative discourse exploits people's vulnerabilities by targeting mental models, memory, "knowledge, attitudes and ideologies," as well as by reshaping normative standards, Van Dijk explains. Manipulative discourse engages the masses' "feelings and perceptions," blending stories and affect as politicians help people make sense of their circumstances while offering "simplistic solutions" with good media coverage. With curated settings, attire, and style to enhance the authority of the speaker, manipulative discourse presents positions and beliefs as irrefutable, even when drawing on uncheckable facts. Ultimately, manipulative discourse portrays dissent and criticisms as unpatriotic and stifles debate. Manipulating people through fear can make militarization and restrictions of rights and liberties look acceptable.[67]

State agents may assert that the outcome will not be that negative. Or resort to "strategies of transformation" and gaslighting. The latter, a term originating from a 1944 film, describes manipulation that makes people distrust their own perceptions and accept a " false reality," as Peter Wehner writes in The Atlantic. Sometimes, "an entire nation" can be targeted. The assertions may seem trivial—as when the White House' press secretary claimed that, in 2017, President Trump attracted "the largest audience to ever witness an inauguration, period," while photographs showed otherwise. Others involve international matters, as when in 2002 US Defense Secretary Donald Rumsfeld declared that Guantanamo prisoners were being treated in ways "reasonably consistent with the Geneva Conventions," just as he claimed that "unlawful combatants" did not deserve legal protection, in flagrant violation of treaty obligations at a time that images of prisoners in cages were released. Eventually, in 2018, President Trump became associated with gaslighting with telling the audience: "Just remember—what you are seeing and what you are reading is not what's happening." In all cases, manipulative discourse denies the speaker's responsibility while blaming choices made by antagonists whose actions are demonized.

Sometimes, we witness apologies, even exemplary prosecutions. Images of police officers kneeling to Black Lives Matter protesters across the US received media coverage in the summer 2020. The gesture, introduced by football player Colin Kaepernick in denouncing racial violence, was taken as a sign of solidarity with victims of racist violence. Yet in some cases the same kneeling cops were later seen repressing protesters. At the time, a New York Police Department lieutenant wrote an email to his peers expressing shame and regret for his "horrible decision to give into a crowd of protesters demands" by kneeling together with other members of the force.

In disputing "which stories" will be adopted by governments, Michelle Bonner notes, politicians provide journalists with "packaged" news. Mainstream journalism validates these positions in their reporting and treats the opinions of high-raking government officials and the police as facts. Considering that media representations produce "legal effects," Ieva Jusyionite notes, by adopting the state's viewpoint and accepting the official "moral binary discourse to define what is legal and what is illegal," the media helps frame and establish narratives.[68]

To shut down criticism, state agents may proceed to the selective recognition of stories of rights violations (and the deliberate silencing of others) when reaching out to specific constituencies. Flaws of current policies tend to be kept "hidden, limited or . . . discursively deemphasized," and officials may invoke alternative laws or regulations "considered either more important or more appropriate to the circumstances at hand," as John Bellamy Foster notes. Acting as gatekeepers, the established media may simply refuse to cover events.

These are a few ways in which torture, extrajudicial killings, illegal detentions, and other forms of state unlawfulness get trivialized. Official denial and censorship, legalisms and technicalities, euphemisms, and mislabeling (e.g., "enhanced interrogation"), the aestheticizing and trivializing of state violence by the media and entertainment industries, all make unlawful governance normalized.

On her part, the recalcitrant investigative journalist should expect silencing and attacks. As should those engaging with critical, community-based online reporting, from professionals to include activists and common citizens, many of whom become targeted by "those who want to control the flow of information," often linked to the government or with state protection. As state secrecy and unlawful practices expand and investigative reporting becomes all the more crucial, "the number of acts of censorship also increases," including legal attacks and imprisonment, fines, and confiscations.

At its most brutal, killings of journalists have been on the rise. Between 1992 and 2025, the Committee to Protect Journalists documents 2,458 killings of journalists and media workers, while 361 journalists were imprisoned and 68 went missing in 2024 alone. During 2024, 124 journalists and media workers were killed, the highest number since records started in 1992, with "nearly two-thirds of them Palestinians killed by Israel."[69]

Photojournalists and camera operators have become the target of attacks, kidnappings, and murders. Indeed, as shown by the international outrage following the release of torture scenes from Abu Ghraib, the video of the brutal police treatment of Rodney King, or the videotaped murders of Michael Brown or George Floyd by police officers, images feel threatening to those in power. Among the countries with the most killings of journalists, the UN Rapporteur lists Colombia, India, Mexico, Brazil, Turkey, Bosnia and Herzegovina, Bangladesh, Israel and the occupied Palestinian territory, and Nigeria, all of which also exhibit the highest levels of immunity.[70]

Invoking partial truths to disqualify critics, politicians claim to tell who the real journalists and legitimate protesters and human rights groups are. The smearing of independent voices through media and social media campaigns, with trolls or AI bots harassing journalists can overwhelm those targeted and confuse the public. The consumerist imperatives of neoliberal capitalism require a sense of normalcy to function, including the elision and denial of ongoing, actual crises whose acknowledgment threatens the spectacles of capital.

Thus information about highly complex, "wicked problems" from the unprecedented levels of accelerating warming, mounting disasters and crop failures to millions of people displaced, rising wars and casualties, the threat of fascism, or the persistence of COVID-19 infections and deaths can get "neutralized or evaded," minimized, or disqualified, in ways that help things feel "back to normal." Banning terms such as "climate crisis," "exclusion," or "inequality" in government websites and in grant applications promotes their invisibility. The one common thread is protecting consumption levels and the smooth flow and perpetual expansion of capital.[71]

Caught in the webs of the spectacle, under its spell, we are kept busy, entertained, pacified, and isolated. Once no dissenting voices are left, the spectacle self-referentially focuses "upon itself and its own imagined enemies," Tom Bunyard observes. So from large-scale crises to the routine, police-driven governance of (in)security, threats and enemies help justify extraordinary measures. The need for security, for people to accept the Hobbesian bargain, relies on threats and enemies. And the discursive construction and treatment of enemies anticipates their physical destruction as officials reclaim authority.

Crush 1. Finding Enemies

"The Movement has enemies abroad and enemies within. Whoever does not fight the enemy or defend everyday life is a traitor. Whoever fights the enemy and defends the cause of the people is a partner. And who fights a partner is either an enemy or a traitor." In an interview in 1971, Juan Domingo Perón restates main ideas inspiring his politics. In particular, Perón notes the importance of distinguishing between friends and enemies, to then make sure to give "to the friend, everything; to the enemy, not even justice." In this matter, he observes, there is no room for ambiguity. "Everyone who fights for the same cause than we do is a partner," Perón adds, "an ally." In contrast, "the enemies of the motherland are the enemies of the people." In the end, Perón calls for solidarity among the people, noting that "for us, all of those who fight the enemies of our country are our friends." Perón's formula formidably captures the intimate links between the (extralegal) logic of the emergency and definitions of the People. Views of the people, the enemy, and loyalty such as those conveyed by Perón materialize in exceptional measures, which political discourse anticipates.

Thrilling, charismatic, and polemical, political discourse can quickly shift from festive and celebratory to threatening and antagonizing as it defines identities. Representations of the People, of who "we" are, get defined in contrast to those portrayed as endangering our collective existence as a Nation—our enemies. Pivoting on a logic of inclusions and exclusions—even destruction—of those perceived as threats, political discourse delineates supporters and adversaries, a group of the indecisive whom the speaker attempts to persuade, as well as enemies. After presenting their credentials as a representative of the People, the political speaker introduces explicit addressees who are greeted with praise and promises. As with promises, the speech makes significant use of warnings and threats. Then, María Marta García Negroni and Mónica Graciela Zoppi Fontana observe, there is the hidden addressee. Hardly ever mentioned, the hidden addressee gets alluded to only vaguely through dark references and threats. Eventually, in times of crisis, the hidden addressee is made explicit as the enemy and target of threats. Rallying the audience against the enemy to justify bypassing rights and legal norms involves affective, emotional appeals. This is one point at which populist interpellations and emergency politics meet.[72]

In his 1932 book, Carl Schmitt characterizes the political as an identity-shaping dialectics through which "the most intense and extreme antagonism" develops in defining friend and enemy. The enemy, Schmitt notes, is "the other, the stranger . . . in an especially intense way." In the end, the identification of friends and enemies results from a political decision by the "sovereign body," he concludes. Describing the play of identities against the background of the state of exception, Schmitt stresses the importance of antagonism. The definition of the people and "the unity of the body politic" require and get imagined alongside the figure of the enemy.

Schmitt's theory captures the dialectic of identity unfolding under the arch of the state-centered political imagination. The state body, Neocleous notes, needs to be secured from threats. Never neatly defined, the enemy stands in "a place both at the gates and inside the territory." As threats are detected, any means seem warranted to neutralize or eliminate them. "The security–identity–loyalty complex" pushes those who resist further into this dialectic, with a veiled threat that unless they align with the hegemonic, sovereign story, they could themselves be labeled as enemies.[73]

State-defined antagonisms and strangers come in various formats and combinations. While friends, allies, adversaries, and enemies populate political life, exacerbating antagonisms is politics' trademark. Antagonizing speech may seem softened by euphemisms or justifications, by appealing to common interests, or even by humor as the same statements appear as a promise to some and a threat to others—just think of the motto "Make America Great Again." In moments of crisis, the speaker appeals to both her supporters and to the indecisive to rally against the enemy that she identifies. As this motto is raised against those defined as not belonging, it becomes a call for securitization and criminalizing immigration in the US.

Enemies can be domestic. In contexts of economic crisis, it is tempting for politicians to "appeal to fear of an internal enemy—the fear of violent crime," Paul Chevigny notes, as with the populism of fear. Amid heightened fear of crime, reflected in polls and the media, politicians campaign on a rhetoric that divides society into citizens and criminals, making promises of tougher policing and imprisonment. And if the figure of the terrorist serves to justify emergencies, so does the criminal in everyday life.[74]

Enemies can be (or be made) foreign. The foreigner, the refugee, the alien keep being targeted. Their strangeness helps politicians delimit the People's collective identity. Portrayed as contaminating the nation's body, their expulsion is presented as a matter of "social hygiene" alongside "a view of statecraft as a therapeutic art," Neocleous observes. Thus the border stands as a preeminent territory for "the stabilization of order," Neocleous notes.[75]

The "alien," however, can be a plastic notion, as political definitions of threats and enemies blend crime, migration, and the poor with victims of natural disasters. Boundaries get blurry and definitions can change quickly, with enemies potentially everywhere. With the "spectacle of terrorism" established after New York, Madrid, Paris, and London underwent attacks, the figure of the terrorist sets an evanescent but omnipresent threat.

"In our fight against Islamist terrorism, we will never give in," French president Emmanuel Macron reminded citizens after the killing of a policewoman in 2021 in Rambouillet, following his call to "the entire nation" to mobilize against terrorism. "Emotionally exploited," fear of terrorism helps politicians and the media make citizens accept irregular operations and weakened rights crowned by illegal detentions and the use of torture while absolving governments from responsibility. Appealing to French greatness while rallying against a revitalized "enemy within" represented as Islamic terrorists, helped French politicians win elections despite their unpopular austerity policies.[76]

Terrorism serves to identify internal enemies. In the summer of 2020, as thousands of protests followed the murder of George Floyd in Minneapolis by the police, Trump blamed some violent incidents on "Antifa," which he characterized as terrorists as he threatened to ban the group. A short for antifascism, Antifa describes no particular group. Still, the president's Antifa invention seemed "an excuse for military escalation—and for impunity," a *Washington Post* editorial noted, as unidentified federal forces entered Seattle and detained protesters, attesting to the material implications of threatening speech.

Ultimately, the enemy can be portrayed as "a parasite or a waste product to be eliminated," Neocleous notes, just as mutually reinforcing mechanisms of exclusion strip individuals and groups of legal protections. With its storytelling about migrants, terrorists, and criminals, spectacular politics naturalizes exclusion, silences the excluded, and makes their exclusion invisible and irrelevant.[77]

In its escalation into an endless global crusade to maintain and restore order, the US global war on terror further complicates Perón's Schmittian views of the enemy. How does one prepare to identify and combat omnipresent but evanescent and changing enemies? This preemptive war, Neocleous notes, has introduced a new figure, the "Universal Adversary." Attacks can be brought by the usual "foreign terrorists, domestic radical groups, state-sponsored adversaries," as well as by "disgruntled employees," according to a 2005 US Homeland Security Council document. In anticipation of these threats, Neocleous observes, Homeland Security defined its target as "the Universal Adversary." For training purposes, with a view of unpredictable enemies yet trying not to stigmatize any group, emergency planning initiatives in the US have adopted imaginary figures, such as zombies. Intendedly or not, the use of such figures makes the dehumanization of the enemy absolute.[78]

In any case, unless one responds appropriately, the threat remains latent for anyone to be turned into an enemy, with "not even justice!" as Perón put it. Repressive practices continue to be justified as necessary for reasons of "national security, law and order, and the protection of national values." And the more open the appeals "to 'cure', 'purge' and 'invigorate'" the body of the Nation, the more intense the biopolitical rhetoric, the closer we get to fascism, state terror, and genocide.

We thus reach the darkest, ugliest underbelly of the sovereign state and its productive matrix, the neoliberal reason of state. "While it remains true that even in the most desperate situations people can exert agency, to ignore the asymmetry of power in many relations is naive and dangerous," Kathleen Arnold reminds us. Indeed, governments regulate and limit rights, access, and protections. As part of their sovereign claims, they also exercise the prerogative to take life.[79]

Crush 2. We Kill

"We kill suspects whose names we know, and whose names we don't; we kill the guilty and the not guilty; we kill men, but also women and children; we kill by day and by night; we fire missiles at confirmed visual targets, but also at cellphone numbers we hope belong to targets." This account of drone killings by the US government captures the dimension of state terror embedded in the same networks that connect and entertain us. "The cell phone is the new cigarette in the foxhole . . . your cell phone can get you killed," a U.S. military commander alerts his soldiers. Supported on "artificial intelligence, autonomy, and greater intelligence," drone surveillance and targeting rely on signals from satellites, Khalil Dewan explains. The same cell phone that people use to access the last series on Netflix, to call their loved ones, or to share memes on social media lets AI systems and police and military apparatuses track and, a few algorithms and drone controls later, even kill them. As the center of the military-industrial complex moves to Silicon Valley, the same spectacular apparatus that enchants us also can exploit our labor, spy on us, keeps us under control, and even take our lives. At its core, the design of algorithms, Dardot observes, defines neoliberalism's "privileged battlefield," helped by sexist, racist, and ideological biases embedded in instructions that enable things such as AI pattern recognition or decision-making. Here the spectacle first described by Debord comes full circle to blend with the traditional sovereign prerogative to take lives through twenty-first-century "seamless connectivity."[80]

Since 2023, "large-scale assassination operations" conducted in Gaza by the Israeli military relied on "Absora" or "The Gospel," an artificial intelligence-driven system that generated "automatic recommendations" of suspected Hamas operatives' residences for attacks. Another AI-based program, "Lavender," identifies "targets for assassination." At least 37,000 individuals were identified in Gaza this way, barely checked for accuracy before bombing them (targets were checked for twenty seconds at the most, to make sure they were male). Both systems were trained and fed with intelligence about the entire population, including pictures, social media, phone information, and contacts. "They wanted to allow us to attack automatically. That's the Holy Grail. Once you go automatic, target generation goes crazy," a soldier observed.[81]

It is the same with drones. More than 100 countries had a drone program in 2022, many of them armed, and drones are accessible to more actors. In the US, killings by drone gained visibility when President Obama's Disposition Matrix or "kill list" was leaked, following the government's killings of sixteen-year-old US citizen Abdulrahman Al-Aulaqi and two of his American relatives in Yemen. The secret list, decided by the president in consultation with security advisors, classified people as "targeting for capture, interrogation, or assassination by drone." Every week, on "Terror Tuesdays," the President met with his advisors to make decisions about the list.[82]

Obama expanded drone strikes tenfold compared to the Bush years, and their use was estimated to have increased four- or fivefold under Trump. In early August 2022, Biden announced the killing of al-Qaeda leader Ayman al-Zawahiri in Afghanistan through a drone attack. "I authorized a precision strike that would remove him from the battlefield, once and for all," Biden declared. While Biden claimed to have delivered "justice," drone strikes leave only death and destruction with no clear claims to legality. More so since the United States normalized the use of "over-the-horizon strikes," drone attacks conducted from outside the target country's borders. A next step is the use of Lethal Autonomous Weapons Systems (LAWS) or "killer robots" by making machines autonomously identify targets and conduct an attack.[83]

Trust in drones or AI's "precision" echoes broader "scientific" claims across the security fields. In her book *The Truth Machines*, Jinee Lokaneeta examines the use of narcoanalysis and brain scanning by the Indian police, on—unproven—claims of scientificity. The use of lie detectors, brain monitoring, or truth serums for confessions was introduced in India in recent decades in response to reports of abuse and torture. Despite numerous studies showing the inaccuracy of the new methods, in an effort "to apply science" police and courts have upheld these tools. Even in the best-case scenario, when technologies are precise, biases in collecting and coding data compromise their use. In the end, "the prejudices in our society live in our data-sets, our categories, our labels and our algorithms," the Campaign to Ban Killer Robots notes. No technology, as sophisticated as it may be, can solve ideologically biased definitions of who a "terrorist" or a "criminal" are.[84]

In 2023, in response to a lawsuit by the American Civil Liberties Union, the Biden administration released the guidelines used in drone strikes. In response, the ACLU reminds the public that "only Congress has the power to authorize use of force abroad." Concerned about the expansion of executive prerogatives through new technologies, the ACLU objects to the president's vague language such as "'imminence' and 'near certainty'" to justify the use of lethal force, and that not even these loose rules are demanded from attacks by "US partner forces." Moreover, the ACLU decries the "appalling toll" that the US drone program continues to take on "Muslim, Brown, and Black civilians around the world."[85]

Deterritorializing unlawful exercises, as with the US government torturing detainees on Cuban soil, or outsourcing unlawful practices through contractors to then invoking immunity through secret laws and "evidentiary problems" helps state agents escape domestic and international law. Regardless of what language is used, claims to traditional prerogatives and reserve powers linked to "personal (and charismatic) authority" stand behind instances of executive clemency as much as behind the setting of "legal black holes."[86]

By 2024, the Pentagon had accelerated demand for technologies, data, and data storage supporting its use of drones and AI in Ukraine and Gaza. The war in Ukraine, in particular, saw a fast expansion in the use of drones, which turned into "one of the most important and widely used weapons on the battlefield." As drone divisions became fully integrated within the Ukrainian military structure, AI-driven autonomous drone systems capable of both identifying and attacking targets without human intervention are being developed.[87] Warfare makes for profitable industries.

Costs are going up. From 2003 to 2023, Neta Crawford documents the $2.89 trillion cost of US military operations in Iraq and Syria, where over half a million people were killed, "several times as many" likely died from indirect causes, over seven million people from the two countries became refugees, and eight million more were internally displaced. Meanwhile, with a $883.7 billion national defense budget in 2024, and $21 trillion spent on defense and security between 2001 and 2021, budgets keep skyrocketing, helped by the "rally around the flag effect," where members of Congress give the military more funds that requested to show troops their support, Crawford notes.[88]

Hundreds of protesters are killed around the world every year. As with other forms of acclamation, demonstrations are welcome only when those in power benefit from them. In the aftermath of recent historical cycles of protest, state repression has intensified "globally," Amnesty

International notes, by 2025 including the US revoking student visas and arresting those taking part in demonstrations. "Efforts to choke off civil society," Kenneth Roth observes, draw on increasingly refined though no less "brutal" repressive modalities across authoritarian and democratic regimes. Laws constrain NGOs and their funding. Victims of police violence are smeared and ignored, just as media campaigns discredit protesters and their grievances.[89]

The refulgent sword of Leviathan intends to keep the multitude orderly. Both charming and terrifying, the sovereign play amplified by the spectacular maintains the population in awe and fear, with the threat of terror in the back. At the end of the governing chain, its agents and performances, celebrations and military parades, the fetishistic sovereign state shines as a violent mechanism. Threats are everywhere, we are told. Besides the ever-expanding spectacular, surveillance, and coercive apparatuses, entire industries develop in response. Among them are what Barbara Sutton calls the "fashion of fear," offering outfits and accessories to maximize personal safety. Bulletproof backpacks and apparel for schoolchildren, but also elegant outfits for men and women, together with accessories, hide their bulletproof or other safety-related properties. While protective, the bulletproof fashion may function more as "a talisman," Sutton cites a war correspondent's memories of reporting from conflict zones. "Nothing's bulletproof" in the end, a salesperson observes. Still, the bulletproof garment industry is expected to reach $5.8 billion a decade from now.[90]

What happens when people lose fear? What happens when the state, rather than as a sobering protector, starts to be perceived as a threat? This is a problem for the Hobbesian who acts as if fear of one another was the defining human experience. It is also a problem for the Schmittian and other friends of sovereignty. The state of exception, in which the sovereign suspends the law for the people but keeps them subjected, only works if people believe both that the rest of us are a threat and that sovereignty is the response for their protection. Otherwise, potentially any crisis can devolve into what Walter Benjamin characterized as a real state of exception. "The tradition of the oppressed," Benjamin notes, "teaches us that the 'state of emergency' in which we live is not the exception but the rule." Against the violence of fascism, we must, "it is our task," he adds, to "bring about a real state of emergency" that moves beyond violence and emergencies.[91]

In order for sovereignty to exist, for its emergency apparatus to perpetuate itself, the threat of terror needs to be felt as absolute while kept under control by the state. One inch further and the state itself could collapse. Avoiding this collapse demands keeping people more afraid of one another than of the Leviathan. Otherwise, again hinted by Benjamin, the ambiguous territory opened by the emergency governmental apparatus could develop into a revolutionary direction.

As with any patriarchal figure, if only in this case a fetish, the state offers citizens its threatening protection. The hooded, tortured camp prisoner in Guantanamo, the drone-obliterated victim, the individuals killed in the streets by the police, make the millions of people in prisons look fortunate, and those of us allowed to live in freedom incredibly privileged and grateful to the state. "The divine grace that has been transformed into the grace conceded to us by the State may have the face of a Clinton, or a Menem . . . but it also has the face of the duty officer or the illegal employer." In any case, León Rozitchner reminds us, we are being "graced with the consolation prize: they let us off with our lives," and for this "we say thank you to them." Every day, regardless of how precarious our lives may be, Rozitchner reminds us that we're even unknowingly grateful to those in power for letting us live. State performances and rituals not only impress us, but they also constitute and reconstitute us as fearing, obedient subjects.[92]

As democracy and rights are presented as a "grace granted to us," to borrow from Rozitchner, the threat of state terror remains "in the innermost recesses of our bodies." State terrorism has been continuously used "by Northern liberal democratic states," Ruth Blakeley explains, with mostly complicit silence of the media and academia. Its signature and insignia are present even in the most glamorous political moments. It is the sword in the hand of Leviathan, the military commanders surrounding the president, the fully armored cops, weapon and immunity laden in our neighborhoods. They are there for our protection, we are told. Unless, that is, all of the sudden we happen to be defined as their threat.[93]

Under spectacular capitalism, the porous state of exception blends with its legitimating practices. Exposing the contingent character of state storytelling, myths, and liturgies takes away its "supernatural resplendence," as Jens Bartelson puts it, and challenges its legitimacy. And why shouldn't it? In contrast to effigies and sovereign stories, the image of people speaking and acting together, held by the power they create, as Arendt presents it, captures the heart of the political experience. In gathering, people may seek and generate distinct modalities of power and action. None of which, Arendt observes, match sovereignty and its fictions. And the plurality of voices of people in the streets reminds us that there is still, always, the possibility for politics to disrupt.[94]

4 | When the Spell Breaks Down

The tactic of opposing the state of exception with more law will be
inadequate. It may be necessary but will not be sufficient.
—Bonnie Honig

"Que se vayan todos!" Every politician must go. The declaration of a state
of siege in 2001 in Argentina brought masses of enraged citizens to the
streets and precipitated the government's fall. After winning the 1999 elections with the promise to revert a decade of neoliberal austerity, the left-
of-center Alianza government proved unable to address the crisis. The
external debt had burdened the nation while policies remained subject to
IMF experts imposing budget cuts to health, education, and social programs. Between November and December 2001, the government's proposal to restructure the debt was rejected, and the IMF's refusal of a $1.3
billion emergency loan put Argentina on the brink of default.

In a matter of days, the crisis worsened. The government restricted citizens' bank withdrawals to eventually take over people's funds. On December 19, protests and looting spread throughout the country. After meeting
with the Committee of Crisis, President Fernando De la Rúa went on TV
to announce the state of siege for thirty days through an executive decree
(of "necessity and urgency"). The measure, the president explained, was
the necessary response to the violence of those who "in an organized
manner promote riots and looting in shops of diverse nature," endangering persons and property and creating "a state of internal commotion."
Broadcasting nationally, De la Rúa's speech acknowledged people's "suffering" while differentiating between "the needy" and the "violent or criminals" and raised the need to put limits on those "who take advantage" of
the circumstances, as he blamed opposition leaders for encouraging politically motivated looting.

At the time of De la Rúa's speech, a state of siege had been declared
fifty-three times since the passing of the 1853 Constitution. During the

twentieth century, states of emergency were in place for almost three decades—with the longest one running between the November 6, 1974, declaration by President Isabel Perón until October 29, 1983, when the military dictatorship lifted it one day before the elections, just as the numbers of the *desaparecidos* and death camps started to come to light.

Historical precedent made De la Rúa's announcement frightening. Yet in 2001, rather than appease or scare the population, the declaration of a new state of siege triggered people's anger as they joined protests across cities. Hundreds of thousands gathered in Plaza de Mayo and Congress, with the motto "¡Que se vayan todos!" demanding all politicians to go. In response to the state of siege, massive protests acted as a government recall. On December 20, 2001, President De la Rúa resigned, leaving in a helicopter amid protests and a violent crackdown that left thirty-six dead.[1]

Tropes and stories cement institutions and social order. But they can also disrupt them. In a nation with a past of state terror, as citizens assembled and mobilized, the declaration of the state of siege evoked truly frightening memories. But, in 2001, it led to an unlikely outcome. Breaking up the circle of fear, citizens went into the streets and took power back. As the country saw a flurry of interim presidents (five in ten days), citizens gathered in the streets and hundreds of popular assemblies in public squares across the nation to deliberate and make decisions on their own lives.

As in Argentina in 2001, states of emergency can backfire when citizens find the government's exceptional measures arbitrary and react. In 2024, it was the turn of South Korea. President Yoon Suk Yeol, a conservative former prosecutor, elected in 2021 by a slim margin, got involved in scandals and clashes with the opposition since early in his government. His antifeminist agenda, hawkish foreign policy, and attacks on the opposition and journalists had raised concerns.

On December 3, Yoon declared martial law, but it was withdrawn through a unanimous vote of the National Assembly two hours later. Yoon justified his martial law declaration as a response to a "paralysis" of the government due to the opposition's budget cuts, constant threat of impeachment, and mismanagement of the electronic voting systems, which he alleged were posing economic and political security threats. This was the first time martial law had been declared since South Korea became a democracy in the late 1980s.

Thousands of protesters poured into the streets and the city center and went to the National Assembly asking for Yoon's impeachment. Dominated by youths singing and dancing to K-Pop music, with glow sticks, candles, in colorful attire, protesters' chants asked for the president's resignation, arrest, and impeachment.

Isolated since mid-December, formally detained in January, Yoon was suspended from his office to undergo impeachment procedures—and potential charges of insurrection for sending troops into the National Assembly after declaring martial law—before the Constitutional Court.[2]

These moments, when the limits of consensus come into view, have been characterized as negative acclamations, when people directly repudiate a leader or government—captured by the "thumbs down," among us a Facebook icon, whose origins go back to people's reactions to Roman gladiators when deciding their fate. They also bring back John Locke's Appeal to Heaven when, confronted with abuses, citizens resume the direct exercise of their authority. Indeed, challenging emergency powers may call for "political resistance" or citizen-concerted efforts, Nancy Rosenblum acknowledges. Under certain conditions, people can make governments' legitimacy crumble and precipitate their demise.[3]

Argentine protesters coined the term *horizontalidad* to describe the egalitarian, dialogical relations made possible by forms of direct democracy grounding "affective politics and mutual empowerment" out of the December 2001protests. Since then, as Marina Sitrin documented, horizontalism was adopted by assembly movements in Spain, Greece, the Occupy movement, and in 2016 France.[4]

Ordinary people make history, including through "contentious interactions," Charles Tilly observes. Protests follow identifiable patterns, which Donatella Della Porta describes as "chains, series, waves, cycles, and tides," revealing their recurrent and structured nature. Cycles of protests often gain international significance, as in 1848, the aftermath of World War I, 1968, 1989, 2008, 2011, and 2019. A historic wave of mass demonstrations around the world started in the 1980s, and their number tripled since 2006, with "real democracy" as participants' main demand. After reaching new levels in the 2010s, 2019 was described as the "year of global protests" when millions took their demand for democracy and rights protections to the streets across sixty-three countries. In raw numbers, GDELT (Global Database of Events, Language, and Tone) records 280,716 media-reported protest events in 2019. Chile, Algeria, Colombia, Ecuador, Bolivia, Hong Kong, Lebanon, Spain, France, Greece, India, and Tunisia stood out among the countries with the most protests that year.[5]

Countering state abuses, exclusions, and abandonment, street protests bring people together. Protests, demonstrations, and assemblies involve major forms of political action. Through them, participants break with the routine reproduction of the status quo in articulating demands and identities, redefining common horizons, renewing democratic politics, and radically transforming societies and themselves.

These moments epitomize what Andreas Kalyvas calls the "democratic extraordinary" that disrupts established politics to redefine principles, goals, and practices. These extraordinary moments offer glimpses of new emancipatory political possibilities and the life to come. Only the "living power of a community acting in concert" can counter abuses and violence, Kalyvas writes after Arendt. As the "resource of the powerless," distinct and unique, protests in recent years have converged in rejecting precarity.[6]

This chapter scrutinizes citizen resistance to state abuses and exclusions, attentive to moments when state wrongdoing becomes evident, the spectacular spell gets cracked, and citizens mobilize. In so doing, protesters' initiatives and repertoires revitalize core traditions of democratic life. Drawing on media, database, and archival records and on the insights of theorists, with a view of on popular resistance to neoliberal enclosures, this chapter revisits extraordinary democratic moments in the streets.

Through a plurality of voices and demands, protesters denounce policies that subject many to precarious conditions exacerbated by neoliberal austerity and state abandonment and abuses accompanying them. Precarity describes a range of substandard conditions, including low-paid temporary jobs with no safety nets, in societies turned into "jungle" capitalism—as discussed in the first chapter. For years, IMF-sponsored cuts to pensions, wages, healthcare, and social programs were adopted together with labor flexibilization, indirect taxes, public-private partnerships and the privatization of public assets and services, impacting 143 countries in 2023 alone. People have mobilized in response. In over half of the major global protests, participants demand economic justice and better living conditions. These claims are part of protesters' broader demands for real democracy, political representation, and rights.[7]

Austerity and emergency work together. By confronting austerity policies, protesters are acting against the neoliberal reason of state that presides over resources, rights, and life. Protests bring together those austerity most hurts, from Indigenous groups and farmers to students, workers, and middle-class citizens. Together with long-term activists, new generations and groups go "newly into the streets." Frustrated and disillusioned with the political and economic status quo, their voices converge in "a demand for more direct democracy."[8]

With a main focus on popular protests and their theorizing, the analysis of people's reclaiming rights and "real" democracy draws on insights from theorists including Jacques Rancière on politics and democracy and Andreas Kalyvas on the democratic politics of the extraordinary. In what follows, the chapter presents an overview of trends in global protests and their repertoires, and how protesters resist and reject precarity while advancing shared demands for rights and democracy. I then revisit questions of effectiveness that acknowledge protests as an expression of the democratic extraordinary, even in the face of heightened state repression.

Protests, the Demos's Voices and Actions

Expanding civil and political rights and setting limits to government abandonment and abuse, protests can merge into social movements, revolts, and revolutions. Often, as in 1848 or 1968, protest movements diffused transnationally in cycles and waves. Protests spread with electoral and labor campaigns and international networks in distinct modalities that help expand democratic horizons. By giving visibility to their grievances, the voices of ordinary citizens cement new identities and forms of agency that open democratic horizons and new languages of rights. Ultimately, as deliberate breaks with the past seeking to eradicate "all forms of domination and inequality," as Kalyvas puts it, modern revolutions condensed egalitarian forms of the democratic extraordinary and infused them in everyday life.

It is the moments when those who are not expected to act politically defy the "perpetual privatization of public life" that Jacques Rancière finds the most significant. As with the first women demanding voting rights or undocumented migrants demanding rights and protections, by acting and speaking together in public, the excluded turn themselves into political subjects and redefine the limits of the visible and the sayable. And as they do so, their presence destabilizes hierarchies, categories, and forms of order—at once political, symbolic, and epistemic. It is these instances of democratic politics that Rancière defines as the disruption of the status quo by those who "have no part." Their appearance transforms the political scene.[9]

Protests vary in modalities, targets, or levels (e.g., local, national) as contextual conditions and prior trajectories shape them. Sometimes, protests are brief, while others combine with electoral campaigns or labor struggles. They may develop links with established networks or political parties, with participants then running for office. At the grassroots level, rights and land defenders report rights violations, assist victims, and help communities organize. This translates into small, local demonstrations that rarely make national or international headlines. At times, protests start with a specific focus and, after being ignored, grow more ambitious demands. From time to time, protests gain salience and spiral into mass demonstrations that can expand regionally and globally by connecting related agendas or campaigns.

New political parties may emerge out of protests, as with Syriza in Greece and Podemos in Spain. In all cases, protests need to "nurture and sustain" participants while defining goals and forms of action to get media attention and influence politics. While receiving media coverage is essential, social media offers tools to help develop narratives and reach the public directly. Thus the "relatively powerless," as Michael Lipsky notes, gain visibility, recognition, and resources to sustain concerted action over time. In the end, a movement's strength lies in its ability "to set the narrative, to affect electoral or institutional changes, and to disrupt the status quo," as Zeynep Tufekci puts it.[10]

Scholars acknowledge peaks of political mobilization with often unique dynamics. Protests may seem to weaken and disperse only to reappear, reinvigorated. At times, movements may "go through periods . . . of rest." In other cases, the idea of cycles may not be applicable—the Madres of the Plaza de Mayo have been demonstrating every Thursday in Buenos Aires since April 30, 1977.[11]

While studies converge in assessing trends, definitions of protests and how to count them vary. Characterizing a protest as one or more occurrences "ignited by identifiable grievances or set of demands" extending up to a year, Isabel Ortiz et al. examined nearly 3,000 major protests and more than 900 protest movements in 101 countries between 2006 and 2020. The sample comprised over 93 percent of the world's population, with events at times spreading across countries. During those years, the number of protests increased threefold. Growing "frustration with politicians" and loss of trust in government officials, as well as concerns with rising inequality, youth unemployment, government corruption, and repression, were behind these protests.[12]

Researchers of protests traditionally have relied on newspaper records to identify events. With a focus on single events as units of analysis, the "protest event analysis" method, first developed by Charles Tilly, makes it possible to identify claims, sites, participants, frequency, size, modalities, responses, and immediate outcomes. Initially recorded by hand, the rise of online newspapers and powerful search tools have made it possible to survey an unprecedented number of sources in tracking "street protest, riots, rallies, boycotts, road blockages and strikes" that express discontent.[13]

Considering changes in coverage associated with digital media, it is difficult to decide whether the data shows "a world awakening to the potential of mass civil action to overthrow governments," as a GDELT document notes, or merely reflects an intensified coverage—or "information effect." The absolute increase in the numbers in fact reflects both. There is no single way to identify and count protests, which may extend from a single day to weeks- or months-long mobilization. In the end, what matters is the identification of patterns, cycles, peaks, and trends. Over the last decade, researchers coincide that protests have increased in number, scale, and intensity as they agree about trends and cycles.[14]

"A very real escalation in global protest intensity" has taken place in recent history, V-Dem analysts observe, both in the number of protests and participants. At least 52 global protests had a million participants since 2006, including a strike joined by 100 million people in India in 2013 and a 2011 protest with 18 million people in Egypt, not to mention the 2019 protests in Chile and Colombia, the 26 million joining 11,000 Black Lives protests since May 2020, the January 2023 anti-austerity protests in France, or the thousands of protests to denounce Israeli violence in Gaza. Before 2019, characterized as the "year of global protests," spikes were identified in 1989, 2001–2, 2005, 2008, and 2011.[15]

Considering a billion media events between 1990 and 2024 recorded on GDELT, the following graph shows unique occurrences under "Protest," including rallies, protests, demonstrations, civil disobedience, or hunger strikes. The GDELT database captures events, large and minuscule, that are reported by the media. The graph shows the number of unique media records of protests recorded globally.[16]

Visibly in all databases, the 2011 Arab Spring led to an abrupt spike, followed by a rise of protests across regions. The number of events is significant, but so is their public visibility. Assessing the impact of media coverage is important to compensate for the "information effect."

No methodological sophistication in the study of protests can compensate for uneven reporting. Media coverage of protests privileges powerful, picturesque, or "scandalous" actors and violent and disruptive events with "high news-value." News reporting also tends to echo the view of police and government agents, as it reflects the weight of countries in the global economy. "Wide disparity" in media coverage of protests in the Global North and South is striking. A small protest in London or New York may get broad coverage, and a large rally in India may not—unless it involves violence.[17]

In turn, the sources privileged by researchers in the Global North intensify those biases. For the case of Argentina, a study led by Federico

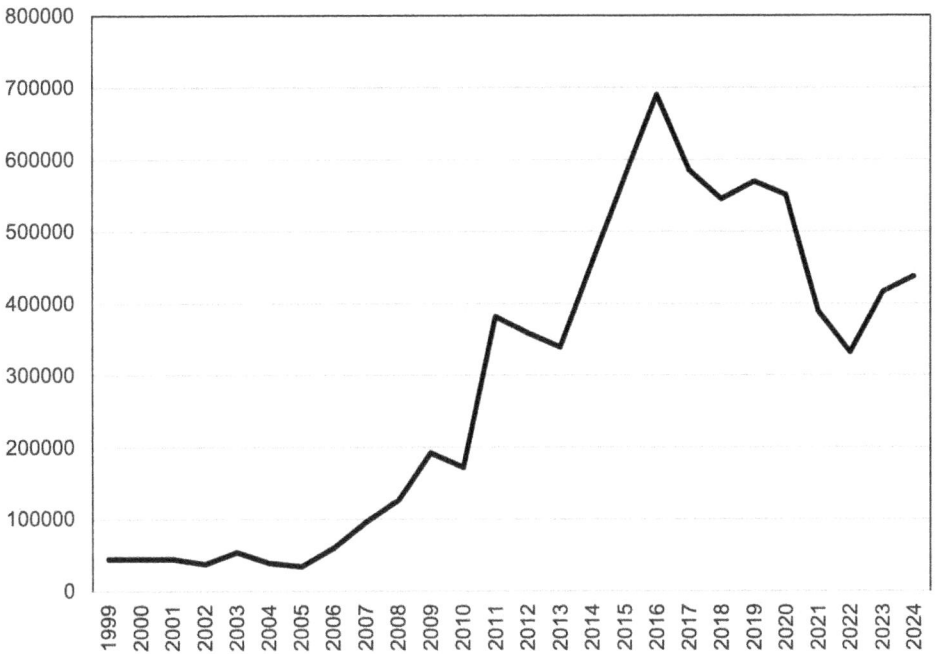

Figure 4: Newspaper-recorded number of world protests, 1999–2024
(Source: GDELT)

Schuster at the University of Buenos Aires recorded 5,268 protests from 1989 through May 2003, drawing on Argentine newspapers. For the same period, GDELT identifies 940 events and the SPEED database—based on the *New York Times* and the *Washington Post*—lists only 18. The magnitude of the gaps in media coverage is dramatic and more pronounced than previously acknowledged. The implications for the understanding of politics and societies are significant.

Thabi Myeni, writing from South Africa, notices how things such as the 2020 transnational surge of protests in support of Black Lives Matter rarely go the other way. Global South citizens learn about and support causes from the North, but as with episodes of police brutality in the Global South, most of these stories remain internationally invisible. Despite the use of social media, both activists and the public are subjected to what US and Western European media outlets define as "worthy of social outrage," Myeni writes. Overall, "stories outside the US are rarely told on a global scale." Such uneven visibility affects our present as it shapes the archive.[18]

While it took almost two decades for the neoliberal credo to be visibly put into question in the Global North, since the 1980s, millions mobilized across Eastern Europe and Latin America denouncing neoliberal austerity and demanding political and social rights and democracy. In Latin America, massive protests included the 1989 Caracazo. In the US media, however, with scant coverage, such movements were portrayed as a combination of citizens from the former Soviet bloc demanding capitalist freedoms or as problems of unstable, "new" democracies.

Only in 1999, with the "battle of Seattle," protesters critical of neoliberal policies gained visibility when 40,000 protesters showed up during the World Trade Organization meeting. Global in its demands, the movement stood as the "most internationally minded, globally linked" initiative up to that point, Naomi Klein notes. In turn, Klein points out, the Seattle protests were the first to come out of "the anarchic pathways of the Internet," without hierarchies or organized leadership and deliberative in nature. Organized through the Direct Action Network, an international coordinator of grassroots groups, protesters in Seattle introduced new modalities of political action with transnational agendas and digital technologies—at the time, email and chat. From that point on, digitally supported, nonhierarchical, networked grassroots organizing prevailed.[19]

In 2003, the first simultaneous global protest took place when millions gathered to reject the US invasion of Iraq. The largest global protest in history up to that point, it brought 36 million protesters demonstrating in 3,000 events over four months. Anti-war protests and Seattle were key moments in a long chain of international organizing and resistance going back to the 1994 Zapatista uprising. As in this case, by the end of a cycle of protests, innovations became part of available repertoires.[20]

Repertoires

In articulating their demands, protesters shape "repertoires of contention," Tilly observes. The idea of repertoire brings the performative dimension of collective action to the forefront. Over centuries, "contentious performances" including demonstrations, strikes, revolts, and revolutions have changed the rhythm of popular struggles. In organizing, people draw on past experiences as they renew local, "parochial," and cosmopolitan practices and forms of expression.[21]

Speeches, declarations, murals and graffiti, digital materials, films, plays, theatrical performances, marches, assemblies, walkouts, boycotts, strikes, and sit-downs are well-established modalities of collective action.

They undergo transformations as smaller, cumulative changes combine with significant shifts following major protests such as those of May 1968 in France.[22]

Besides the ways in which laws and policies become themselves the object of contention, governments influence collective action through regulations, as when banning or restricting forms of expression, in ways that compel activists to innovate. Thus grassroots political action gets shaped by participants' concerns and ideas as by political conditions, legal restrictions, past struggles, and cultural and technological possibilities, combining the traditional and "improvisational." They all help define strategies that protesters adopt to be seen and heard as well as entire repertoires of contention.[23]

Technology reshapes activism. The 1991 Rodney King beating, filmed by George Holliday on VHS, and the 2020 murder of George Floyd, recorded by Darnella Frazier on her phone, mobilized millions. Over this period, electronic technologies reshaped the conditions and arenas where collective action takes place, helping expand their reach and modalities. Cell phones with cameras, instant messaging, live streaming, and instant sharing of pictures and video on social media have made documenting police and other government wrongdoing easier. They also allow direct, expedient forms of interaction and the prompt organization of events.

Decentralized and widely accessible, digital technologies and social media make it possible for large numbers of people without previous acquaintance to gather and organize in ways that "would have seemed miraculous to earlier generations," Tufekci notes. These resources have helped people circumvent censorship and media blackouts as they reclaim political agency. No wonder social media has been characterized as a virtual public sphere. It makes it possible to share information on state abuses and offers forums to explore new forms of political imagination, vocabularies, and ideas. Through these channels, local grievances can reach hundreds of millions around the world.[24]

Pioneered by the Zapatistas and the Seattle protesters, these possibilities gained salience in the aftermath of the 2008 financial crisis and the 2011 democratic "Springs." Through them, digitally networked protesters entered the streets in massive horizontal movements. The repertoire expanded with hundreds of public squares and parks occupations, from the 15M movement in Madrid's Plaza del Sol to the Occupy movement, and other groups forming part of the "movement of the squares," still recognizable in the 2020 Seattle's Capitol Hill autonomous protest zone or in 2024 US Gaza campus occupations and protests.

For all this vibrancy, even if they open "a new vocabulary of performative political imaginaries," as Yaron Ezhari acknowledges, digital technologies do not seem to have fundamentally changed protest dynamics. Half of the protests in recent years adopted classical modalities of demonstrations in the form of rallies and strikes. Still today, "collective decision making" and resilience empower movements in the long run.[25]

Electronic communications may allow people to organize and coordinate, yet participants often lack the time and resources to consolidate gains into political change. Gaining—and maintaining—visibility and public attention remains challenging, including the efforts, labor, and resources that come with it. In turn, being ignored or distorted by powerful media, eclipsed by generously funded astroturfing and hostile social media campaigns, and made invisible by algorithms channeling users away makes things difficult for movements.[26]

Moreover, technologies are not neutral, and pushing activism into social media has "perverse repercussions," Jodi Dean observes. Social media challenges people to create content to attract audiences in ways that transform them into unpaid labor through forms of digital extractivism while exposing them to surveillance and harassment by revealing "the locations, intentions, and associations of those who are fighting," Dean concludes. And this takes place just when—as Paul Passavant shows—the policing of protests has become "more aggressive, violent, and cruel" and structurally committed to protecting authoritarian neoliberalism. Ultimately, networked activism is easier to control and neutralize, even without considering the possibilities opened by AI tools in the hands of corporations and states.[27]

Resisting Precarity

Austerity measures hurt jobs, wages, pensions, access to essential services, and citizen protections. Recognizing them at the heart of "a global human rights crisis," in its 2018 Annual Report Amnesty International warned about an impending "austerity apocalypse." The organization reported "formidable" social frustration as people were "denied access to fundamental rights to food, clean water, healthcare and shelter." Austerity can also bring artificial food and housing crises, poverty, and worsening social exclusions. No wonder mass protests in Chile came in 2019 in response to neoliberal reforms. Often imposed through International Monetary Fund packages, neoliberal austerity reached 159 countries and 6.6 billion people in 2022.

As discussed in the introduction, waves of neoliberal precarity have kept being imposed since its brutal entrance in General Augusto Pinochet's Chile in 1973, often supported by emergency regimes and ever-evolving surveillance and repressive technologies. Neoliberal reforms come with new enclosures, which people keep fighting against in local, regional, and transnational movements converging in a global horizon to demand rights. This section revisits the course of global protests in recent years, voicing their rejection of precarity and rights exclusions and abuses, including the social, economic, and environmental consequences of neoliberal extractivism and violence and abuse by the police and other state agents, often as part of the forceful imposition of these policies.[28]

By the late 1990s, within ten months of "the battle of Seattle," over fifty major protests against IMF-sponsored austerity were held across thirteen countries. A myriad constituency, including factory workers, teachers, and farmers, denounced the damaging conditionalities of IMF loans with their cuts to education, health, and social services, wage freezes, layoffs, and increasing food and transportation prices. Often, government repression was the main response.[29]

With millions resisting austerity in countries like Colombia, Costa Rica, Honduras, Kenya, Malawi, South Africa, Zambia, and France, a new cycle of protests expanded since 2000. As failed neoliberal experiments brought staggering social crises, a few governments, like Argentina in 2001 and Bolivia in 2003, collapsed. Bolivia's "water wars" protests, repudiating expensive privatized water services, started in the streets of Cochabamba and escalated nationwide despite the killings and declaration of a state of emergency. In Ecuador, 3,000 protesters occupied the legislature, supported by 10,000 people rejecting IMF austerity. To protest the privatization of phone, water, and public transportation, Paraguayans went on a two-day general strike. So did Nigerians. Meanwhile, with their "Cry of the Excluded," Brazilians denounced neoliberal reforms.

While citizens in countries like France had been mobilizing for years, the world was "shaken by protests" with the 2008 global financial crisis, as it burdened the poor and the middle classes. Millions protested the loss of jobs, health services, housing, and rising socioeconomic inequality, just as billionaires behaved like celebrities, corruption kept rising, and citizens felt betrayed by their elected authorities.

Across countries, protesters occupied squares and joined in assemblies, inspired by ideas of autonomy and solidarity. In Iceland, struck by the 2008 financial crisis, citizens banging pots and pans outside the Parliament demanded the resignation of the prime minister and the head of the

Central Bank. Their "kitchenware revolution" and "Anthill" movement celebrated the wisdom of ordinary people and inspired the reorganization of the country's legislative body in 2009. With 1,200 citizens selected by lot, a fourth of them representing institutions, principles for a new constitution were set. In two referendums in 2010 and 2011, citizens rejected honoring the foreign debt and a repayment program.

Starting in May 2010, massive demonstrations were held across Greece's major cities, following the occupation of Athens' Syntagma Square in rejection of austerity imposed as a condition to renegotiate the country's debt. Spaniards of the Indignados movement mobilized against austerity and occupied Madrid's Puerta del Sol in 2011, with rallies of half a million people in Madrid and Barcelona. Both movements included epic cultural and political experimenting, including direct democracy in hundreds of popular assemblies for months.

Global protests reached new levels following the 2011 Arab Spring and Occupy movement. Demonstrations were sparked by the self-inflicted death of Mohamed Bouazizi, a twenty-six-year-old Tunisian street vendor who set himself on fire after being subjected to constant humiliation and police abuses. Beginning in December 2010, protests spread rapidly through the region, from Tunisia, Egypt, Algeria, Syria, Libya, Morocco, Bahrain, and Yemen, just as a democratic "Jasmine revolution" started in Tunisia.

As eighteen million people demonstrated in Egypt, the largest demonstration in history up to that point, protests spread across countries like wildfire. Meanwhile, "the world watched transfixed" the reporting of common citizens from across the Middle East.[30]

In September 2011, heeding calls by the online magazine *Adbusters* to protest inequality and the broken political system, a group set up tents in Wall Street's Zuccotti Park. A month later, Occupy went global with a "day of rage" joined by protesters in 950 cities across eighty-two countries, in defiance of the political elites' "unchecked" power. As in Spain, they raised demands for "Real Democracy." Occupy's original "We are the 99 percent" made visible neoliberal inequality in the Global North. A main goal of the movement, Occupy organizer Marisa Holmes notes, was "transforming a public space into a commons." In a few weeks, Occupy was running a community kitchen, a library, a clinic, and providing winterized tents. Sixty percent of the US public supported Occupy's demands, Nancy Fraser notes, coming from "besieged unions, indebted students, struggling middle-class families and the growing 'precariat.'"[31]

Occupations continued across world capitals in the following years. Protests denouncing neoliberal austerity were led by students in Chile,

France, and Italy, rallying against budget cuts and attempts to commodify education. While voicing their grievances, people joined in "creating new social relationships and ways of being," as Marina Sitrin notes.[32]

Extending what Jayson Harsin describes as the post-2011 "movements of the squares," protesters in Istanbul's Gezi Park led massive protests and occupation in 2013. The protest started with rejecting the government's decision to build a shopping mall on the site. In late May, Cigdem Çıdam observes, members of the park association saw workers preparing to cut trees. Preventing the destruction of the park led to the occupation, and in a few days, many people had joined in. Film screenings and music gave the protest a festive flavor, until repression started, with the police beating and arresting people while burning their tents. But then, "hundreds" of groups— from feminists to LGBTQ to soccer fans to leftist activists to environmentalists to religious conservatives—joined and found themselves resisting police attacks together in defense of the park. This "completely new experience" of solidarity went further by turning into organized sharing and collaboration. Under the heightened stress of militarized police violence, for almost three months, protestors "created a shared world comprised of diverse groups of people . . . as political friends," Çıdam notes. The protests brought out 3.5 million people in 5,000 protests over two weeks, with the initial grievances evolving into broad, sweeping demands.[33]

In France, in 2016, following the government's sponsorship of a law that made labor contracts more precarious, under a state of emergency, popular assemblies resurfaced in the Nuit Debout movement. Demonstrations to reject labor flexibilization were scheduled across the country for late March 2016. At the time, a state of emergency in place since the November 2015 attacks banned public meetings. People still protested, and were met with an "enormous" mass of heavily armed riot police and gendarmes. High school and university students were hurt and arrested, just as port, railway, steel, and aviation workers joined rallies, demonstrations, and bridge and road blocking.[34]

Citizens in France have mobilized against neoliberal austerity for decades. Mass protests peaked in the mid-1990s when the Jacques Chirac government sought to freeze public sector wages, cut social benefits, and delay retirement. Hundreds of thousands of aviation, railway, port, university, and healthcare workers took to the streets. Another massive wave followed in the early 2000s, led by air traffic controllers, teachers, and postal workers demanding better wages and working conditions.[35]

In 2005, protests exposed France's racial exclusions. The deaths of 15-year-old Bouna Traore and 17-year-old Zyed Benna inside an electric station while fleeing police sparked the "largest rebellion" in four decades. In days, protests spread to 300 cities, with thousands of cars and buildings burned in clashes with police.[36]

In early 2006, youths protesting a labor flexibilization bill joined anti-austerity demonstrations. Months of student-led actions culminated in 1.5 million people going in the streets and threatening with a general strike, which forced Chirac to withdraw the bill. Austerity policies persisted. In 2009, 1.2 million workers protested Sarkozy's pension reforms, followed by 3.5 million mobilizing in late 2010.[37]

A renewed wave of protests confronted Hollande, a socialist, after 2012, for embracing neoliberal austerity. Numerous protests had taken place when the 2015 state of emergency let the government restrict demonstrations. Curfews, in turn, limited public meetings to between 6 pm and midnight and were enforced more strictly as the weeks progressed. Then came Nuit Debout.

It started at the end of March with the screening of François Ruffin's film *Merci, Patron!* at Paris's Place of the Republique. Ruffin had invited the public through a Facebook page named "Nuit Debout." Attendees were encouraged to stay and spend the night at the square "to resist and create!" In a matter of days, the Nuit Debout assembly spread to over thirty cities despite the state of emergency and local bans.

Nuit Debout occupations rapidly expanded into direct democratic practices and cultural and organizational experimenting. Assemblies ran every night until 10 p.m., giving room to various activities that often extended until the morning. "Activism needs storytelling," Ruffin noted. Speeches, presentations, debates, music, dancing, singing, and acting alternated with health and legal services or lending books at the square. In parallel, specialized committees addressed economic, educational, and strategic issues including feminism, education, or the writing of manifestos.[38]

"Horizontality, radical democracy and leaderless organization" characterized Nuit Debout, where two-thirds of interviewees reported to have spoken up at assemblies. A solid communications and social media presence, with press reports, safe messaging, and apps for democratic decision-making, supported the movement. Despite hostile media coverage and politicians and police blaming protesters for violence, Nuit Debout meetings extended every night across dozens of squares, for weeks—until mid-June at the Place of the Republique. Popular assemblies gathered every evening in 300 cities across the country, supported by 200 street protests, and joined by about 1.2 million people.

In parallel, rallies brought together over 100,000 people in Paris, Toulouse, and Marseille, and student occupations of 250 high schools. As university students and port, railway, steel, and aviation workers joined, protesters rejected Hollande's austerity measures that sought to extend the work week while shrinking labor protections.[39]

Targeted with state repression, Nuit Debout meetings were still being held weekly in October. "A movement is never really over," noted Geoffrey Pleyers, a Belgian academic and activist, observing how protests extend into other activities—and back.

In April 2016, as Nuit Debout was in full swing, leaks from a Panama law firm exposed massive international elite tax evasion. Protesters in Iceland forced the prime minister—mentioned in the leaked documents—to resign. Protests were carried out in countries including Italy, Portugal, Iceland, Brazil, France, Chile, and Argentina as a new wave started around the world to peak in 2019. The epicenter was Chile.[40]

October 2019 in Chile was described as "the citizen insurrection that shook the world." Protests started when high school students' fare evasion against a subway fare hike escalated and brought hundreds of thousands to the streets. On October 18, as fires were reported in stations, President Sebastián Piñera declared a state of emergency, deployed the military, and imposed a curfew in the capital.[41]

As in Argentina two decades earlier, the president's declaration of emergency backfired. Piñera framed the unrest as a war against an "invisible enemy . . . who is willing to use violence and crime with no limits." Challenging the president's attempt to securitize a conflict that they saw as preeminently political, about neoliberalism, protesters poured into the streets across Chilean cities and towns.[42]

"We are not at war," a giant Chilean flag read at a 1.2 million people demonstration. "Chile woke up," was echoed in placards, graffiti, and singing, as people marched for weeks and deliberated in hundreds of assemblies and cabildos. Santiago was transformed, as the protests exposed the deep inequalities behind Chile's so-called neoliberal "miracle." Protests continued for months despite the brutal repression by the military police and the carabineros that left dozens of protesters killed, hundreds wounded, and thousands arrested.[43]

The leading student role in the protests had precedents. In 2006, high school students—dubbed the "penguin" movement for their black-and-white uniforms—led "the largest protest movement seen in Chile since the transition to electoral democracy in 1990," Mary Rose Kubal and Eloy Fisher note, mobilizing against Pinochet's voucher-driven school system. Deliberative assemblies, strikes, and school occupations gave the protests visibility.[44]

In 2011, university students protested against Chile's "privatized higher education system" that led nonwealthy students into unbearable debt. For two years, student protests mobilized hundreds of thousands and produced a generation of new leaders, including Gabriel Boric, elected president in 2021.

In 2019, by early November, over 10,000 people were joining more than 300 assemblies under the Mesa de Unidad Social, a coalition of 150 groups. Their *Manifesto* denounced the neoliberal system under Pinochet's constitution, as "a social, institutional and economic framework that prevents democratic change and the recovery of fundamental rights" while calling for democratic renewal. Capturing the demands was the graffiti *"El neoliberalismo nace y muere en Chile"* (Neoliberalism was born and comes to die in Chile).[45]

Unlike in 2001 in Argentina, Piñera dismissed most of his ministers and scheduled a referendum for a new constitution. Under Boric's left-of-center government, Chileans drafted a progressive charter that incorporated the most advanced world standards by recognizing women and Indigenous representation, the rights of nature, and the state's duty to protect the "natural commons," as well as the rights to "live with dignity" and to a healthy environment. In 2022, a right-wing campaign led to its rejection, only to have their own arch-conservative alternative rejected the following year as well.[46]

Besides Chile, 2019 saw significant protests across Bolivia, Ecuador, Peru, Colombia, the US, Spain, Israel, and India, followed by Greece and Brazil, and Gazans protesting against abuses under the Israeli occupation and Hamas. In Colombia, in November 2019, citizens went to the streets to denounce and challenge a long history of emergency rule and state abuses. Emergency measures had been traditionally used to control the population and to "reduce specific sectors to bare life," David Vásquez Hurtado, Carlos Mejía Suárez, and Carlos Gardeazabal Bravo write. In defiance, Colombians from different walks of life came together to confront persisting conditions of exception. Facing repressive forces in the streets, they "changed the official narrative, empowered marginalized people, and produced a new landscape of political possibilities." In the streets, people turned themselves from bare life into "subjects of rights," empowered to "undoing state repression," the authors conclude. Not only did protesters make visible the persistence of an "undeclared but operative" state of exception in breach of the constitution, but they helped bring a historic progressive coalition to power in Colombia's government for the first time.[47]

While Chileans are still living with Pinochet's legacy, people in the streets made the constitutional convention possible. In fact, protests are among the "most important extraconstitutional factor constraining government emergency power," Nancy Rosenblum notes, as constitutionalists like Roberto Gargarella affirm protesting as the first, most fundamental right. The Argentine, Chilean, Colombian, French—and South Korean—examples expose the ambiguous potential of suspending laws through emergency measures or securitizing crises, as the expected citizen submission can turn into rage. Not only does this attest to the unpredictable political territory opened by emergency rule and suggests that "overblown claims of national security rarely stand the test of time," as Ben Wizner of the American Civil Liberties Union puts it, but it also shows that exceptional conditions can be appropriated and redirected by the people in potentially radical ways.[48]

Neoliberal reason has made life on earth more precarious through deforestation, pollution, and accelerating climate warming caused by the extraction of fossil fuels and the expansion of commodity frontiers. In driving a new wave of enclosures, neoliberal capitalism exacerbates the destruction of lives, ecosystems, and communities. Not surprisingly, protests against extractive activities have grown in number. By mid-2025, the Global Atlas of Environmental Justice documented 4,333 ongoing conflicts worldwide. In countries including Bolivia, Peru, Ecuador, Argentina, Canada, Brazil, Colombia, Chile, and the US, groups have denounced corporate violations of Indigenous sovereignty, environmental regulations, and workers' rights. Indigenous and peasant communities, often led by women, have mobilized. In April 2016, US protesters gathered to resist the building of a pipeline and to protect water sources and Indigenous sacred space at Standing Rock. The protest was "the largest mobilization of Native American peoples in decades," supported by widespread popular solidarity, Brendan McQuade notes. Repression was brutal. Three hundred people were injured, and two dozen protesters had to be taken to the hospital while others were arrested. The state response to the protesters put on display modalities including the "aggressive disruption of protest; psychological warfare; and wholesale surveillance and intelligence-gathering," McQuade concludes.[49]

Resistance to extractive projects and enclosures is widespread across Latin America, with 1,126, or 25 percent, of recorded conflicts documented by EJAtlas. From Standing Rock to Isiboro-Sécure to Halkadiki, demands conflate environmental and socioeconomic grievances with matters of rights. Protests have been met with brutal repression, however, including charges of terrorism, and hundreds of protesters and land and rights activists have been targeted and killed.

In January 2023, the first environmental activist was killed in the US. Manuel Esteban Paez Terán, "Tortuguita," was taking part in nonviolent action to protect the Weelaunee forest from the construction of a "Cop City" police training center in Atlanta. Paez Terán was killed with eighteen bullets in summary-execution style, followed by the arrests of protesters who were charged with domestic terrorism. Around the world, one environmental defender was killed every other day between 2012 and 2022, Global Witness reports. Violence continues as governments side with corporations and intimidate activists with the help of lawyers, legislators, the police, private guards, mercenaries, AI, and gangs.[50]

Real Democracy

Public opinion surveys in recent years show citizen support for democracy and frustration with their current governments. After spreading in unprecedented numbers, popularly elected governments face difficulties in "genuinely engaging, inspiring, and benefiting ordinary citizens." Accordingly, the most important demand in protests worldwide is "real democracy," Ortiz et al. note., which participants associate with openness, inclusiveness, and the ascendancy of the common people. Since the mid-2000s, demands for real democracy tripled and, in most protests, they rank together with calls for expanded rights (which protesters see threatened by neoliberal precarity).

In their call for more democracy, movements denounce the roots of persistent, structural exclusions. This is the case of Black Lives Matter. African Americans have long faced systemic oppression, from slavery to Jim Crow terror to ongoing socioeconomic exclusion, criminalization, and voter suppression—despite the historic significance of the civil rights movement in the 1960s. In this story, the figure of the police looms large.[51]

Black Lives Matter was founded in 2013 by Patrisse Khan-Cullors, Alicia Garza, and Opal Tometi, following the acquittal of George Zimmerman, a neighborhood watch guard who killed teenager Trayvon Martin in Florida. Started as a hashtag, #BlacksLivesMatter describes itself as an online community "to help combat anti-Black racism," as Khan-Cullors writes.[52]

The police killing of Michael Brown by the police in Ferguson, Missouri, in 2014, caught on tape, brought the movement into the streets. *#Black Lives Matter* Ferguson demonstrations were met with Missouri's declaration of a state of emergency and deployment of the National Guard.

Protests expanded to other cities. In dozens of demonstrations, protesters demanded justice for Michael Brown, while videos of dozens of police attacks of unarmed African American citizens—often deadly, such as those of Eric Garner, Tamir Rice, and Freddie Gray—further fueled the movement. Participants recalled earlier protests over the police beatings of Rodney King and the killing of Amadou Diallo and triggering a wave of protests and public debate.[53]

Dozens of Black Lives Matter chapters were organized across the nation. On May 1, 2015, thousands marched in major cities with "Black Lives Matter" and "No Justice No Peace" banners, demanding police accountability, fair wages, and social investment. In New York City, demonstrations called to disarm the police. In Los Angeles, they denounced the mistreatment of immigrants. Despite limited media coverage, the movement became embedded in US political, cultural, and intellectual life, with its grassroots activism amplified by celebrities like Colin Kaepernick and showcased in books, museums, and the arts.[54]

Black Lives Matter reached an unprecedented scale in the summer of 2020, following the release video of the murder of George Floyd by the Minneapolis police. During Floyd's funeral, Reverend William Lawson called it "a worldwide movement." Within a month, despite pandemic restrictions, over twenty-six million people participated in 4,000 Black Lives Matter protests across the US and globally. Calls for divesting from bloated police budgets into education, health, housing, and local communities, and even for police abolition, grew with the protests.

While movements such as Black Lives Matter challenge state abuse, others, including right-wing and white supremacist groups, exploit grievances to attract those hurt by precarity in ways that reinforce social hierarchies and exclusions. Varieties of Democracy classifies protests as pro-democracy when they explicitly advocate for rights, freedoms, and democratic institutions, while demonstrations supporting authoritarianism, racist and gender-driven exclusion, electoral suppression, or military rule are labeled as antidemocratic.[55]

Drawing on this criterion, with expert-assessed levels of protest, the following graph shows the prevalence of pro-democratic and pro-authoritarian protests since 1900:

The graph in figure 5 represents the average scores of pro-democracy protests (v2cademmob_ord) and pro-autocracy protests (v2caautmob_ord) respectively for each year across electoral democracies. Within democratic countries, the steady rise of pro-democracy protests seems striking, as 2019 appears as the year with the highest average of democratic

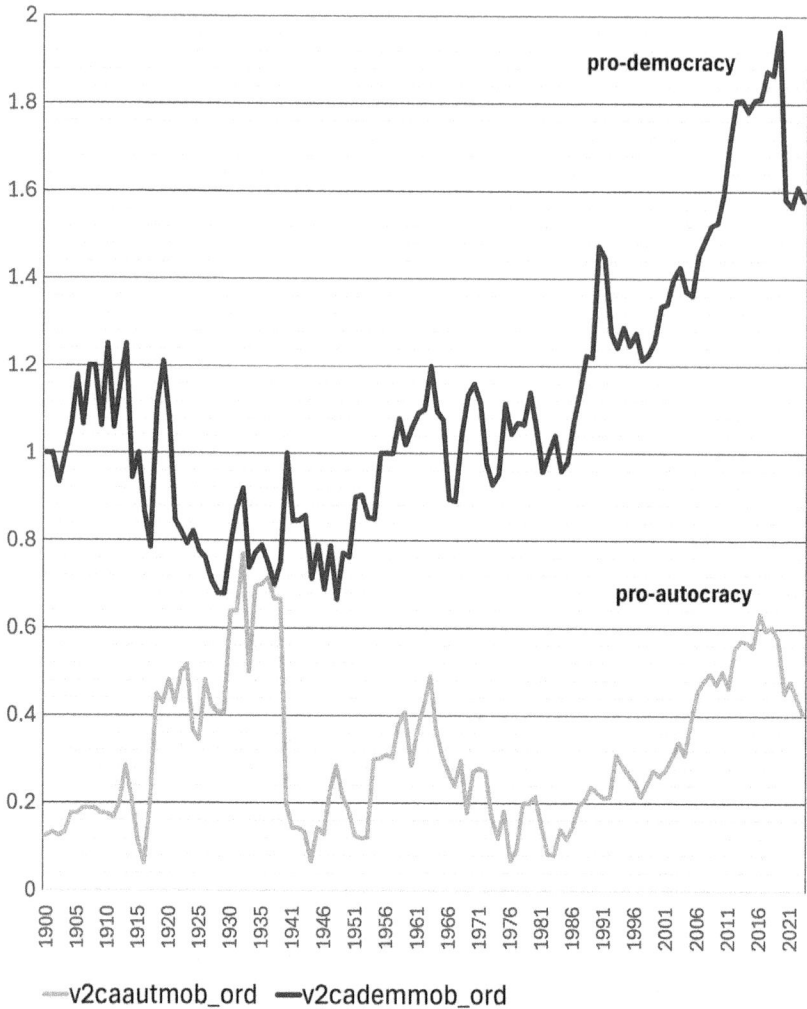

Figure 5: Pro-democracy vs. pro-autocracy protests in (electoral) democracies, 1900–2023 (Source: V-Dem)

mobilization. Pro-autocracy protests, in turn, following a rise of antidemocratic demonstrations in the years leading to World War II, stayed at a much lower level than pro-democracy protests and the pattern of growth over time is irregular. Overall, this confirms the rising trend of demands for more democracy described by Ortiz et al. If no doubt a crucial distinction, with plenty of salient examples from both camps, the challenges of labeling protests pro- or antidemocratic in some cases suggest approaching these numbers with caution.

Around the world, people "from Bolivia to the Niger Delta," including long-term activists and union members, Indigenous and peasant groups, students, unions, and middle-class citizens, young and older, were "brought newly into the streets." Many were driven by a "lack of trust and disillusionment" in view of persistent neoliberal austerity and their governments' disregard for rights and liberties. People opposed surveillance, repression, and militarism, an unresponsive political system plagued by corruption and austerity amid flagrant socioeconomic inequalities and exclusions. Protesters demanded fair representation, accountability, and better and "more direct democracy" as they called for global justice to advance "environmental justice and the global commons."

As surveyed by Ortiz and coauthors, demands converge around the right to the commons. From Argentina to Brazil, Chile to Mexico, the United States to Canada, the UK to Italy, Spain to Portugal to Turkey, protesters asked for recognition of their right to the commons. In three out of ten protests worldwide, the protection and expansion of "digital, land, cultural, atmospheric" commons came together with claims regarding the rights of people. In fact, protests often re-create forms of the commons by building solidarity and resisting enclosures. Despite their defensive character, protest movements can lead to "changes in paradigms, redefinition of sense horizons, clarification of the nature and structure of fields of power relations, and new connections with other movements," Massimo De Angelis notes. From real democracy to the commons to the full recognition of rights to workers, Indigenous, ethnic, and religious groups, women, LGBT, immigrants, and prisoners, to traditional individual rights of assembly and expression, "antiauthoritarianism, distrust of authority, and desire for participation" formed part of protesters' demands around the world.[56]

Success?

"When ordinary people resisted vigorously," history shows that the authorities often responded with concessions, including granting rights, guarantees, or representative institutions. Even when their intrinsic normative and political significance is acknowledged, protests tend to be considered for their impact on policy and legislative changes. "Full response, Preemption, Co-optation, and Collapse" are the terms identified by Marco Giugni to assess protests. Indeed, over one-third of protesters' demands studied by Ortiz et al. were met by governments, and an additional third addressed through legislation. The authorities often changed policies to increase transparency, called elections, formed new governments, called for constitutional reform—as in Iceland, Morocco, and Chile—and even adopted democratic institutions as in Tunisia. From pay raises to improving labor regulations and contracts to fairer taxation, labor and economic gains amounted to roughly one-third of outcomes. In environmental protests, protesters succeeded in their demands in one out of five cases by having projects interrupted and regulations passed.[57]

The instrumental approach to protests tends to focus on short-term outcomes. But how can we ensure this is the right criterion to evaluate success? What if the Arab Spring was just the initial step of a decades-long movement to transform the region? Protests can be defeated in the short term only for their demands to be brought back by a broader movement that becomes dominant. Movements influence one another across countries and regions, even after decades, just as their impact may take a long time to materialize.

Important demands of a movement may not be immediately assessable in terms of outcomes. Policy reforms, for example, may help but never fulfill protesters' demands for real democracy, while symbols and practices of protesters can raise people's awareness with cumulative effects. The shifts in public discourse by Occupy's "We are the 99%," brought the scope of inequality and exclusion to the global mainstream. Likewise, "Black Lives Matter" gave visibility to persistent police brutality while exposing layers of structural racism in the US and beyond. In both cases, the racist and violent conditions of neoliberal precarity, depriving millions of access to essential goods and supported on repressive policing, came into full view. Hence the motto "Abolish the police," which the 2020 Black Lives Matter protests brought from the fringes of critical theory to the streets— even to *New York Times* headlines—in a matter of days.

Along these lines, Çıdam stresses the importance of democratic moments as transformational political experiences, which she scrutinizes in the case of the Gezi protests in Istanbul. Initially gathering to defend a park from being turned into a shopping mall, people from the most diverse walks of life came together in what she describes as forms of political friendship. "The experience of solidarity and altruism within communities engaged in collective rebellion," Çıdam notes, took people into a different time and space—as participants described—and defined a highlight of the protests. The significance of democratic moments, Çıdam continues, lies not in their success in achieving specific goals but in their possibility of reconfiguring "the existing order by challenging and altering the universe of possibilities here and now in ways that are not foreseeable ahead of time." As participants in the Nuit Debout movement pointed out, their experiences were crucial for their democratic and creative qualities. Protests can generate new relations of power, institutions, subjectivities—and horizons.[58]

Recognition of protests' intrinsic value led Madrid's Plaza del Sol 15-M participants to refuse to define goals for their occupations. The experience was so enriching and multifaceted that it should not be reduced to any one of its dimensions, protesters conveyed. The 15-M movement was about "being there" with the community, a participant expressed in an interview. There is undoubtedly immanent value in the democratic extraordinary, worth experiencing in itself. If legal and policy changes addressing protesters' demands are welcome, the instrumental outcome-driven effectiveness of protests should not obscure their inherent significance. Surely the antiausterity agenda of the 15-M movement matters, as much as concrete gains do. The popular vote, democracy, and social and political rights were all won by the people in the streets.[59]

Protests and Politics

Power and politics may not always exist. Ephemeral, power arises as people speak and act together and disappears with "the activities themselves," Hannah Arendt observes. Distinctively "acting and speaking together" reenacts political experiences and communities. Fueled by shared stories, this acting together precedes institutions and the public sphere and stands as their ultimate source.[60]

And yet, "speech and deed are not representable qualities." The political, Arendt adds, can only be re-created through deliberative practices. Thus, when citizen deliberation-based self-government gets shunned by state institutions invoking "the public good," governments disempower and marginalize citizens in what is experienced as "a form of political dispossession," Kalyvas observes. An enclosure, we could also say. And with citizens' capacity to act and deliberate, so goes the political.[61]

Studies of world protests acknowledge widespread demands for deliberative democratic practices. Through protests and other forms of direct action, the common people, the demos, make themselves noticeable in the streets. Their power, as Kristin Ross puts it, is "rather the power of anybody," with their ever-changing voices, faces, and demands. In their appearances and interventions, participants give themselves different names as they defy and put into question traditional political identities and practices. And it is those previously excluded for their lack of wealth or social status, treated as they "who do not count," as Rancière puts it, it is their voices and actions that disrupt the status quo. In acting together, they *become* political subjects and redefine what counts as political.[62]

Rancière objects to treating democracy as a form of government or "a juridico-political form." Democracy involves dislocating exclusionary forms of hierarchical order, he contends. Rather than a political regime, democracy defines a series of "rare" and "sporadic" fleeting moments in which the otherwise silenced demos gains visibility. It is in this sense that Rancière describes democracy as a "state of exception" brought about by the common people in their disrupting of expected roles and hierarchies. Against the institutionalized politics that shrinks opportunities for democratic politics, which Rancière refers to as *police*, politics describes people's actions that challenge, push, and erase the boundaries of the established order.[63]

Political representation, Rancière makes clear, is oligarchical, based on the selection of a minority of individuals allegedly qualified to rule. At the same time, governments can be receptive to people's voices and demands, Rancière acknowledges, in ways that our oligarchies "can be said to be more or less democratic." Ultimately, however, democracy can never be conflated with a form of government. Even at its most democratic, governments reinscribe people's initiatives along hierarchies that leave aside those who do not fit in. On their part, democratic struggles push to enlarge the public sphere by demanding "the government of anyone and everyone."[64]

Illuminating democracy as a performative event, Rancière brings to the forefront the politics and "practices of ordinary people" who go in the streets often "against all odds," Çıdam observes. The concrete instances of democracy brought about by demonstrators are both meaningful and impactful. While events always have the potential to make history, the "democratic significance" of the actions of common citizens speaks directly to "us today," Çıdam notes, an observation that echoes those of protesters themselves.[65]

Original, insightful, and productive, Rancière's portrayal of democracy and politics as contingent, fleeting moments of direct action leaves out, however, the crucial organizing and coordinating in their support. For all its merits in recognizing the demos and its politics, the importance of organizing behind people's appearance in the streets tends to get lost in Rancière's account. This is a problem, considering that political interventions rely on less visible, labor-intensive, sustained organizing. Protesters emphasize the vital role of organization, strategizing, and training in bringing together events.

Spontaneity itself often results from "years of organizing and outreach." Ordinary citizens "acquire power primarily through organization," which serves as the mortar of collective action as protesters find themselves forced to deal with repression and censorship creatively. No less important or political, the savvy combination of methods, leadership, timing, and demands in coordination with political organizations, parties, and NGOs is key to supporting people in the streets.[66]

Çidam rejects claims that Rancière dismisses organization. Spontaneity is not "the other of organization," she notes, since organizing is inseparable from the political performances in the streets. True, but Rancière's emphasis on street protests tends to leave people's organizing in the dark. In between politics and police, the need for planning for collective action and its supporting structures somehow remains undertheorized. This leaves the reader poorly equipped to explore the processes, practices, networking, and organizing supporting those moments.[67]

Great efforts go into organizing, from logistics to communications to funding, as activists, scholars, and organizers including Gene Sharp, Marisa Holmes, and Roger Hallam acknowledge and discuss. Holmes, for example, recalls working with others "from the early planning process" of Occupy Wall Street to then devoting years to building the movement's legacy. Her work included debunking distorting narratives that dismissed Occupy participants as being disorganized and unprepared, accepting that the movement had "evolved" into party politics, or highlighting Occupy's coincidences with the far right.[68]

In turn, in countries like France or the US, protest organizers need to navigate a maze of restrictions and regulations, which in France led creatively to Nuit Debout. Special laws securitizing sites and criminalizing protests make it difficult to access public spaces. Organizing involves significant work and preparation, starting with identifying sites where demonstrations can be held and obtaining permits. Paul Passavant describes the rise of a "negotiated management model of protest policing" introduced in the 1970s in the US. Accompanying the rise of the neoliberal, business-friendly city, the model was portrayed as an attempt to make the police embrace their role in protecting citizens' freedom of expression while forcing citizens to collaborate. By making citizens plan their protests with the police, including how arrests would be conducted, protests become highly staged. How should we think of these and other efforts preparing for protests within the framework of democratic politics that Rancière so beautifully theorizes?[69]

Still, most of the demos's resistance may take place out of the streets.

"Most resistance in history did not speak its name," James C. Scott reminds us, opening to the world that does not make it to the public sphere but remains hidden. Protests are the tip of a maze of forms of resistance supported on undercurrents that may be perceived more clearly in retrospect. By highlighting only the visible, "formal organization and public demonstrations," Scott adds, scholars tend to miss "most acts of resistance throughout history," including the ones he judges most important. "Alienation and withdrawal," Scott notes, have served as resources for those in vulnerable positions who cannot participate in street protests. The "weapon[s] of the powerless" include less visible forms of resistance, from "foot-dragging" to "internal migration." These are strategies of those with no social power or effective access to citizenship protections, conditions shared by "most of the world's population most of the time," Scott reminds us. In the end, protests stand as a moment of the democratic extraordinary that can decisively change "fundamental norms, values, and institutions" even by shaping everyday politics. But protests are also the tip of a massive, if formless, network, of forms of resistance that are also political.[70]

The Democratic Extraordinary

Protests epitomize the democratic extraordinary, most visibly when people reclaim the exercise of their authority. Extraordinary democratic politics brings back practices of direct, deliberative democracy and articulates public space in defiance of the status quo. Going beyond institutionalized politics, people can redefine values and practices, including "political, symbolic, and constitutional principles," Kalyvas notes. Direct action impacts ordinary politics and can lead to institutional transformation—eventually even of the state itself. Yet there is more to popular politics than "constant mobilization and permanent participation," Kalyvas contends, as he reminds the reader that direct democracy "is not the only available version of radical democracy." A range of possibilities opens between direct democratic experiences and electoral politics, with protests falling in between. In all cases, radical democratic action closes the gap "between rulers and ruled, active and passive citizens, representatives and represented" to open new ideas that can transform politics. These possibilities have been acknowledged in constitutions that recognize a right to resist oppression, from Germany to Greece, Ecuador, Argentina, and Portugal. In the end, popular resistance is founded on a "right to insurrection" that acknowledges the people as sovereign.[71]

By acknowledging people, from the streets to their presence in the constitution, Kalyvas addresses the democratic extraordinary in its distinct modalities. The founding of political communities, the institutionalization of power, and direct democratic participation define three main forms. They all help generate "legitimacy and legality, sovereignty and representation, power and law, freedom and authority" that empower communities and can take distinct forms.[72]

Legal and constitutional recognition is fundamental for advancing rights and political participation. As Gargarella observes, it is difficult to claim rights that are not written. Still, for its awesome constitution, the Ecuadoran government did not care much about its provisos in crushing protests in October 2019. Shortly after, officials acknowledged eleven protesters dead, over 1,300 people wounded, and over a thousand arrests, including minors. In 2022, Chileans put up to a vote what, at the time, many considered the best constitutional text in the world. They lost. Kalyvas's nuanced approach to the democratic extraordinary productively acknowledges different forms of radical democratic action and how they reinforce one another. The study of protests suggests that the democratic extraordinary ultimately draws on people's direct action and its radical transformational possibilities.[73]

While protests, including disobedience, "presuppose fundamental rights," as Kalyvas notes, the source of those rights includes, but cannot be limited by, the constitution. Rights are immanent, prior to any specific institution, and they do not derive from any natural or legal foundation. The right to have rights, as Butler notes, "comes into being when it is exercised" by a group acting in concert. Ordinary people go into the streets and, through demonstrations, reclaim and recognize their rights and turn themselves into political agents. While the legal and constitutional recognition of rights is essential, it is their embodiment by the people claiming them and the "back-and-forth" between the two that make them concrete.[74]

Through self-empowering performances, claiming rights in the streets (and elsewhere), people exercise their lawmaking power with authoritative status. And not just people. Diego Rossello highlights the role of two stray dogs, Loukanikos and the "negro matapacos," rising to legend status due to their active support for antiausterity protests in Athens in 2010 and Chile in 2019. These "enraged democratic dogs," Rossello observes, show their teeth to the state as their inner wolf defies Hobbes and his Leviathan. In the end, democratic extraordinary moments show that rights get recognized and validated through their exercise by the ultimate authority of the people. As Rossello's "democratic dogs" gesture, we are overdue to revisit our relationship with the "morethanhuman." But I will come back to this in chapter 5.[75]

When Politics Turns Sour: State Repression

In the decade following the Arab Spring and Occupy, governments met the surge of protests with increasingly sophisticated surveillance and censorship while still with brutal force in the streets. Sixty-two percent of major world protests between 2006 and 2020 were met with repression. In turn, global media records of episodes of the use of coercion by states suggest their significantly larger growth vis-à-vis protests. This is shown in the graph (fig. 6) below. GDELT automates its data collection into categories. "Coerce" includes the repression of protests, the seizure of property, arrests, the imposition of states of emergency, martial law, or curfews, deportations, political bans, or the illegal state spying on people; "Protest" includes a variety of modalities of collective action, from demonstrations, rallies, and forms of civil disobedience to hunger strikes. The graph shows the number of episodes recorded by the media globally. Drawing on media records of unique events of protests and state coercion (or repression) collected by GDELT for 1999–2024, we see the trends captured in Figure 6 on the next page.[76]

While media reports of protests have risen since 1990, protests pale compared to the dramatic rise of media-recorded episodes of state coercion (repression). The rising levels of state coercion against citizens are sobering. At the same time, we may wonder if this suggests that states have to spend more coercive resources in trying to quell a robust expansion of citizen demands—a good sign for democracy.

Democratic governments are expected to tolerate a wider variety of "claim-making performances," Tilly notes, and not to resort to violence, considering constitutional checks and institutional and legal mechanisms to deal with conflict. And yet the relation between repression and democracy appears to be "nonlinear"—initially low, repression can go up fast, more so if it has been used in the past, as Christian Davenport has shown. And no surprises here, "repression works"; governments that intervene more heavily to prevent and repress citizens "have fewer protests," Ortiz et al. note.[77]

Democratic regimes, with their variations, are essential to political life. Yet the expectations that democratic governments would make a difference in honoring the rights of demonstration and protest have been fulfilled only in part. Governments go to great lengths to monitor, control, and repress protests, trying to make them unviable. As part of these efforts, "digital repression" makes interfering with citizens' activities easier.

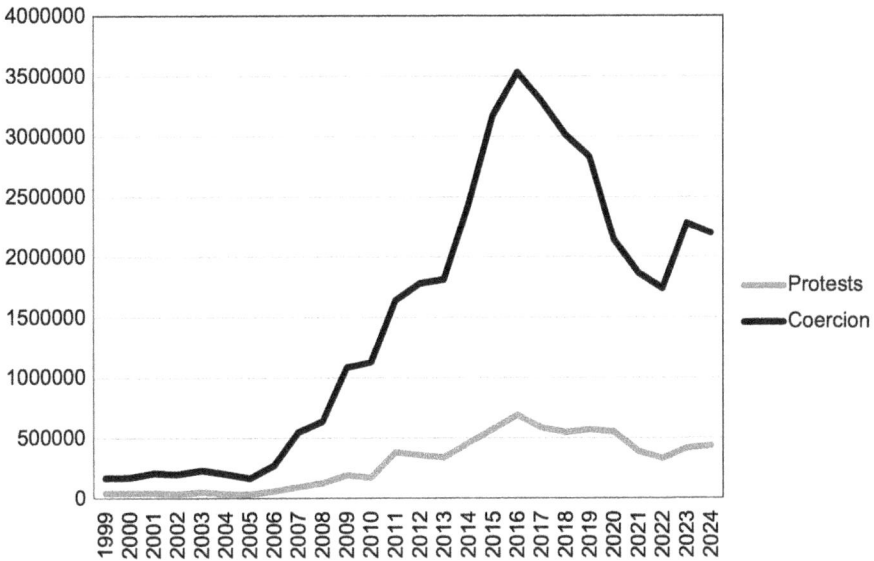

Figure 6: Newspaper-recorded number of world protests vs. coercion, 1999–2024 (Source: GDELT)

AI-powered surveillance technologies allow the authorities "to intercept entire populations" while making repression more effective. The massive automated scanning of social media and personal communications allows state agents to "identify, monitor, and selectively detain" participants and supporters. By targeting "crowd formations" early, surveillance makes it possible for police and other security agents to intervene preemptively. In its "elegant simplicity," Steven Feldstein notes, digital repression involves fewer agents, promises unprecedented reach, reduces the use of physical coercion, and is cheaper. Furthermore, awareness of AI surveillance can effectively deter potential participants from getting involved.[78]

As protests take place, those in the government tend to initially ignore protesters as political actors, up to the point when people force them to respond by mobilizing in large numbers at central, visible sites. Sometimes, in response, protests and protesters can be securitized, and the securitizing rationale, as discussed in chapter 2, helps normalize exceptional measures, legislation, and practices.

Governments may target activists and rights and land defenders with harassment and smear campaigns. Seeking to "reduce their support base, win over public opinion or to justify criminalization," Frontline Defenders reports, online attacks on defenders have been expanding. Any single episode of violence linked to the protests is used by the state to blame it on protesters and escalate repression. Repressive measures are claimed to restore order and national security, which also help excuse police preroga- tives and legal immunity. And while citizens are subjected to increasing restrictions, the police can "arrest protesters for the most minor viola- tions," even preventively, Passavant observes.[79]

Protesters often find themselves criminalized through "unfair or fabri- cated judicial proceedings," having to endure lengthy and costly prosecutions—many under detention. From Standing Rock to Chile, demonstrations have been treated as "threats to state authority," securi- tized, and linked to terrorism. The trend toward criminalizing politics reframes political questions in police terms. In the US, the International Center for Not-for-Profit Law documents a record number of bills restrict- ing and criminalizing public protests that were introduced in recent years across forty-five states—92 in 2021 and 51 in 2024. They target demonstra- tions at gas and oil facilities for obstructing traffic, access to facilities, or causing "economic disruption," with penalties of hundreds of thousands of dollars and years in jail.

Things have not gotten better since then. Since 2023, with a wave of "unlawful restrictions," governments including Germany, France, and Austria "preemptively" banned protests denouncing the killing of civilians in Gaza, just as politicians and the media across the US and Europe used rhetoric that dehumanized Palestinians, and anti-Semitic and anti-Muslim hate crimes increased.[80]

Like antiterrorist laws, protest protocols travel around the world. An expansive definition of terrorism has been promoted internationally as a needed legislative update for countries to catch up with the world, under pressure from organizations such as FATF (Financial Action Task Force) and international financial institutions. New antiterrorist legislation has been adopted for years, even by progressive governments in Argentina, Ecuador, and Uruguay.[81]

In Chile, the figure of terrorism has been used against members of Mapuche communities since 2001 in response to their quest to reclaim ancestral lands. By 2014, 108 Chilean citizens, most of them Indigenous, had been indicted under the figure of terrorism, and twenty-three new cases were added in 2017 alone. Antiterrorist protocols, used since the 1980s in the US against environmental activists, equate terrorism to trying to "coerce policy changes." Loose interpretation of the term "coercion" leads to arrests and indictments. Indeed, in their study of major protest movements, Ortiz et al. identified 192 killings of protesters. In Argentina,

CORREPI documented ninety-three. Indigenous communities and land and environmental defenders have been targeted across countries, and thousands have been killed. Now, the rise of far right-wing governments is making things worse.[82]

Accompanying these trends, protests have increasingly become the object of declarations of emergency. Emergency measures and laws restricting the right to demonstrate expand notions of "crimes of public disorder" and terrorism. As the authorities respond with exceptional, repressive measures, and the police are given blank checks, people exercising their right to peacefully demonstrate get treated as criminals and enemies of the state. Used in response to protests, states of emergency and antiterrorist laws help states "mask human rights abuses" while undermining political and civil rights.[83]

Of New Beginnings?

"Out of the entrails of neoliberalism emerge new forms of human cooperation and resistance that reject the extractivism of humanity and seek to expand democracy and free time," Orellana Calderón wrote about the Chilean protests in 2019. On his part, Rajesh Makwana highlights the number and significance of protests in the recent decade as announcing "a new expression of democracy that is still in its infancy," but that has proven its potential to transform politics. Overall, we can see two trends. On the one hand, there is a steady rise in people's mobilizing to demand more democracy and rights. Indeed, major protests between 2023 and 2024 mobilized on climate and environmental issues, the rejection of austerity, and more democracy and rights. In the UK and the Netherlands, groups like Greenpeace and Extinction Rebellion demonstrated against government inaction on climate change. In Sweden, people demanded urgent protections for wetlands, while in the United States, activists resisted the construction of the controversial "Cop City" in Atlanta's forests. Antiausterity protests gained new strength. In Argentina, 1.5 million people marched in defense of public universities against the drastic cuts imposed by President Javier Milei. In France, protesters rejected pension reforms, and in Italy they rallied against budget cuts while protesters questioned the government housing policies in Portugal. Across fifty-one countries, people protested Israel's actions in Gaza while, between October 2023 and January 2025, over 22,000 pro-Palestine protests took place in the US alone. Also in the US, as protests against ICE raids continue, demonstrations critical of the Trump administration's policies have been significant.

By the end of March 2025, protests had tripled 2017 levels, and numbers continued to rise, with over 1,100 "Hands Off" protests across all states on April 5, and thousands of "No Kings" protests with millions in attendance. In this light, Erica Chenoweth et al. wonder if we are witnessing an "American Spring."[84]

On the other hand, Makwana notes, the far right has won elections in several countries, and rights—including the right to protest, arguably the most fundamental right—are facing "a rising, unprecedented threat across all world regions," as Amnesty International reports. In dozens of countries, at all levels, laws and regulations restrict protests, and protesters are criminalized and subjected to violence just as surveillance and the use of state force reach new heights. Does the latter suggest that states are becoming more successful in preventing and crushing protests or that the people in the streets are a force difficult to contain? In either case, the unprecedented rise in protests has helped carve room for democratic experiences. Giving visibility and voice to grievances, street protests bring snippets of the democratic extraordinary into everyday life, at times with radical implications that set limits to the neoliberal reason of state.[85]

In perspective, demands for participatory democracy arise from "the best in the revolutionary tradition—the council system, the always defeated but only authentic outgrowth of all revolutions since the eighteenth century," Arendt contends. Commenting on Arendt, Kalyvas notes the "continuing practices of political participation, regulated contests, and public deliberation" associated with councils. This tradition comes to life again and again in the "movement of squares" that, prefigured in Argentina in 2001, spread after Tahrir Square and Occupy.[86]

The extraordinary expressions of autonomy, self-government, and creativity conveyed by people in the streets as on the electronic sphere can be interpreted along the lines of popular sovereignty. For Agamben, however, that would be a mistake. While direct democratic expressions can be seen as a materialization of popular sovereignty, considering the complicated history and implications of the tradition, linking the democratic extraordinary to sovereign claims may constrain the possibilities of the very same people who are being acknowledged as in charge of their lives. Echoing these concerns, which he shares with Arendt, instead of following on the tradition of [sovereign] constituent power, Agamben calls for "a 'purely destituent power' that cannot be captured in the spiral of security."[87]

In ways that connect to the gist of the commons, Agamben emphasizes the need to think and act beyond categories such as sovereignty and security. Sovereignty and its reason of state and apparatuses are not well suited to a democratic people. In fact, they keep hurting us. Foucault would agree, as he points out the need for forms of rights "emancipated from the principle of sovereignty." Their quest continues for the most appropriate forms to conceptualize and organize people's power other than as expressions of a constitutional order driven by sovereignty. Supported on ancestral traditions, an appropriate candidate is the commons—as we saw, voiced by protesters themselves. In Massimo de Angelis's view, taking ownership of our lives calls for the freedom that only the commons can offer, by ending enclosures and separations "to reclaim commons at every scale" through communities both immediate and virtual.[88]

5 | "An All Powerful Social Barrier"

Rights as Commons

Reappropriating the Language of Rights

"We demand the right to a future." In the summer of 2022, the UN General Assembly recognized "the human right to a clean, healthy, and sustainable environment." Addressing the triple crisis of climate, species extinctions, and pollution, this new right shows the possibilities of popular struggles to succeed. "At the forefront of world protests," Isabel Ortiz et al. note, demands for "real" or more democracy converge with demands for rights. Seventy-three percent of a world survey respondents find protecting people's rights against oppression essential to democracy. The language of rights decisively shapes democratic politics. "Every demand (and there are many) that reality match rhetoric is a challenge to the status quo," William Edmunson writes. The rights we have are the result of past battles. They "function as forms of power," shaping possibilities and practices both as mechanisms for empowerment and "capture and inscription," as Ben Golder notes after Foucault. This idea is also present in Marx's discussions. Rights are grounded on democratic traditions, including the commons, which can acknowledge and protect rights anywhere as we advance toward cosmopolitan, inclusive forms of community and membership. These possibilities gain salience from time to time, when crises bring people into the streets. As in Seattle in 1999, Argentina in 2001, Bolivia in 2000 and 2003, Athens in 2010, Madrid in 2011, France in 2016, the US in 2011 and 2020, or in Colombia and Chile in 2019, demands for rights keep informing people's politics. Students, women, workers, members of Indigenous groups, LGBTQ people, and immigrants have spoken against neoliberal austerity and class, racist, and sexist exclusions, as well as for abolishing police and prisons toward a livable future. These and other grievances gain salience in the streets. And protesters code their demands in the language of rights.[1]

After mapping the apparatus of neoliberal reason of state, its governmental and legitimating mechanisms, and how people resist through political action, this chapter explores the possibilities of rights to inform and expand democratic practices, within and beyond the state. In so doing, I acknowledge the importance of rights while trying to think "outside the statist imaginary," as Neocleous puts it, to identify alternative grounds, the commons in particular, with potential to support rights beyond their instrumentalization by states. The word "commons" describes forms of communal, collective property historically associated with land, its uses, and the products of shared labor. Recognizing rights as forms of commons, to borrow from Massimo De Angelis, makes it possible to support, or rebuild them, on an immanent, solid ground. Yet since modern rights developed together with enclosures against the commons, the commoning of rights calls for a critique of their appropriation by the state and capital.[2]

Let us see. Rights delimit "a boundary around the individual, or at least around certain crucial aspects of her freedom" and, as such, they are central in political theory, Duncan Ivison notes. Offering a "straightforward moral-legal template" to demand judicial review, in modern societies rights provide a common vocabulary for legal, political, and interpersonal forms of recognition that travels well across countries, cultures, and fields.[3]

As both "mediums and ends of social practice," as Boaventura de Sousa Santos puts it, rights help people articulate demands for protections and resources. John Searle describes rights as resulting from assigning roles and status with support from some form of authority with a collective mandate. They may take the form of "claim-rights," "privileges (or permissions, or liberties)," "powers," and "immunities," as well as "political liberties or rights." Generally introduced through declarations, invoking political or moral ground, rights tend to be written into laws once recognized by states.[4]

As popular struggles succeed, rights gain legal and constitutional standing. In the way of a "moral armor," they protect individuals from abuses and expand personal and collective possibilities. Of course, things are not so simple. Laws can narrow and distort the spirit of the demands that originated them. Even when promulgated, gaining effective access to rights requires significant resources to navigate courts and bureaucracies. When rights recognize people for who they are, they may force individuals to perform these legalized identities. Questions like these make many, including political theorists, skeptical of rights. Still, despite constraints and reversals, most democratic demands, including those of people in the streets, continue to take the form and adopt the language of rights.[5]

The importance of rights becomes evident especially when they are withheld or withdrawn. In the summer of 2022, over the course of a few days, the US Supreme Court carried out what Naomi Klein describes as "a shock-and-awe judicial coup," taking away the right to have abortions, weakening Indigenous sovereignty, eroding states' rights to limit firearm carrying, allowing schools to force students to pray, and shrinking the Environmental Protection Agency's ability to regulate CO_2 emissions. Meanwhile, the UK government attempted to downgrade the Human Rights Act into a "more limited" Bill of Rights.[6]

With ubiquity in our lives, rights, as Stefan-Ludwig Hoffman notes, have become the "lingua franca of global moral thought." From the freedoms of expression and association, voting, the civil and social rights discussed by T. H. Marshall, or the 1948 Universal Declaration of Human Rights and ensuing protocols, their evolution makes the need for "inalienable rights accorded to every human being" as a self-evident new *doxa*.[7]

Starting with the right to life, "from which all other rights flow," as David Garcia Bondia puts it, recent history has seen new series of "emerging" legal protections. Among those protections are the right to migrate, to defining one's own identity, gender, and forms of family, to guaranteed access to food, water, and a basic citizen income, and to living in a healthy environment. They also include expansive access to education and healthcare while extending to communities' protections previously afforded only to individuals. Meanwhile, amid worsening climate and planetary conditions, both in the streets and in court children demand a right to a future. Environmental and Indigenous movements, in turn, lead in the collective recognition of what Danielle Celermajer et al. describe as "morethanhuman," or the beings and bonds that frame our lives and coexist with us on the planet. Finally, others reclaim collective rights to the commons, a demand present in 30 percent of major world protests since 2006.[8]

Marked by the accelerated loss of forests and glaciers, voices call us to save the "global commons," which Pascal Grohmann describes as the "very life support of Earth that connects us all and on which we all depend."[9] On this, he draws on a long tradition. In Britain, the 1215 Magna Carta and the 1217 Charters of Liberties and the Forest acknowledged commons rights while a number of laws were "about managing them." People were recognized rights and responsibilities in ways to "support life and the community." Commons rights included the use of the forest for collecting wood for fuel and repairing homes and tools, letting animals graze, picking berries, and gathering honey, herbs, or fish. Rights "to self-organize their own governance rules, and civil liberties and rights to protect them from the sovereign's arbitrary abuses of power" were also listed, David Bollier notes, founded on "fundamental needs and long-standing traditions" preceding written law.[10]

Widespread across medieval Europe, from the German Mark's democratic decisions to support the needs of members and guests to the commons in Britain, similar institutions have been traced back to what is now Peru, Mexico, the US, Canada, India, and Algeria. An ample repertoire of communal rights and institutions has been identified across societies "from time immemorial." Whether including only a few households or entire communities, rights were held collectively under customary norms and membership linked to—and inherited through—households or residence.[11]

Among us, the commons have gained room in recent years, driven by street protests and the work of radical theorists alerting about neoliberal enclosures, Dardot observes. Even mainstream social science has been impacted after Elinor Ostrom received the 2009 Economics Nobel Prize for her work on the commons' superior performance to regulate the sustainable use of resources.[12]

Behind the commons, a universal institution with ancient roots, stands the living fabric of social practices. Andreas Exner, Stephan Hochleithner, and Sarah Kumnig characterize the commons as "a way of world-making" arising from practices of commoning that are distinctively "collective and non-commodified." Likewise, following Cesare Casarino, Jodi Dean describes the commons as what we do and create together. They involve a "global network of social relations" made of labor power, creativity, and thinking and acting together, itself "infinite and characterized by surplus," Dean concludes. Through a variety of perspectives, studies of the commons converge in acknowledging ordinary people's creativity and political wisdom. They offer relevant insight at a time when neoliberal enclosures, including privatizations (e.g., healthcare, education, water, pensions), massive land grabs and forced displacements, as well as the trampling of the right of privacy that turns our personal data—including genetic information and networks—into extractive sources, threaten our world.[13]

Rights themselves, De Angelis observes, are "forms of social commons" that develop by "being exercised." Surely the people stand as the ultimate source of authority grounding rights in modern constitutions. And yet the legal field—decisive in defining and regulating rights—has not echoed the term. Except for niches like intellectual property and environmental law, legal theory has overlooked the commons, as Filippo Valguarnera notes. This silence seems odd considering the law's central place as "the main normative tool of the West" and plenty of evidence that "our survival on the planet requires a different approach to law."[14]

Indeed, as Exner, Hochleithner, and Kumnig note, the perspective framing most of our current laws treats people as self-contained agents with fixed identities that enter (hierarchical) relations of domination, even involving violence, in their individual pursuit of survival. Unlike this imagination of entities fighting for survival, the tradition of the commons compels us to consider that we exist amid multiple relations "with a multitude of nonhuman living beings, natural forces, natural objects, and artifacts." Survival occurs through collaboration among human and "morethanhuman" beings. Without addressing the commons and its perspectives, urgent questions seem impossible to articulate. And yet the very "core of the Western legal tradition," Valguarnera writes, developed as "an ideological reaction against the commons" in defense of private property.[15]

Over centuries, carried out by feudal lords, the gentry, the bourgeoisie, and corporations, enclosures took away "rights of access to land and livelihoods" and "contested and eroded" the commons with fences and legislation. In their unfolding, laws banned customary practices while favoring the spread of mercantile exchange and commodity production. The dominance of capital, waged labor, and exploitative and destructive relations to the nonhuman came about as a result. Supported by recurrent enclosures, in the end, "capitalism is the negation of the commons," John Bellamy Foster, Brett Clark, and Hannah Holleman observe.[16]

Modern theories of rights centered on individuals and property were instrumental to enclosure campaigns. So has been social science discourse such as the "tragedy of the commons" argument. Without ever referring to any existent commons, Garrett Hardin's unfounded but popular rational choice story imagines self-maximizing individuals exhausting common goods. No matter that it has been refuted even at the heart of economics. As neoliberal enclosures and struggles over rights continue, the "tragedy of the commons" tropes keep nurturing a neoliberal common sense.[17]

Commons are crucial. Both ancient and new commons, I show in this chapter, offer insight into democratic rights. In acknowledging distinct forms of rights and rights recognition, I turn to Marx. Rights, he writes in *Capital*, stand as "social barriers" key to protecting people's lives. Pivotal in empowering individuals and groups, rights ground new forms of community, relationships, and agency. Yet, more intensely under neoliberal reason, the state privileges the rights of propertied individuals or corporations while disowning the many.[18]

In a dialogue with Marxian insights as well as with political and legal theorists including Jessica Whyte, Jacques Rancière, Eugeny Pashukanis, Nasser Hussain, and Bhikhu Parekh, this chapter interrogates rights traditions and emancipatory possibilities. Unleashing this potential requires challenging the ongoing neoliberal hijacking of rights. In what follows, sections revisit main tenets of rights, from the ancient principle of isonomia to modern cosmopolitanism and contemporary debates. The role of rights in enclosures—ancient and current—as in informing democratic struggles leads to the commons—both to the right of commons and to the commons as a foundation for rights. If laws "predate recorded history," as Peter Nardulli, Buddy Peyton, and Joseph Bajjalieh observe, rights precede sovereign states and will survive them.[19]

Rights and the Promise of Rights

The word "right" may have been coined only in the late Middle Ages, but the concept and associated practices, including popular demands and litigation, have been present since ancient times. A "vigorous" understanding of rights in the Greek Isonomia and the Roman *ius gentium* seems "essentially continuous" with enduring personal and collective protections, Edmunson notes. In Athens, Solon's Constitution put power "in the hands of the people" by banning debt slavery, introducing the selection of public officials by lot, and making courts accessible even to the poorest citizens. However, it was Cleisthenes' advocacy for Isonomia that truly invigorated the Athenian democracy. Inspired by the Ionian tradition that Gowder describes as "political equality through legal equality," the principle of Isonomia protected citizens from the "depredations of the powerful" while allowing them to serve on juries and as lawmakers. In communities of self-governing assemblies, the empowered demos blurred the "division between rulers and ruled," which is why Arendt portrays Isonomia as a form of "no-rule."[20]

Praising the law became standard. Even a caustic critic of democracy like Plato endorsed governments in which rulers are "servants" of the law as second best to the rule of the wise. Aware of the changing terms of freedom and citizenship across governments, Aristotle went further to theorize the rule of law. The law, he argues, "ought to be supreme over all," as he praised taking turns in governing as the alternative to despotic rule. Both written and unwritten, as embodied practical wisdom, only the law can preserve fair, egalitarian conditions in a city. Compelling citizens to exercise self-restraint, virtue, and prudence, the law calls for free and

equal individuals deliberating and making laws in conditions of "autonomy, or self-government."[21] With his view of "human existence as participation," Aristotle argues that political involvement sets the path for developing human potential—an argument that still nurtures the language of
democratic rights.[22]

In ancient Rome, notably after the *ius civile* and the Twelve Tables, citizens were free and, since the third century BC, citizen assemblies gained
authority to pass laws. The Roman principle of *ius gentium* or "law of peoples" recognized legal protections for noncitizens and, eventually, for all
persons. If rudimentary, its standards included treating others as "innately
free," inviting impartial mediation to solve conflicts, and honoring promises and agreements. And when Emperor Caracalla extended citizenship
throughout the empire in the third century, the *ius gentium* became applicable to all peoples.[23]

While acknowledging such earlier references, historians trace the idea
of rights to medieval debates on whether the authority of pope and
emperor needed limits or if the poor should take some surplus from the
wealthy. Still, the language of rights is distinctly modern. As "an invention
of the Enlightenment," its early expansion followed debates on popular
sovereignty, equality, and natural rights. William of Ockham is credited
with conceiving of rights as a person's power or *potentia* and Hugo Grotius
for introducing a distinct language. Rights, in his view, amount to a person's "moral quality" that allows them "to have or to do something law-
fully." Justice, in turn, consists of respecting rights, and rights violations
are a justified cause of war.[24]

Critical of Grotius, Thomas Hobbes radicalized the notion of natural
rights. The latter, as he puts it, involve "the Liberty each man hath, to use
his own power . . . for the preservation of his own Nature; that is to say, of
his own Life." In Hobbes's hypothetical state of nature, rights are unlimited. Everyone has "a Right to every thing; even to one another's body."
Individual, natural rights stand at the heart of Hobbes' arguments, if only,
in the end, he judges it rational to renounce those rights for self-
preservation. But I will come back to this.

A few decades later, just as the 1688 Glorious Revolution was bringing
a massive wave of enclosures to England, John Locke linked rights to
property. Individual property rights proved pivotal in supporting "bodily
integrity, freedom from arbitrary detention, and freedom from torture,"
Celermajer et al. acknowledge. At the same time, they were instrumental
to, and part of, the giant capitalist enclosure movement.

Locke's *Second Treatise* recognizes an original, God-given right to use the earth in common. Yet it is only individuals, in his account, who can take possession of the land through their labor. Taking distance from Hobbes, Locke imagines a state of nature where people have rights and possessions. He acknowledges men as "free, equal, and independent," and natural rights as inalienable. Self-protection and freedom are tied to property, however, the most crucial right that includes "life, liberty, and estate" as an extension of one's body. The appropriation of nature is individual, and so are property rights.[25]

Property is a central, defining concept in Locke. Propertied individuals alone can be the full subject of rights. Since rights are unevenly enforced in the state of nature, individuals create a political society with the main purpose of making laws to defend property. "Third party justice," supported by clear norms and impartial judicial authorities, thus perfects the protection of rights and property in Locke's view.

With a true "ideological passion for individual property," William Blackstone goes further to judge it "the sole and despotic dominion" of one man "in total exclusion of the right of any other individual in the universe." Not surprisingly, by the late eighteenth century, the right to private property had become "sacred," as Adam Smith put it.[26]

Those without property, whether women or the enslaved, were seen as defective and in need of subjection. By giving legal status to "natural claims," Christoph Menke observes, modern theories of rights only protect what individuals already possess and authorize them to be what they were already in their private lives. In an individualistic and depoliticizing manner, these rights privilege "the enjoyment of security in private pleasures" and define liberty according to them. This way, bourgeois rights accommodate "the non-legal," Menke notes, by legally sanctioning prior status and possessions as "natural," or as the "legal power to exercise prelegal power." Among political philosophers, legal scholars, lawmakers, and courts, a focus on individual property-driven private law dominated modern thought by theorizing rights alongside a legal public-private split that echoed "the state-market dichotomy."[27]

Capital accumulation progressed through enclosures, by dispossessing peasants and entire communities, reorganizing maps, expanding markets, and violently subjecting people to differential recognition. In India, village commons described as an "ocean of trees teeming with wildlife" were taken over by British colonial administrators to exhaust land and workers. In early nineteenth-century New Mexico, US usurpers succeeded in claiming ownership of commons through "subterfuge and legal loopholes" to split the land with the state. It continues. Ultimately, the instrumental views of nature as resources to exploit advanced by Locke and others condense the logic now leading to "social, economic, and environmental catastrophes," Celermajer et al. note.[28]

Still, despite these private, individualizing, property-centered emphases, a long tradition of rights declarations conveys the "collective instituting power" transpiring intense moments of direct political action, as Kalyvas observes. The first explicit, institutional reference to universal rights appeared with the French 1789 *Declaration of les droits of homme and le citoyen*. For the first time, ordinary people became "the immediate bearer of sovereignty," expanding on the 1776 US Declaration of Independence's recognition of "unalienable rights" to "life, liberty and the pursuit of happiness," Agamben observes.[29]

"Men," the gendered first article of the French Declaration reads, "are born and remain free and equal in rights." They enter political associations to preserve their "natural and imprescriptible rights," namely "liberty, property, security, and resistance of oppression." Introduced by revolutions on the two sides of the Atlantic, supported on Immanuel Kant's claim of human autonomy, freedom, and the duty to treat individuals as ends in themselves, universal rights set standards for "an emergent global citizenry," Hussain observes. Still, this conception of rights legalizes a preexistent natural condition while making room for a sovereign state that guarantees and limits their exercise through laws.

Critics of natural rights pointed out that rights do not exist before the laws that recognize them, adds Menke. Among them, Jeremy Bentham contends that rights can be valid only to the extent that they are "advantageous" to society. In turn, the idea of natural, imprescriptible rights seemed to him "simple nonsense . . . rhetorical nonsense,—nonsense upon stilts."[30]

Along these lines, modern states took control over rights by regulating them through laws. "In themselves acts of sovereignty," Foucault writes, laws let states advance over the rights they grant. Social and political emancipation was made "into one more object of juridical regulation," as de Sousa Santos notes. By treating rights as objects of governance, legal provisos constrained their reach to state-sanctioned practices alone. Paradoxically, built on "the primacy of rights over law," modern states ended up subsuming rights, Menke concludes.[31]

Nineteenth-century revolutionaries and protesters succeeded in abolishing slavery and servitude, limiting and regulating the labor day, protecting the freedoms of conscience, expression, and association and, starting in New Zealand in 1893, granting voting rights to women. Twentieth-century revolutionaries went further. On the steps of 1789, the

Mexican Revolution first gave "the sacred rights of the workers" constitutional standing. Mexico's 1917 Constitution consecrated social rights as the "safeguards . . . to shield the individual from various forms of economic oppression." Introducing the social rights later adopted by Weimar and the Soviet Union, in Article 123 the Mexican Constitution mandated labor laws and made employers responsible for fair and safe working conditions. It also canceled any debt owed to employers, established the eight-hour labor day and a minimum wage, allowed workers to share profits, and protected them from arbitrary dismissal. The article also guaranteed the rights to unionize, collective bargaining, and going on strike, as it recognized the need for public housing, hospitals, and schools. Regarding land, Article 27 establishes that the land belongs to the nation, while acknowledging collective land rights and limiting private property based on public interest.[32]

Supporting people's life needs, social rights sought to compensate for the bourgeois right of property. Acknowledging collective property and people's ownership of the land, water, forests, factories, large farms, mines, banks, and means of transportation and communication, the Soviet Constitution introduced rights to "rest and leisure, health protection, care in old age and sickness, education, and cultural benefits." Revolutions and democratic experiments brought forward an expansive repertoire of rights.[33]

In 1948, the American Declaration of the Rights and Duties of Man was passed in Bogotá. Including education, health, social programs, fair pay, culture, and leisure, with twenty-eight articles listing rights, the Bogotá document helped Latin American delegates' efforts to enshrine these rights among "the basic purposes" of the United Nations, Kathryn Sikkink notes.[34]

"It is essential, if man is not to be compelled to have recourse, as a last resort, to rebellion against tyranny and oppression, that human rights should be protected by the rule of law," the 1948 UN Universal Declaration of Human Rights states as it acknowledges a fundamental right to rebel. By affirming people's "inherent dignity" and "equal and inalienable" rights, binding covenants and domestic and international laws transformed universal rights from "an aspirational statement to a body of norms," Thomas Poole observes. Thus radical constitutionalists treat human rights as "interdependent and indivisible" in ways that highlight the coherence of an agenda in constant expansion.[35]

To the 1948 Charter, the 1966 Covenants added civil, political, economic, social, and cultural rights. Further conventions recognized the rights of women, children, migrants and their families, the Indigenous, and persons with disabilities. Banning all forms of discrimination, the death penalty, torture, and mandating protections against forced disappearances—the latter coming into effect in 2010—these legal instruments invite countries to join as signatories.[36]

Concerns about states' failure to protect rights as well as about state violence, including genocide, led to internationalizing human rights law and advocacy in the late twentieth century. Making crimes against humanity imprescriptible, human rights trials and the principle of universal jurisdiction defined milestones toward people's self-protection. In parallel, democratic protests and agendas brought expansive rights "revolutions" and constitutional reforms. In Latin America alone, nineteen constitutions included new rights. Afrodescendants and the Indigenous gained constitutional protections in 1991 in Colombia. In 1994, the Argentine Constitution defined advancing the "inherent rights" of citizens as the main state duty as it made international human rights treaties the law of the land. In 1998, Venezuelans rewrote their constitution through a participatory process. Human rights, guaranteed education, healthcare, food, housing, participatory mechanisms, and ethnicities were recognized. Both "constitutional or cosmopolitan" agendas, as Bonnie Honig notes, help advance new rights.[37]

The 2008 Ecuadoran Constitution went further to redefine Ecuador as "a state of rights." It enshrined guaranteed access to food and water as key steps toward "Buen Vivir," the revitalized ancient tradition of living in harmony with nature. Eduardo Gudynas highlights Buen Vivir's "commitments on quality of life" and expansive definition of communities. The latter, including "some non-human elements or even the whole environment," involves the recognition of rights to other species and nature itself. The following year, Bolivia joined in, by incorporating its own tradition of suma qamaña or "Buen Vivir" in the Constitution, in "harmony with nature," followed by a 2011 Pachamama or "Mother Earth" bill that acknowledged rights for nonsentient beings and for nature itself. Bolivians also gave the right to water constitutional standing. "From the moment the provision of water is a private business, human rights are being violated," President Evo Morales declared, defending water as a public good.[38]

Following on these steps, the defense of water as an "inappropriable" common good and human right has been gaining leverage globally. So have claims about clean air and access to housing as the urban correlate of cultivable land. Finally, views that "all earth beings are entangled and interdependent" continue to gain legal recognition around the world.[39]

Despite reversals, these examples show how, as people's voices gain

salience, the democratic "uncommon and . . . extraordinary emerge"—
Kalyvas cites Arendt—as "a new, lasting form of legality." It is especially by
"granting rights to the most vulnerable in society" that legal and constitutional reforms can improve the lives of the many and advance democratic
agendas, Roberto Gargarella notes.[40]

Collective, cultural, and environmental rights, deliberative initiatives,
and new branches of government have also entered legal reforms and constitutions. In 2004, Brazil was the first country to pass a universal basic
income law. In 2010, the Argentine Congress legalized same-sex, egalitarian marriage, followed two years later by the world's most progressive gender law. Earlier, in 1989, the Convention on the Rights of the Child introduced the right to identity, one of the "Argentine Articles" sponsored by
the Grandmothers of the Plaza de Mayo. Rights, Kathryn Sikkink argues,
progress in a self-reinforcing manner, in what she describes as a "cascad-
ing" effect.[41]

Rights agendas keep expanding. Besides water, food, energy, and housing, emerging rights include access to the best available healthcare, freedom and legal and political equality in plural conditions, privacy, education, knowledge, and science alongside social protections, leisure, and
personal and collective "economic, social, cultural and political" development. Freedom of movement and access to information and communication technologies, together with the protection of personal data, further
expand the repertoire of rights.

Control over the product of one's labor, to a basic universal income, to
a healthy, biodiverse environment, and to defend it for the future are
among new rights. Personal integrity, gender identity, "the choice of personal ties" in forming romantic bonds, and protected access to reproductive health and family support are now recognized. The rights to live in
peace, to conscientious objection, to unionize, organize, and protest, and
to resist "direct or indirect foreign oppression, of military, political, economic or cultural nature," as well as to request international help are
included, as well as the right to a "worthy," decent death. Rights are being
extended to sentient and nonsentient beings and the planet through different forms of recognition of the "morethanhuman."[42]

Participatory democracy, a right to the city, public space, and to enjoy
beauty are additional emerging rights. So is access to the "universal common good," the "cultural heritage of humanity," the human genome, spaces
on Earth and beyond, and the right to a future now mobilizing youths
around the world. Moreover, a fundamental right is spelled out to be
granted effective access to all these rights. The struggle for rights has been

accompanied by a myriad state and nonstate organization monitoring initiatives, yearly reports, and datasets.[43]

The mesmerizing progress made in terms of rights suggests that we may be coming full circle, from the conceptual and practical erasure of the commons to mounting demands for their return. Still, for all their ambitious portrayal of a better world, rights have achieved "little to bring that world about," as Samuel Moyn notes. Indeed, governments have failed to join rights treaties, delayed their implementation, or introduced restrictive rules for people to qualify for access, adding to their selective suspension under emergencies. As women, minorities, and the poor have known for centuries, the formal recognition of rights does not guarantee access to them. States may endorse human rights to improve their image as "an index of good government" to help their trade and credit opportunities. In turn, countries like the US have used human rights to undermine their enemies and to justify military intervention. Turned into imperial tools and instruments supporting new enclosures, human rights have been used to justify actions from neoliberal reforms to military campaigns for "humanitarian" reasons to protect people made into helpless victims.[44]

Besides presiding over the discourse on the rule of law, the neoliberal takeover extended to human rights. Human rights gained notoriety in the 1970s driven by NGO campaigns denouncing "the torture and disappearances that accompanied neoliberal shock treatment in the Southern Cone," Jessica Whyte notes. At the time, various progressive groups embraced the language of human rights. Over time, however, neoliberal reason infused the human rights agenda in ways that need to be addressed, Whyte contends.[45]

Embarked on "re-making societies on the model of the market," as Whyte puts it, neoliberal discourse portrays human rights as part of a global system of freedom driven by markets. Emphases on civil and political rights and individual property to the exclusion of social or economic matters accompanied definitions of the role of the state as narrowly focused on providing physical security. A "neoliberal rights consensus" agenda thus mimicked the Washington Consensus, Whyte shows. Drawing on "a very selective vision of the western tradition," as Sousa Santos observes, neoliberal ideas managed to become mainstream.[46]

Markets and their main agents, the fetishistic but too real corporations, were afforded free speech and other rights as legal persons in the United States. Disregarding entire groups of people while personifying artificial capitalist entities, "recasting" rights and citizenship alongside markets, neoliberal reason dilutes democracy, even politics, as Wendy Brown observes, making rights other than private property "largely irrelevant." Neoliberal appropriations of the rule of law and rights that treat markets and property rights as synonymous with both give a patina of legitimacy to the near absolute dominion of capital. States, it is clear, must prevent and repress "those unable to adjust themselves" to the market, whether by using laws or emergency measures, war, coups d'état, or state terror in imposing neoliberal austerity.[47]

Still, the problem with rights may not lie merely in their (mis)appropriation. Far from neutral, modern rights and laws have taken shape as "a special system of social relationships" intertwined "with the logic of the social relationship of commodity production" and their historical forms, as Evgeny Pashukanis reminds us. Along these lines, to revolutionary demands for equality, the liberal state responds with abstract, individual rights that constrain those demands into "equal claims to private spheres of and capacities for self-will," as Menke notes. Thus the state turns radical demands into an "equal right to consideration" that transforms people into abstractly equal, passive subjects dispensed from participating in governing their own lives. And as those in subordinate positions fight for a chance to be considered, the powerful invest themselves with the supreme "right to create values," with no need for rights.[48]

A Problem with Rights Themselves?

Post–World War II rights declarations coincided with an unprecedented number of war refugees and migrant crises. Concerned with the difficulties of accessing legal protections, in a 1946 essay Arendt warns against the potential for racism and extermination to continue. Considering refugees, the ultimate citizens of the world who should represent the triumph of human rights, she observes: "The Rights of Man, supposedly inalienable, proved to be unenforceable," even when enshrined in constitutions, as soon as "people appeared who were no longer citizens of any sovereign state." Rather than being recognized and protected, refugees found themselves denationalized and deported. Those most in need of rights had no way to claim them from outside the citizenship not recognized to them. Prevented from claiming the rights that states recognize to citizens alone, abandoned to their fate, their plight exposed the gap between abstract human rights and the concrete, enforceable rights granted by states. Without legal protections, not acknowledged a voice, and prevented from having a home and access to rights forces people into a condition that Arendt described as "radical *poverty in world*." Writing about concentration camps and the stateless, as about the fundamental "right to have rights," Arendt anticipated that things would only get worse. She was right. Or so suggests the estimated 120 million displaced people, including 63.3 million internally displaced, 6.9 million asylum-seekers, 43.4 million refugees, plus over 4 million stateless people in 2024.[49]

At least in part, Agamben suggests, the problem may lie with legal rights themselves. On the one hand, he notes, "spaces . . . liberties, and . . . rights" are won by ordinary people in confronting state powers. Still, the status of rights is fragile. Not only can states limit their access, but the rights they acknowledge inscribe "individuals' lives within the state order" in ways that expand the state's sovereign orbit and potential for abuses that people resisted by demanding rights in the first place.[50]

In his view, the issue transcends human rights lacking "teeth" or proper enforcement. Hierarchical distinctions between worthy and unworthy lives "lacking every political value" have persisted since ancient times. Among the ancient Greeks, the life of the citizen recognized dignity, political voice, and full rights stood in contrast to the merely living, lesser forms of life that humans could share with animals and plants, zoē, which amounted to a factual existence without worth or legal standing, which Agamben calls "bare life."[51]

Determining which lives are alternatively granted rights or deemed unworthy and expendable defines a core aspect of sovereign power, Agamben observes. Through (sovereign) decisions, entire groups can be excluded from legal protections and stripped of their rights. The cycle is unending, as sovereign power, Agamben argues, perpetuates itself by classifying lives according to their perceived worth.

Throughout history, groups including the enslaved, Jews, Roma, Indigenous peoples, citizens of "enemy" origin, camp detainees, Palestinians, and the stateless, among others, have been treated as if they had no rights. Subjected to this condition through forms of "exclusive inclusion," groups and individuals are not left out, however, but kept trapped in legal limbos.[52] Turned into a sovereign instrument, part of the reason of state repertoire, the law thrives in reproducing biopolitical hierarchies even through its own suspension. For a (sovereign) law that "nourishes itself" on the exception, Menke observes, rights are "forms of law's inclusion of life" that normalize biopolitical hierarchies. Embedded in the law, rights can help inscribe people in the legal order through their exclusion, as bare life, Agamben notes, by identifying the rights they are not recognized. This rationale seems to be at play in the abandonment of migrants at sea in the desert, prisons, or camps, and even the criminalization of those assisting them, with thousands of deaths for which no authorities take responsibility.[53]

Such expressions cast a shadow on the rights that promise to protect us, as a minimal denominator that can paradoxically serve to exclude. Skeptical of rights declarations, Agamben observes that rights are made accessible to some at the cost of excluding others as a mechanism of sovereignty. The modern state, he notes, has no place for human life "as such." Under these conditions, human rights risk reducing people to "the zero-level of being simply human," as Eric Santner puts it, pushing individuals into a "juridical no-man's-land." From this bottom, as we will see later, things get worse for those with no chances to be considered human. Indeed, it is hard having to rely on Leviathan for protecting our rights.[54]

"Can Leviathan incorporate its subjects without disintegrating them?" Diego Rossello asks.[55] Doubtfully so. Portraying freedom, equal rights, autonomy, and reason as inherent to all humans, Hobbes's theory of natural rights was radical for the time. No less radical was his support for renouncing those same rights. Natural equality is unsustainable, Hobbes tells us. Our unlimited natural rights to everything lead individuals to compete for resources, and ultimately to a state of constant war. The only way to gain peace, to increase our chances of survival, is by renouncing our natural rights and equality. All rights, then, except "to defend my selfe from force, by force," must be surrendered for the sake of self-preservation, he argues. Thus a multitude unite through a covenant to institute a sovereign and proceed to subject themselves and enjoy the limited freedoms and protections that the sovereign may decide to concede. Or not.

Hobbes's radical claim to equal natural rights leads to a no less radical support for absolute subjection, with the compelling argument that such a move is in our own interest. The sovereign, however, remains in the state of nature, bound by no obligations or laws. Survival, not rights, is what the Hobbesian bargain is supposed to be about. It is precisely the exclusion of rights in his theory that keep conservatives bringing back Hobbes, Perry Anderson observes. "There is no place for rights in his scheme of things," only duties, in a political theory that justifies absolute rule and that portrays rights as untenable—other than as a sovereign-given, contingent privilege.[56]

Hierarchical views of life and rights persisted, not sparing modern revolutions. Soon after the French proclaimed the common people sovereign, Abbe Sieyes distinguished between "active rights and passive rights," as he considered "children, the insane, minors, women" and prisoners unable to contribute to the public good. The latter, Sieyes argued, should be excluded from "active" citizenship. This was just one way in which newly revamped hierarchies served to justify rights exclusions. Concerned with the persistence of exclusionary biopolitical hierarchies, Agamben "persuasively argues" for the need to address some "paradoxically violent effects of the human rights discourse," Ayten Gündoğdu writes. In fact, revisiting rights may call for "a new ontology," Agamben suggests. Aware of the impossibility of escaping a sovereign rationale that extends over its own outside, Agamben hints at the possibility of deactivating the sovereign apparatus and its law while exploring forms of "destituent" power that "cannot be captured" by security or sovereign mechanisms.[57]

Jacques Rancière disagrees with Agamben. The problem, he observes, is not rights in themselves but their depoliticization into fixed categories. Treating rights as a dichotomous thing that we either have or not turns them into "a void or a tautology," Rancière notes. To the excluded, rights may seem ineffective and useless. To those already enjoying the protections of citizenship, they may appear as redundant. Rancière is concerned that Arendt's and Agamben's discussions on rights as available to only some may unintendedly echo Edmund Burke's conservative critique of the Rights of Man as abstract and inapplicable. It is this treatment of rights, not rights themselves, that Rancière finds problematic.

Taking distance from Agamben, Rancière contends that "man is not the void term opposed to the actual rights of the citizen." Like freedom or equality, rights are the object of political contention that helps define the terms of membership. Rather than an empty container opposite those enjoying rights, "man and citizen" suggests a distance that is always politically constructed. And as such, the politics can be challenged. Universal rights are "the rights of the demos" or the ordinary people who won them "through democratic action." Lacking qualifications for rule such as money, rank, and expertise, the ordinary people are simply the mass of those who are not supposed to speak and appear in public, Rancière notes. Yet through politics, especially through forms of direct action like "pronouncements and demonstrations," people reclaim political agency and breach barriers to effectively access rights. By acknowledging rights as "inscriptions of the community as free and equal," people activate those rights and make them their own. The lack of access to rights opens room for inclusion through political struggles, and democratic action stands as the only guarantee for people to make rights "a reality."[58]

Political action bridges the distance between written and unwritten rights and lived experience. Democracy gets reenacted every time the common people make themselves visible, and movements demanding rights have shown the possibility of altering deeply unequal conditions. Rights, Rancière reminds us, are always available to the oppressed and excluded, who can invoke them to resist and overcome those conditions. While formal recognition matters, it is the people reclaiming rights in the "back-and-forth" that makes them concrete.[59]

Indeed, the emancipatory potential of rights seems clear to "socially oppressed groups and classes" who, in their struggle, turn to local, national, and international laws. These struggles, Sousa Santos adds, reaffirm the law's "insurgent, emancipatory character." Hence, if not without difficulties, always at risk of reversal, legal rights provide citizens with key resources, including awakening "dormant" rights. Through common action, protests, contention, and litigation, people "put to test" rights and their scope. Judith Butler presents a similar view by observing that even when deprived of access to rights, life "is still within the sphere of the political." Excluding someone from rights involves a complex political operation that needs to be reproduced and can be reversed. Moreover, lack of rights recognition does not lead to their loss. Like Rancière, Butler sees people's actions as what makes otherwise abstract rights real.[60] Struggles for rights can take place independently of the state. As such, the "rights of man" both codify rights and invite us to go further in reclaiming effective access and recognition through political action. In the end, rights claims lie in the fundamental right of insurrection. As a constitutionalist, Gargarella agrees: "the right to protest should be understood as a *first right*," the ultimate right "that helps us keep all the other rights intact." If the right to protest is not recognized, "all the structure of rights starts crumbling," Gargarella notes. The defense of the right to "social protest and resistance to oppression" is the ultimate defense of democratic politics of a law conceived as a dialogue between equals, he concludes.[61]

If these uses of rights may betray or fail both the concept and its traditions, and if formal recognition may not suffice to guarantee access, this does not make rights into mere "poetry," however, Gargarella contends. It is difficult for people to claim, and for judges to grant, rights that are not written, as "the absence of these rights works against their materialization." Formal recognition is essential, as it opens the door for demanding and accessing even "dormant" rights. In other words, if being recognized as a subject of rights may not guarantee legal protections, not being granted that status leaves individuals and groups in an extremely fragile position. This is in part why protesters consistently demand rights.[62]

Still, it is important to remain aware of the structural limitations of both politics and rights under our present conditions. "Right can never be higher than the economic structure of society and its cultural develop-ment," Marx notes, as he questions the "narrow horizon" of bourgeois rights. In fact, as he and others have shown, modern individual rights developed in parallel and were instrumental to the enclosure movement against the commons, as discussed in the next section. As such, they indi-vidualize and depoliticize our demands, naturalize our conditions, and position us as passive recipients of recognition by the powerful. They are central to capitalist societies, where "the *regulation* of social relationships *assumes a legal character*" that turns individuals into legal subjects and "bearers of rights," as Pashukanis observes. These are all conditions that neoliberalism only intensifies.[63]

If the law grounds rights, it also makes bodies and territories legible and easier to control, helping create the subjects it describes. This is in part why the language of rights has become suspect. For if serving as "an indis-putable force of emancipation," as Brown puts it, rights can be used to neutralize or block radical democratic agendas.[64]

Whereas Marx exposed the law's involvement with various forms of exploitation and dispossession, Foucault showed how, once made into law, the rights we claim are turned into disciplining devices that subject and reshape us. Far from neutral, as Golder notes following Foucault, rights are "immanent and not exterior to the field of political combat." They work as governmental devices that penetrate communities and bodies through differential recognition and take power away from them. In the 1979 lectures, Foucault describes two "absolutely heterogeneous" views of freedom. The first, developed in the tradition of "the rights of man," would basically coincide with the overview of the evolution of rights presented here earlier. The second, he notes, is the tradition of "the independence of the governed."

Concerned with the disciplining role of rights, Foucault increasingly moved to explore the problematic of the rights of the governed. "More historically determinate than the rights of man," he writes in 1977, using the term for the first time, it is necessary to explore the "legitimate defense with regard to governments." No government can be assumed to be truly committed to protecting human rights, Foucault reminds us, as he con-cluded by assimilating human rights to those of the governed, as J. L. Ferreira-Neto notes.[65]

While the question of how to become a subject without being sub-jected would define Foucault's later works, his uncompromising commit-ment, Whyte notes, was to "the suffering of men." The latter, which Whyte reminds us recurs in his work, grounds "an absolute right to stand up and speak to those who hold power." Concern with the oppression and suffering of the governed thus delineates a blueprint in Foucault's work for "a new form of right," one that moves away from both discipline and sovereignty.[66]

A similar awareness is present in Marx, concerned with how bourgeois rights continue to "merely reinscribe" capitalist values and subjectivities. The latter would make the rights we have potentially incompatible with a postcapitalist society, David Harvey notes. Laws express capitalist social relations in "juridic language," shaping "isolated, egoistic agents," hostile to one another and subjecting us to constant uncertainty and (in)security. Even when recognizing rights, the state tends to curtail them in the name of "public safety" or the "rights of others," Marx observes, as he ironizes about "the pompous catalogue of the 'inalienable rights of man'" and bourgeois law's denial of humans' communal "species being." Still, distrust of the legal language of rights as ambiguous and treacherous should not prevent us from appreciating their possibilities for "counter-investment and appropriation," as Foucault points out.[67]

Appropriating rights, of course, goes both ways. In the 1970s, Amnesty International remarkably exposed the torture, forced disappearances, camps, and extrajudicial killings under military dictatorships in countries like Argentina and Chile. Yet, as Whyte notes, visibility came at a cost. Human rights NGOs replaced previous comprehensive initiatives to "enshrine rights to housing, food, education and medical care" with "a narrow focus on civil and political rights" that avoided structural questions. Added to the UN treatment of social rights as unenforceable "flexible standards," this narrow emphasis gave human rights currency while shrinking their scope and easing their neoliberal takeover. Over the following decades, cast as "rigidities" obstructing the economy, wage and labor standards and safety nets have been dismantled across countries under waves of neoliberal austerity. This calls to interrogate the uses of rights in ongoing enclosures, as well as of the enclosures targeting rights themselves.[68]

Rights and the Struggle over Enclosures

"For the poor, the marginalized, the excluded, the 'rule of law' means the targeted assassinations and collective massacres that we have endured," Bolivian president Evo Morales declared in 2005. In some light, Morales's words may sound counterintuitive. Across comparable institutions including the German *Reichstaat*, the British common law, the Spanish *Estado de*

Derecho, and the French *état de droit*, the rule of law predicates public, general, clear, stable, and consistent norms that are impartially enforced and applied proactively. Government actions must be articulated in legal terms "that limit them in advance," as Foucault describes it.[69]

Laws define and regulate people's "status, obligations, and rights" while determining enforcement mechanisms, limiting discretionary power, and holding those in positions of authority accountable. Besides its key role in governing, the law stands as a source of legitimacy by validating norms according to their coherence with the legal system. Only within the space defined by law can the authorities use force. Features like these give the law its "allure," and have made scholars see the rule of law synonymous with freedom and human rights, a defining "arena" of democratization, and a major facet of rights and citizenship.[70]

For all their virtues, laws never work in isolation but within assemblages of knowledge and institutional practices. Diverging meanings of the law transpire in available indicators. Varieties of Democracy focuses on whether laws are "transparently, independently, predictably, impartially, and equally enforced" along with government compliance. Freedom House emphasizes the need for an independent judiciary, legal equality, civil control of the police, and safeguards against unjustified detentions, torture, exile, and political terror. The World Bank, with a more openly neoliberal perspective, stresses "the quality of contract enforcement, property rights, the police, and the courts, as well as the likelihood of crime and violence" as synonymous with the rule of law.[71]

Yet narratives on the rule of law tend to omit questions about laws' meaning and reach, such as "who makes them, interprets them, and applies them for what purposes," as Stephen Holmes points out. In their obliviousness to power and market and political exclusions, rule of law narratives appear complicit with them. These biases, silences, and formal language serve the status quo well.[72]

At times, technical claims about the law can turn highly ideological. Consider Hayek. He describes the rule of law as a condition in which the government is "bound by rules fixed and announced beforehand." Laws, he continues, must apply universally, as they set up the rules "of the game," which the state must strictly enforce. At first sight, nothing seems out of order. Yet, Hayek continues, the law must protect property rights, enforce market rules, fulfill contracts, and lower transaction costs, all of which he portrays as unproblematic and neutral. Only truly universal rights such as freedom of thought or owning property deserve recognition for Hayek. Social rights or special protections for any group seem to him illegitimate entitlements and a threat to freedom. Such rights must be fiercely opposed and eliminated as if "the fate of civilisation depended on it," he concludes.[73]

Pushing narrow, formal, allegedly neutral meanings of rights, the law, and government against popular democratic politics seems part of the neoliberal tradition. Along these lines, Hayek's views of rights and the law reveal themselves to be all about protecting the market, (individual and corporate) property rights, self-interest, and individual responsibility. He portrays market freedom as the source of all freedoms. In his view, only rights compatible with the market should be honored. Moreover, Hayek acknowledges that protecting the market is no "laissez-faire" and that its preservation may require sacrificing freedom under authoritarian rule—no doubt, a peculiar claim.

Revealing moments like these are rarely spelled out. Ludwig Von Mises is also eloquent: "Men are altogether unequal," he contends, as he finds claims about human equality absurd. Only trade equality seems, in his view, necessary to keep the market going and make people responsible for their own fate. The neoliberal worship for "competition," barely conceals its dismissal of rights and democracy.

Claims that markets would offer rights "ample opportunities," as Sheldon Wolin puts it, have been debunked by persistent exclusions and inequalities. Behind the storytelling of a self-regulating market that delivers wealth, order, and justice lie the differential effects of the law on the propertied and the poor, and the worsening of living conditions and rights protections for the many, conveyed by Morales in his inauguration speech.[74]

The private-property-centered, neoliberal hijacking of rule of law rhetoric has been contested with claims about the need to distill a "democratic" law, as Guillermo O'Donnell hoped for, that protects rights, liberties, and equality against "potential abuses of state power." Far from an anomaly, however, neoliberal restrictive views on rights have a long pedigree. Hayek's portrayal of markets as the heart of freedom goes back at least to Adam Smith, as Warren Montag shows. For all his praise of freedom and the "invisible hand," the state, Smith argues, must guarantee cheap commodities through laws that preserve the "useful inequality in the fortunes of mankind," and protect the wealthy, starting with banning workers from unionizing. Likewise, Locke's celebration of the law, together with his claim that "government has no other end but the preservation of property," all of this supported by prerogative power, such as his neglect of the fate of those without property, gain full meaning under neoliberal regimes. These emphases and historical continuities serve as a reminder of the preeminent role of Western law in privatizing common resources through enclosures.[75]

"The neoliberal market order, as assisted by the state, has proven to be as zealous and ruthless in enclosing the commons as King John," David Bollier notes. In Colombia, for decades, the authorities bypassed constitutional provisos, invoking efficiency and national interest, to give corporations access to exploiting protected Afro Colombian and Indigenous land while preventing local communities from accessing water. They did so by differentiating governing surfaces, distinguishing between water sources, the soil, the subsoil, and the airspace to create distinct spheres of use and regulation that favor the dispossession of local communities, even when explicitly protected by law. Thanks to these governing tactics, the law can at once recognize communities' ownership over territories while granting its subsoil exploitation to extractive companies, which makes staying on the land virtually impossible. As in the past, the law, as Marx writes, still serves as an "instrument by which the people's land is stolen," and assets and labor are privately appropriated. Whereas this appropriation is just part of neoliberalism's enclosures or the "seizure of what is common," as Jodi Dean puts it, it instrumentalizes laws and rights. In turn, democratic laws and constitutional reforms are resisted by transnational corporations, which sue governments in private courts on grounds of profit loss caused by expanded people's rights.[76]

In Colombia, with close to nine million internally displaced people, over a million people killed, and 157 killings of human rights defenders in 2024 alone, defenders—women, in particular—face harassment, violence, and criminalization, Frontline Defenders reports. While the 1991 Constitution recognizes the rights of Indigenous and Afrodescendant Colombians, including their rights to the land, on the ground people are still targeted with forced displacements and land dispossession campaigns.[77]

Milena Quiroz Jiménez is one of them. A leader in Southern Bolívar's Arenal, a region plagued by extractive operations, Quiroz Jiménez was active in local organizations, including a radio station. First arrested by the military in 2017 with eleven other people, she was charged for helping organize protests, accused of "'rebellion,' 'conspiracy to commit a crime' and 'financing terrorist groups'"—an accusation of terrorism too common in targeting grassroots activists. Imprisoned without trial for over eight years, Quiroz Jiménez shares this condition with countless grassroots land and rights defenders targeted with violence and criminalized as part of a new extractive wave—300 of whom were killed in 2023.[78]

As in her case, or as with the Indigenous peoples who endure "the highest proportion of killings of rights defenders" documented by the UN Special Rapporteur, the treatment of ordinary people as criminals when exercising their rights has recurred since the earliest enclosures. Visibly since the fourteenth century in Europe, new forms of law and governmental practices supported expelling people from their land and denying their communal rights. Communities lost access to forests, rivers, and farmland. Through "endless expropriation, even extermination, of populations and of the earth itself," in disregard of ancient rights and legal traditions, the enclosure movement resorted to legislation and violence to impose forms of private property and force the dispossessed to work for a wage. Through land and other forms of enclosure, a relentless destruction of the commons took place.[79]

Massive land grabs set the foundation of capitalism through the accumulation of wealth. Those in a position of power—the gentry and nobles earlier, then clan chiefs and capitalists—used new laws to rob peasants and claim the land as their personal property. Dispossessing peasants became "perfectly legal," Michael Perelman notes. Communal rights were dismissed as feudal relics, vague, "uncertain," and even irrational, and their subjects treated as usurpers and punished. Besides mass dispossession, the enclosures helped naturalize the wage relation while criminalizing nonmercantile lifestyles. Supported by laws, various waves of enclosures erased commons and rights while separating people from one another and from their means of living.[80]

With antecedents going back to the eleventh century, Britain was the first place where massive enclosures were documented as powerful feudal landlords started taking over common land. Marx, who grew up in a region with a strong tradition of commons, began his critical studies of political economy with a series of pieces on the theft of wood. Through enclosures, he notes, a "complete separation" took place, pulling people apart from their homes, communities, and means of living in sheer disregard for centuries-old rights. Marx identified five waves of enclosures, intensified with the rise of Protestantism and, in England, when Henry VIII confiscated the Catholic Church's property. Land was distributed among feudal lords just as peasants found their rights denied, were expelled from the land, and even put to death by the tens of thousands, with executions extending under the time of the Elizabethan "poor laws." A second wave of enclosures unfolded during and after the English Civil War, and a third wave started with the 1688 Glorious Revolution. It was then that the Parliament and the Orange monarchy took over "extensive state lands, most of which were forest commons" to distribute among wealthy landlords.[81]

Laws were strategic in advancing land appropriations, with "thousands of 'Bills for Inclosure of commons'" in the eighteenth and nineteenth centuries. Backed by soldiers, clan leaders took over common land In Scotland through "Highland Clearances," including by "burning and destroying villages" to set up giant private farms. Up to a third of the population was dispossessed by the mid-nineteenth century, M. T. Devine shows. The privatization of water and drainage of rivers accompanied enclosures and forced people to leave. Targeted by successive waves of expropriation, the "traditional rights of the poor" were made "irrelevant."[82]

Increasingly, liberal laws treated commons and commons rights, from collecting firewood or peat to animal grazing, as feudal remnants. Private property was made "absolute," and "all the tolerated 'rights' that the peasantry had acquired or preserved . . . were now rejected," Perelman writes, citing Foucault. Bourgeois property rights displaced poor people's rights, Perelman adds. Mounted on the law, state, capital, and private property expanded around the world.[83]

For centuries, just as waves of waves of dispossession and the destruction of "forests and larger wildlife" continued, British colonial administrators perfected the enclosure model overseas. Through the "conquest, enslavement, robbery, murder" described by Marx, British colonialism forced population displacements and the rise of slave plantations. The private appropriation of what Jason Moore describes as "biophysical reproduction (labor-power, forestry, agriculture)" and "geological extractions (energy and minerals)" drove enclosures—and the destruction of communities and habitats—worldwide.[84]

While the propertied classes in the metropolis succeeded in having their rights recognized, "the law itself" had turned into a colonial tool. Colonized or enslaved others were judged "an error of arrested evolution" and entire groups were not considered fully human. Under the law in the metropolis, Indigenous peoples' rights and lives "did not merit even a trifle of concern," Perelman notes. Natives were treated as part of nature and made into the law's Other. Rights, in turn, were assumed not to apply to societies dominated by "custom, tribe, and savagery," Nasser Hussain observes. Even those supporting the humanity of the Indigenous peoples, such as Francisco de Vitoria, justified subjecting, dispossessing, and killing those resisting the forces of trade, as Neocleous points out.[85]

The brutal treatment of colonial subjects was justified on grounds of their presumably "barbarous" character, a story that helped colonial administrators ignore their own barbarism. In the "moral and legal no man's land" thus created, as Tayyab Mahmud puts it, theft, forced displacements, land grabbing, the banning of communal forms of labor and ownership, unpaid labor—or its ultimate form, enslavement—and the appropriation of assets or capital goods were dominant.[86]

Claiming that nothing counted as a sin below the Equator, colonial administrators used the law to justify exploitation, dispossession, enslavement, and genocide, just as North Atlantic myths of altruism, Christian salvation, and civilizing "missions" or "manifest destiny" concealed those practices. No wonder modern law has been portrayed as a form of "white mythology" that proclaims itself coherent, objective, rational, and impartial—along the lines of the rule of law—against its ambiguous, contradictory character and not-so-hidden violence. This violence, Mahmud reminds us, "threatens" the law "from within," by legitimizing an "extrajudicial" foundation of the order that the law is set to protect.[87]

"To characterize any conduct whatever towards a barbarous people as a violation of the law of nations, only shows that he who so speaks has never considered the subject," wrote John Stuart Mill. Such peoples, he added, were incapable of following rules, noting that "their minds are not capable of so great an effort, nor their will sufficiently under the influence of distant motives." Otherwise known as a defender of rights, even as a nineteenth-century avant-garde feminist, Mill dismissed so-called Barbarians in a racist, bold defense of colonialism.[88]

Better than anyone else's, Mill's words epitomize the differential recognition of dignity, voice, and rights discussed by Agamben and its shadow looming over the liberal defense of freedoms and the rule of law. Still, as Foucault reminds us, liberalism has nothing to do with rights. New forms of power require new foundations, and liberalism found it in the law. The liberal state embraced the law as a "technology of government," Foucault notes. No less than it imposed markets and wage labor through unlawful, brutal violence. Still, out of sheer political contingency, a semantic association between "liberalism, law and representative democracy" was born.[89]

Colonial hierarchies and governing traditions eventually came home to infuse the law back in the metropolis. Its enduring legacies include a racist "color line" built into the law and the politics of emergency. Law and the emergency are "powerfully and intimately connected," as Hussain puts it. Together with pacification campaigns, security, and interconnected police apparatuses, emergency regimes let "a system of a rule of law" support extralegal state action while giving corporate and state agents immunity.[90]

In the end, Arendt acknowledges, the rule of law, which intended "to eliminate violence and the war of all against all," depends on "instruments of violence in order to assure its own existence." By violence Arendt means state crimes, which she notes governments sometimes must commit for their "own survival and the survival of lawfulness." This is hardly surprising, if we consider the genealogical imbrication of the modern, bourgeois rule of law with enclosures and colonialism.[91]

Enclosures never ended. The destruction of the commons and the expropriation of previously shared resources sanctioned by laws and institutions "were a continuous characteristic of capital development," De Angelis notes. Through successive, cumulative waves, appropriating people's labor, products, and ideas while privatizing access to both natural and cultural resources, enclosures commodify additional facets of life.[92]

The attack on Indigenous land, forests, rivers, and rights supported on (neo)colonial and racist narratives, re-creates practices of original expropriation or "primitive accumulation." Visibly in the hundreds of land grabs by agroindustry and mining conglomerates, neoliberal enclosures advance by turning our habits, social networks, and even DNA into a source of appropriation, with no end in sight, as corporations and states come for "what's left."[93]

Revealing "integral" bonds with war, violence, and exploitation, neoliberal reason's "endless emergency" lets powerful states claim "a new right to 'humanitarian interference'" over countries and communities. Lawfare is a form of war that uses laws to achieve military goals. In so doing, it exposes the ways in which "'law' and 'war' are contained" within each other, Tawia Ansah argues. As part of the repertoire of pacification, Neocleous shows how lawfare involves multiple cultural, economic, and violent resources seeking to consolidate military gains politically and keep the population docile. Under these conditions, the law helps war overflow into daily life while operating as a legitimizing mechanism that makes state-authorized agents immune to prosecution. Thus laws have been oblivious to state terror policies securing the expansion of markets, from the early mass expropriation to colonial rule to dictatorships and emergency regimes "entrench[ing] neoliberalism" over the last fifty years, as Ruth Blakeley shows. Through the law, Foucault reminds us, "war continues to rage."

Through a combination of laws and emergency measures, governments support enclosures while neglecting citizens' rights and state obligations toward them and preventing people and communities from being self-sustaining. As a result, the population is made into a passive object of governance, with the law mostly used as a disciplining tool as neoliberal reason pushes toward "abolishing people's remaining rights," De Angelis notes.[94]

Critical Foundations: Rights as "Social Barriers."

"For 'protection' against the serpent of their agonies, the workers have to put their heads together and, as a class, compel the passing of a law, an all-powerful social barrier by which they can be prevented from selling themselves and their families into slavery and death by voluntary contract with capital."[95] Skeptical of "pompous" legal declarations and the privileges they hide, Marx highlights the importance of the struggle for rights. In the passage above, from *Capital*, he treats the legal regulation of the working day as an example of how workers use laws to win labor protections—and the protection of their lives. If bourgeois rights and laws structurally support capital, Marx acknowledges that they can also serve as a "social barrier" allowing people to shelter their bodies, families, and communities from exploitation and enclosures. The image brings in the notion of a "limit beyond which capital cannot go," as De Angelis observes, in the form of a true commons.[96]

In his writings, Marx is sensitive to the contradictions between bourgeois individual rights and the collective needs of workers. Struggling for better wages and conditions of labor, including "the codification of legal rights," is simply necessary. If in itself it does not challenge the normal capitalist dynamics, the "learning and radicalization" that comes with taking part in the struggle leads to overcoming "fetishistic forms of thought and perception," he observes. In addition, for all their treacherous aspects, laws convey elements of popular justice, that, even if distorted and idealized, anticipate the overcoming of "structural inequalities, unfreedoms, and lack of collective power over existence." The context is one of alienation, but other possibilities are also present. The challenge, then, is not simply demanding "a moral 'right' to an unscathed existence"; Marx expects that workers will mobilize as they learn about capitalism's destructive character.[97]

A revolutionary society would grant everybody "equal power to politically govern" while advancing a "true democracy," one that is egalitarian and participatory. Under truly democratic conditions, (formal?) rights would not be needed, Menke interprets Marx. By relying on individuals' equal rights and duties to self-govern, with his focus on participation Marx envisions the emancipated individuals in the way of Nietzschean masters, which would make rights irrelevant. The notion that participatory practices may in the end make rights redundant, displaced by people's straightforward decisions over their own lives, is intriguing. And yet Marx shows a clear appreciation for rights.[98]

Bhiku Parekh stresses the "subtle and discriminating" character of the Marxian approach to rights. Marx "did not intend to reject the modern theory of rights," Parekh observes, but only "its perverted forms." To Marx, under capitalist conditions, rights can "in fact restrain the state, subject the capitalist class to certain norms and provide the conditions under which the working class can organize and grow." Surely, as discussed earlier, states limit rights through regulations and can use them as governmental devices to discipline individuals and groups. Often, in their discretionary enforcement of the law, bureaucrats, courts, or the police use rights intended to empower citizens to control and even exclude them. Moreover, the state can and does suspend laws. And states can fully dismiss the rights of the people and abuse and kill them. Governments do all these things on our behalf in representative democracies; it is horrific, and they get away with it. But the state "cannot do so all the time," Parekh observes, as constantly bypassing laws "weakens its authority."[99]

That law and rights can be co-opted for antagonistic political projects does not mean "that the state creates the legal superstructure by its arbitrary will," Pashukanis notes. E. P. Thompson agrees. If "partly the vehicle of a mystifying ideology and of class interests," the law, Thompson writes, cannot effectively help governments other than by at least from time to time "actually being just."[100]

Despite their limits, laws have shown potential to enhance social life by making it more predictable and to offer protections while moving toward "conditions of social ownership," T. B. Bottomore writes. Likewise, the history of legal protections attests to their—ancient, modern, and revolutionary—possibilities to create sanctuary for individuals and communities. Along these lines, Gargarella helps think of a democratic approach to rights by thinking of law as a dialogue between equals that involves everyone in defining how we want to live and the "principles and rules that will define and organize our social lives." Equality, disagreement, deliberation, and inclusiveness are the main principles supporting such a continuous dialogue.[101]

Popular struggles expose the "insurgent and emancipatory" possibilities of rights. Local, state, international, written and unwritten, informed by traditions of legal pluralism, multicultural constitutionalism, or Indigenous, communal, and popular forms of "legality from below" push toward a critical "cosmopolitan legality," Sousa Santos notes. While the law can serve as an exclusionary instrument under the state, it also helps to confront the "demoliberal state legality" in global struggles for inclusion. Key in this regard, Sousa Santos argues, is determining whether alternative legal traditions can help expand and improve equality and inclusion.[102]

In the perspective opened by Marx, striving for "the maximum rights compatible" with capitalist conditions seems strategic for advancing solidarity. Rights and laws matter. They can help people protect gains from (centuries of) struggles. The struggles for the commons and for rights, in this regard, are the same.[103]

Insights like these point out to the potential for laws to serve universal, species-like interests, and for rights to protect expansive dimensions of life. For even the content of our established laws "is bound to have features that point beyond the bourgeois society and require to be preserved," Parekh contends, just as the law anticipates universal, emancipatory possibilities. Law, as the "legal expression" of social relationships, can be transformed in a revolutionary fashion, Pashukanis observes. In the meantime, in the way of a social barrier protecting individuals and communities that Marx describes, rights stand as a *dispositif* of protection for both individuals and groups available any time to anyone. Furthermore, adding more layers, new forms of rights seem essential to welcome the "morethanhuman" to our communities, through "multi-species entanglements that cast their nets across the planet, into the spheres of justice," as Celermajer et al. put it.[104]

Rights can be co-opted, but they precede and exceed the project of the sovereign capitalist state and are central to furthering the democratic horizon. If vulnerable to (mis)appropriation, they stand out for their resilience and enduring value. In the end, as Parekh notes, even a society emancipated from exploitation by an empowered people and revitalized commons will likely need "a theory of rights" that defines rights' bearers. Conflicts and potential for forms of interpersonal—and we can add, interspecies—abuse would not just simply vanish.[105]

Critics from Marx to Foucault to Pashukanis have identified the need for new forms of rights. If, following Marx, Pashukanis explores the prospect of the "struggle for revolutionary legality," Foucault identifies the need for an "art of not being governed so much," and Menke calls for a new form of rights—or counter-rights—which he links to a democratic politics based on the intentional and reflective "*self-government of practice*." Besides equality, rights need to protect everyone's judgment, including on whether and how to participate. Menke imagines a deliberative exercise of judgment that "itself issues laws." These hypothetical "new rights decisions" and laws would be ephemeral. They would understand themselves and their legal products as "claims to a transitory *and* recurring—moment in the political process of law." In articulating decisions on the present, we would rely on laws without a need to obey or force them on others in the future. Open, flexible, democratic, drawing on people's customary self-governing and creativity and attuned to local conditions, the counter-rights theorized by Menke echo the principles of commoning as a fundamental right. Acknowledging the commons and its ancient norms and practices is becoming increasingly central to reinvigorating the meaning of life, democracy, and rights.[106]

Reclaiming the Commons and Rights as Commons

"Estovers, turbary, pannage . . . And this weekend millions of Britons will be enjoying a relatively recent addition to their ancient rights to collect firewood, cut peat, and graze pigs on common land—the right of access." Thus Geoffrey Lean encourages Britons to exercise their commons rights in a 2015 piece in the *Telegraph*. With about 36,000 rights in use across 7,000 commons extending over 574,880 hectares or 5 percent of the UK territory, if down from having covered over half of the territory centuries ago, commons are showing "signs of revival," Lean reports. Along waterways such as the River Cam, people gather to defend their access to water and to assert "the *rights* of rivers to exist and be properly maintained." Mobilizing for clean water, riding horses, and going on visits or walks may be "a long way" from their old uses, but they offer "hope of a new age for our ancient common land," as Lean puts it.[107]

Not reducible to either public or private, the commons describe social forms of ownership of "lands, territories, forests, meadows, and streams, or communicative spaces" that a group of people "collectively owns, manages, and controls," by involving "intense social cooperation," Silvia Federici notes. The concept of the commons allows us to see the parallels between massive forms of expropriation and resistance across continents and eras, from Irish and English peasants to Indigenous people in the Americas to engineers and activists advocating for open source software.[108]

A shared use of the land characterizes "the primitive institution of the common," Karl Polanyi observes. Together with the land, commons included access to key public goods, from water to food, traditionally seen in Western cultures as the "inheritance of humanity." Further analysis reveals also "knowledges, languages, codes, information, affects," as well as care. Universal rights standards building on *ius gentium* and other forms of common law are part of the commons as well, De Angelis notes. In fact, commons' definitions and limits are "entirely contextual and political," and they evolve together with communities and technologies.[109]

Widespread and resilient, open, egalitarian commons were an established presence across Europe. The Campine region of what is now Belgium hosted an extended communal system since the twelfth century. By the 1500s, "98 per cent of households actively used the commons," Maïka De Keyzer observes, with no restrictions or exclusions despite population growth. The Campine commons were successful, ecologically efficient, and sustainable, with rules protecting shared resources and guaranteeing a fair distribution of the surplus.[110]

Sharing land and resources prevailed across continents until capitalist groups enclosed commons through expropriations and privatizations. Even at the peak of enclosures in England, however, the authorities had to respond to grassroots pressure. In 1795, the Speenhamland Law was passed to introduce an allowance that guaranteed "a minimum income" to the poor to supplement wages or serve as sole support in an amount that was set according to the price of bread. Abolished in 1834 under market pressure, the allowance recognized a "right to live" and the "unconditional right of the poor to relief." Likewise, the Campine commons functioned until arbitrary decisions ended them in the late eighteenth century. Without romanticizing a past tainted by patriarchal and other biopolitical hierarchies, Rosa Luxemburg acknowledged "important social protections" in these traditions. This helps understand why ordinary people persisted in defending their commons and forced their recognition—and preservation—throughout England, Wales, France, and the Swiss Alps, some of them extending to the present.[111]

Indeed, although the commons may sound like an "archaic idea," ongoing enclosures through privatization, dispossession, and rights losses under neoliberal austerity and legislation have made visible "a world of communal properties and relations that many had believed to be extinct," Federici notes. No wonder then that the historical and philosophical traditions of the commons are making a comeback.[112]

Federici shows that forms of communal land tenure have survived across Africa more extensively than anywhere else. A significant number of rural dwellers live under arrangements including urban communal gardens. Women, in particular, have traditionally cultivated the land, primarily to secure food for their families and to sell the surplus. Federici stresses women's historic reliance on the communal and "commoning" as "the primary mechanism" of social reproduction and forming social bonds.[113]

In recent decades, fueled by debt crises and the recommendations of international financial institutions, the communal land system came under attack. Ending communal land arrangements was an explicit goal of the World Bank, on grounds that only market uses of the land are productive. Privatizing public land, promoting land titling and crops for export, and letting foreign investors buy land were imposed as part of loan conditionalities. Moreover, the World Bank promoted land privatization as beneficial to women. And yet market initiatives led to selling land to foreign investors and to "dispossess[ing] millions of farmers, many of them women," Federici explains.

People resisted and communal land arrangements were allowed to continue. As all land was made sellable, however, Federici notes that displaced women turned to growing food in vacant public lots, parks, alongside roads or sidewalks in Kampala, Lusaka, Kinshasa, and other major African cities. Movements like these illustrate what has been described as a revolution of the poor and the resilience of commoning. "New commons are being created" around the world, as neoliberal exclusions force people to come up with alternatives to markets and money.[114]

On its part, the World Bank campaign to privatize land in Africa is part of a global attack on the commons and a neoliberal attempt to enclose even the idea of the commons itself. Federici discusses the "many manipulations and appropriations" of the concept of the commons by the same institutions and actors that "have made the abolition of communal property their mission." The World Bank, for example, has adopted the language of the "global commons" following the UN definition that includes the open seas, atmosphere, Antarctica, outer space, and tropical rainforests, all treated as resources not owned by any nation. While the UN invites inclusive, equitable, and sustainable forms of development to honor humans' "common heritage," in the name of protecting these "global commons," the World Bank questions "open access" or unclear property rights. In fact, the World Bank's claims for good governance and stewardship of the global commons help justify new enclosures that exclude even Indigenous groups from access to their lands. In this neoliberal appropriation, the concept of commons becomes code for the financialization of nature.[115]

The financialization of nature, Foster explains, involves transforming "natural capital" such as lakes or forests into physical assets with monetary value to facilitate the creation of bonds and other "green" financial products. Examples include "water-quality trading," or assigning monetary value to the "natural carbon sequestration" provided by forests. Investors have advocated for monetizing tens of trillions of US dollars' worth of "global natural capital and ecosystems," as a strategy to favor "sustainable growth." Still, this represents only a fraction of the estimated 4,000 trillion US dollars in total global natural capital. The financialization of nature, which claims to "save nature 'by turning it into a market'," would be the largest wave of expropriation of the commons ever conceived, Foster notes. This is the context of the World Bank's demand for responsible stewardship of the global commons.[116]

In the meantime, enclosures combine with the co-optation of the commons, De Angelis observes, in such a way to put them "to work for capital." This way, to advance development in the Global South, the World Bank promotes community participation and sharing resources while encouraging people to take on bank loans or microcredit that make them dependent on capital.[117]

Financial elites notwithstanding, whether involving ecosystems, ideas, material goods, or social networks, the struggle is always about "re-appropriating the common" as a way of being, in the broadest sense, Antonio Negri notes. "Commons exist in the here and now," De Angelis stresses, highlighting their coexistence with markets and states. If most visible when formally recognized or when under attack, commons shape significant dimensions of our lives. People have fought for centuries for their commons rights, forcing the authorities to recognize and "confirm" them. This seems echoed by protesters demanding a "right to the commons" that de-commodifies access to land, culture, digital technologies, the internet, or the environment. Initiatives to protect the commons include General Public and Creative Commons licenses, cooperatives extending common property into new areas, biocultural protocols preserving Indigenous technologies, demands to make all software and algorithms open-source, legal limits to "corporate enclosures" like fracking or industrial agriculture, "stakeholder trusts" aiming at protecting from "the atmosphere to minerals to groundwater" to commons' productive activities. For these and other initiatives, organizations such as the P2P Foundation compile initiatives and norms.[118]

Among the commons, rights stand out. Discussions of rights tend to be linked to the law. Yet, I hope the earlier discussion made clear that, if embedded within legal regimes, rights both precede and transcend them. As "a social practice with a history," rights exceed legislation and stand as independent "regalia endowed with authority," as Sousa Santos puts it.

Self-referential, instituted by the people themselves, commons rights come into being when "exercised by those who act in concert," as Butler notes. The commons' process of self-creation and recognition independent from the state echoes the dynamics that Honig describes as "taking." Indeed, rights and rights recognition can be gained without "rights-talk," even beyond or outside the state. In claiming rights, people invest themselves with the authority that Searle describes as distinctive of instituting rights, in this case confirmed, justified, and legitimized through their exercise.[119]

Indeed, personal and collective rights define "forms of social commons," De Angelis observes:

> Commoning is also constituent of rights, the "commons rights," which should not be confused with "legal rights." The latter are granted within the context of the state, by the powerful. Commons rights instead originate in their being exercised, and therefore the state can only, at most, acknowledge them, and confirm them (or else deny, restrict them, etc.).[120]

Commons are autonomous, self-generating, and self-supporting. The origin of common rights "is in commoning," and "the right to common" generally expands from the bottom up, De Angelis explains. If constrained by structural conditions, the commons can "develop their own politics," to expand their "autonomy vis-à-vis capital and the top-down logic of states." The tradition of the commons shows promise to nurture forms of labor and production that promote "the all-around development of the individual, and all the springs of co-operative wealth flow more abundantly."[121]

Commoning can support egalitarian, fair, and democratic relations between us and with the rest of the beings on Earth. "*Vasudhaiva kutumbakam*, the world is one family"; these words, written on the walls of the Indian parliament, acknowledge commons and treating other species, trees, or water courses "as part of their community." These moments and examples delineate a path toward rebuilding forms of "communal existence," Foster, Clark, and Holleman note. The commons, ancient and still ongoing, provide an appropriate framework to devise forms of living and working together that honor the organic relations between humans, other species, and the planet in protecting, supporting, and making life thrive.[122]

As "existing regimes of law and governance" fail people and the planet, "commoning and laws to enable it" can address needs and promote egalitarian, fair, and democratic practices in conditions of "dignity, respect and equality." Regarding the fundamental question of access, Etienne Balibar calls for moving "beyond the *exclusive* membership in one community." Moving away from states' sovereign exclusionary dynamics, people should be given "permanent *access*" to rights wherever they happen to work and live.[123]

In considering moving in this direction, it seems important to challenge views that reduce the commons to "natural resources" and treat the world as one seamless space. Both the human and "morethanhuman" multispecies relationships amount to much more than the instrumental, unilateral approach that the term "resources" suggests. This is what Mario Blaser and Marisol de la Cadena remind us in their discussion of "the uncommon." The latter acknowledges multiple perspectives involved in the encounters between "heterogeneous assemblages of life" that make our actual worlds. It is the plurality and radical heterogeneity of the uncommon—encompassing both human and nonhuman elements—that form "the condition of possibility for the common good and for the commons" themselves, Blaser and de la Cadena note.[124]

Respect, care, and ethical obligations are just a few of the bonds linking different groups, entities, and their worlds into "indissoluble wholes of human and non-humans," Blaser and de la Cadena add, that expose the commons as an activity. "Ongoing, always in the making," the commons reminds us of its possibilities to both practically and normatively organize fairer, non-exploitative forms of life. In this endeavor, recognition of the uncommon and the multiplicity of perspectives and experiences involved seems key to expand the horizon of democracy and to embark on "types of flourishing nourished through relational lifeways" referred to by Celermajer et al.[125]

While granting rights to other species and the nonsentient, as in Bolivia, even at the constitutional level as in Ecuador, is just the beginning, Diego Rossello cautions that the endeavor involves more than simply expanding rights. Notions of dignity supporting the 1948 UN Declaration of Human Rights ultimately rely on a human-centered hierarchical approach to rights, Rossello observes after Will Kymlicka. More so, being recognized as human with dignity seems contingent not just on not being perceived as "animal," but also on (sovereign) "mechanisms of investiture" that are not radically different from the ones studied by Ernst Kantorowicz in the institution of a new monarch. If so, ongoing attempts to extend rights to the "morethanhuman" may call for revisiting speciesist notions of dignity and sovereign mechanisms still embedded in rights. Hopefully, as Rossello suggests, human rights find ways to support themselves beyond speciesism and biopolitical hierarchies.[126]

Only once exploitative labor conditions and the destruction of nature are overcome will life flourish. In the meantime, rights can help us progress toward free and equal societies that "would no longer be represented in the institutions of law and State but embodied in the very forms of concrete life and sensible experience" that Rancière anticipates. Transformed by political experiences, rights offer a universal vocabulary to confront state abuses and expand democratic imagination, horizons, and demands ever beyond. If preliminary and fragile, every new right anticipates and helps deliver a new world, with the relationships, practices, and possibilities it presupposes, as Bonnie Honig observes. In so doing, the need to advance a politics of rights independent from and beyond the state seems overdue.

6 | Capital Unleashed

Neoliberal Reason Returns with a Vengeance

Argentina is in decline and because of this damn political caste. . . .
The caste model is born from a disastrous premise, which says that
where there is a need, a right is born. The problem is that needs are
infinite and someone has to pay for the rights, and that implies that
you have to have resources, and resources are finite.[1]
 —Javier Milei, 2023 presidential debate

Ten days after taking office, in December 2023, Argentina's president,
Javier Milei, issued a "mega" emergency decree abolishing over 300 laws
that governed areas from tourism to internet services to groceries to medicine or regulated rental housing. Followed by an additional bill sent to
Congress, such extraordinary measures sought to begin the "reconstruc-
tion" of a "free" Argentina. The endeavor involved advancing the "widest
deregulation" of industry, trade, and services to eliminate market "distortions" obstructing "private initiative" and the "spontaneous play of supply
and demand." Meanwhile, taxes were raised, rents and prices deregulated,
salaries frozen (despite a 25 percent inflation in December 2023 alone),
thousands of public servants fired, and decades-old labor and social security protections were abolished by decree. Next, Milei's comprehensive
Bases law (with more than 200 articles and a tax section) set conditions
for privatizations, lowering labor standards, and attracting foreign investors. It granted the president special powers to declare an economic emergency and discretionary authority to shut down state agencies and sell
public assets. Never before in Argentine history had a president attempted
such a radical economic, political, institutional, and legal takeover accompanied by unprecedented claims of executive authority. Not an elected
president at least.

Milei, Maria Esperanza Casullo points out, has real chances to transform Argentina "in a very different thing than what it was until now." In a matter of months, he tried to achieve what it took Conservatives forty-five years in the UK to accomplish, George Monbiot wrote in *The Guardian*. Perhaps more. Milei describes the market, "where property rights are voluntarily exchanged" alongside the price system, as the "main inventions in the history of humankind." The neoliberal faith pivots on the idea that, for any individual or collective problem, a market solution is always best. Milei, who brags about being the first "Liberal-Libertarian" to preside over a country, prides himself on implementing "the largest adjustment program in the history of humanity," affecting 15 percent of the GDP in just five months. This, in a country with over half of the population living in poverty.[2]

And while on the night of December 20, 2023, concerned citizens did not wait for the end of the televised speech to go into the streets banging pots and pans, over the next months, the government started severely limiting protests by making them a felony and charging protesters for their own policing. Participants and bystanders were randomly arrested, in some cases charged with terrorism—even with attempts of coup d'état. Over a thousand people were hurt during Milei's first year, including at least fifty journalists—one of them left blind and another one with head injuries that required months in the ICU. At least for those who care about the environment, feminism, LGTBQ, and rights, all of them Milei's targets, things got worse.[3]

With degrees in economics, and a past as a rock musician, a soccer player, and a TV personality, despite his "El loco" nickname, "Lion" signature hairstyle, furious social media posts, and religious mysticism, Milei is far from a simple madman. Helped by his visibility as a guest in TV shows, a unique AI-supported, cosplay-inspired social media and campaign aesthetics, and his trademark chainsaw, at the cry of "Long Live Freedom, dammit!" supported by an influencer fan-base, Milei's message reached millions of Argentines.

Presenting himself as a true outsider against establishment corrupt politicians, with what Rocio Annunziata et al. characterize as his "politicized antipolitics," Milei capitalized on citizen frustration. This helped him to rise, in just a couple of years, from the fringes of reality TV to representative in Congress, to then become Argentina's president with 56 percent of the vote.[4]

Besides the wealthy, pro-market groups of the middle class, and disenchanted citizens, a group of workers—many in informal jobs—supported

Milei. Millions of Argentines work by themselves without labor protections. For some poor citizens, living precariously often with no access to running water, sewers, hospitals, schools, or jobs, previous governments' invoking "'Community', 'dignity', and 'human rights'" had become meaningless, a Milei sympathizer from a shantytown observes.[5]

In endorsing Milei's politics, many among the poor echo what Verónica Gago calls "neoliberalism from below," embracing a cost-benefit calculating logic "tactically while putting it in crisis" from time to time. Not represented by unions, ignored by politicians, excluded, they found Milei's antipolitics rhetoric and praise of market and entrepreneurial opportunities appealing. This celebration of individual entrepreneurship equates the self-employed delivery worker with the wealthy business leader, together with a defense of privilege and the idea that rights are only for "those who deserve them," as Marcela Schenck points out.[6]

The sacrificial aspects of neoliberalism were denounced early, as a "policy of economic genocide" under Friedman's signature "shock therapy" during Augusto Pinochet's military dictatorship. The Chilean dictatorship imposed a novel radical experiment in deregulated capitalism just as the military conducted killings and forced disappearances.

Then, since 1989, Washington Consensus–driven economic and environmental deregulations were key to expanding fossil fuels, mining, logging, and industrial agriculture on a planetary scale. Driven by a paradigm of endless growth, these policies doubled and even quadrupled extraction levels. Labor productivity, GDP, energy, and financial markets skyrocketed. Inequality and precarity accelerated together with the destruction of habitats.

Decades later, the far right's "creative forms of cultural activism" have made Latin America once again a testing ground for radical market experiments. Now, with accelerating climate change, the enclosures of neoliberal accumulation call for "a double shock therapy that reregulates natural resource governance and blocks dissent," Alejandro Artiga-Purcell et al. note. These scenarios anticipate new "sacrifice zones" and more "disaster extractivism," a vicious cycle that pushes regions heavily impacted into more extraction, with further destructive consequences for communities and habitats. Moreover, in the way of new Poor Laws, neoliberal enclosures demand "the destruction of existing social rights and the criminalization of popular resistance," as Daniel Bensaïd puts it.[7]

Milei represents this new cycle. At the forefront of a global right-wing network that blends market libertarianism with authoritarian populism in dismantling rights, public services, and social protections while accelerating climate and environmental crises and undermining democracy, Milei helps illuminate the politics of extinction embedded in neoliberal experiments. The neoliberal privileging of markets and profits over the state's role in social reproduction does not sit well with rights and democracy. Fundamental ideals of equality, fraternity, rights, and freedom come under attack as neoliberal reason reigns. Rights are the ultimate neoliberal enclosure, and leaders like Milei are going for them.[8]

Drawing on Foucault's analytics of governmentality and neoliberalism and the Marxian critique, this book sought to map a distinctive neoliberal form of reason of state, its governmental mechanisms and practices, and their impact on democracy, rights, and life. This concluding chapter revisits Javier Milei's turning Argentina into a "world's social laboratory" for the most radical global neoliberal experiment so far. In what follows, I revisit Milei's rise to power and distinct populist brand as well as his program as a politics of extinction. Through experiments like Milei's in Argentina, neoliberal reason drives the unchecked growth of capital, opening the planet's final frontiers—including the deep seas—to exploitation in conditions of global precarity. In this context, the neoliberal business-as-usual can only accelerate climate catastrophe and threaten life on Earth. The scope of the ongoing destruction and the prospects of collapse and alternatives to collapse are addressed at the end.

Time Traveler

In June 2024, in Madrid, Milei claimed to be coming "from the future," as Argentina had already gone through the crises other countries were experiencing, as he described his "chainsaw" austerity program as a global blueprint. "I am today one of the two most relevant politicians on planet Earth. One is Trump, and the other is me." If the claim may betray an inflated ego, *Time* magazine once again including him on its cover suggests that Milei is right, including for different reasons than the ones he invoked.[9]

Javier Milei stands "at the forefront of innovations within right-wing politics," exemplifying what Paulo Ravecca calls "right-wing intersectionality"—or a "multilayered, integrated, and holistic reactionary project" uniting conservatives and the far right in a "cultural battle" against the left. Indeed, the battles of neoliberalism are "total," Dardot observes, simultaneously waged on cultural, economic, social, legal, and environmental fronts. As a host of the Conservative Political Action Conference in Buenos Aires, Milei highlighted CPAC's role as "guardians of ideas" as he called for international coordination to take the "historic opportunity" to make impossible a return of the left and its "politically correct" agenda. As part of these efforts, President Milei has traveled the world to meet with pals and admired figures such as Nayib Bukele, Jair Bolsonaro, Giorgia Meloni, Benjamin Netanyahu, and Donald Trump, and with billionaires like Elon Musk. Together, they are part of a recent populist right-wing wave, with "transgressive" performances denouncing political elites—the "caste," in Milei's terms—bolstered by social media effects of "unmediated communication," as Anthony Pereira puts it. Among them, Milei has been a pioneer in radicalizing the far right-wing by daring "to go where nobody has gone" and "showing others the way," Dardot notes.[10]

In Argentina, within months, Milei's government imposed mass layoffs, slashed health services, pensions, and school funding, with drastic budget cuts to higher education, including the University of Buenos Aires, Latin America's top-ranked university.[11] While rhetorically targeting the political "caste," the actual victims of Milei's austerity were pensioners, students, public employees, teachers, and the poor. Adding insult to injury, Milei vetoed laws aimed at securing funds for public universities and adjusting pensions for inflation. By August 2024, over a million and a half children were skipping dinner in Argentina.[12]

Citizens pushed back. Massive demonstrations and grassroots campaigns in defense of public universities, public health, human rights, and retirees' conditions have been constant. Still, the dizzying pace of government dismissals of public servants, announcements of budget cuts, the closure of state offices, and Milei's vetoes on laws and lack of concern about citizen demands seemed unprecedented.

In the meantime, President Milei found time to give a concert at a packed Luna Park Stadium to present a new book and to publicize his romantic affairs with showbiz figures. President Milei adores his dogs, named after economists, "Conan, Murray, Milton, Robert, and Lucas," and he described their daily routines. Controversy arose, however, as Conan, from whom the other four are cloned and Milei declared to have taken political counsel, died in 2017. The light and curated naivete of Milei's stories contrast to not so light details and the drastic impact of his policies. For all his eccentricities, however, there is nothing crazy about Milei, Elian Chali notes, observing that he is just a "healthy son of neoliberalism."[13]

At once simplistic and all-encompassing, neoliberal reasoning approaches the world as a market and focuses on individual maximizing alongside a logic of cost/benefit analysis. Modeled after firms and corporations, individuals, groups, societies, and states are all expected to expand their assets and "enhance their future value . . . through practices of entre-preneurialism, self-investment, and/or attracting investors," as Wendy Brown puts it. If reducing every single dimension of life to markets seems radical, Milei represents an intensification of these ideas. Giving a speech in Davos, going further than the staunchest neoliberals, he declared that "there are no market failures." Neoliberalism is back in office, and Milei is neoliberal reason, personified.[14]

"There Is No Money!" Milei, a Populist

"He is a MAGA guy. But it is a slightly different form of MAGA. It's 'Make Argentina Great Again.' That's pretty good!," Donald Trump said about Milei. Indeed, the Argentine claims that in the late nineteenth century Argentina was "the wealthiest country in the world," and that the pains Argentines have endured since then result from the "damage and deca-dence" caused by "socialism." That Argentina was never the world's wealthiest country or socialist does not deter its current president or his followers from repeating the story.[15]

Launched to English-speaking audiences by his August 2023 interview with Tucker Carlson, with 435 million views, Milei is remarkably active on social media. With his unique style amplified by AI and an army of influ-encers, just like other populists, he thrives on conflict and antagonisms, as well as on claims of speaking directly for the people while denouncing and blaming political elites. Milei has been prolific in defining enemies. They range from the "caste" of allegedly corrupt professional politicians to femi-nists, "communists," people demanding "social justice," those who he does not deem "personas de bien" or good people, or fellow presidents he calls "terrorist" and "murderer" on Twitter and CNN.

By fueling antagonisms, in scenarios portrayed as severe crises, the populist rallies citizens into "a mobilized and convinced 'we.'" In so doing, populists usually display "bad manners," as Benjamin Moffitt and Simon Tormey put it, transgressing norms of action and speech considered appropriate. These elements define populism as a political style involving discourse, visuals, aesthetics, and theatrical performances. Through them, a leader presents herself as a "singular redemptive or extraordinary figure," Moffit observes, with intense emotional appeals that can "obfuscate facts," as Illouz shows. In the end, the performances that we call populist were addressed half a millennia ago by Giovanni Botero, as "the arts which win for a ruler the love and admiration of his people" to impress citizens and enemies alike as the ultimate display of state might if, only in this case, the rationale is neoliberal.[16]

For all this novelty, Milei builds on a 1990s neoliberal wave of Latin American populism that included Alberto Fujimori in Peru, Abdala Bucaram in Ecuador, Fernando Collor de Mello in Brazil, and Carlos Menem in Argentina. In gaining popularity while advancing neoliberal reforms, they appeared to "violate" the rules of classical populism, as Kurt Weyland notes. Up to that point, market reforms were associated with military dictatorships, not with elected governments, just as populism was seen as synonymous with expanding jobs, education, health, and social programs. Indeed, the 1990s neoliberal populists went against the legacy of leaders such as Getulio Vargas or Juan Domingo Perón, often privatizing "what their populist predecessors had nationalized."[17]

The contrast was striking in Argentina, where Carlos Menem, a former Peronist governor from the northwest, won the 1989 presidential election promising higher salaries and to revitalize local industries only to soon abandon that agenda. "If I had said 'I will privatize the telephones, the railways, and Aerolíneas Argentinas', the whole labor movement would have been against me," Menem later explained. Menem presented himself as having rescued society from hyperinflation, promoting investments and growth, and bringing Argentina back into the world. The formula succeeded, and he was reelected in 1995.

Waning down with the decade, the neoliberal dream ended badly, however, with the largest country debt default up to that point, followed by the collapse of the economy and the government amid mass protests at the cry "Que se vayan todos!" in December 2001.

Argentina recovered, to the point of thriving for years. A China-led cycle of rising commodity prices, soybeans in particular, made possible a new redistributive cycle and the Kirchnerista era. However, the looming shadow of IMF conditionality-driven austerity policies never really went away. By the mid-2010s, the exhaustion of the commodity boom behind "export-oriented populism" became clear, when not even a pro-market government was able to attract foreign investments. Since 2019, the return of a Peronist coalition had to navigate crises intensified by the pandemic, with a series of erratic policies and scandals that paved the conditions for Milei's rise.

Milei, who claims to lead "the best government in history," recognizes Menem as his predecessor. Acknowledging that Menem introduced the largest market reforms in Argentina, Milei claims that his own reforms are "eight times larger," as he surrounds himself with members of the Menem family.[18]

"I am the utmost representative of freedom in the world"; Milei's neoliberal populist style draws on intense, bombastic performances and declarations. His constant invocation of freedom contrasts with his authoritarian politics. Eager to share international media coverage featuring him, even critical pieces such as an interview in *Time* magazine or an article in the *New Yorker*, when it comes to the Argentine media, Milei does not appreciate dissent. Too often, the president gets irritated seeing or hearing anything that contradicts his beliefs. He may respond with angry tirades, including insults and threats, often targeting journalists, even in personal terms. Scholars, public intellectuals, and artists have also endured his attacks—often escalating into a "violent and intolerant confrontation," amplified by his supporters, lesser officials, influencers, and trolls.[19]

Milei's government turned Argentina into a reactionary international outlier, voting against basic protections for women or children, and rejecting the UN Agenda 2030. Argentina's military, security, and defense budgets were doubled and a new Artificial Intelligence Security Unit raised the prospects of mass surveillance, targeting, and breaches of privacy. The government increased state opacity by expanding officials' discretion in classifying and restricting access to information. Milei also considered privatizing prisons and explored adopting the "Bukele Model" of mass imprisonment.[20]

With his singular blend of authoritarian populism, the governmentalities of emergency and the semiotic and spectacular resources discussed in chapters 2 and 3 are on full display, in support of the "Liberal-Libertarian" encounters with the public, his international celebrity status, and his obsession with eradicating any alternative to the market he reveres.[21]

Forces of Heaven and the "Cultural Battle"

In a speech delivered in Rome, Milei outlined a "decalogue," in which he praised right-wing politics, criticized the idea of compromise, and portrayed politics as a zero-sum game. Commending his own politics as a "just and noble cause," he defended the use of force and escalation to defeat adversaries. In reference to his own "cultural battle," he observed that individuals are "mere instruments" who must be "willing to give their lives" for the cause.

Since entering politics in 2021, Milei has frequently invoked religious imagery. One powerful motif is that f the "forces of heaven." A biblical expression from the book of Maccabees, the line reads: "Victory in war does not depend upon the size of the army, but on strength that comes from Heaven." Investing his initially small group of followers with quasi-religious strength, heaven and images of light over darkness have become a staple of his movement. In late 2024, during an event with fascist-looking décor, the Forces of Heaven went from a metaphor into an elite of right-wing activists that presented themselves as Milei's "armed wing" just as they invoked "God, freedom, life, the motherland, the family, and property."[22]

Such mystical and religious references may seem strange for a Libertarian economist. Still, as Adam Kotsko notes, at the core of neoliberalism lies a political theology, in fact "the most coherent and self-reinforcing political theology ever devised." Indeed, this neoliberal political theology comprises a "deeply compelling account of how the world works and what matters most." For all the numbers that economists like Milei like to show, in the end, faith in market forces as a source of truth and the common good informs their arguments. Freedom is market freedom, and individuals are free only when making good choices through the market. Not only is the market a site of veridiction, as Foucault discussed, but there are also no market failures, Milei now claims.[23]

"There is going to be a time when people are going to die of hunger, with which, let's say, somehow, they are going to decide not to die. I don't need [as a state] to intervene," he declared during a talk at Stanford. In his perspective, people are solely responsible for their destiny, as they have the market as a universally accessible instrument to obtain what they need. It is only a matter of selling what one has, even our organs or children, possibilities that Milei considered in different interviews. In this view, markets and market competition are believed to be inherently good and, as Kotsko puts it, "the purest instantiation of human freedom," if only freedom comes to be recursively defined as acting by market principles.

Ending all speeches with "Long live freedom, dammit!" with scruffy references to prophets and "forces of heaven," in his market fundamentalism, Milei brushes aside the crises of our times, as his "cultural battle" targets what he imagines as "the left."[24]

In so doing, he has embarked on a systematic attack on rights and institutions foundational to four decades of Argentine democracy. From the start, the government moved toward eliminating sexual education from schools, defunding cultural programs, universities, science, and education, and dismantling human rights programs, institutions, ongoing prosecutions, and archives, as well as the politics and sites of memory, in an attempt to "modify the historical memory of the dictatorship," as Daniel Feierstein notes. Denying women's pay gap, reproductive rights, nonbinary identities, and feminicide, calling global warming "a socialist lie" and environmentalism "sinister" while authorizing deforestation and mining in protected zones are part of the attack. Meanwhile, public employees were banned from mentioning the climate crisis, environmental issues, sustainable development, feminism, LGTBQ, or the last military dictatorship.

President Milei opposes social justice and rights as "truly aberrant." The only legitimate rights, in his view, are "life, liberty and property," and he claims that these original negative rights were distorted into "an endless list of positive rights," including education and housing, and what he defines as "absurdities like access to the internet, televised football, theatre, cosmetic treatments and an endless number of other desires that were turned into fundamental human rights." In the name of the market, Milei attacks rights.[25]

It makes sense. As discussed earlier, rights protect us in the form of "social barriers." As such, they are central to democratic politics and life, starting with our own lives. The repertoire of rights, vibrant and expansive, evolving to include the "morethanhuman," nonexploitative, and democratic, is part of what countless struggles of a mobilized people gave us. So are the concepts I have used, including those revealing Marx's concerns with the common people and Foucault's insights on neoliberal reason and the focus on the governed. At the front of a radical neoliberal experiment accompanying a new, unprecedented extractive wave, Milei's attack on rights, social standards, and institutions attests to the ultimate enclosure aiming to make it impossible for us to be or choose to live otherwise.

Over the past half century, neoliberalism has reshaped our common sense, fostering a world of isolated individuals increasingly connecting solely through the market. Today, the stakes are even higher, driven by the unprecedented scale and speed of the extractive wave underway. Milei's "cultural battle," as Feierstein observes, seems aimed to "dissolve social bonds," to transform Argentina into a society defined by "ferocious individualism" and extreme isolation, where relationships are reduced to market exchanges. On this, Argentina is serving as a world laboratory—the Milei model is for export.[26]

A (Neoliberal) Politics of Extinction

"Argentina Is About to Unleash a Wave of Lithium in a Global Glut," Bloomberg reported in mid-2024, with several mining operations set to increase lithium production 80 percent in months. Argentina is part of the

"Lithium Triangle" and holds some of the world's largest reserves. Milei promotes mining and fossil fuels. While imposing austerity, the president has pressured governors to sell assets and embark on extractivist projects to obtain funds. Milei is, additionally, an enthusiastic climate change denier, which he defines as "a cycle that exists regardless of men."[27]

Outside Milei's world, scientists track whether we have already definitively crossed the 1.5C threshold as well as the rate of acceleration, chances of reversibility, and implications of the ongoing warming of the planet. "The rate of global warming really is accelerating," legendary NASA scientist James Hansen observes. "The two large humanmade climate forcings— greenhouse gases (GHGs) and aerosols—account for accelerated global warming. The growth rate of these two forcings accelerated in the past 15 years," he adds. As the world's energy imbalance and warming speed up, disasters, crop losses, and unlivable conditions move from dystopian fiction into news headlines.[28]

CO_2 levels have risen from 280 parts per million at the start of the Industrial Revolution to 425 parts per million by late 2024. The accelerated greenhouse emissions and warming have no precedent. Most of it has happened in a matter of decades. The "Great Acceleration," as Foster describes it, peaked in the aftermath of World War II and then again since the 1960s, never to stop. Since 1970, the extraction of metals has grown by 273 percent, fossil fuels by 158 percent, and nonmetallic minerals by 402 percent.[29]

Moving forward, the extraction of lithium and rare minerals will increase fivefold over the next two decades, the World Bank now projects. This is the future that Milei represents. No capitalist "greening" or technoutopia can make the largest extractive effort ever attempted across rainforests, mountains, and the deep seas sustainable.

Milei personifies the capitalist project that propels us toward the edge, blindly, indifferent to the fact that the ledge is far closer than even the most critical anticipated. It's a mass experiment in neoliberal reason, unleashed. As we see the Amazon or cities like Los Angeles burn, and these and other vistas reach us through the news cycle, the climate denier right-wing global network and their billionaire supporters oscillate between monetizing and denial. In the meantime, new extractive waves keep "destroying the Earth's system as a place of human habitability," as Foster observes, in ways that make capitalism not "commensurate with any plausible scenario of human survival," concludes the Salvage Collective.[30]

The Ultimate Enclosure

"There are no such things as limits to growth, because there are no limits on the human capacity for intelligence, imagination, and wonder," Ronald Reagan told graduates during a Commencement speech. He was responding to the Club of Rome's 1972 *Limits of Growth* report, which Milton Friedman had already discredited. The belief is that there are no limits, and that, in case there were any, markets would take care of any necessary adjustments.[31]

If neoliberal storytelling makes the main challenges of our times appear to dissolve, the unprecedented conditions created by climate change intensify extreme weather at a speed that no technology, market innovation, or human effort can beat. There is a point beyond which the planet "simply cannot accommodate anymore," Meadows, one of the authors of the *Limits of Growth* report, notes. Overshoot leads to "disease, scarcity, climate" as life and physical systems, and the articulations between them, get disrupted. Still, governments and corporations are embarking on even more expansive extractive initiatives.[32]

The neoliberal take on climate catastrophe consists in commodifying the response. In 2018, the story that Kim Kardashian and Kayne West had their $60 million Calabasas home saved by private firefighters broke in the news. Wildfire Defense Systems, a company supplying insurance companies, reports to have conducted "more than 1,300 wildfire responses on behalf of insurers." By early 2025, as LA burned, private firefighters could be hired for $2,000 an hour. In what Raymond Craib describes as "'exit' projects," fans of private government—including Patri Friedman, Milton's grandson—have been experimenting with things including from "seasteading to special economic zones to proprietary cities." Imbued with technoutopian faith, love for entrepreneurship, and the assimilation of "private property rights with freedom," these wealthy groups are basically planning to escape from the disasters and from the rest of us.[33]

"If you're going to be able to survive underground, we want you to be having fun," declares Al Corbi, a leading bunker designer, to CNN. Bowling alleys, flying and outside climate simulators, operating rooms, lavish décor, thirty-year supplies, James Bond-like hideouts, and secret passages are some of the features that the ultra-wealthy include in their "uber-prime" bunkers. Bill Gates is said to have one such bunker connected to each of his homes.[34]

Resource-intensive, securitized private communities sheltered from the climate are available to the wealthy. For now. The ever larger fires in

California show that, when dry weather combines with 100 mph gusts, fire spreads so fast that fire hydrants may run dry and helicopters cannot fly—not even for the uber-wealthy.[35] "There's no number of helicopters or trucks that we can buy, no number of firefighters that we can have, no amount of brush that we can clear that will stop this," observed the mayor of Los Angeles, Eric Garcetti, in a 2019 interview.[36]

In its pursuit of ever-increasing profits, capital reveals a self-destructing dynamic, which threatens "its own substance," Nancy Fraser points out, and, of course, our lives. In what Craig Collins describes as "catabolic" and Fraser as "cannibal," ongoing capitalist practices—overexploiting waged and unpaid labor, profiting from public works and goods while undermining them, corrupting and corroding democracy, and destroying entire habitats, supported on militarism—capital accelerates a multipronged crisis impacting all areas of life.

The current, rapid change of Earth systems is "closely associated with the system of capital accumulation and is pointing society toward an Anthropocene-extinction event," Foster notes. For all its scientific conservatism, the Intergovernmental Panel on Climate Change (IPCC), formed in 1988 by the United Nations Environmental Programme, projects a potential increase of 4C by the end of this century. And yet nobody knows how Earth and oceanic systems will behave as we get closer to even 2C degrees.

On their part, driven by climate collapse, the COVID-19 pandemic, and AI, the world's most powerful are planning for some literal end of the world. "We are up against end times fascism," warn Naomi Klein and Astra Taylor. The austerity and authoritarianism we are experiencing are not just a revival of "the old marriage of neoliberalism and neoconservatism," they argue, not even of the "Chicago Boys" and Pinochet. The wealthiest and most powerful, Klein and Taylor argue, have given up on liberal democracy as much as on "the livability of our shared world," and they have "made peace with mass death." They are planning for an exit plan for themselves and a select few to luxury bunkers and private cities, to "transhumanism," or even to Mars. And they are determined to "expel and imprison unwanted humans" as they are to "violently claim the land and resources" needed for their survival, whether it is food, water, or an entire continent. Meanwhile, ongoing deregulations dismantling health, environmental, energy, and social policies, or disaster planning for the masses, accelerate the prospects of collapse. In fact, "crisis, conflict and collapse can be extremely profitable" in the short term, Collins observes. Corporations profit from mining and oil extraction as permafrost thaws and the deep sea exploration continues, while governments, whether they are market faithful, desperate, corrupt—or all the above—lift environmental protections.[37]

We have a better understanding of the mechanics of climate change than of how to change the politics supporting them, Joel Wainwright and Geoff Mann note. The IPCC has for decades brought together hundreds of scientists to assess the climate, summarizing the state of the art about climate across fields, and offering policy blueprints. While sharing increasingly sobering data and projections, IPCC reports sound mostly optimistic. Urging governments to meet climate goals—that keep being bypassed—documents call for "climate resilient development," through forms of "effective and equitable climate action" that "secure a livable future for all." While such efforts are crucial, the IPCC privileges mainstream consensus that has "consistently underestimated the real pace of climate change." Mann and Wainwright thus revisit the unrealistic assumptions and lack of political analysis in IPCC reports. In their narrative, massive climate and environmental disruptions seem not to have more than a "modest" impact on a global economy that gets treated as stable across mounting disasters. Trusting that humans "will figure out how to live in a hotter planet" and that adaptation will continue to be possible seem questionable at least, as is the IPCC's hopeful framing of its damning data.[38]

Wainwright and Mann look for the politics that can help us navigate the challenging conditions to come. Unfolding scenarios, they argue, will be shaped by competing political responses to planetary changes along capitalist vs. noncapitalist and pro-sovereign vs. pro-autonomous lines. Four types result from these alignments. The first one, Climate Leviathan, represents the "dream of a sustainable capitalist status quo," in the form of a planetary sovereign imposing adaptation efforts by monitoring and governing resources and populations. The authors call a noncapitalist sovereign alternative Climate Mao. Moving away from centralized state responses, arise, first, a libertarian capitalist antistate whose politics Wainwright and Mann describe as "a reactionary capitalist Behemoth." Finally, the anticapitalist decentralized alternative involves a grassroots-based "anti-sovereign Climate X." The latter, which the authors judge "ethically and politically superior" considering its democratic and inclusive possibilities, seems to be the direction that dominates among those on the left. Among them, Pierre Dardot calls for the state to undergo a "considerable" transformation alongside the "logic of the common" that lets people take democratic control of their lives.[39]

On their part, echoing these arguments, Jodi Dean and Kai Heron emphasize the imperative to move beyond the capitalist system that brought us here. "We need to break from capitalism. It really is ruin or revolution," they contend. No Green New Deal or communal systems will take us anywhere, less so diluting the capitalist core of the crisis with euphemisms such as "Anthropocene." Capital is at the very center of the changing climate, and responses require "a state-led, centrally planned, and global response," they argue, that takes advantage of government instruments and resources. The state, as Dean and Heron put it, stands as "a ready-made apparatus for responding to the climate crisis," superior to the dominant imagination of localized responses. State resources can and should be steered to effectively research, plan for, and reorganize our food, production, communications, transportation, energy, and systems, ultimately "backed by a standing army," Dean and Heron note. The challenge then is to put all state resources at the service of workers' collective power to rebuild egalitarian, nonexploitative, and sustainable social relations from the bottom-up, the authors conclude. They call their proposal Climate Leninism.[40]

One idea central to our societies that gets put into question is that of growth. Too bad for Ronald Reagan's enthusiasm, unlimited growth is "not possible," Dennis Meadows reflects decades after coauthoring the 1972 *Limits of Growth* report. Not only is unlimited growth not possible, he notes, but going beyond "the physical limits of the planet leads to collapse."[41]

Back in the 1970s, Flavia Boffroni reports, scientists from the Bariloche Foundation responded to the *Limits of Growth* report. Inequality in resource distribution was at the root of the crisis, they argued, as they noted that "other alternatives" were available. Along these lines, experiences of what Thea Riofrancos calls resource nationalism developed that sought to use the revenue from extractive exports to promote egalitarian and democratic forms of development and redistribute wealth. Yet, as Eduardo Gudynas notes, resource nationalism often ended up resorting to "similar conventional strategies" that hurt rural communities and the environment.[42]

Recent years saw the development of the paradigm of degrowth, which seeks "a planned reduction of energy and resource throughput designed to bring the economy back into balance with the living world," as Jason Hickel explains. In response to the environmental and climate crises, through planning, destructive activities can be minimized while still expanding wherever is needed to support marginalized communities, Hickel argues. Accompanied by and making "universal public goods and services" such as education and healthcare widely available, we could "achieve a rapid transition to renewable energy, restore soils and biodiversity, and reverse ecological breakdown," Hickel notes.[43]

And yet, some argue that societal collapse is already underway. "Polycrisis, multicrisis . . . collapse" are just some of the words used by scientists to describe our trajectory, Flavia Boffroni observes. Gathering a wealth of scientific research, Jem Bendell concludes that we are at the start of "an uneven ending of industrial consumer modes of sustenance, shelter, health, security, pleasure, identity and meaning." This process, "irreversible," he notes, signals the start of "societal collapse." Bendell offers insights on how to best transit societal breakdown through "less-oppressive ways of being and behaving." Resources, he argues, should become "commonly-owned" through appropriate organizations and platforms to allow for "a gentler and fairer collapse."[44]

On their part, Pablo Servigne, Raphaël Stevens, and Gauthier Chapelle describe "global systemic collapse" as a series of interconnected events worsened by pandemics, industrial disasters, desertification, pollution, mass extinctions, economic and political crisis, or war. The collapse of what they call "thermo-industrial civilization" unravels across numerous locations and—they contend—"it has already begun."

Adding a practical perspective, Boffroni points out that when essential needs including "water, food, housing, clothing, energy" are no longer accessible at an affordable cost, "that is collapse." In the end, societal collapse leads to "a loss of complexity." The end of oil, in particular, as a viable energy source, and the lack of a replacement to keep "business as usual," makes Alice Friedemann hopeful that we will be able to avoid the worst of climate catastrophe. With the decline of oil, societies "will revert to biomass for thermal energy, as well as muscle, river, and wind power just as in the past," she notes. The "Great Simplification" of life conditions will pose countless challenges, though.[45]

These perspectives offer a glimpse of the difficulties and possibilities that lie ahead, as they call for further research and debate—and political organizing. One such challenge is that "right-wing religions, politicians, and capitalists would seem to prefer the Four Horsemen to arrive in the future rather than to forgo ever-increasing profits," Friedemann notes.[46]

Neither the politics of extinction of neoliberal reason nor its governmentalities of emergency are destiny, however. Economic growth is only necessary under capitalism, as De Angelis observes, while commons-based societies can "survive with alternative means of livelihood and exchange that are not directly measured in terms of economic growth." We have the rights, the commons, and repertoires ranging from protests to assemblies to revolutions, in forms that will keep expanding as political and planetary conditions change. And as we learn to best repair and take care of our world, we must start with dismantling neoliberal reason.[47]

Notes

CHAPTER I

1. Nelson Sandoval Díaz, "Las frases más controvertidas del ex dictador Augusto Pinochet," *Efenoticia*, December 11, 2006; "Pinochet 'Diritti umani? Che Cosa Sono?," *La Stampa*, August 5, 1995; Winn, "Pinochet Regime," *Victims of the Chilean Miracle*, 19; Snyder, "Dirty Legal War." The measures included a state of siege that subjected civilians to military tribunals, a state of emergency, and a state of danger or disturbance to internal peace; Hobsbawm, "Chile: Year One," 231; Waldstein, "In Chile's National Stadium."

2. Friedman, "Free Markets and the Generals"; Sebastian Edwards, *The Chile Project: The Story of the Chicago Boys and the Downfall of Neoliberalism* (Princeton: Princeton University Press, 2023), 14; Guillermina Seri and David Siegel , "Between Marx and Foucault: Blending Critical Epistemologies in the Study of Neoliberalism." *Critical Review*, December 2025, 1–33.

3. Sebastian Edwards, "Social Revolt in Chile: The End of Neoliberalism?," *Milken Review*, May 4, 2020, www.milkenreview.org/articles/social-revolt-in-chile-the-end-of-neoliberalism; Saad-Filho, "From COVID-19 to the End of Neoliberalism," 479.

4. Louis Menand, "The Rise and Fall of Neoliberalism," *New Yorker*, July 17, 2023; "What Comes After Neoliberalism?," *Project Syndicate*, June 4, 2024; Louis Menand; "Joe Biden's Radical Legacy," *More Perfect Union*, YouTube, min. 15:30–16:10 www.youtube.com/watch?v=BHUGVEThmsg; Jamieson, David, "Trump's Protectionist Turn Is a Death Blow for Neoliberalism," Jacobin, April 3, 2025.

5. Jen Moore and Manuel Pérez Rocha, *Extraction Casino*, Institute for Policy Studies, 2019, 16; "What Comes After Neoliberalism?," *Project Syndicate*, June 4, 2024,

6. Friedman, "Neo-Liberalism and Its Prospects," 3; Harvey, *Brief History*, 3; Kotsko, "Neoliberalism's Demons," 494; Robert A. Packenham and William Ratliff, "What Pinochet Did for Chile," Hoover Institution, January 30, 2007.

7. Foster, "Absolute Capitalism," 1.

8. Gudynas, "Beyond Varieties of Development," 725; Riofrancos, *Resource Radicals*, 11, 38–50; "Javier Milei: 'Soy el máximo exponente de la libertad a nivel mundial,'" *Letra P*, May 21, 2024, www.letrap.com.ar/

9. Pascale Bonnefoy, "With Pensions Like This ($315 a Month), Chileans Wonder How They'll Ever Retire," *New York Times*, September 13, 2016; Andre Gunder Frank's letters, www.rrojasdatabank.info/agfrank/index.html; Mandel, "Origins of National Socialism"; Fraser, "Can Society Be Commodities All the Way Down?," 542; Davis-Hamel, "Successful Neoliberalism?"; Taylor, "Historical-Materialist Critique," 53.

10. Letelier, "'Chicago Boys' in Chile"; Valdés and Rojas Martini, "Neoliberal Chilean Process," 29; Federico Glodowsky, "A 45 años del inicio del régimen de valorización financiera de la dictadura cívico-militar: El modelo económico de Martínez de Hoz," *Pagina12*, March 28, 2021.

11. O'Donnell, *Democracia en la Argentina*, 10.

12. Since 1958, a USAID-funded program brought dozens of Chileans to the University of Chicago, six of whom got their PhDs trained in neoclassical economics under Friedman and others. Sebastian Edwards, *The Chile Project: The Story of the Chicago Boys and the Downfall of Neoliberalism* (Princeton: Princeton University Press, 2023), 1; Renée Sallas, "Friedrich von Hayek, Leader and Master of Liberalism" (interview with Friedrich Hayek), *El Mercurio*, Santiago de Chile, April 12, 1981, D8-D9.

13. Hayek, *Road to Serfdom*, 110; Montes, "Friedman's Two Visits to Chile," 11; Robin, *Reactionary Mind*, 74–75; Robin, "Nietzsche, Hayek," 110.

14. Arnol Kremer, "Review of *El dictador: The Secret and Public History of Jorge Rafael Videla* (Maria Seoane, Vicente Muleiro)," *Insumisos*, Southern Cone edition, April 22, 2001; Foster, "Absolute Capitalism."

15. World Bank, "World Development Indicators," GDP (current U$S), data.worldbank.org/indicator/NY.GDP.MKTP.CD; Ortiz and Cummins, "Austerity," 5.

16. Robert A. Packenham and William Ratliff, "What Pinochet Did for Chile," Hoover Institution, January 30, 2007

17. Edurne Garde, "Las cifras de la dictadura" *La Vanguardia*, March 3, 2020; Enrique Gutiérrez, "Batalla campal en provocador homenaje a Pinochet en Chile," *La Jornada*, June 11, 2012; Winn, "Pinochet Regime," 21; Davis-Hamel, "Successful Neoliberalism?"; Orellana Calderón, "In Chile," 105; Pérez, Angélica, "Chile dice adiós a la Constitución de los 'Chicago Boys,'" *Radio France Internationale*, October 16, 2020; Leiva, *Left Hand of Capital*, 11.

18. O'Donnell, *Democracia en la Argentina*, 10; Herre, Bastian, "The 'Regimes of the World' data: how do researchers measure democracy?" *OurWorldInData*, 2021; Whyte, *Morals of the Market*, 4.

19. Mattei, qtd. in Justin Villamil, "New Age of Austerity," *Inkstick*, March 13, 2024.

20. Davidson and Ward. *Cities Under Austerity*, 8; O'Connor, "Marxism and the Three Movements of Neoliberalism," 700.

21. Ong, *Neoliberalism as Exception*, 5; Kasmir, "Precarity"; Butler, *Performative Theory of Assembly*, 33.

22. Lührmann et al., *Autocratization Surges*, 7; Aislinn Laing and Natalia A. Ramos, "Chile's Piñera Extends State of Emergency," Reuters, October 21, 2019; Dave Sherwood and Natalia A. Ramos Miranda, "One Million Chileans March in Santiago," *Reuters*, October 25, 2019.

23. Alexis Cortés, "El octubre chileno: El neoliberalismo ¿nació y morirá en Chile?" *Open Democracy*, January 23, 2020.

24. Alicia Trabucco Terán, "Chile: Estado de Emergencia," *Palabra Pública*, November 10, 2019.

25. Pérez, "Chile dice adiós a la Constitución de los 'Chicago Boys.'"

26. Cortés, "El octubre chileno: El neoliberalismo ¿nació y morirá en Chile?," *Open Democracy*, January 23, 2020; Gerbaudo, "Pandemic Crowd," 62; Boese et al., *Autocratization Changing Nature?*, 26; Nord et al., *Democracy Report 2024*, 6, 9.

27. The United States dropped below the "democracy threshold" (+6) on the Polity scale in 2020.

28. Nazifa Alisada et al. "Autocratization Turns Viral," *Democracy Report* 2021, V-Dem Institute, University of Gothenburg: Lührmann et al., *Autocratization Surges*, 2, 9, 19, 28, 26, 6.

29. Galtung, "Violence, Peace, and Peace Research."

30. Friedman, qtd. in Whyte, *Morals of the Market*, 238.

31. Brown, *Undoing the Demos*, 142, 151.

32. Foucault, *Security, Territory, Population*, 108; Foucault, *Birth of Biopolitics*, 14, 131; The expression *conduire des conduits* appeared originally in French (*Dits et écrits IV*, 237).

33. Blakeley, *State Terrorism and Neoliberalism*, 160; Oksala, "Violence and Neoliberal Governmentality," 475.

34. Zamora, introduction to *Foucault and Neoliberalism*, 4; Behrent, "Liberalism without Humanism," 53. Foucault's endorsement of neoliberalism would be consistent with the view advanced by François Ewald, one of his students, collaborators, and editors. In this account, disenchanted with the authoritarian turn in socialist countries and the crisis of social democracy in Europe, Foucault would have seen "new possibilities for liberty" in neoliberalism, as Ewald put it. Indeed, in the 1970s, a number of French leftists were becoming neoliberals—including Ewald, a former Maoist—and even socialist governments were adopting market policies. Picturing this scenario, together with Zamora, Dean, and others, Behrent has made the case regarding Foucault's endorsement of neoliberal ideas that the dominant reception of his work by the left may have overlooked. Foucault's interest in neoliberalism, these authors point out, seems related to the expectation of a "far less intrusive technique of population management" and human interactions that could potentially expand room for personal autonomy. Foucault, Zamora observes, sees neoliberalism as the state's "withdrawal of its techniques of subjection." The idea in Foucault's lectures that neoliberalism makes the market the ultimate site of truth and veridiction, highlighted by Dean, can be seen as part of expectations of less state intrusiveness.

Ewald went further. In a meeting with Gary Becker, a prominent neoliberal scholar whose assimilation of human behavior to a self-maximizing model of market gains and losses Foucault discusses in his lectures, Ewald expressed that Becker's *Homo Oeconomicus* was "what Foucault searched for with his theory of the subject and of subjectivity," Dean writes (Mitchell Dean, "Foucault, Ewald, and Neoliberalism," in *Foucault and Neoliberalism*, ed. Daniel Zamora and Michael C. Behrent [Cambridge: Polity, 2016], 90). On his part, in reference to Foucault's work, Becker notes: "I like most of it, and I do not disagree with much. I also cannot tell whether Foucault is disagreeing with me."

To Zamora, Becker's finding "himself in perfect agreement with Foucault's analysis of his own text" serves as the ultimate proof of Foucault's neoliberal sympathies. Once Foucault's neoliberal credentials are supposedly established, Zamora objects to drawing on Foucault to support a critique of neoliberalism on grounds that Foucault declared that he was trying "to 'get rid of Marxism.'"

Taking distance from such interpretations, Dean identifies Antonio Negri, Colin Gordon, and Thomas Lemke as among those who position Foucault on the left. Surely Foucault's relation to Marx and Marxism has been the subject of debate. Revisiting such questions, Bob Jessop refers to Foucault's paradoxical "outspoken opposition to official and vulgar Marxist positions and an implicit appropriation and development of insights from Marx himself" (Jessop, "From Micro-Powers to Governmentality," 3). Indeed, while Foucault did object to "Marxism," in an interview published in *Power/Knowledge*, he acknowledges that he "often quote[s] concepts, texts and phrases from Marx, but without feeling obliged to add the authenticating label of a footnote with a laudatory phrase to accompany the quotation. . . . I quote Marx without saying so, without quotation marks" (Foucault, "Prison Talk," *Power/Knowledge*, 52).

Comparing his use of Marx's texts to physicists who do not need to quote Isaac Newton as everyone in the field recognizes his theories, Foucault adds: "It is impossible at the present time to write history without using a whole range of concepts directly or indirectly linked to Marx's thought and situating oneself within a horizon of thought which has been defined and described by Marx" (Foucault, "Prison Talk," *Power/Knowledge*, 53).

Along these lines, after listing various "Marxisms" criticized by Foucault, Jessop reminds us of his "uninterrupted dialogue" with Marx and acknowledges his seminal contributions to illuminate capital's radical remaking of power and subjectivities. In agreement with Jessop's assessment, my engagement with neoliberal reason and its governmentalities summons the Marxian critique of capital as much as Foucault's work and contributions.

35. Whyte, "Is Revolution Desirable?," Foucault, *Birth of Biopolitics*, 118. Ravecca, *Politics of Political Science*, 26. Ferreira-Neto, "Right of the Governed," 86.

36. Foster, "Absolute Capitalism."

37. Davidson-Harden, "Interrogating the University,'" 578; John Bew, "Revenge of the Nation-State," *New Statesman*, November 2018.

38. Thucydides, *Peloponnesian War*, 145. Laclau and Mouffe, *Hegemony and Socialist Strategy*, 188. Rancière, *Hatred of Democracy*, 72.

39. Marx, *Capital*, 1:415–16; Rancière, "Who Is the Subject, 305.

40. Kotsko, "Neoliberalism's Demons," 493.

41. Orellana Calderón, "Post-Neoliberal Future," 105; Hayek, *Road to Serfdom*, 110.

42. Foucault, *Birth of Biopolitics*, 28.

43. Foucault, *Security, Territory, Population*, 377; Foucault, *Birth of Biopolitics*, 5.

44. Foucault, *Security, Territory, Population*, 241, 289.

45. Foucault, *Security, Territory, Population*, 241, 289; Viroli, "Reason of State," 73.

46. Foucault, *Security, Territory, Population*, 289, 343, 452.

47. Meinecke, *Machiavellism*; Rosenblum, "Constitutional Reason of State," 147; Botero, *Reason of State*, 3.

48. Foucault, *Birth of Biopolitics*, 4. Foucault, *Security, Territory, Population*, 248.

49. Foucault, *Birth of Biopolitics*, 313, 28.

50. Hobbes, *Leviathan*, 32, 1; Agamben, *Leviathan's Riddle*, 28; Neocleous, *Imagining the State*, 4; Kalmo and Skinner, "Sovereign State," 3.

51. Brown, *States of Injury*, 176; Poole, *Reason of State*, 2.

52. Butler, *Precarious Life*, 54; Loughlin, *Public Law*, 380; Poole, *Reason of State*, 17.

53. Locke, *Two Treatises of Government*, 374–80; Neocleous, "Security, Liberty and the Myth of Balance," 136.

54. Poole, *Reason of State*, 129, 148, 150, 17; Smith, *Wealth of Nations*, 456; Nigro, "From Reason of State to Liberalism," 132–33.

55. Foucault, *Birth of Biopolitics*, 102, 294, 28, 321, 102, 33, 45; Foucault, *Security, Territory, Population*, 448, 13, 15; Poole, *Reason of State*, 129.

56. Foucault, *Birth of Biopolitics*, 22.

57. Foucault, *Birth of Biopolitics*, 28.

58. Arendt, *Eichmann in Jerusalem*, 291.

59. Madra and Adaman, *Neoliberal Reason*, 700.

60. Friedman, "Neo-Liberalism and Its Prospects," 3; Friedrich, "Road to Serfdom," 575–79.

61. Hayek, *Constitution of Liberty*, 6, 11, 29, 37.

62. Hayek, *Road to Serfdom*, 156, 112, and *Constitution of Liberty*, 21; Poole, *Reason of State*, 231, 229, 234, 239, 233.

63. Hayek, *Constitution of Liberty*, 217, 159; Poole, *Reason of State*, 234.

64. Friedman, *Capitalism and Freedom*, 9, 13, 25; Poole, *Reason of State*, 231, 229, 234, 239; Stedman Jones, *Masters of the Universe*, 69; Hayek, *Road to Serfdom*, 112.

65. Friedman, *Capitalism and Freedom*, 27, 34.

66. Friedman, *Capitalism and Freedom*, 191, 34; Hayek, *Constitution of Liberty*, 285.

67. Hayek, *Constitution of Liberty*, 297.

68. Hayek, *Road to Serfdom*, 110, and *Constitution of Liberty*, 103.

69. Bonefeld, "Free Economy and the Strong State," 16–17; see Hayek's 1981 declarations to *El Mercurio*, endnote 12; Runciman, *Confidence Trap*, 207; Friedman, "Free Markets and the Generals," 59.

70. Tucker Carlson, interview with Javier Milei, September 14, 2023, x.com/Tucker Carlson/status/1702442099814342725?lang=en

71. Brown, *Undoing the Demos*, 179; Prados-de-la-Escosura, "History of Economic Freedom."

72. Bew, "Revenge of the Nation-State," 45; Neocleous, *Fabrication of Social Order*, xii.

73. Abhijit Banerjee and Esther Duflo, "Foreword," in Lucas Chancel et al. *World Inequality Report* 2022. Cambridge: Harvard University Press, 2022; Djelic and Mousavi, "How the Neoliberal Think Tank Went Global."

74. Wiliamson, "What Washington Means by Policy Reform"; Rodrik, "Goodbye Washington Consensus," 973.

75. Dey, "Fall of Market Democracy in Europe," *Economic & Political Weekly*, August 13, 2016. The GINI Index measures wealth inequality, with 0 representing perfect equality and 1 representing perfect inequality. For 2023, the World Inequality Database estimates a 0.63 GINI for the US, UBS puts it at 0.75, and the World Bank at 0.398—the gap between these different estimates is puzzling; *UBS 2024 Global Wealth Report*, 23.

76. O'Connor, "Three Movements of Neoliberalism," 696.

77. International Monetary Fund, "IMF Conditionality," www.imf.org/en/About/Fa ctsheets/Sheets/2016/08/02/21/28/IMF-Conditionality

78. "Bolivia Now Under State of Siege," Associated Press, September 20, 1985.

79. Williamson, "What Washington Means"; Klein, *Shock Doctrine*, 18–19.

80. G. Fuchs and L. Brown, "Venezuela's Caracazo: How neoliberal failure led to state repression," *Green Left*, 2016.

81. Stokes, *Mandates and Democracy*; Men T. et al., "Russian Mortality Trends for 1991–2001: analysis by cause and region," BMJ. October 25;327(7421):964 (2003).

82. Fukuyama, "Capitalism and Democracy"; O'Donnell, *Democracia en la Argentina*, 16.

83. Fraser, *The Old Is Dying*, 8.

84. Josefina L. Martínez, "El espejismo del thatcherismo y las nuevas derechas en el declive," *La Izquierda Diario*, March 3, 2024.

85. Marso, *Feminism*, 42–44; Marso, " Feeling Like a Barbie: On Greta Gerwig and Chantal Akerman," *Los Angeles Review of Books*. August 18, 2023.

86. Ravecca, *Politics of Political Science*, 148.

87. Foucault, *Birth of Biopolitics*, 224–27.

88. Foucault, *Birth of Biopolitics*, 229, 244; Madra and Adaman, "Neoliberal Reason," 708.

89. Oksala, "Violence and Neoliberal Governmentality," 475; Brown, *Undoing the Demos*, 109.

90. Fraser, "Commodities All the Way Down," 542.

91. Han, *Psychopolitics*, 36–37, 25.

92. Sabuktay, "Extra-Legal Activities," 512; Blakeley, *State Terrorism and Neoliberalism*, 7.

93. Amy Goodman, "Bolivian Activist Oscar Olivera on Bechtel's Privatization of Rainwater and Why Evo Morales Should Remember the Ongoing Struggle over Water," *Democracy Now*, October 5, 2006; "Management: A Tale of Three Cities," *Précis 222*, World Bank, 1; Emily Achtenberg, "From Water Wars to Water Scarcity: Bolivia's Cautionary Tale," *ReVista. Harvard Review of Latin America* XII(2).

94. Tosa, "Anarchical Governance," 414; Wright, *Emergency Politics*, xiii.

95. Brian Kenety, "Development: Report Details Pattern of Southern Resistance," *Interpress Service*, September 25, 2000.

96. Kotz, "Financial and Economic Crisis of 2008," 307; Exner, Hochleithner, and Kumnig, "Expanding the Scope," 5; Laliotis, Ioannidis, and Stavropoulou, "Total and Cause-Specific Mortality," e56-e65; Lizarraga, "Las cifras ocultas de los suicidios por desahucio"; Melanie Haiken, "More Than 10,000 Suicides Tied to Economic Crisis, Study Says," *Forbes*, June 12, 2014.

97. Lucas, qtd. in Harbert, "Here's How Much the 2008 Bailouts Really Cost," *MIT Management Sloan School*, www.mitsloan.mit.edu/ideas-made-to-matter/heres-how-much-2008-bailouts-really-cost

98. Elizabeth Jackson, "Timeline: Notable Government Bailout, Relief Programs in U.S. History," *USA Today*, November 13, 2023; Gerald Epstein and Robert Pollin, "Neoliberalism's Bailout Problem," *Boston Review*, June 24, 2021.

99. Ostry, Loungani, and Furceri, "Neoliberalism, Oversold?"; Dey, "Fall of Market Democracy in Europe"; Ortiz and Cummins, "Austerity," 21.

100. Murphy, "Rise of the Precariat?," 74–75; Standing, "Precariat," 10; International Labor Organization, *World Employment and Social Outlook Trends 2020* and *World Employment and Social Outlook Trends 2023*, 49; Tosa, "Anarchical Governance," 427.

101. Ong, *Neoliberalism as Exception*, 202; Agamben, *Homo Sacer*, 12.

102. Marx, *Capital*, 1:896 and note on 1:1141; de Boever, "Agamben and Marx," 259.

103. Marx, *Capital*, vol. 1, chapters 26 and 27.

104. Moore, *Web of Life*, 27.

105. Otto et al., *Mining Royalties*; Artiga-Purcell et al., "Disaster Extractivism," 2.

106. Svampa, "El 'Consenso de los Commodities'"; Brand, Dietz, and Lang, "Neo-Extractivism in Latin America."

107. Harvey, qtd. in Moore, *Web of Life*, 164; Sly, M. "Argentine Portion of the Soy Commodity Chain," *Palgrave Communication* 3, 17095 (2017) fig. 1; Stephan Lutter, Ste-

fan Giljum and Julia Kreimel, "Domestic Extraction of World in 1970–2024, by Material Group," *Material Flows.Net*, www.materialflows.net

108. Weinberg: "Bolivia's New Water Wars," 23; Valdivia, "Sacrificial Zones"; Artiga-Purcell et al., "Disaster Extractivism," 2.

109. Hund et al., *Minerals for Climate Action*; Montalván Zambrano and Wences, "Transición energética," 436.

110. Scheidel, "Renewables Grabbing," 189; EJAtlas ejatlas.org; Araghi and Karides, "Land Dispossession and Global Crisis," 1–5.

111. Weinberg: "Bolivia's New Water Wars," 23; Schwenk, "Wall Street Is Buying Up Entire Neighborhoods."

112. Mariani, "Law, Order, and Neoliberalism," 4; Montalván Zambrano and Wences, "Transición energética y litio," 419.

113. Blakeley, *State Terrorism and Neoliberalism*, 160; Valcárcel and Samudio, "Colombia: Durable Solutions."

114. "Jared Kushner Says Gaza's 'Waterfront Property Could Be Very Valuable,'" *Guardian*, March 19, 2024; Yuval Barnea, "From Crisis to Prosperity: Netanyahu's Vision for Gaza 2035 Revealed Online," *Jerusalem Post*, May 3, 2024.

115. International Criminal Court, "Report of the Panel of Experts in International Law," May 20, 2024, www.icc-cpi.int/sites/default/files/2024-05/240520-panel-report-eng.pdf; Barlow, Rich, "Trump Says the United States Should Seize and Develop Gaza. Is That a Good Idea?" *Boston University Today*, February 6, 2025; OCHA (United Nations Office for the Coordination of Humanitarian Affairs), "Reported Impact Snapshot," November 6, 2025, http://www.ochaopt.org/content/reported-impact-snapshot-gaza-strip-5-november-2025.

116. Foster, "Nature as a Mode of Accumulation."

117. Statista, und Global Carbon Budget, "Annual carbon dioxide (CO_2) emissions worldwide from 1940 to 2024 (in billion metric tons)," Chart. November 13, 2024.

118. Moore, *Web of Life*, 195; H. Lee and J. Romero, "Climate Change 2023: Synthesis Report. Contribution of Working Groups I, II and III to the Sixth Assessment Report of the Intergovernmental Panel on Climate Change," Geneva, Switzerland," IPCC, 68, 4; Foster, "Absolute Capitalism."

119. Mandel, "Origins of National Socialism."

120. Foster, "Absolute Capitalism"; De Angelis, *Omnia Sunt Communia*, 136; Dardot and Laval, *Dominar*, 34.

121. Moses, "Collapse of Civilisation"; Orellana Calderón, "Post-Neoliberal Future," 107.

122. Davis, "Crimes"; Agamben, *State of Exception*, 14.

CHAPTER 2

1. Swati Sharma, "'It Is Horror'. French President's Remarks after Paris terrorist attacks," *Washington Post*, November 15, 2015.

2. EM-DAT, *The International Disaster Database*, public.emdat.be/data; Heifer, "Rethinking Derogations," 20, 7; Wright, *Emergency Politics*, xiii.

3. Jennifer C. Rubenstein, "Canonical Emergency Stories," paper presented at the Association for Political Theory 22nd annual conference, November 21–23, Virginia Tech, Blacksburg, VA, 2024.

4. Bremner, "This Is War and Our Enemy Will Strike Again, French Told," *Times*, November 17, 2015.

5. Cypel, "Hollande's War on Liberties," *The New York Times*, November 25, 2015.

6. Paye, "Sovereignty and the State of Emergency."

7. Louise Nordstrom, "In Numbers: Behind France's Two-Year State of Emergency," *France 24*, November 7, 2017.

8. Amnesty International, "A Right Not a Threat: Disproportionate Restrictions on Demonstrations Under the State of Emergency in France," May 30, 2017, 12, 14, 16, 24.

9. "France: State of Emergency Officially Ends as New Security Measures Come into Force," *Global Legal Monitor*, November 29, 2017; Amnesty International, *Report 2017/18: The State of the World's Human Rights*, February 22, 2018, 14.

10. Lisa Bryant, "In France, Drones, Apps and Racial Profiling," *Voice of America*, June 23, 2020; French Constitution, Article 49.3; Aurelien Breeden, "France Adopts Laws to Combat Terrorism, but Critics Call Them Overreaching," *New York Times*, July 23, 2021; Amnesty International, "France 2021."

11. Sheeran, "States of Emergency," 504.

12. United Nations. *International Covenant on Civil and Political Rights*; Heifer, "Rethinking Derogations"; Council of Europe, "France Informs Secretary General of Article 15," November 25, 2015.

13. Torbisco Casals, "Covid-19 and States of Emergency"; Amanda B. Edgell et al. "Pandemic Backsliding: Democracy during COVID-19 (PanDem). V-Dem Institute, www.v-dem.net/pandem

14. Agamben, "State of Exception," 87, 164; Poole, "Judicial Review," 83; Neocleous, "Problem with Normality"; Prozorov, "Farewell to Homo Sacer," 67; Conor Bean, "Potential without Exception: Emergency Powers After Agamben and Schmitt," paper presented at the Association for Political Theory 22nd annual conference, November 21–23, Virginia Tech, Blacksburg, VA, 2024, 3–8, 20–22.

15. "Paraguay: Many Confused as 33 Years of State of Siege Expires," *Inter Press Service*, April 10, 1987.

16. Gross, "What 'Emergency Regime'"? 78; Ferejohn and Pasquino, "Emergency Powers"; National Defense Authorization Act for Fiscal Year 2012; Carey and Shugart, *Executive Decree Authority*, 3, 5, 9, 13, 16.

17. Hussain, *Jurisprudence of Emergency*, 17; Agamben, *State of Exception*, 50.

18. Neocleous, "Martial Law," 15, 18; Poole, *Reason of State*, 16; Sir Frederick Pollock, qtd. in "Martial Law," *Encyclopedia Britannica*.

19. Neocleous, "Martial Law," 15.

20. Hussain, *Jurisprudence of Emergency*, 3; Neocleous, *Critique of Security*, 8; Dafnos, Thompson, and French, "Surveillance and the Colonial Dream," 20.

21. Agamben, *State of Exception*, 13; Poole, *Reason of State*, 16; Jeffrey Herf, "Emergency Powers Helped Hitler's Rise: Germany Has Avoided Them Ever Since," *Washington Post*, February 19, 2019; Scheppele, "Symposium: Emergency Powers"; Neocleous, "Problem with Normality," 194–95.

22. Ferejohn and Pasquino, "Emergency Powers," 339.

23. Despouy, "Report by the UN Special Rapporteur"; Calloni, "Los Archivos del Horror del Operativo Cóndor," NIZKOR, www.derechos.org/nizkor/doc/condor/calloni.html #Ibid; Dunkerley, *Pacification of Central America*.

24. Narkunas, "Human Rights and States of Emergency"; Gross and Aoláin, *Law in Times of Crisis*, 3.

25. Katharina Buchholz, "Natural Disasters on the Rise around the Globe," *Statista*, August 25, 2020; EM-DAT, CRED / UCLouvain, 2025, Brussels, Belgium – www.emdat .be; Scheppele, "Underreaction"; Varieties of Democracy Dataset, see Codebook, "State of Emergency (Variable: v2casoe)" www.v-dem.net/documents/55/codebook.pdf/ Frontline Defenders. *Global Analysis on the Situation of Human Rights Defenders (HRDs) at Risk Around the World*, February 23, 2021, 29.

26. Tanguay-Renaud, "Intelligibility of Extra-Legal State Action," 163; Noah Feldman, "What Ferguson's State of Emergency Means," *Denver Post*, August 13, 2015.

27. Scheppele, "Symposium: Emergency Powers," 835.

28. Noah Feldman, "One Man Now Rules Ferguson," *Denver Post*, April 22, 2016.

29. Ferejohn and Pasquino, "Law of the Exception," 216.

30. Roberts, "Age of Emergency"; Mizock, "Legality of the State of Emergency," 225; Glenn Frankel, "Crisis without End," *Washington Post*, June 12, 2004.

31. Sapir, *Israeli Constitution*, 153–71; Mehozay, "Fluid Jurisprudence," 142.

32. Mehozay, "Fluid Jurisprudence," 142.

33. Venegas, "Colombian Truth Commission's Final Report," Geneva International Centre for Justice, July 20, 2022, www.gicj.org/positions-opinons/gicj-positions-and-op inions/2810-colombian-truth-commission-s-final-report

34. Kernaghan, *Coca's Gone*, 16; Wright, *Emergency Politics*, 63; *Front Line Defenders' Global Analysis 2024/25*
May 13, 2025, humanrightsdefenders.blog/2025/05/13/front-line-defenders-global-analysis-2024-25/.

35. The Federal Register, www.federalregister.gov/documents; "US Sanctions on the International Criminal Court," *Human Rights Watch*, December 14, 2020; Linda Pearson, "US War Crimes Immunity and the International Criminal Court," *Verso Blog*, September 13, 2018; White House, "Statement of President Barack Obama on Release of OLC Memos," April 16, 2009.

36. With the invaluable support of student research assistants, declarations of the state of exception and emergency legislation were identified through Lexis-Nexis (now Nexis-Uni), checked against the UN Rapporteur 1997 list of states of emergency, databases (e.g., SPEED, Political Terror Scale, GDELT) and—more recently—Varieties of Democracy records. Countries are listed as democratic (≥ 6) and nondemocratic (≤ 5), according to Polity IV. Eventually, V-Dem introduced a variable on states of emergency, on which I have been drawing as well.

37. Menichelli, "National Picture," 269.

38. Ellen Nakashima and Shane Harris, "Congress Extends Controversial Warrantless Surveillance Law for Two Years," *Washington Post*, April 20, 2024.

39. Manin, "Emergency Paradigm," 3; Scheppele, "Underreaction"; "Trinidadian Columnist Sees 'Sophistry' behind State of Emergency Declaration," *BBC Monitoring Latin America*, November 14, 2011.

40. "President's Remarks at National Day of Prayer and Remembrance," White House, September 14, 2001; Lokaneeta, *Transnational Torture*, 24; Agamben, "State of Exception," 165; Scarry, *Thinking in an Emergency*, 4.

41. "Declared National Emergencies under the National Emergencies Act," Brennan Center for Justice.

42. Scarry, *Thinking in an Emergency*, 6; John Mecklin, "Closer Than Ever: It Is Now 89 Seconds to Midnight," *Bulletin of the Atomic Scientists*, January 28, 2025, thebulletin.org/doomsday-clock/2025-statement/

43. Tariq Ali, "America's Selective Vigilantism will make as many Enemies as Friends," *The Guardian*, September 6, 2011; "Uniting and Strengthening America by Providing Appropriate Tools Required to Intercept and Obstruct Terrorism (USA Patriot Act) Act of 2001," Public Law 107–56—October 26, 2001.

44. Agamben, "State of Exception," 165; "Military Order of November 13, 2001: Detention, Treatment, and Trial of Certain Non-Citizens in the WaraAgainst Terrorism," *Presidential Documents*, Federal Register: vol. 66, no. 222, 57831–57836, https://irp.fas.org/offdocs/eo/mo-111301.htm

45. Butler, *Precarious Life*, 64.

46. "Convention against Torture and Other Cruel, Inhuman or Degrading Treatment or Punishment," General Assembly Res. 39/46, December 10, 1984, article 27 (1).

47. Gross, "What 'Emergency' Regime?," 79; Feldman, "Police Violence," 2.

48. Rejali, *Torture and Democracy*, 35; Dershowitz, *Why Terrorism Works*, 156–59; Lokaneeta, *Transnational Torture*; Greenwald, "The Suppressed Fact: Deaths by US Torture," *Salon*, June 30, 2009.

49. "President Obama Signs Indefinite Detention Bill into Law," ACLU, December 31, 2011; National Defense Authorization Act 2012.

50. Neta Crawford, figures of "Post-9/11 Wars," "Cost of War," Watson Institute, watson.brown.edu/costsofwar/figures

51. Scheppele, "International Standardization"; Agamben, "What Is a Camp?," 40; Kotek, "Concentration Camps," 196; Caroline Kelly, "Ocasio-Cortez Compares Migrant Detention Facilities to Concentration Camps," *CNN*, June 18, 2019; Agamben, *Homo Sacer*, 72; Hyslop, "Invention of the Concentration Camp," 258–61.

52. Dorothy Chao, "In Nogales, More Deported US Residents," *No More Deaths*, November 5, 2017, nomoredeaths.org/in-nogales-more-deported-us-residents/; "National Emergency Concerning the Southern Border of the United States," February 15, 2019 (Proclamation 9844); Obed Manuel, "No Shower for 23 Days: US Citizen Says Conditions Were So Bad That He Almost Self-Deported," *Dallas Morning News*, July 24, 2019.

53. "Disappeared: How the US Border Enforcement Agencies Are Fueling a Missing Persons Crisis," *Missing Persons*, missingpersons.icrc.org/; ICE, "Detainee Death Reporting," www.ice.gov/detain/detainee-death-reporting; "Protecting the American people against invasion," The White House, January 20, 2025 .

54. Gruber, "État de siege"; Agamben, "State of Exception," 284.

55. Machiavelli, *Discourses on Livy*, 71; Wright, "Going beyond the Roman Dictator."

56. Wright, *Emergency Politics*, 1–22; Gross and Ni Aoláin, *Law in Times of Crisis*, 11.

57. Rosenblum, "Constitutional Reason of State," 150; Fatovic, "Emergency," 1.

58. Schmitt, *Political Theology*, 12.

59. Schmitt, *Political Theology*, 12, 66; Poole, *Reason of State*, 219.

60. Lowy, *Fire Alarm*, 58; Agamben, *State of Exception*, 50.

61. Schmitt, *Political Theology*, 12, 7; Neocleous, *Critique of Security*, 40; Murray, "State of Exception," 185.

62. Scheuerman, "States of Emergency," 566.

63. Hayek, *Constitution of Liberty*, 217.

64. Agamben, "State of Exception," 167; McLoughlin, "Giorgio Agamben on Security," 683.

65. Kotsko, "Neoliberalism's Demons," 502.

66. Agamben, "State of Exception," 164; Huysmans, "Jargon of Exception," 179; Rossello, *Teoría política en el antropoceno*, 89, 91; Agamben, *Homo Sacer*, 12.

67. International Organization for Migration, "Number of Recorded Deaths in the Mediterranean Sea from 2014 to 2024," *Statista*, July 4, 2024.

68. Rossello, *Teoría política en el antropoceno*, 54.

69. Agamben, "Destituent Power," and *State of Exception*, 14; Neocleous, *Critique of Security*, 8.

70. Ian Smith, "State of Siege; Tanks Roll in to UK's Biggest Airport to Stop Missile Attack," *Daily Record*, February 12, 2003.

71. Homeland Security, National Terrorism Advisory System, www.dhs.gov/nation al-terrorism-advisory-system.

72. Feierstein, "National Security Doctrine," 489; Seri and Kubal, "How Policy Fields Are Born," 139; Waever, "Securitization and Desecuritization"; Koshgarian, Siddique, and Steichen, *State of Insecurity*, 4; "Size of the Security Services Market Worldwide from 2011 to 2020," *Statista*.

73. Hobbes, *Leviathan*, 97, 102, 357.

74. Agamben, "For a Theory of Destituent Power" and "Security and Terror"; Foucault, *Security, Territory, Population*, 56, 68, 25–35; 69, 93, 60.

75. Neocleous, *Critique of Security*, 8, 4.

76. Rousseau, "*Discourse on the Origin of Inequality*," *The Social Contract*,105; Hegel, *Philosophy of Right*, §289, 235.

77. Neocleous, *Critique of Security*, 87; Marx, "On the Jewish Question," *Selected Writings*, 17.

78. Neocleous, *Critique of Security* 4.

79. Neocleous, *Critique of Security*, 8; Poole, "Judicial Review," 83.

80. "France: State of Emergency Officially Ends as New Security Measures Come into Force," *Global Legal Monitor*, November 29, 2017; Nicolas Boring, "France: President Signs New Antiterrorism Law," *Global Legal Monitor*, August 23, 2021; Sudhir Hazareesingh, "Macron, Le Pen and France's Long Battle between Order and Dissent," *Financial Times*, April 23, 2022.

81. Zuboff, *Surveillance Capitalism*, 115, 103–4; McQuade, *Pacifying the Homeland*, 21–22.

82. Cathy Gwin and Jackie Fox, "Inaugural Global Health Security Index" *GHS Index, October 24, 2019*; also see the World Economic Forum's *Global Risk Report* series.

83. Shepardson, "U.S. Airline CEOs Urge Biden to Lift COVID Mask Mandate"; Gregg Gonsalves, "Welcome to the 'You Do You' Pandemic," *The Nation*, September 1, 2023; Meghan Bartels, "Rampant COVID Poses New Challenges in the Fifth Year of the Pandemic," *Scientific American*, February 6, 2024; Joshua Cohen, "From Mask Mandates to Bans: Some Jurisdictions in U.S. Are Doing a 180," *Forbes*, July 1, 2024; "WHO press conference on global health issues," June 27, 2025.

84. Neocleous and Rigakos, *Anti-Security*.

85. Agamben, "Destituent Power."

86. Poole, "Judicial Review," 87, 83.

87. Melanie Kruvelis, "Florida Cop Told Teenager: "I Am the Law . . . I Can Fuck You Up and No One Will Say Anything about It," *Reason*, March 7, 2021.

88. Neocleous, *Fabrication*, 1–6; Knemeyer, "Polizei"; Foucault, *Discipline and Punish*, 220–21; Foucault, *Security, Territory, Population*, 318; Vitale, *End of Policing*, 36–37; Gascon et al., *Police and State Crime in the Americas*, 8–9.

89. Mitchell, *Critical and Effective Histories*, 176.

90. Novak, "Police Power," 55; Foucault, *Security, Territory, Population*, 316–28.

91. Bayley, "Police and Political Development in Europe," 329.

92. N'dea Yancey-Bragg, "Police Robots Are on Patrol: Now the Questions about Them Are Piling Up," *USA Today*, October 31, 2023.

93. Neocleous, "Original, Absolute, Indefeasible," 29; Dubber, *Police Power*, 135.

94. Feldman, "Police Violence," 2, 8; Agamben, "Sovereign Police," *Means without End*, 104.

95. Feldman, "Police Violence," 1; Schott, "Qualified Immunity," 22–32; *Malley v. Briggs* 475 U.S. 335, 1986.

96. Adam Andrzejewski, "FBI And Other Agencies Paid Informants $548 Million in Recent Years with Many Committing Authorized Crimes," *Forbes*, November 18, 2021; Eric Lichtblau and William M. Arkin, "More Federal Agencies Are Using Undercover Operations," *New York Times*, November 15, 2014.

97. Seri, *Seguridad*, 175.

98. "Mannheim, Germany Stabbing: Police Officer Who Intervened to Save Others at Anti-Islam Rally Dies," *Times Now*, June 2, 2024; Cohen et al., "Trust and Street-Level Bureaucrats"; Butler, *Precarious Life*, 64.

99. Barkan, "Use beyond Value," 256; Vitale, *End of Policing*, 26; Seri and Lokaneeta, "Police as State."

100. Joe Sandler Clarke, "Exclusive: VICE Data Shows Virtually No London Cops Get Fired for Complaints of Assault," *Vice*, November 10, 2015; "Police Complaints: Statistics for England and Wales 2019/20," Independent Office for Police Conduct, UK, 3; "Violent Deaths Due to Legal Interventions," *SAS Research* #53 (2015), 1, note 53.

101. Terrence McCoy, "Rio Police Were Ordered to Limit Favela Raids during the Pandemic: They're Still Killing Hundreds of People," *Washington Post*, May 20, 2021; "Brazil: At Least 21 People Killed during Police Raid in Rio Favela," *Guardian*, May 24, 2022; "Brazil: Police Killings of Black Youths Continue, 25 Years after the Candelária Massacre," *Amnesty International*, July 21, 2018; CORREPI, *Archivo de Casos 2024*, www.correpi.org

102. Anne Branigin, "Officer-Involved Killings: Now a Leading Cause of Death for Young Men in America," *The Root*, August 10, 2019; *Mapping Police Violence*, mappingpoliceviolence.org/; *Washington Post*'s Police Shootings database, www.washingtonpost.com/graphics/investigations/police-shootings-database/

103. Edgell et al., "Pandemic Backsliding," 5; "A Right Not a Threat," *Amnesty International*, 40, 29, www.gov.uk/government/news/new-protest-laws-on-face-coverings-and-pyrotechnics; John Parkinson, "Intersection of Masks and the Law," *ContagionLive*, May 16, 2024.

104. Taylor, *#BlackLivesMatter*, 121; Schrader, *Badges without Borders*, 6.

105. Poole, "Judicial Review," 85.

106. Frost, *Nixon Interviews*, 254–56, 266–71.

107. Helen Dewar, "President Isn't above the Law," *Washington Post*, June 4, 1977.

108. Ross, *Democracy and Violence*, 53; Barak, *Crimes by the Capitalist State*.

109. Neocleous, *Critique of Security*, 42.

110. Artiga-Purcell et al., "Disaster Extractivism," 2; Butler, *Precarious Life*, 61.

111. Lowy, *Fire Alarm*, 60; Agamben, "State of Exception," 170; Neocleous, and Riga-kos, *Anti-Security*, 21.

CHAPTER 3

1. President Donald Trump's Inauguration Speech, January 20, 2017, trumpwhiteh ouse.archives.gov/briefings-statements/the-inaugural-address/

2. McBride, *Collective Dreams*, 14.

3. Beetham, "Legitimacy"; Hardin, "Compliance, Consent, and Legitimacy."

4. Moffitt and Tormey, "Rethinking Populism"; Agamben, *Kingdom and Glory*, 181; Santner, *Royal Remains*, 4.

5. Botero, *Reason of State*, 12, 75; Foucault, *Security, Territory, Population*, 347.

6. Agamben, *Means without End*, 95; Butler, *Precarious Life*, xx.

7. Ani Petrosyan, "Internet Usage Worldwide," *Statista*, April 11, 2025.

8. Tufekci, *Twitter and Tear Gas*, 29; Kenneth Olmstead et al. "News Video on the Web: A Growing, if Uncertain, Part of News," Pew Research Center, March 26, 2014; "YouTube by the Numbers: Stats, Demographics & Fun Facts," February 10, 2020, www .omnicoreagency.com/youtube-statistics/; "Value of the Entertainment and Media Mar-ket Worldwide," *Statista*, 2024.

9. Foucault, *Security, Territory, Population*, 126.

10. Foucault, *Security, Territory, Population*, 265; Bartelson, "Making Exceptions."

11. President Donald Trump's Inaugural Address, January 20, 2025, www.whitehou se.gov/remarks/2025/01/the-inaugural-address/; Aaron Blake, "6 Takeaways from Trump's Inaugural Address," *Washington Post*, January 20, 2025.

12. Laclau, *Populist Reason*, 176.

13. Moffitt and Tormey, "Rethinking Populism"; Reyes, "Strategies of Legitimiza-tion," 783.

14. "Trump 'Lit That Fire' of Capitol Insurrection, Jan 6 Committee Report Says," *NPR*, December 23, 2022; Nina Totenberg, "Supreme Court Says Trump Has Absolute Immunity for Core Acts Only," *NPR*, July 1, 2024; Carrie Johnson, "Trump offers long-promised pardons to some 1,500 January 6 rioters," *NPR*, January 20, 2025.

15. Murtaza Hussain, "Democracy Dies in the Blinding Light of Day," *The Intercept*, July 4, 2018.

16. Foucault, *Society Must Be Defended*, 33.

17. Viroli, *Liberty of Servants*, 28, 37; Santner, *Royal Remains*, 45.

18. Henkin, "That 'S' Word," 5.

19. Walker, "Invention of the Royal Courts," 17.

20. Kantorowicz, *King's Two Bodies*, 141.

21. Kantorowicz, *King's Two Bodies*, 506.

22. Kantorowicz, *King's Two Bodies*, 305.

23. Kantorowicz, *Laudes Regiae*, 79.

24. Loughlin, *Foundations*, 380.

25. Jeffrey Merrick, Book Review, 927–29.

26. Hobsbawm, "Inventing Traditions," 7.

27. Santner, *Royal Remains*, 46–7, 4; Rossello, "Fleshing Out"; Rossello, *Teoría política en el antropoceno*, 108, 144.

28. Guénoun and Kavanagh, "Jacques Rancière," 19.

29. Neocleous, *Imagining the State*, 18.

30. Kalmo and Skinner, "Sovereign State," 3.

31. Giroux, *Spectacle of Terrorism*, 30.

32. Foucault, *Security, Territory, Population*, 344; Feldman, "Necessity"; Arnold, "'Domestic War.'"

33. Agamben, *State of Exception*, 6; Engelhardt, "Documenting Darkness"; Feldman, "Police Violence."

34. Eriksson, "Threat Framing"; Bellow, Heather, "Masked, armed ICE agents arrest two men in Great Barrington as witnesses taunt, shoot video," *The Lakeville Journal*, May 9, 2025; Annaleise Azevedo Lohr, "Reuters/Ipsos Issues Survey May 2025," *Ipsos*, May 16, 2025.

35. Jessop, "Bringing the State Back In," 163.

36. Baranger, "Apparition of Sovereignty," 61.

37. Neocleous, *Imagining the State*, 18.

38. Debord, *Society of the Spectacle*, 24; Kellner, "Media Spectacles and Media Events," 78–79; Agamben, *Means without End*, 81

39. Debord, *Society of the Spectacle*, 12.

40. Ani Petrosyan, "Worldwide Digital Population 2024," *Statista*, May 22, 2024; Bernard Marr, "20 Mind-Blowing AI Statistics Everyone Must Know About Now," *Forbes*, June 3, 2025.

41. Rodilosso, "Bubbles," 70.

42. Rodilosso, "Bubbles," 70–71.

43. Jonathan Taplin, "How Musk, Thiel, Zuckerberg, and Andreessen—Four Billionaire Techno-Oligarchs—Are Creating an Alternate, Autocratic Reality," *Vanity Fair*, August 22, 2023; *Statista*, www.statista.com/outlook/dmo/digital-media/worldwide

44. Murray and Zartaloudis, "Power of Thought," 209.

45. Jonathan Taplin, "How Musk, Thiel, Zuckerberg, and Andreessen—Four Billionaire Techno-Oligarchs—Are Creating an Alternate, Autocratic Reality," *Vanity Fair*, August 22, 2023

46. Gago and Mezzadra, "Extractive Operations," 579; Gandesha and Hartle, "Reification and Spectacle," 10; Hesmondhalgh, "User-Generated Content," 275.

47. Agamben, *Means without End*, 115.

48. Office of the Press Secretary, "At O'Hare, President Says 'Get on Board'," *George W. Bush White House Archives*, September 27, 2001; Ruby Lott-Lavigna, "Johnson: 'I Didn't Know Scientists Weren't Consulted," *Open Democracy*, December 7, 2023.

49. Holmes, "Spider's Web," 124.

50. Aditya Mani Jha, "The Gray Man and how the CIA took over Hollywood," Firstpost, July 25, 2022; CIA, "Entertainment Industry Guidelines" FOIA Collection, Case Number: F-2016-00356, March 26, 2014; Tanner Mirrlees, "The militarization of Movies and Television," *Cost of War*, Watson Institute, February 25, 2025.

51. Gerardo Papalia, "Just a Berlusclone?," *PORTAL Journal of Multidisciplinary International Studies*, Vol. 14, No. 1, April 2017, 30–32.

52. Dean, "Political Acclamation," 13.

53. Han, *Psychopolitics*, 57, 58; Dean, "Political Acclamation," 3.

54. Dominic Casciani, "The Undercover Cop, His Lover, and Their Son," *BBC*, October 24, 2014; Paul Lewis, Rob Evans, and Sorcha Pollak, "Trauma of Spy's Girlfriend: 'Like Being Raped by the State,'" *Guardian*, June 24, 2013.

55. Brezovšek and Črnčec, "Secrecy in Democracy," 31; Loughlin, *Public Law*, 381; Foucault, *Security, Territory, Population*, 355.

56. Brezovšek and Črnčec, "Secrecy in Democracy," 28.

57. Executive Order 13526, "Classified National Security Information"; German Lopez, "Too Many Top Secrets," *New York Times*, January 27, 2023; Henderson, Adelia, and Gabe Rottman, "Overclassification Is an Even Bigger Problem in an Age of Leak-Hunting," Reporters Committee on the Freedom of the Press, August 26, 2019, www.rcfp.org/

58. Bryan Bender, "White House Launches New War on Secrecy," *Politico*, August 23, 2022; Engelhardt, "Documenting Darkness."

59. Steven Aftergood, "Leakers May Be Worse Than Spies, Gov't Says," Federation of American Scientists, October 3, 2019, fas.org/publication/leakers-spies-hale/

60. Richard McGregor, "James Clapper, Director of National Intelligence," *Financial Times*, August 29, 2013.

61. "What Are State Secrets," Center for Constitutional Rights, ccrjustice.org/home/get-involved/tools-resources/fact-sheets-and-faqs/faqs-what-are-state-secrets

62. "The State Secrets Privilege: National Security Information in Civil Litigation," Congressional Research Service, April 28, 2022.

63. Brezovšek and Črnčec, "Secrecy in Democracy," 37.

64. Bovard, James, "Federal Secrecy Protects the Crimes of Every President," *Counterpunch*, January 28, 2021.

65. "Obama: '"We Tortured Some Folks" After 9/11," *CBS/AP*, August 1, 2014.

66. Berlant, "Epistemology of State Emotion," 67.

67. Van Dijk, "Discourse and Manipulation," 375; Kellner, "Media Spectacles," 79.

68. Jusionyte, "On and Off," 234.

69. "2024 is Deadliest Year for Journalists in CPJ history; almost 70% Killed by Israel," Committee to Protect Journalists, February 12, 2025, cpj.org/special-reports/2024-is-deadliest-year-for-journalists-in-cpj-history-almost-70-percent-killed-by-israel/

70. "Journalist Casualties in the Israel-Gaza War," Committee to Protect Journalists, cpj.org/2023/10/journalist-casualties-in-the-israel-gaza-conflict/; Christof Heyns, "Report of the Special Rapporteur on Extrajudicial, Summary or Arbitrary Executions," United Nations, 2013, 5, https://digitallibrary.un.org/record/755741?ln=en&v=pdf

71. Cooper and Voronov, "We've Hit Peak Denial"; Karen Yourish, Annie Daniel, Saurabh Datar, Isaac White, and Lazaro Gamio, "These Words Are Disappearing in the New Trump Administration," *The New York Times*, March 7, 2025.

72. García Negroni and Zoppi Fontana, *Análisis lingüístico y discurso político*.

73. Neocleous, "Fate of the Body Politic," 36.

74. Chevigny, "Populism of Fear," 2.

75. Neocleous, *Imagining the State*, 36.

76. Casali, Clovis, "France Will 'Never Give In to Islamist terrorism,' says Macron after policewoman's killing," France 24, April 23, 2021; "Terrorism—Macron Calls on 'Entire Nation' to Mobilise against Terrorism," *RFI*, October 8, 2019.

77. Neocleous, "Fate of the Body Politic," 33.

78. Neocleous, *Universal Adversary*, 22, 37.

79. Arnold, *Homelessness*, 157.

80. Matt Taibbi, "How to Survive America's Kill List," *Rolling Stone*, July 19, 2018, www.rollingstone.com; Detsch, Jack, "America's Next Soldiers Will Be Machines," *Foreign Policy*, April 6, 2024; "Pierre Dardot: 'Las guerras civiles del neoliberalismo'"; Roberto J. González, "How Big Tech and Silicon Valley Are Transforming the Military-Industrial Complex," *Costs of War*, April 17, 2024, 2.

81. Yuval Abraham, "'A Mass Assassination Factory': Inside Israel's Calculated Bombing of Gaza," *972 Magazine*, November 30, 2023; Yuval Abraham, "'Lavender': The AI Machine Directing Israel's Bombing Spree in Gaza," *972 Magazine*, April 3, 2024.

82. Marcus, Jonathan "Combat Drones: We are in a new era of warfare - here's why," *BBC*, February 4, 2022.

83. Kevin Liptak et al. ,"US Kills al Qaeda Leader Ayman al-Zawahiri," *CNN*, August 22, 2022.

84. Lokaneeta, *Truth Machines*, 1–2; "Problems with Autonomous Weapons," Campaign to Ban Killer Robots, www.stopkillerrobots.org

85. "ACLU Statement on President Biden's Overdue Release of Rules Governing Drone Strikes and Lethal Force Abroad," *ACLU*, June 30, 2023.

86. Engelhardt, "Documenting Darkness."

87. Roberto J. González, "Big Tech and Silicon Valley Are Transforming the Military-Industrial Complex," *Costs of War*, April 17, 2024, 2.

88. Crawford, "Blood and Treasure: United States Budgetary Costs and Human Costs of 20 Years of War in Iraq and Syria, 2003–2023," Watson Institute; Koshgarian, "Military Budget"; Koshgarian, Siddique, and Steichen, *State of Insecurity*.

89. Roth, "Great Civil Society Choke-Out"; Alex Woodward, "Trump resumes student visa interviews," *The Independent*, June 19, 2025.

90. Sutton, *Bulletproof Fashion*, 2, 10, 11, 87.

91. Benjamin, *Illuminations*, 257.

92. Rozitchner, "Terror and Grace," 148.

93. Rozitchner, "Terror and Grace," 148.

94. Bartelson, "Making Exceptions," 336.

CHAPTER 4

1. Michael J. Sullivan, "Argentina's Political Upheaval," Congressional Research Service, The Library of Congress, Order Code RS21113, January 25, 2002; "Los muertos del 19/20 de diciembre de 2001," *La Vaca*, September 4, 2011, lavaca.org/recuadros/los-muertos-del-1920-de-diciembre-de-2001/; "'Olla a presión': Original y punzante análisis de la crisis en Argentina," *La República*, June 10, 2002.

2. "South Korea's Yoon Attends Impeachment Trial for First Time," *EFE*, January 21, 2025.

3. Dean, "Political Acclamation," 32.

4. Sitrin, "Horizontalism and Autonomy."

5. Tarrow, "Charles Tilly," 228; Della Porta, "Protest Cycles," 450; Ortiz et al., *World Protests*, 3, 86; GDELT.

6. Kalyvas, *Democracy*, 272; Lipsky, qtd. in Della Porta, "Protest Cycles."

7. Murphy, "Rise of the Precariat?," 74–5; Ortiz and Cummins, *End Austerity*, 17, 21; Ortiz et al., *Brief: World Protest*, 21–24.

8. "Political Conditions: France," *CountryWatch Reviews*, June 21, 2018.

9. Rancière, *Hatred of Democracy*, 62; Rancière, "Ten Theses on Politics."

10. Carothers and Youngs, "Complexities"; Lipsky, "Protest as a Political Resource," 1147; Tufekci, *Twitter and Tear Gas*, 191.

11. Della Porta, "Protest Cycles," 450; Roudabeh Kishi et al. "A Year of Racial Justice Protests: Key Trends in Demonstrations Supporting the BLM Movement," *The Armed Conflict Location & Event Data Project*, May 2021; Harsin, "Nuit Debout," 1832.

12. Ortiz et al., *World Protests*, 3.

13. Della Porta, "Protest Cycles," 451; GDELT, "Mapping Global Protest Trends 1979–2019 through One Billion News Articles," November 24, 2019; Mass Mobilization Project, massmobilization.github.io/; Carnegie's Global Protest Tracker, carnegieendowment.org/features/global-protest-tracker?lang=en

14. Della Porta, "Protest Cycles," 450; GDELT.

15. V-Dem, *2020 Report*, 21; Ortiz et al., *World Protests*.

16. Philip A. Schrodt, "CAMEO Conflict and Mediation Event Observations: Event and Actor Codebook," data.gdeltproject.org/documentation/CAMEO.Manual.1.1b3.pdf

17. Della Porta, "Protest Cycles," 451; Mansley, *Collective Violence*, 5; Ortiz et al., *World Protests*, 74.

18. Thabi Myeni, "Black Lives Matter and the trap of performative activism," *Al Jazeera*, June 20, 2020.

19. Naomi Klein, "Revisiting *No Logo*, Ten Years Later," *The Huffington Post*, March 18, 2010.

20. Kenety, "Development."

21. Tilly, *Regimes and Repertoires*, 44; Tarrow, "Contentious Politics," 238.

22. Sharp, "*198 Methods of Nonviolent Action*," *War Resisters' International*, wri-irg.org/en/resources/2008/gene-sharps-198-methods-nonviolent-action.

23. Tarrow, "Contentious Politics," 237.

24. Tufekci, *Twitter and Tear Gas*, xxii.

25. Ezrahi, *Imagined Democracies*, 3; Tufekci, *Twitter and Tear Gas*, xiii; Ortiz et al., *World Protests*, 437.

26. Tufekci, *Twitter and Tear Gas*, 269, xii–xiii; Harsin, "Nuit Debout," 1830.

27. Dean, *Communist Horizon*, 110; Passavant, *Policing Protest*, 1, 13; Adrienne Russel, qtd. in Harsin, "Nuit Debout," 1830.

28. Amnesty International, 2017/2018 Report, 15 16; Ortiz and Cummins, "Global Austerity Alert," 11; Butler, *Performative Theory of Assembly*, 91.

29. Mark Ellis-Jones, *States of Unrest: Resistance to IMF Policies in Poor Countries*. World Development Movement, 2003.

30. Jillian Kestler-D'Amours, "Sidi Bouzid: Hardship bites where Arab Spring began," Al Jazeera, January 14, 2018; Tufekci, *Twitter and Tear Gas*, x

31. Tufekci, *Twitter and Tear Gas*, 210; Holmes, *Organizing Occupy Wall Street*, 145; Fraser, *The Old Is Dying*.

32. Sitrin, "Main Foreword," *Organizing Occupy Wall Street*, xii.

33. Çıdam, *In the Street*, 169, 180, 170, 184.

34. Anthony Torres, "French Workers, Youth Defy State of Emergency," *World Socialist Website*, April 1, 2016.

35. Lowry, "French Pensions"; Boyer et al., "Origins of the 'Yellow Vests' Movement."

36. Safdar Anealla, "Clichy-sous-Bois: A Suburb Scarred by 2005 French Riots," *Al Jazeera*, June 12, 2017."; "Political Conditions: France," CountryWatch; Christine Ollivier, "France Declares State of Emergency to Impose Curfews against Rioting," *Associated Press*, November 8, 2005.

37. Anealla, "Clichy-sous-Bois"; "Political Conditions: France," *CountryWatch*.

38. Harsin, "Nuit Debout," 1821, 1830, 1825, 1828.

39. Harsin, "Nuit Debout," 1823, 1821.

40. Steven Erlanger, Stephen Castle, and Rick Gladstone, "Iceland's Prime Minister Steps Down amid Panama Papers Scandal," *New York Times*, April 5, 2016.

41. Editorial Collective, "La casa no está en orden," *Crisis*, October 14, 2020.

42. "Protestas en Chile: 'Estamos en guerra', la frase de Piñera que se le volvió en contra en medio de las fuertes manifestaciones," *BBC Mundo*, October 22, 2019.

43. Jeria, "Impresionante bandera chilena gigante desplegada en Plaza Italia: 'Chile despertó, no estamos en guerra," *Redgol*, October 25, 2019; "Chile: Con protestas cabildos y asambleas"; Orellana Calderón, "Post-Neoliberal Future," 100.

44. Kubal and Fisher, "Student Protest," 221, 217; Leiva, *Left Hand of Capital*, 94.

45. "Chile: Con protestas cabildos y asambleas"; "Mesa de unidad social"; Unidad Social Chile—Manifiesto"; Orellana Calderón, "Post-Neoliberal Future," 101.

46. Ciara Nugent, "Chile's Conservatives Push Ahead with Rightwing Constitution," Financial Times, October 4, 2023.

47. Vásquez Hurtado, Mejía Suarez, and Gardeazabal Bravo, "Politics in the Streets."

48. Rosenblum, "Constitutional Reason of State," 162; Gargarella, *Manifiesto*, 85–86, my translation; Ellen Nakashima, "Obama, Lawmakers Discuss Whether to End NSA Collection of Americans' Phone Records," *Washington Post*, January 9, 2014.

49. Brandan McQuade, "Guns, Grenades, and Facebook," *Jacobin*, December 5, 2016.

50. Amanda Lumpkin, "'Stop Cop City' Activist Shot 50+ Times: DeKalb Autopsy Report," *Patch*, Apr 20, 2023; Global Witness. *Annual report 2022: Rising to the challenge of a world in crisis*, October 6, 2023, 21.

51. Taylor, *#BlackLivesMatter*; Steven Donziger, "Environmentalist Manuel Esteban Paez Terán's Death Is Part of a Disturbing Trend," *Guardian*, February 2, 2023.

52. Black Lives Matter, "Her Story," blacklivesmatter.com/herstory/

53. Black Lives Matter, "Her Story," blacklivesmatter.com/herstory/; "Timeline of Events in Shooting of Michael Brown in Ferguson," Associated Press, August 8, 2019.

54. Taylor, *#BlackLivesMatter*; Larry Buchanan, Quoctrung Bui, and Jugal K. Patel, "Black Lives Matter May Be the Largest Movement in U.S. History," *The New York Times*, July 3, 2020.

55. Variables: "Mobilization for Democracy" (v2cademmob) and "Mobilization for Autocracy" (v2caautmob), Varieties of Democracy Codebook v14—March 2024, 235–36.

56. Ortiz et al., *World Protests*; De Angelis, *Omnia Sunt Communia*, 369.

57. Giugni, "Was It Worth the Effort?," 386, 382; Ortiz et al., *World Protests*.

58. Çıdam, *In the Street*, 122.

59. *15 M*, directed by Stéphane M. Grueso, Pragda, 2012.

60. Arendt, *Human Condition*, 203, 192–93.

61. Kalyvas, *Politics of the Extraordinary*, 273.

62. Kristin Ross, "Democracy for Sale," in Agamben, *Democracy in What State?*, 89.

63. Rancière, *Hatred of Democracy*, 54; Guénoun and Kavanagh, "Jacques Rancière"; Rancière, *Disagreement*; Rancière, "Ten Theses on Politics."

64. Rancière, *Hatred of Democracy*, 72, 55.

65. Çıdam, "Disagreeing about Democracy."

66. Carothers and Youngs, "Global Protests," 14; Rueschemeyer, Huber Stephens, and Stephens, *Capitalist Development and Democracy*, 66.

67. Çıdam, "Disagreeing about Democracy."

68. Sharp; *From Dictatorship to Democracy*; Hallam, "Common Sense"; Holmes, *Organizing Occupy Wall Street*.

69. Passavant, *Policing Protest*, 4.

70. Francis Wade, "Most Resistance Does Not Speak Its Name: An Interview with James C. Scott," *LA Review of Books*, January 22, 2018.

71. Tanguay-Renaud, "Extra-Legal State Action"; Kalyvas, *Politics of the Extraordinary*, 7, 295, 13, 291; Tarrow, "Contentious Politics," 227.

72. Kalyvas, *Politics of the Extraordinary*, 2.

73. Resmini, "Long Coup in Ecuador"; Kalyvas, *Politics of the Extraordinary*, 5.

74. Kalyvas, *Politics of the Extraordinary*, 290; Guénoun and Kavanagh, "Rancière"; Rancière, "Who Is the Subject," 303; Butler, *Performative Theory of Assembly*, 80.

75. Rossello, *Teoría política en el antropoceno*, 63; Celermajer et al., "Political Theory."

76. Schrodt et al. "The CAMEO (Conflict and Mediation Event Observations) Actor Coding Framework," Prepared for delivery at the 2005 Annual Meeting of the American Political Science Association, 1 – 4 September 2005, eventdata.parusanalytics.com/papers.dir/APSA.2005.pdf.

77. Tilly, *Regimes and Repertoires*, 76; Tarrow, "Contentious Politics," 239; Ortiz et al., *World Protests*, 57.

78. Feldstein, "Road to Digital Unfreedom," 42, 43.

79. Front Line Defenders, *Global Analysis 2019*, January 11, 2019, 8; Instituto Nacional de Derechos Humanos (INDH) and Alto Comisionado de las Naciones Unidas para los Derechos Humanos (ACNUDH), "Protesta social y derechos humanos: Estándares internacionales y nacionales," Santiago de Chile, December 2014, 211; Passavant, *Policing Protest*, 5.

80. Amnesty International, *State of the World's Human Rights 2024*, 16; Erica Chenoweth, Soha Hamman, and Christopher Shay, "Crowd Counting Consortium," Ash Center for Democratic Governance and Innovation, Harvard University.

81. Martín Rodríguez Rocha, "Ya tenemos ley antiterrorista," *4 Semanas*, June 14, 2007.

82. "Aplicación de Ley Antiterrorista en Chile," *Cejil*, October 5, 2017; Carpenter and Williams, "Since Standing Rock" *The Nation*, February 16, 2018; CORREPI, Casos 2023, www.correpi.org/; INDH & ACNUDH, "Protesta social y derechos humanos," 98.

83. INDH & ACNUDH, "Protesta social y derechos humanos," 12.

84. "Global Protest Tracker," Carnegie Endowment for International Peace, carnegi eendowment.org/features/global-protest-tracker?lang=en

85. Orellana Calderón, "Post-Neoliberal Future," 107; Rajesh Makwana, "A New Era of Global Protest Begins," *Common Dreams*, January 14, 2016; Amnesty International, *Human Rights 2024*, 16.

86. Arendt, "Reflections on Violence," 22; Kalyvas, *Politics of the Extraordinary*, 15.

87. Agamben, "Destituent Power."

88. Agamben, "Destituent Power"; Foucault, *Society Must Be Defended*, 40; Abramsky and De Angelis, "Energy Crisis," 13.

CHAPTER 5

1. Edmunson, *Introduction to Rights*, 11; Golder, *Foucault and the Politics of Right*, 6; UN General Assembly A/76/L.75, "The Human Right to a Clean, Healthy and Sustainable Environment," July 26, 2022; Ortiz et al., *World Protests*, 7; World Values Survey, Wave 7, question 246, www.worldvaluessurvey.org/; Tamara O'Laughlin Toles, "The Fight to Stop the Climate Crisis Is Local," *Common Dreams*, October 2, 2019; "UN General Assembly Declares Access to Clean and Healthy Environment a Universal Human Right," *UN News*, July 28, 2022; Wilde, "Communal Councils and Participatory Democracy," 154; Ivison, *Rights*, 7.

2. Neocleous, *Imagining the State*, 1.

3. Ivison, *Rights*, 1; Poole, *Reason of State*, 253.

4. Santos, *Derecho y emancipación*, 103; Searle, "Derechos humanos," 20; Searle, *Making the Social World*, 9.

5. Hoffman, *Human Rights*, 2; Edmundson, *Introduction to Rights*, xi.

6. Naomi Klein, "The Supreme Court's Shock and Awe Judicial Coup," *Intercept*, June 30, 2022; "Rights Removal Bill Is 'Giant Leap Backwards' for Ordinary People," *Impact News Service*, June 23, 2022.

7. Hoffmann, *Human Rights*, 2.

8. Bondia Garcia, "Emerging Human Rights Revolution," 68.

9. Grohmann, "One Earth: Stockholm+50," *CE Noticias Financieras English*, June 16, 2022.

10. Geoffrey Lean, "Our Right to Ramble on Common Land," qtd. in Rodgers and Mackay, "Creating 'New' Commons"; Foster, Clark, and Holleman, "Marx and the Commons," 3, 2; Bollier, "Who May Use the King's Forest?"

11. De Keyzer, *Inclusive Commons*, 3, 2–3; Polanyi, *Great Transformation*, 37.

12. Dardot and Laval, *Common*, 76; Benjamin Selwyn, "The Economist Who Solved the Free-Rider Problem," Jacobin, June 3, 2025.

13. Exner, Hochleithner, and Kumnig, "Expanding the Scope"; Dean, *Communist Horizon*, 134.

14. De Angelis, "Marx's Theory of Primitive Accumulation"; Valguarnera, "Legal Ideology and the Commons."

15. Exner, Hochleithner, and Kumnig, "Expanding the Scope"; Valguarnera, "Legal ideology and the Commons," 205–207.

16. Foster, Clark, and Holleman, "Marx and the Commons," 2; 4, 15.

17. Moyn, *Human Rights*, xiv.

18. Marx, *Capital*, 1:416.

19. Nardulli, Peyton, and Bajjalieh, "Conceptualizing and Measuring," 139.

20. Edmunson, *Rights*, 10; Gowder, "Isonomia," 84, 88, 95; Arendt, *On Revolution*, 30.

21. Gowder, "Isonomia," 90; Plato. Laws. Luton, Bedfordshire: Andrews UK Limited, 2012, 273; Aristotle, Politics, 157.

22. Aristotle, *Politics*, 140.

23. Lacey, "Patria Potestas," 124; "Roman Law," *Encyclopædia Britannica*.

24. Wenar, "Rights"; Hoffman, *Human Rights*, 5; Edmunson, *Rights*, 10, 15.

25. Valguarnera, "Legal Ideology," 208. Locke, *Two Treatises of Government*, 323.

26. Valguarnera, "Legal Ideology," 208.

27. Celermajer et al., "Multispecies," 44; Menke, *Critique of Rights*, 257, 5, 269, 34; Pashukanis, *Selected Writings*, 73; Valguarnera, "Legal Ideology," 206.

28. "Crowning Fury: New Mexico Wildfire Reignites Long-Standing Tensions," *Rolling Stone*, June 8, 2022; Celermajer et al., "Multispecies," 44.

29. Kalyvas, *Politics of the Extraordinary*, 257; Agamben, *Homo Sacer*, 76.

30. Foucault, *Birth of Biopolitics*, 39, 275, 40; Menke, *Critique of Rights*, 15; Edmundson, *An Introduction to Rights*, 49.

31. Foucault, *Birth of Biopolitics*, 169–70; Santos, *Derecho y emancipación*, 64; Menke, *Critique of Rights*, 16.

32. Yllanes Ramos, "Social Rights Enshrined in the Mexican Constitution," 601, 602–4, 605–6, 601.

33. Soviet Union 1936 (art. 6) and 1977 constitutions.

34. Sikkink, "Latin American Countries," 395.

35. Hussain, *Jurisprudence of Emergency*, 141; Poole, *Reason of State*, 249; Nolte and Schilling-Vacaflor, *New Constitutionalism*, 21.

36. "The Core International Human Rights Instruments and Their Monitoring Bodies," UN Human Rights Office of the High Commissioner, www.ohchr.org/EN/Professio nalInterest/Pages/CoreInstruments.aspx

37. Daniel Lozano, "Los derechos humanos, una bandera que a Chávez se le volvió en contra," *La Nación*, September 28, 2012; Nolte and Schilling-Vacaflor, *New Constitutionalism* 3–5, 18; Honig, *Emergency Politics*, 54.

38. Rafael Correa, "Inauguration Speech," May 24, 2013; Evo Morales, "Inauguration Speech," qtd. in Roberto Gargarella, "Latin American Constitutionalism Then and Now: Promises and Questions," in Nolte and Schilling Vacaflor, *New Constitutionalism in Latin America*, 145.

39. Bensaïd, *Dispossessed*, 46; Celermajer et al. "Multispecies," 50.

40. Roberto Gargarella, "Latin American Constitutionalism Then and Now: Promises and Questions," in Nolte and Schilling Vacaflor, *New Constitutionalism in Latin America*, 168.

41. Brazil, Law #10.835/2004; Sikkink and Walling, *International Human Rights Regimes*, 319; Sikkink, "Transnational Politics," 516.

42. "Charter of Emerging Human Rights Human Rights in a Globalised World," Universal Forum of Cultures, Monterrey, 2007; "Charter of Emerging Human Rights," Barcelona, 2004; Bondia Garcia, "Emerging Human Rights Revolution."

43. Brook, Clay, and Randolph, "Human Rights Data for Everyone," humanrightsm easurement.org/about hrmi/our purpose/

44. Moyn, "Human Rights," xiii; *World Values Survey*, Wave 7 (2017 2020), question 253; Poole, *Reason of State*, 250; Clark, "Democracy and Human Rights," 397.

45. Whyte, *Morals of the Market*, 34.

46. Whyte, "Is Revolution Desirable?," 209; Regilme, "Constitutional Order"; Santos, *Derecho y emancipación*, 72.

47. Brown, *Undoing the Demos*, 151.

48. Menke, *Critique of Rights*, 244, 250; Pashukanis, *Selected Writings*, 51, 69.

49. Arendt, "Perplexities of the Rights of Man"; UNHCR (United Nations High Commissioner for Refugees), "Refugee Facts," www.unrefugees.org/refugee-facts/statistics

50. Agamben, *Homo Sacer*, 72.

51. Agamben, *Homo Sacer*, 12.

52. Agamben, *Homo Sacer*, 107, 97; Mehozay, "Fluid Jurisprudence," 138.

53. Menke, *Critique of Rights*, 113; Tranchina Giulia, "Italy's Criminalisation of Migrant Rescue: The Luventa Case," *euobserver*, December 13, 2022.

54. Santner, *Royal Remains*, 59; Agamben, *Homo Sacer*, 80.

55. Rossello, *Teoría política en el antropoceno*, 42.

56. Anderson, "Intransigent Right."

57. Sieyes, "Rights of Man and Citizen," 127; Gündoğdu, "Potentialities of Human Rights," 10.

58. Rancière, "Rights of Man," 304; Rancière, *Hatred of Democracy*, 74.

59. Rancière "Rights of Man," 304, 305–6.

60. Santos, *Derecho y emancipación*, 59.

61. Rancière, "Rights of Man," 305–6; Gargarella, *Manifiesto*, 85–86, my translation; Butler, *Performative Theory of Assembly*; Searle, "Derechos humanos," 26; Rancière, "Rights of Man," 306–7; Menke, *Critique of Rights*, 284; Gargarella, *Manifiesto*, 85.

62. Gargarella, "Latin American Constitutionalism," 153.

63. Marx, "Critique of the Gotha Program," *Selected Writings, 321*; Pashukanis, *Selected Writings*, 58, 342.

64. Brown, *States of Injury*, 98.

65. Senellart, "Course Context," *Birth of Biopolitics*, 480, 42; Ferreira-Neto, "Rights of the Governed," 89.

66. Whyte, *Morals of the Market*, 211; Foucault, *Power/Knowledge*, 108.

67. Harvey, *Companion*, 51; Pashukanis, *Selected Writings*, 51; Golder, *Foucault and the Politics of Rights*, 6, 22.

68. Whyte, *Morals of the Market*.

69. Evo Morales. Inauguration Speech: Excerpts, BBC, January 22, 2006.

70. Nardulli, Peyton, and Bajjalieh, "Conceptualizing and Measuring," 143–44; Louglin, *Foundations of Public Law*, 443.

71. *Varieties of Democracy Codebook*, v-dem.net/documents/55/codebook.pdf, 312. World Bank Governance Indicators, "Rule of Law," www.worldbank.org/content/dam/sites/govindicators/doc/rl.pdf /

72. Holmes, "Spider's Web"; Nardulli, Peyton, and Bajjalieh, "Conceptualizing and Measuring," 141.

73. Hayek, *Road to Serfdom*, 112.

74. Wolin, *Politics and Vision*, 525.

75. O'Donnell, "Quality of Democracy," 45, 32; Montag, "Necroeconomics"; Locke, *Two Treatises of Government*, 329.

76. Bollier, "Who May Use the King's Forest?"; Marx, *Capital*, 885; Dean, *Communist Horizon*, 119; Moore and Perez-Rocha, *Extraction Casino*.

77. The Colombian government's Registro Único de Víctimas lists 8,736,196 of the forcefully displaced in 2024, cifras.unidadvictimas.gov.co/Cifras/#!/infografia; Front Line Defenders. *Global Analysis 2024–25*, 9.

78. "Colombia: Over 2,000 Days of Criminalisation and Persecution against Milena Quiroz Jiménez, Woman Human Rights Defender in the Region of Sur de Bolívar, Colombia," *Frontline Defenders*, July 28, 2022.

79. Roa Avendaño and Toloza, "Songful Resistance," 188; Front Line Defenders, *Global Analysis 2023–24*, 11; Foster, Clark, and Holleman, "Marx and the Commons," 21, 14; Polanyi, *Great Transformation*, 37.

80. Ansah, "Lawfare," 88, 104; Perelman, *Invention of Capitalism*, 14, 141.

81. Marx, *Capital*, vol. 1, chap. 26; Bensaïd, *Dispossessed*, 48; Foster, Clark, and Holleman, "Marx and the Commons," 10–11; Perelman, *Invention*, 13–14.

82. Kathleen Jamie, "Uncovering the Facts of the Scottish Clearances," The *New Statesman*, January 16, 2019.

83. Foucault, *Birth of Biopolitics*, 85; Perelman, *Invention*, 39.

84. Marx, *Capital*, vol. 1, chap. 26; Madhav Gadgil, "Biodiversity Is for the People. Protect it," *Hindustan Times*, February 18, 2022; Moore, *Web of Life*, 149.

85. Perelman, *Invention*, 331; Hussain, *Jurisprudence of Emergency*, 28; Neocleous, *War Power, Police Power*, 32.

86. Mahmud, "Law of Geography," 79.

87. Mignolo, "Coloniality," 40; Fitzpatrick, *Mythology*; Mahmud, "Law of Geography."

88. Mill, "Treatment of Barbarous Nations," 252–53.

89. Foucault, *Birth of Biopolitics*, 42; Dean, "Political Acclamation," 120.

90. Hussain, *Jurisprudence of Emergency*, 28.

91. Arendt, *Eichmann in Jerusalem*, 291.

92. De Angelis, *Omnia Sunt Communia*, 173, 179; Bensaïd, *Dispossessed*, 39.

93. Front Line Defenders, *Global Analysis 2019*, 7; EJAtlas; Klare, *Race for What Is Left*.

94. De Angelis, *Omnia Sunt Communia* 25.

95. Marx, *Capital*, 1:416.

96. Ucelli, "Janus and My Ode to Capital"; Marx, *Capital*, 1:416; De Angelis, "Marx's Theory of Primitive Accumulation, 18.

97. Ucelli, "Janus"; Heinrich, *Introduction*, 195, 36; Brown, *Undoing the Demos*, 206.

98. Menke, *Critique of Rights*, 256, 260; Marx, qtd. in Menke, *Critique of Rights*, 244.

99. Parekh, "Modern Conception of Right," 19, 20, 18.

100. Pashukanis, *Selected Writings*, 291, Hay, "E. P. Thompson and the Rule of Law."

101. Bottomore, *Dictionary*; Gargarella, *Law as a Conversation between Equals*, 19, 21–25.

102. Santos, *Derecho y emancipación*, 59, 105

103. Cotterrell, *Law's Community*, 119; Parekh, "Modern Conception of Right," 18.

104. Parekh, "Modern Conception of Right," 19; Pashukanis, *Selected Writings*, 288; Celermajer et al., "Political Theory," 40.

105. Parekh, "Modern Conception of Right," 20.

106. Pashukanis, *Selected Writings*, 290; Golder, *Foucault and the Politics of Rights*, 22; Menke, *Critique of Rights*, 245, 248, 226, 287, 290, 281, 290.

107. Lean, qtd. in Rodgers and Mackay, "Creating 'New' Commons."

108. Federici, "Women's Struggles for Land in Africa."

109. Polanyi, *Great Transformation*, 37; Bensaïd, *Dispossessed*, 15; De Angelis, *Omnia Sunt Communia*, 63.

110. De Keyzer, *Inclusive Commons*, 7

111. Polanyi, *Great Transformation*, 82, 86; De Keyzer, *Inclusive Commons*, 5; Polanyi, *Great Transformation*, 86

112. Federici, *Revolution at Point Zero*, 140

113. Federici, *Revolution at Point Zero*, 144.

114. Federici, "Women's Struggles for Land in Africa."

115. Federici, "Women's Struggles for Land in Africa."

116. Foster, "Nature as a Mode of Accumulation."

117. De Angelis, *Omnia Sunt Communia*, 317.

118. Pascal Gielen and Sonja Lavaert, "The Salt of the Earth. On Commonism: An Interview with Antonio Negri," *Open!*, August 18, 2018; De Angelis, *Omnia Sunt Communia*, 13, 63; De Keyzer, *Inclusive Commons*, 7; Ramos, "Ethics of AI"; "The P2P Foundation's Wiki Compiles Extensive Data on Commons Experiences and Laws," wiki.p2pfoundation.net/Main_Page

119. Ivison, *Rights*, 10; Santos, *Derecho y emancipación*, 102.

120. De Angelis, *Omnia Sunt Communia*, 223–24.

121. De Angelis, *Omnia Sunt Communia*, 224–25, 13.

122. Gadgil, "Biodiversity"; Foster, Clark, and Holleman, "Marx and the Commons," 20, 22.

123. Bollier, "Who May Use the King's Forest?"; Balibar, "Outlines," 28.

124. Blaser and de la Cadena, "Uncommons."

125. Blaser and de la Cadena, "Uncommons," 186; Celermajer et al., "Political Theory," 44.

126. Rossello, *Teoría política en el antropoceno*, 177, 122.

CHAPTER 6

1. Gastón Valderrama, "Con varios momentos destacados, así fue el Debate Presidencial 2023," *Vox Populi*, October 1, 2023.

2. Astrid Pikielny, "María Esperanza Casullo, sobre la batalla 'épica y moral' de Javier Milei," *La Nación*, October 22, 2024; George Monbiot, "What Links Rishi Sunak, Javier Milei and Donald Trump?," *Guardian*, January 6, 2024; "Milei habló en España y advirtió 'Venimos del futuro,'" *Urgente Milei*, YouTube, minute 15:55, www.youtube.com/watch?v=xAmYCWl786E; "Milei aseguró que hizo 'el ajuste más grande de la humanidad' y llamó a invertir en la Argentina," *El Cronista*, April 7, 2024.

3. "Argentina's Protests Have Only Gained Momentum in the Ensuing Months"; "Massive Crowds March against Milei's Cuts to State Universities," *BA Times*, April 23, 2024.

4. Annunziata et al., "Anti-Political Politicization," 19.

5. Jon Lee Anderson, "Javier Milei Wages War on Argentina's Government," *New Yorker*, December 2, 2024.

6. Gago, *Razón neoliberal*, 303–4; Schenck, "Doblar hasta quebrar," p. 357, 360, 351

7. Gunder Frank, "Official Website"; Ravecca, Robaina, and Zannier, "Javier Milei's Global Leadership," 2; Artiga Purcell et al., "Disaster Extractivism," 12, 3; Bensaid, *Dispossessed*.

8. Jorge Fontevecchia, "La muerte del padre," *Perfil*, December 16, 2024.

9. Jon Lee Anderson, "Javier Milei Wages War on Argentina's Government," *New Yorker*, December 2, 2024; "Milei habló en España."

10. Ravecca, Robaina, and Zannier, "Reading the Far-Right," 3; Ravecca et al., "What Are They Doing *Right*?," 17; Pereira, "Understanding Right-Wing Populism," 17; "Pierre Dardot: 'Las guerras civiles del neoliberalismo son guerras totales,'" interview by Jorge Fontevecchia, Perfil, May 31, 2025.

11. QS Top Universities, www.topuniversities.com/world-university-rankings?region=Latin%20America

12. "Un millón de chicos se van a dormir sin cenar en Argentina, según una encuesta de UNICEF," *Infobae*, August 12, 2024.

13. "Milei Makes It Official: Amalia 'Yuyito' González Is His New Girlfriend," *Buenos Aires Times*, August 25, 2024; "Exclusivo: Javier Milei, en Oppenheimer presenta, parte 1," CNN, April 1, 2024, minutes 36:45 and 37:55, youtu.be/6fer15t-hKI?si=vQjhsAu9RXmzc2ql&t=2266; "El Gobierno argentino rechaza dar información sobre los perros de Milei," *El Pais*, July 26, 2024; Elian Chali, "Fingir demencia," *Anfibia*, April 29, 2024.

14. Brown, *Undoing the Demos*, 22; "Davos 2025: Special Address by Javier Milei, President of Argentina," January 23, 2025.

15. Donald Trump, campaign speech in Richmond, VA, on March 3, 2024; "Milei habló en España."

16. Moffitt, *Global Rise*; Botero, *Reason of State*, 12; Illouz, *Emotional Life of Populism*, vii.

17. Weyland, "Populism," 203; de la Torre, "Populism," 200.

18. Richardson, "Export-Oriented Populism"; Jon Lee Anderson, "Javier Milei"; "El guiño de Milei a los aliados y una dura definición del 'enemigo,'" *MDZ Política*, November 20, 2024; Cadahia, "democracia en disputa," 320.

19. Amnesty International, *DDHH en Argentina*, 2024.

20. "Busca Milei 'importar' método de seguridad de Bukele," *El Porvenir*, June 20, 2024; "Milei's Key Reforms, 'Ley de Bases' and Fiscal Package, Become Law in Argentina," *BA Times*, July 8, 2024; Ailin Bullentini, "Más allá del desfile: Javier Milei duplicó el presupuesto de Seguridad y las FFAA con la protesta en la mira," *Letra P*, July 12, 2024.

21. Amnesty International, *DDHH en Argentina*, 2024, 30–31; "Javier Milei: 'Soy el máximo exponente de la libertad a nivel mundial,'" *Letra P*.

22. "Milei habló de traiciones en el Circo Máximo de Roma, citó a Lenin y leyó su decálogo de acción política," *Perfil*, December 14, 2024; Celeste Murillo, "El Círculo Rojo. ¿Qué son las fuerzas del cielo?," *La Izquierda Diario*, December 15, 2023; Pablo Duer, "Milei avanza con su batalla cultural para transformar los valores de la sociedad argentina," *EFE*, December 6, 2024.

23. Kotsko, *Neoliberalism's Demons*, 500, 497.

24. Milei, "Interview with Tucker Carlson"; Agustina Ramos, "La libertad para censurar del gobierno de Javier Milei," *Presentes*, September 10, 2024; "Censura en el INTA: Prohíben hablar de 'cambio climático', 'agroecología' y 'sustentabilidad'," *Pagina12*, July 15, 2024.

25. Serrano, Julian, Interview with Javier Milei, August 4, 2021, www.youtube.com /watch?v=rAdtDxJnvB8&t=4069s; "Milei habló en España."

26. Kotsko, *Neoliberalism's Demons*, 500; Harvey, *Brief History*, 3; Pablo Duer, "Milei avanza con su batalla cultural para transformar los valores de la sociedad argentina," *EFE*, December 6, 2024.

27. Jonathan Gilbert and James Attwood, "Argentina Is about to Unleash a Wave of Lithium in a Global Glut," *Bloomberg*, June 28, 2024.

28. James Hansen, "The World Will Cool Off—a Bit—And Other Good News!" *Dr. James Hansen Communications*, Columbia University, June 27, 2024; Madeleine Cuff, "Three Years of High Temperatures Will Mean We Have Breached 1.5°C," *New Scientist*, May 24, 2024; Climate Science, Awareness and Solutions Program, June 27, 2024, www .columbia.edu/~jeh1/

29. Rebecca Lindsey, "Climate Change: Atmospheric Carbon Dioxide," *NOAA*, April 29, 2024, www.climate.gov; IPCC, "Summary for Policymakers," 13, www.ipcc.ch; Material Flows, www.materialflows.ne

30. Foster, "Extractivism in the Anthropocene"; Salvage Collective, *Tragedy of the Worker*, 88.

31. Ronald Reagan, "Remarks at Convocation Ceremonies at the University of South Carolina in Columbia, September 20, 1983," Ronald Reagan Presidential Library.

32. Dennis Meadows, "Growing, Growing, Gone: Reaching the Limits," interview, *Great Transition Initiative*, June 2015, www.greattransition.org/publication/growing-gro wing-gone

33. "Hire Private Firefighters . . . Save Neighbors' Homes Too," *TMZ*, November 12, 2018; Alexis Madrigal, "Kim Kardashian's Private Firefighters Expose America's Fault," *The Atlantic*, November 14, 2018; Jared Downing, "LA Millionaires Shell Out for $2,000/ Hour Private Firefighters as Overwhelmed City Abandons Neighborhoods to the Flames," *New York Post*, January 12, 2025; Raymond B. Craib, "Egotopia," *Counterpunch*, August 24, 2018.

34. "How the Super-Rich Are Building Their Luxury 'Safe House' Bunkers," *CNN*, August 7, 2024.

35. Matt Hamilton and David Zahniser, "Fire Hydrants Ran Dry as Pacific Palisades Burned: L.A. City Officials Blame 'Tremendous Demand'," *Los Angeles Times*, January 8, 2025; Rong-Gong Lin II, et al., "5 Dead, More Than 1,100 Structures Destroyed as Firestorm Besieges L.A. County," *Los Angeles Times*, January 8, 2025.

36. David Wallace-Wells, "Los Angeles Fire Season Is Beginning Again. And It Will Never End: A Bulletin from Our Climate Future," *Intelligencer*, May 12, 2019.

37. Naomi Klein and Astra Taylor, "The rise of end times fascism," *The Guardian*, Apr 13, 2025; Craig Collins, "Catabolism: Capitalism's Frightening Future," *Counterpunch*, November 1, 2018.

38. Salvage Collective, *Tragedy of the Worker*, 29; Wainwright and Mann, *Climate Leviathan*, 62.

39. Wainwright and Mann, *Climate Leviathan*, 28–30; "Pierre Dardot: 'Las guerras civiles del neoliberalismo.'"

40. Heron and Dean, "Climate Leninism and Revolutionary Transition," *Spectre*, June 26, 2022.

41. Meadows, qtd. in Boffroni, *Colapso*, 34.

42. Gudynas, "Varieties of Development," 725; Riofrancos, *Resource Radicals*, 11, 38–50; Boffroni, *Colapso*, 31; "Sobre la Fundación Bariloche," fundacionbariloche.org.ar /historia/

43. Hickel, "What Does Degrowth Mean?," 1106.

44. Boffroni, *Colapso*, 15; Bendell, *Breaking Together*, 32

45. Boffroni, *Colapso*, 35, 40; Servigne, Stevens, and Chapelle, *Another End of the World*, 2; Friedemann, *Life After Fossil Fuels*, 193.

46. De Angelis, *Omnia Sunt Communia*, 313.

47. Friedeman, *Life After Fossil Fuels*, 93; Eve Ottenberg, "Markets and Technology Won't Solve Climate Crisis," *Thruthout*, December 26, 2022.

Bibliography

Aaronson, D. E., C. T. Dienes, and M. C. Musheno. *Public Policy and Police Discretion: Processes of Decriminalization*. New York: Clark Boardman, 1984.

Abramsky, Kolya, and Massimo De Angelis. "Introduction: Energy Crisis (among Others) Is in the Air." *The Commoner* 13 (Winter 2008–9): 1–14.

Agamben, Giorgio. "For a Theory of Destituent Power." *Critical Legal Thinking*, February 5, 2014. criticallegalthinking.com

Agamben, Giorgio. *Democracy in What State?* New York: Columbia University Press, 2011.

Agamben, Giorgio. *Homo Sacer: Sovereign Power and Bare Life*. Stanford: Stanford University Press, 1998.

Agamben, Giorgio. *The Kingdom and the Glory: For a Theological Genealogy of Economy and Government*. Stanford, California: Stanford University Press, 2011.

Agamben, Giorgio. *Means without End*. Minneapolis: University of Minnesota Press, 2000.

Agamben, Giorgio. "Security and Terror." *Theory and Event* 5, no. 4 (2002).

Agamben, Giorgio. "State of Exception." *Phainomena* 21: 82–83 (2012).

Agamben, Giorgio. *State of Exception*. Chicago: University of Chicago Press, 2005.

Agamben, Giorgio. "What Is a Camp?" In *Means without End*. Minneapolis: University of Minnesota Press, 2000.

Agamben, Giorgio, Friedrich Hermanni, and Paul Silas Peterson. *Leviathans Rätsel Lucas-Preis 2013*. Tübingen: Mohr Siebeck, 2021.

Agamben, Giorgio, and William McCuaig. *Democracy in What State?* New York: Columbia University Press, 2011.

Ajao, Khadijat Oluwatoyin. "Citizen Journalism and Conflict in Africa: The Ushahidi Platform in Kenya's 2008 Post-Election Violence." PhD diss., University of Pretoria, October 2017.

Al-Aly, Z., H. Davis, L. McCorkell, et al. "Long COVID Science, Research and Policy." *Nature Medicine* 30 (2024): 2148–64.

Anderson, Benedict. *Imagined Communities: Reflections on the Origin and Spread of Nationalism*. London: Verso, 1991.

Anderson, Perry. "The Intransigent Right at the End of the Century." *London Review of Books* 14, no. 18 (1992).

Anderson, Scott R. "The Constitutional Quandary Already at the Border." *Lawfare*, January 22, 2019.

Annunziata, Rocío, Andrea Ariza, Valeria Romina March, and Sofía Torres. "The Anti-Political Politicization: Analysis of the Javier Milei's Phenomenon." *Revista SAAP* 18, no. 1 (May 2024): 13–42.

Ansah, Tawia. "Lawfare: A Rhetorical Analysis." 43 *Case Western Reserve Journal of International Law* 87 (2010).

Araghi, Farshad, and Marina Karides. "Land Dispossession and Global Crisis: Introduction to the Special Section on Land Rights in the World-System." *Journal of World-Systems Research* 18, no. 1 (2012): 1–5. https://doi.org/10.5195/jwsr.2012.487

Arendt, Hannah. *Eichmann in Jerusalem*. New York: Penguin, 2006.

Arendt, Hannah. *The Human Condition*. Chicago: University of Chicago Press, 1998.

Arendt, Hannah. *Life of the Mind*. New York: Harcourt Brace Jovanovich, 1978.

Arendt, Hannah. *On Revolution*. New York: Viking Press, 1970.

Arendt, Hannah. "The Perplexities of the Rights of Man." *Headline Series*, no. 318 (1998): 88–100.

Arendt, Hannah. "A Special Supplement: Reflections on Violence." *New York Review of Books* 12, no. 4 (February 27, 1969).

Aristotle. *Politics*. Translated by Benjamin Jowett. Oxford: Clarendon, 1967.

Arnold, Kathleen. "'Domestic War: Locke's Concept of Prerogative and Implications for US 'Wars' Today." *Polity* 39, no. 1 (2007): 1–27.

Artiga-Purcell, James Alejandro, Thomas Chiasson-LeBel, Fernando Ignacio Leiva, and Alejandra Watanabe-Farro. "Disaster Extractivism: Latin America's Extractive Shock Therapy in the Age of Covid-19." *Latin American Perspectives* 20, no. 30 (2023).

Balibar, Etienne. "Outlines of a Topography of Cruelty: Citizenship and Civility in the Era of Global Violence." *Constellations* 8, no. 1 (2002). https://doi.org/10.1111/1467-8675.00213

Barak, Gregg. *Crimes by the Capitalist State: An Introduction to State Criminality*. Albany: State University of New York Press, 1991.

Baranger, Denis. "The Apparition of Sovereignty." In *Sovereignty in Fragments*, edited by Quentin Skinner and Hent Kalmo. Cambridge: Cambridge University Press, 2010.

Barkan, Joshua. "Use beyond Value: Giorgio Agamben and a Critique of Capitalism." *Rethinking Marxism: A Journal of Economics, Culture & Society* 21, no. 2 (2009): 243–59.

Bartelson, Jens. "Making Exceptions: Some Remarks on the Concept of Coup d'État and Its History." *Political Theory* 25, no. 3 (1997).

Bayley, David H. "The Police and Political Development in Europe." In *The Formation of National States in Western Europe*, edited by Charles Tilly. Princeton: Princeton University Press, 1975.

Bean, Conor. "Potential without Exception: Emergency Powers after Agamben and Schmitt." Paper presented at the Association for Political Theory Conference, Blackburn, VA, November 21–23, 2024.

Beetham, David. "Legitimacy." In *International Encyclopedia of Political Science*, edited by Bertrand Badie, Dirk Berg-Schlosser, and Leonardo Morlino. Thousand Oaks, CA: Sage, 2011.

Behrent, Michael. "Liberalism without Humanism: Michel Foucault and the Free-Market Creed." In *Foucault and Neoliberalism*, edited by Daniel Zamora and Michael C. Behrent. Cambridge: Polity, 2016.

Behrman, Simon. "Police Killings and the Law." *International Socialism* 129 (January 4, 2011). https://isj.org.uk/police-killings-and-the-law/

Bendell, Jem. *Breaking Together: A Freedom-Loving Response to Collapse.* Bristol, UK: Good Works, an imprint of the Schumacher Institute, 2023.

Benjamin, Walter. *Illuminations.* New York: Schocken, 1968.

Bensaïd, Daniel. *The Dispossessed: Karl Marx's Debates on Wood Theft and the Rights of the Poor.* Minneapolis: University of Minnesota Press, 2021.

Berlant, Lauren. "The Epistemology of State Emotion." In *Dissent in Dangerous Times*, edited by Austin Sarat. Ann Arbor: University of Michigan Press, 2010.

Blake, Megan K. "More Than Just Food: Food Insecurity and Resilient Place Making through Community Self-Organising." *Sustainability* 11, no. 10 (2019).

Blakeley, Ruth. *State Terrorism and Neoliberalism: The North in the South.* London: Routledge, 2009.

Blaser, Mario, and Marisol de la Cadena. "The Uncommons: An Introduction." *Anthropologica* 59, no. 2 (2017): 185–93.

Boese, Vanessa A., Nazifa Alizada, Martin Lundstedt, Kelly Morrison, Natalia Natsika, Yuko Sato, Hugo Tai, and Staffan I. Lindberg. *Autocratization Changing Nature? Democracy Report 2022.* Gothenburg, Sweden: Varieties of Democracy Institute (V-Dem), 2022.

Boffroni, Flavia. *Colapso: Cómo transitar el umbral de los mundos por venir?* Buenos Aires: Sudamericana, 2024.

Bollier, David. "Who May Use the King's Forest? The Meaning of Magna Carta, Commons and Law in Our Time." September 14, 2015. www.bollier.org

Bondia Garcia, David. "The Emerging Human Rights Revolution: The Beginning of the Fifth Historical Process in the Consolidation of Human Rights." *Age of Human Rights Journal* 3 (2014): 63–101.

Bonefeld, Werner. "Free Economy and the Strong State: Some Notes on the State." *Capital & Class* 34, no. 1 (2010).

Bonner, Michelle D. *Policing Protest in Argentina and Chile.* Boulder, CO: Lynne Rienner, 2014.

Botero, Giovanni. *The Reason of State.* New Haven: Yale University Press, 1956.

Bottomore, T. B. *A Dictionary of Marxist Thought.* Cambridge, MA: Harvard University Press, 1983.

Boyer, Pierre C., Thomas Delemotte, Germain Gauthier, Vincent Rollet, and Benoît Schmutz. "The Origins of the 'Yellow Vests' Movement." *Revue Économique* 71, no. 1 (2020): 109–38.

Brand, Ulrich, Kristina Dietz, and Miriam Lang. "Neo-Extractivism in Latin America: One Side of a New Phase of Global Capitalist Dynamics." *Ciencia Política* 11, no. 21 (2016): 125–59.

Brezovšek, Marjan, and Damir Črnčec. "Secrecy in Democracy." *Journal of Comparative Politics* 2, no. 1 (2009): 27–50.

Brook, Anne Marie, K. Chad Clay, and Susan Randolph. "Human Rights Data for Everyone: Introducing the Human Rights Measurement Initiative (HRMI)." *Journal of Human Rights* 19, no. 3 (2020): 67–82.

Brown, Wendy. *In the Ruins of Neoliberalism.* New York: Columbia University Press, 2019.

Brown, Wendy. "Neo-liberalism and the End of Liberal Democracy." *Theory & Event* 7, no. 1 (2003).

Brown, Wendy. *States of Injury*. Princeton: Princeton University Press, 1995.

Brown, Wendy. *Undoing the Demos: Neoliberalism's Stealth Revolution*. Princeton: Princeton University Press, 2015.

Butler, Judith. *Performative Theory of Assembly*. Cambridge, MA: Harvard University Press, 2015.

Butler, Judith. *Precarious Life: The Powers of Mourning and Violence*. London: Verso, 2006.

Cadahia, Luciana, "La democracia en disputa," *Estado de situación de las democracias en América Latina y el Caribe*, edited by René Ramírez Gallegos. Buenos Aires: CLACSO, 2024.

Carey, John M., and Matthew Soberg Shugart. *Executive Decree Authority*. Cambridge: Cambridge University Press, 2009.

Carothers, Thomas, and Richard Youngs. "The Complexities of Global Protests." Carnegie Endowment for International Peace, 2006.

Castells, Manuel. *Rupture: The Crisis of Liberal Democracy*. Cambridge: Polity, 2019.

Celermajer, Danielle, David Schlosberg, Dinesh Wadiwel, and Christine Winter. "A Political Theory for a Multispecies, Climate-Challenged World: 2050." *Political Theory* 51, no. 1 (2023). https://doi.org/10.1177/00905917221128833

Charter of Emerging Human Rights. Barcelona, 2004.

Charter of Emerging Human Rights. "Human Rights in a Globalised World." Universal Forum of Cultures, Monterrey, 2007.

Chevigny, Paul. "The Populism of Fear: Politics of Crime in the Americas." *Punishment & Society* 5, no. 1 (2003): 77–96.

Chouliaras, Athanasios. "The Reason of State: Theoretical Inquiries and Consequences for the Criminology of State Crime." In *State Crime in the Global Age*, edited by William Chambliss, Raymond Michalowski, and Ronald Kramer, 234–37. London: Routledge, 2010.

Çıdam, Çiğdem. "Disagreeing about Democracy." *Theory & Event* 19, no. 1 (2016).

Çıdam, Çiğdem. *In the Street: Democratic Action, Theatricality, and Political Friendship*. Oxford: Oxford University Press, 2021.

Clark, Rob. "A Tale of Two Trends: Democracy and Human Rights, 1981–2010." *Journal of Human Rights* 13, no. 4 (2014): 395–413.

Cohen, Nissim, Gabriela Lotta, Rafael Alcadipan, and Teddy Lazebnik. "Trust and Street-Level Bureaucrats' Willingness to Risk Their Lives for Others: The Case of Brazilian Law Enforcement." *American Review of Public Administration* 54, no. 2 (2023).

Collins, Craig. "Catabolism: Capitalism's Frightening Future." *Counterpunch*, November 1, 2018.

Cooper, Marianne, and Maxim Voronov. "We've Hit Peak Denial: Here's Why We Can't Turn Away from Reality." *Scientific American*, June 18, 2024.

Cotterrell, Roger. *Law's Community: Legal Theory in Sociological Perspective*. Oxford: Clarendon, 1995.

Dardot, Pierre, and Christian Laval. *Dominar: Estudio Sobre La Soberanía Del Estado de Occidente*. Barcelona: Editorial Gedisa, 2021.

Dardot, Pierre, and Christian Laval. *Common, On Revolution in the 21st Century*. London: Bloomsbury, 2015.

Dafnos, Tia, Scott Thompson, and Martin French. "Surveillance and the Colonial Dream: Canada's Surveillance of Indigenous Self-Determination." In *National Security, Surveillance, and Terror: Canada and Australia in Comparative Research*, edited by Randy K. Lippert, Kevin Walby, and Ian Warren. Basingstoke, UK: Palgrave Macmillan, 2016.

Davidson, Mark, and Kevin Ward. *Cities under Austerity: Restructuring the US Metropolis*. Albany: State University of New York Press, 2018.

Davidson-Harden, Adam. "Interrogating the University as an Engine of Capitalism: Neoliberalism and Academic 'Raison d'État.'" *Policy Futures in Education* 8, no. 5.

Davis, Mike. "Mike Davis on the Crimes of Socialism and Capitalism." *Jacobin*, October 23, 2018.

Davis-Hamel, Ashley. "Successful Neoliberalism? State Policy, Poverty, and Income Inequality in Chile." *International Social Science Review* 87, nos. 3–4 (2021).

Dean, Jodi. *The Communist Horizon*. London: Verso, 2018.

Dean, Mitchell. *Critical and Effective Histories: Foucault's Methods and Historical Sociology*. London: Routledge, 1994.

Dean, Mitchell. "Three Forms of Democratic Political Acclamation." *Telos* 179 (Summer 2017).

Dean, Mitchell. "Political Acclamation, Social Media and the Public Mood." *European Journal of Social Theory* 20, no. 3 (2017): 417–34.

De Angelis, Massimo. "Marx and Primitive Accumulation: The Continuous Character of Capital's 'Enclosures.'" *The Commoner* 2 (September 2001). https://files.libcom.org/files/4_02deangelis.pdf

De Angelis, Massimo. "Marx's Theory of Primitive Accumulation: A Suggested Reinterpretation." 1999. https://libcom.org/library/marx-primitive-accumulation-reinterpretation-massimo-de-angelis

De Angelis, Massimo. *Omnia Sunt Communia*. London: Zed, 2017.

De Boever, Arne. "Agamben and Marx: Sovereignty, Governmentality, Economy." *Law Critique* 20 (2009).

Debord, Guy. *Comments on the Society of the Spectacle*. London: Verso, 1998.

Debord, Guy. *Society of the Spectacle*. New York: Zone Books, 1994.

De Keyzer, Maïka. *Inclusive Commons and the Sustainability of Peasant Communities in the Medieval Low Countries*. Milton, UK: Routledge, 2018.

Della Porta, Donatella. "Protest Cycles and Waves." In *The Wiley-Blackwell Encyclopedia of Social and Political Movements*, edited by David A. Snow, Donatella della Porta, Bert Klandermans, and Doug McAdam. Hoboken, NJ: Wiley-Blackwell, 2013.

de la Torre, Carlos. "Populism in Latin America." In *The Oxford Handbook of Populism*, edited by Cristóbal Rovira Kaltwasser, Paul Taggart, Paulina Ochoa Espejo, and Pierre Ostiguy. Oxford: Oxford University Press, 2017.

De Paula, Claudio Paixao Anastacio. "The Serenity of the Senex: Using Brazilian Folk Tales as an Alternative Approach to 'Entrepreneurship' in University Education." In *Psyche and the Arts: Jungian Approaches to Music, Architecture, Literature, Painting and Film*, edited by Susan Rowland. London: Routledge, 2008.

Dershowitz, Alan M. *Why Terrorism Works*. New Haven: Yale University Press, 2002.

Despouy, Leandro. "Report by the UN Special Rapporteur." New York: United Nations, 1997.

Djelic, Marie-Laure, and Reza Mousavi. "How the Neoliberal Think Tank Went Global: The Atlas Network, 1981 to the Present." In *Nine Lives of Neoliberalism*, edited by Dieter Plehwe, Quinn Slobodian, and Philip Mirowski. London: Verso, 2020.

Dubber, Markus. *The Police Power: Patriarchy and the Foundations of American Government*. New York: Columbia University Press, 2005.

Dubber, Markus D., and Mariana Valverde, eds. "Introduction: Policing the Rechtsstaat." In *Police and the Liberal State*, edited by Markus D. Dubber and Mariana Valverde. Stanford: Stanford University Press, 2008.

Dunkerley, James. *The Pacification of Central America*. London: Verso, 1994.

Edmundson, William A. *An Introduction to Rights*. Cambridge: Cambridge University Press.

Engelhardt, Tom. "Documenting Darkness: How a Thug State Operates." *TomDispatch*, February 20, 2014.

Eriksson, Johan. "Threat Framing." In *The Oxford Research Encyclopedia of Politics*. Oxford: Oxford University Press, 2020.

Exner, Andreas, Stephan Hochleithner, and Sarah Kumnig. "Expanding the Scope: The Commons within and beyond Capitalism in Crisis." In *Capitalism and the Commons: Just Commons in the Era of Multiple Crises*, edited by Andreas Exner, Sarah Kumnig, and Stephan Hochleithner. London: Routledge, 2022.

Ezrahi, Yaron. *Imagined Democracies: Necessary Political Fictions*. Cambridge: Cambridge University Press, 2012.

Fatovic, Clement. "Emergency." In *The Encyclopedia of Political Thought*, edited by Michael T. Gibbons. Hoboken, NJ: John Wiley & Sons, 2015.

Federici, Silvia. *Revolution at Point Zero*. Oakland, CA: PM Press, 2020.

Federici, Silvia. "Women's Struggles for Land in Africa and the Politics of the Commons." In *Re-Enchanting the World: Feminism and the Politics of the Commons*. Oakland, CA: PM Press, 2019.

Feierstein, Daniel. "National Security Doctrine in Latin America: The Genocide Question." In *The Oxford Handbook of Genocide Studies*, edited by Donald Bloxham and A. Dirk Moses. Oxford: Oxford University Press, 2010.

Feldman, Leonard C. "The Banality of Emergency: On the Time and Space of 'Political Necessity.'" In *Sovereignty, Emergency, Legality*, edited by Austin Sarat. Cambridge: Cambridge University Press, 2010.

Feldman, Leonard. "Necessity." In *Encyclopedia of Political Theory*, edited by M. T. Gibbons. Hoboken, NJ: John Wiley, 2014.

Feldman, Leonard. "Police Violence and the Legal Temporalities of Immunity." *Theory & Event* 20, no. 2 (2017).

Feldstein, Steven. "The Road to Digital Unfreedom: How Artificial Intelligence Is Reshaping Repression." *Journal of Democracy* 30, no. 1 (2019): 40–52.

Ferejohn, John, and Pasquale Pasquino. "Emergency Powers." In *Oxford Handbook of Political Theory*, edited by John S. Dryzek, Bonnie Honig, and Anne Phillips. Oxford: Oxford University Press, 2006.

Ferejohn, John, and Pasquale Pasquino. "The Law of the Exception: A Typology of Emergency Powers." *International Journal of Constitutional Law* 2, no. 2.

Ferreira-Neto, J. L. "The Right of the Governed: Foucault's Theoretical Political Turn." *Social Change Review* 15, nos. 1–2 (2017).

Fitzpatrick, Peter. *The Mythology of Modern Law*. London: Routledge, 1992.

Foster, John Bellamy. "Absolute Capitalism." *Monthly Review* 71, no. 1 (2019).

Foster, John Bellamy. "Extractivism in the Anthropocene," *Monthly Review, April 1, 2024*.

Foster, John Bellamy. "Nature as a Mode of Accumulation: Capitalism and the Financialization of the Earth." *Monthly Review* 73, no. 10 (March 2022).

Foster, John Bellamy, Brett Clark, and Hannah Holleman. "Marx and the Commons." *Social Research* 88, no. 1 (2021): 1–30.

Foucault, Michel. *Discipline and Punish. The Birth of the Prison*. New York: Vintage, 1977.

Foucault, Michel. *The Birth of Biopolitics: Lectures at the Collège de France, 1978–79*. Basingstoke, UK: Palgrave Macmillan, 2008.

Foucault, Michel. *Dits et écrits IV*. Paris: Gallimard, 1994.

Foucault, Michel. *Power/Knowledge*. New York: Pantheon, 1980.

Foucault, Michel. *Security, Territory, Population: Lectures at the Collège de France, 1977–1978*. New York: Picador/Palgrave Macmillan, 2009.

Foucault, Michel. *Society Must Be Defended*. New York: Picador, 2003.

Francois, Tanguay-Renaud. "The Intelligibility of Extralegal State Action: A General Lesson for Debates on Public Emergencies and Legality." *Osgoode CLPE Research Paper* 47, no. 6 (2010).

Frankel, Glenn. "The Crisis without End; Israel's Perpetual Emergency Has Become a Political Tool." *Washington Post*, June 13, 2004.

Fraser, Nancy. "Can Society Be Commodities All the Way Down? Post-Polanyian Reflections on the Capitalist Crisis." *Economy and Society* 43, no. 4 (2014).

Fraser, Nancy. *The Old Is Dying and the New Cannot Be Born*. London: Verso, 2019.

Freelona, Deen, and Chris Wells. "Disinformation as Political Communication." *Political Communication* 37, no. 2 (2020).

Friedemann, Alice J. *Life after Fossil Fuels: A Reality Check on Alternative Energy*. Chams, Switzerland: Springer, 2021.

Friedman, Milton. *Capitalism and Freedom*. Chicago: University of Chicago Press, 1982.

Friedman, Milton. "Free Markets and the Generals." *Newsweek*, January 25, 1982.

Friedman, Milton. "Neo-Liberalism and Its Prospects." *Farmand*, February 17, 1951.

Friedrich, Carl J. "The Road to Serfdom by Friedrich A. Hayek." *American Political Science Review* 39, no. 3 (1945).

Frost, David. *Frost/Nixon: Behind the Scenes of the Nixon Interviews*. New York: Harper Perennial, 2007.

Fukuyama, Francis. "Capitalism and Democracy: The Missing Link." *Journal of Democracy* 3, no. 3 (1992): 100–110.

Gago, Verónica. *La razón neoliberal: Economías barrocas y pragmática popular*. Mexico City: Tinta Limón, 2014.

Gago, Verónica, and Sandro Mezzadra. "A Critique of the Extractive Operations of Capital: Toward an Expanded Concept of Extractivism." *Rethinking Marxism* 29, no. 4 (2018): 574–91. https://doi.org/10.1080/08935696.2017.1417087

Galtung, Johan. "Cultural Violence." *Journal of Peace Research* 27, no. 3.

Galtung, Johan. "Violence, Peace, and Peace Research." *Journal of Peace Research* 6, no. 3 (1969).

Gandesha, Samir, and Johan F. Hartle. "Reification and Spectacle: The Timeliness of Western Marxism." In *The Spell of Capital: Reification and Spectacle*, edited by Samir Gandesha and Johan F. Hartle. Amsterdam: Amsterdam University Press, 2017.

García Negroni, María Marta, and Mónica Graciela Zoppi Fontana. *Análisis lingüístico y discurso político: El poder de enunciar*. Centro Editor de América Latina, 1992.

Gargarella, Roberto. *The Law as a Conversation among Equals*. Cambridge: Cambridge University Press, 2022.

Gargarella, Roberto. *Manifiesto por un derecho de izquierda*. Buenos Aires: Siglo XXI, 2023.

Gascon, Daniel, Sebastián Sclofsky, Xavier Perez, Jhon Sanabria, and Analicia Mejia Mesinas, eds. *Police and State Crime in the Americas: Southern and Postcolonial Perspectives*. Basingstoke, UK: Palgrave Macmillan, 2024.

Gawel, Antonia, Nathan Cooper, and Lukas Bester. "What the IPCC Report Tells Us about the Need for Radical Climate Action." *World Economic Forum*, March 3, 2022.

Gerbaudo, Paolo. "The Pandemic Crowd: Protest in the Time of COVID-19." *Journal of International Affairs* 73, no. 2 (2020).

Giroux, Henry A. 2006. *Beyond the Spectacle of Terrorism: Global Uncertainty and the Challenge of the New Media*. Boulder, CO: Paradigm.

Giugni, Marco. "Was It Worth the Effort? The Outcomes and Consequences of Social Movements." *Annual Review of Sociology* 24 (1998).

Golder, Ben. *Foucault and the Politics of Rights*. Stanford: Stanford University Press, 2015.

Gowder, Paul. "Isonomia: The Dawn of Legal Equality." In *The Rule of Law in the Real World*, edited by Paul Gowder. Cambridge: Cambridge University Press, 2016.

Greene, Alan. "Shielding the State of Emergency: Organised Crime in Ireland and the State's Response." *Northern Ireland Legal Quarterly* 62, no. 3 (2020).

Gros, Frédéric. *The Security Principle: From Serenity to Regulation*. London: Verso, 2019.

Gross, Oren. "What 'Emergency' Regime?" *Constellations* 13, no. 1.

Gross, Oren, and Fionnuala Ní Aoláin. *Law in Times of Crisis: Emergency Powers in Theory and Practice*. Cambridge: Cambridge University Press, 2006.

Gross, Oren, Fionnuala Ní Aoláin, Crawford, and Bell. "Accommodation." In *Dominant Perspectives of Constitutional Reason of State*, edited by Rosenblum.

Gruber, Annie. "État de siège." *Encyclopædia Universalis*. www.universalis.fr/encycloped ie/etat-de-siege/

Gudynas, Eduardo. "Beyond Varieties of Development: Disputes and Alternatives." *Third World Quarterly* 37, no. 21.

Guénoun, Solange, and James H. Kavanagh. "Jacques Rancière: Literature, Politics, Aesthetics: Approaches to Democratic Disagreement." *SubStance* 29, no. 2 (2000).

Gunder Frank, Andre. "Andre Gunder Frank official website." www.rrojasdatabank.info /agfrank/index.html

Gündoğdu, Ayten. "Potentialities of Human Rights: Agamben and the Narrative of Fated Necessity." *Contemporary Political Theory* 11, no. 1 (February 2012).

Han, Byung-Chul. *Psychopolitics: Neoliberalism and New Technologies of Power*. London: Verso, 2017.

Hardin, Russell. "Compliance, Consent, and Legitimacy." In *The Oxford Handbook of Comparative Politics*, edited by Carles Boix and Susan C. Stokes. Oxford: Oxford University Press, 2009.

Hardt, Michael. *Commonwealth*. Cambridge, MA: Harvard University Press, 2009.

Harsin, Jayson. "The Nuit Debout Movement: Communication, Politics, and the Counter-Production of 'Everynight Life.'" *International Journal of Communication* 12 (2018): 1819–39.

Harvey, David. *A Brief History of Neoliberalism*. Oxford: Oxford University Press, 2005.

Harvey, David. *A Companion to Marx's Capital*. London: Verso, 2018.

Hay, Douglas. "E. P. Thompson and the Rule of Law: Qualifying the Unqualified Good." In *The Cambridge Companion to the Rule of Law*, edited by David Hay. Cambridge: Cambridge University Press, 2021.

Hayek, Friedrich. *The Constitution of Liberty*. Chicago: University of Chicago Press, 1960.

Hayek, Friedrich. *The Road to Serfdom*. Chicago: University of Chicago Press, 2007.

Hegel, Georg Wilhelm Friedrich. *Philosophy of Right*. Kitchener, Ontario: Batoche Books, 2001.

Heifer, Laurence R. "Rethinking Derogations from Human Rights Treaties." *American Journal of International Law* 115, no. 1.

Heinrich, Michael. *An Introduction to the Three Volumes of Karl Marx's Capital*. New York: Monthly Review Press, 2012.

Henkin, Louis. "That 'S' Word: Sovereignty, and Globalization, and Human Rights." *Fordham Law Review* 68, no. 1 (1999).

Herf, Jeffrey. "Emergency Powers Helped Hitler's Rise: Germany Has Avoided Them Ever Since." *Washington Post*, February 19, 2019.

Heron, Kai, and Jodi Dean. "Climate Leninism and Revolutionary Transition." *Spectre*, June 26, 2022.

Hesmondhalgh, David. "User-Generated Content, Free Labour and the Cultural Industries." *Ephemera* 10, nos. 3–4 (2010).

Hickel, Jason. 2020. "What Does Degrowth Mean? A Few Points of Clarification." *Globalizations* 18, no. 7.

Hirsch, Joachim, and John Kannankulam. "The Spaces of Capital: The Political Form of Capitalism and the Internationalization of the State." *Antipode* 43. https://doi.org/10.1111/j.1467-8330.2010.00809.x

Hobbes, Thomas. *Leviathan*. Oxford: Oxford University Press, 1965.

Hobsbawm, Eric. "Chile: Year One." In *Viva la Revolucion: Hobsbawm on Latin America*. New York: Little, Brown, 2016.

Hobsbawm, Eric. "Introduction: Inventing Traditions." In *Invented Traditions*, edited by Eric Hobsbawm and Terence Ranger. Cambridge: Cambridge University Press, 1983.

Hoffmann, Stefan-Ludwig. *Human Rights in the Twentieth Century*. New York: Cambridge University Press, 2011.

Holmes, Marisa. *Organizing Occupy Wall Street: This Is Just Practice*. Basingstoke, UK: Palgrave Macmillan, 2023.

Holmes, Stephen. "The Spider's Web: How Government Lawbreakers Routinely Elude the Law." In *When Governments Break the Law*, edited by Austin Sarat and Nasser Hussain. New York: NYU Press, 2010.

Honig, Bonnie. *Emergency Politics: Paradox, Law, Democracy*. Princeton: Princeton University Press, 2009.

Hund, Kirsten, Daniele La Porta, Thao P. Fabregas, Tim Laing, and John Drexhage. *Minerals for Climate Action: The Mineral Intensity of the Clean Energy Transition*. New York: World Bank Group, 2020.

Hussain, Nasser. *The Jurisprudence of Emergency: Colonialism and the Rule of Law*. Ann Arbor: University of Michigan Press, 2019.

Huysmans, Jef. "The Jargon of Exception—on Schmitt, Agamben and the Absence of Political Society." *International Political Sociology* 2, no. 2 (2008): 165–83.

Hyslop, Jonathan. "The Invention of the Concentration Camp: Cuba, Southern Africa and the Philippines, 1896–1907." *South African Historical Journal* 63, no. 2 (2011): 251–76.

Illouz, Eva, and Avital Sicron. *The Emotional Life of Populism*. Cambridge, UK: Polity Press, 2023.

Ivison, Duncan. *Rights*. London: Routledge, 2007.

Jessop, Bob. "Bringing the State Back In (Yet Again): Reviews, Revisions, Rejections, and Redirections." *International Review of Sociology* 11, no. 2 (2001).

Jessop, Bob. "From Micro-Powers to Governmentality: Foucault's Work on Statehood, State Formation, Statecraft and State Power," *Political Geography*, Volume 26, Issue 1, 34-40 (2007).

Jusionyte, Ieva. "On and Off the Record: The Production of Legitimacy in an Argentine Border Town." *Political and Legal Anthropology Review* 36, no. 2 (2013).

Kalmo, Hent, and Quentin Skinner. "The Sovereign State: A Genealogy." In *Sovereignty in Fragments: The Past, Present and Future of a Contested Concept*, edited by Hent Kalmo and Quentin Skinner. Cambridge: Cambridge University Press, 2011.

Kalyvas, Andreas. *Democracy and the Politics of the Extraordinary: Max Weber, Carl Schmitt and Hannah Arendt*. Cambridge: Cambridge University Press.

Kantorowicz, Ernst. *The King's Two Bodies: A Study in Medieval Political Theology*. Princeton: Princeton University Press, 1957.

Kantorowicz, Ernst. *Laudes regiae; a Study in Liturgical Acclamations and Mediaeval Ruler Worship*. New York: Kraus, 1974.

Karatani, Kojin. *Isonomia and the Origins of Philosophy*. Durham: Duke University Press, 2017.

Kasmir, Sharryn. "Precarity." In *The Cambridge Encyclopedia of Anthropology*, March 2018. https://www.anthroencyclopedia.com/

Kellner, Douglas. "Media Spectacles and Media Events: Some Critical Reflections." In *Media Events in a Global Age*, edited by Nick Couldry, Andreas Hepp, and Friedrich Krotz. London: Routledge, 2010.

Kernaghan, Richard. *Coca's Gone: Of Might and Right in the Huallaga Post-Boom*. Stanford: Stanford University Press, 2009.

Klare, Michael. *The Race for What's Left*. New York: Metropolitan Books, 2012.

Klein, Naomi. *The Shock Doctrine: The Rise of Disaster Capitalism*. Toronto: Alfred A. Knopf Canada, 2007.

Knemeyer, F. L. "Polizei." *Economy and Society* 9, no. 2 (1980): 72–96.

Koshgarian, Lindsay. "The Nearly $1 Trillion US Military Budget Doesn't Provide Safety, Only Profit." *Truthout*, June 29, 2024.

Koshgarian, Lindsay, Ashik Siddique, and Lorah Steichen. *State of Insecurity: The Cost of Militarization since 9/11*. Washington, DC: Institute for Policy Studies, 2021.

Kotek, Joël. "Concentration Camps." In *Encyclopedia of Genocide and Crimes against Humanity*, edited by Dinah L. Shelton. New York: Macmillan, 2005.

Kotsko, Adam. "Neoliberalism's Demons." *Theory & Event* 20, no. 2 (April 2017).

Kotsko, Adam. *Neoliberalism's Demons: On the Political Theology of Late Capital*. Palo Alto, CA: Stanford University Press, 2018.

Kotz, David M. "The Financial and Economic Crisis of 2008: A Systemic Crisis of Neoliberal Capitalism." *Review of Radical Political Economics* 41, no. 3 (2009): 305–17.

Krausmann, Fridolin, Dominik Wiedenhofer, Christian Lauk, and Helmut Haberl. "Global Socioeconomic Material Stocks Rise 23-Fold over the 20th Century and Require Half of Annual Resource Use." *Proceedings of the National Academy of Sciences* 114, no. 8 (2017).

Kubal, Mary Rose, and Eloy Fisher. "The Politics of Student Protest and Education Reform in Chile: Challenging the Neoliberal State." *Latin Americanist*, June 2016.

Lacey, W.K., "Patria Potestas," *The Family in Ancient Rome: New Perspectives*. Edited by Beryl Rawson. Ithaca, N.Y.: Cornell University Press, 1986.

Laclau, Ernesto. *Populist Reason*. London: Verso, 2005.

Laclau, Ernesto, and Chantal Mouffe. *Hegemony and Socialist Strategy: Towards a Radical Democratic Politics*. London: Verso, 1994.

Laliotis, Ioannis, John P. A. Ioannidis, and Charitini Stavropoulou. "Total and Cause-Specific Mortality before and after the Onset of the Greek Economic Crisis: An Interrupted Time-Series Analysis." *Lancet* 1, no. 2 (2016).

Leiva, Fernando Ignacio. *The Left Hand of Capital*. Albany: State University of New York Press, 2021.

Letelier, Orlando. "The Chicago Boys in Chile: Economic Freedom's Awful Toll," *The Nation* 223, no. 28 (1976): 137–42.

Levitsky, Steven, and Daniel Ziblatt. *How Democracies Die*. New York: Broadway Books, 2018.

Levy, Guillermo, Ricardo Aronskind, Myriam Pelazas, and Lucas Arrimada, et al. *Ensayos urgentes: Para pensar la Argentina que asoma*. Buenos Aires: Marea Editorial, 2023.

Lipsky, Michael. "Protest as a Political Resource." *American Political Science Review* 62, no. 4 (1968): 1144–58.

Lipsky, Michael. *Street Level Bureaucrats: Dilemmas of the Individual in Public Services*. New York: Russell Sage, 1980.

Locke, John. *Two Treatises of Government*. Edited by Peter Laslett. Cambridge: Cambridge University Press, 1988.

Lokaneeta, Jinee. *Transnational Torture: Law, Violence, and State Power in the United States and India*. New York: New York University Press, 2011.

Lokaneeta, Jinee. *The Truth Machines: Policing, Violence, and Scientific Interrogations in India*. Ann Arbor: University of Michigan Press, 2020.

Loughlin, Martin. *Foundations of Public Law*. Oxford: Oxford University Press, 2010.

Lowry, Sam. "The French Pensions Strikes, 1995." libcom.org/history/french-pensions-strikes-1995

Lowy, Michael. *Fire Alarm: Reading Walter Benjamin's 'On the Concept of History'.* London: Verso, 2016.

Lührmann, Anna, et al. *Regimes of the World Classification, and Own Expansions and Refinements*. 2018. v-dem.net/vdemds

Lührmann, Anna, and Staffan I. Lindberg. "A Third Wave of Autocratization Is Here: What Is New about It?" *Democratization* 26, no. 7 (2019): 1095–1113.

Lührmann, Anna, Seraphine F. Maerz, Sandra Grahn, Nazifa Alizada, Lisa Gastaldi, Sebastian Hellmeier, Garry Hindle, and Staffan I. Lindberg. *Autocratization Surges—Resistance Grows. Democracy Report 2020*. Varieties of Democracy Institute (V-Dem), March 2020.

Machiavelli, Niccolò. *Discourses on Livy*. Chicago: University of Chicago Press, 1996.

Madra, Yahya M., and Fikret Adaman. *Neoliberal Reason and Its Forms: De-Politicisation through Economisation*. Paper, Department of Economics, Boğaziçi University, Istanbul. https://courses.umass.edu/econ804/Madra.pdf

Mahmud, Tayyab. "Law of Geography and the Geography of Law: A Post-Colonial Mapping." *Washington University Jurisprudence Review* 3, no. 1 (2011).

Mandel, Ernest. "The Origins of National Socialism: Singularity and Repeatability of the Nazi Crimes." Amsterdam: International Institute for Research and Education, October 23, 2020.

Manin, Bernard. "The Emergency Paradigm and the New Terrorism." In *Les usages de la séparation des pouvoirs*, edited by Sandrine Baume and Biancamaria Fontana. Paris: Michel Houdiard, 2008.

Mansley, David. *Collective Violence, Democracy, and Protest Policing: Protest Events in Great Britain*. London: Routledge, 2013.

Mariani, Philomena. "Overview: Law, Order, and Neoliberalism." *Social Justice* 28, no. 3 (2001): 2–4.

Marso, Lori. *Feminism and the Cinema of Experience*. Durham: Duke University Press, 2024.

Marx, Karl. *Capital: A Critique of Political Economy*. Vol. 1. London: Penguin.

Marx, Karl. *Selected Writings*. Edited by Dan Kirklin. Indianapolis, IN: Hackett, 1994.

Marx, Karl. *Marx: Early Political Writings*. Cambridge: Cambridge University Press, 1994.

Masco, Joseph. Afterword to William Garriott, *Policing and Contemporary Governance: The Anthropology of Police in Practice*. Basingstoke, UK: Palgrave Macmillan, 2013.

McBride, Keally D. *Collective Dreams: Political Imagination and Community*. State College: Pennsylvania State University Press, 2005.

McLoughlin, Daniel. "Giorgio Agamben on Security, Government and the Crisis of Law." *Griffith Law Review* 21, no. 3 (2012).

McQuade, Brendan. *Pacifying the Homeland*. Berkeley: University of California Press, 2019.

Mehozay, Yoav. "The Fluid Jurisprudence of Israel's Emergency Powers: Legal Patchwork as a Governing Norm." *Law & Society Review* 46, no. 1 (2012).

Meinecke, Friedrich. *Machiavellism: The Doctrine of Raison d'État and Its Place in Modern History*. London: Routledge, 1984.

Menichelli, Francesca. "The National Picture: The Reconfiguration of Sovereignty, the Normalization of Emergency and the Rise to Prominence of Urban Security in Italy." *European Journal of Criminology* 12, no. 3 (2013).

Menke, Christoph. *Critique of Rights*. Hoboken, NJ: Wiley, 2020.

Merrick, Jeffrey, "The Entry of Henri II into Paris, 16 June 1549. I. D. McFarlane; Le roi-machine: Spectacle et politique au temps de Louis XIV, Jean-Marie Apostolides; Vive le roi: A History of the French Coronation from Charles V to Charles X, Richard A. Jackson," *The Journal of Modern History*, Volume 58, Number 4, 927–30 (1986).

Mignolo, Walter. "Coloniality Is Far from Over, and So Must Be Decoloniality." *Afterall*, January 1, 2017.

Mill, John Stuart. "On the Treatment of Barbarous Nations" (1874). In *Dissertations and Discussions: Political, Philosophical, and Historical*. Vol. 3. New York, 1874.

Mizock, Adam. "The Legality of the Fifty-Two-Year State of Emergency in Israel." 7 *UC Davis Journal of International Law and Policy* 223.

Mladek, Klaus. "Exception Rules: Contemporary Political Theory and the Police." In *Police Forces: A Cultural History of an Institution*, edited by Klaus Mladek. Basingstoke, UK: Macmillan, 2007.

Moffitt, Benjamin. *The Global Rise of Populism: Performance, Political Style, and Representation*. Stanford: Stanford University Press, 2016.

Moffitt, Benjamin, and Simon Tormey. "Rethinking Populism: Politics, Mediatisation and Political Style." *Political Studies* 62, no. 2 (2013).

Montag, Warren. "Necroeconomics. Adam Smith and Death in the Life of the Universal." *Radical Philosophy* 134 (2005).

Montalván Zambrano, Digno, and Isabel Wences. "Transición energética y litio: Nuevos 'comunes' y otros." *Oñati socio-legal series* 14, no. 2 (2022): 416–46.

Montes, Leonidas. "Friedman's Two Visits to Chile in Context." Summer Institute for the Study of the History of Economics, Duke University, May 31-June 12, 2015.

Moore, Jason W. *Capitalism in the Web of Life: Ecology and the Accumulation of Capital*. London: Verso, 2015.

Moore, Jen, and Manuel Perez-Rocha. *Extraction Casino*. May 1. Washington, DC: Institute for Policy Studies, 2019.

Moses, Asher. "'Collapse of Civilisation Is the Most Likely Outcome': Top Climate Scientists." *Resilience*, June 8, 2020.

Moyn, Samuel. *Human Rights and the Uses of History*. London: Verso, 2014.

Muir, William K., Jr. *Police: Streetcorner Politicians*. Chicago: University of Chicago Press, 1977.

Murphy, John P. "The Rise of the Precariat? Unemployment and Social Identity in a French Outer City." In *Anthropologies of Unemployment: New Perspectives on Work and Its Absence*, edited by Jong Bum Kwon and Carrie M. Lane. Ithaca, NY: Cornell University Press, 2016.

Murray, Alex. "State of Exception." In *The Agamben Dictionary*, edited by Alex Murray and Jessica Whyte. Edinburgh: Edinburgh University Press, 2011.

Murray, Alex, and Thanos Zartaloudis. "The Power of Thought." *Law Critique* 20 (2009): 207–10.

Nardulli, Peter F., Buddy Peyton, and Joseph Bajjalieh. "Conceptualizing and Measuring Rule of Law Constructs, 1850–2010." *Journal of Law and Courts* (Spring 2013).

Narkunas, J. Paul. "Human Rights and States of Emergency: Humanitarians and Governmentality." *Culture, Theory and Critique* 56, no. 2 (2014): 208–27.

Neocleous, Mark. *Critique of Security*. Edinburgh: Edinburgh University Press, 2008.

Neocleous, Mark. *The Fabrication of Social Order*. London: Pluto, 2000.

Neocleous, Mark. "The Fate of the Body Politic." *Radical Philosophy* 108 (July/August 2001).

Neocleous, Mark. *Imagining the State*. New York: McGraw-Hill Education, 2003.

Neocleous, Mark. "Martial Law." *Encyclopedia Britannica*, February 18, 2020.

Neocleous, Mark. "'Original, Absolute, Indefeasible': Or, What We Talk about When We Talk about Police Power." *Social Justice* 47, nos. 3–4 (2020): 9–32.

Neocleous, Mark. "Police, First Emerging between the 15th and 16th Century." In *Three Phases of Security: Westphalia/18th Century French Policies*, 19th Century Institutions, 2020.

Neocleous, Mark. "The Problem with Normality: Taking Exception to 'Permanent Emergency'." *Global, Local, Political* 31, no. 2 (2006).

Neocleous, Mark. 2007. "Security, Liberty and the Myth of Balance: Towards a Critique of Security Politics." *Contemporary Political Theory* 6, no. 2.

Neocleous, Mark. *The Universal Adversary*. London: Routledge, 2016.

Neocleous, Mark. *War Power, Police Power*. Edinburgh: Edinburgh University Press, 2014.

Neocleous, Mark. "Whatever Happened to Martial Law?" *Radical Philosophy* 143 (2007).

Neocleous, Mark, and George S. Rigakos. *Anti-Security*. Ottawa, Ontario: Red Quill Books, 2011.

Nigro, Roberto. "From Reason of State to Liberalism: The Coup d'État as Form of Government." In *The Government of Life: Foucault, Biopolitics, and Neoliberalism*, edited by Vanessa Lemm and Miguel Vatter. New York: Fordham University Press, 2014.

Nolte, Hans-Heinrich, and Almut Schilling-Vacaflor. *New Constitutionalism in Latin America: Promises and Practices*. London: Routledge, 2012.

Nord, Marina, Martin Lundstedt, David Altman, Fabio Angiolillo, Cecilia Borella, Tiago Fernandes, Lisa Gastaldi, Ana Good God, Natalia Natsika, and Staffan I. Lindberg. *Democracy Report 2024: Democracy Winning and Losing at the Ballot*. University of Gothenburg: V-Dem Institute, 2024.

Novak, William J. "Police Power and the Hidden Transformation of the American State." In *Police and the Liberal State*, edited by Markus D. Dubber and Mariana Valverde. Stanford: Stanford University Press, 2008.

O'Connor, John. "Marxism and the Three Movements of Neoliberalism." *Critical Sociology* 36, no. 5 (2010).

O'Donnell, Guillermo A. *Democracia en la Argentina: Micro y macro*. Notre Dame, IN: Helen Kellogg Institute for International Studies, University of Notre Dame, 1983.

O'Donnell, Guillermo. "The Quality of Democracy: Why the Rule of Law Matters." *Journal of Democracy* 15, no. 4 (2004).

O'Kane, Chris. "State Violence, State Control: Marxist State Theory and the Critique of Political Economy." *Viewpoint Magazine*, October 2014.

Oksala, Johanna. "Violence and Neoliberal Governmentality." *Constellations* 18, no. 3 (2011): 474–86.

Ong, Aihwa. *Neoliberalism as Exception*. Durham: Duke University Press, 2006.

Orellana Calderón, Fernando. "In Chile, the Post-Neoliberal Future is Now." *NACLA* (Spring 2020), 100–108. nacla.org

Ortiz, Isabel, Sara Burke, Mohamed Berrada, and Hernán Saenz Cortés. *Brief: World Protests 2021–2022*. New York: Initiative for Policy Dialogue, Columbia University, 2022.

Ortiz, Isabel, Sara Burke, Mohamed Berrada, and Hernán Saenz Cortés. *World Protests: A Study of Key Protest Issues in the 21st Century*. Basingstoke, UK: Palgrave Macmillan, 2022.

Ortiz, Isabel, and Matthew Cummins. "Austerity: The New Normal." October 2019. https://papers.ssrn.com/sol3/papers.cfm?abstract_id=3523562

Ortiz, Isabel, and Matthew Cummins. *End Austerity.* New York: Initiative for Policy Dialogue, Columbia University, 2022.

Ortiz, Isabel, and Matthew Cummins. "Global Austerity Alert: Looming Budget Cuts in 2021–25 and Alternative Pathways." April. New York: Initiative for Policy Dialogue, Columbia University, 2021.

Ortiz-Ospina, Esteban. "The Rise of Social Media." Our World in Data, September 18, 2019. ourworldindata.org/

Ostry, Jonathan D., Prakash Loungani, and Davide Furceri. "Neoliberalism, Oversold?" *Finance & Development* 53, no. 2.

Otto, J., C. Andrews, F. Cawood, M. Doggett, P. Guj, F. Stermole, J. Stermole, and J. Tilto. *Mining Royalties: A Global Study of Their Impact on Investors, Government, and Civil Society.* Washington, DC: World Bank, 2006.

Parekh, Bhikhu. "The Modern Conception of Right and Its Marxist Critique." *India International Centre Quarterly* 13, nos. 3–4 (1986).

Parkinson, John. "The Intersection of Masks and the Law: Public Health vs Public Safety?" *ContagionLive*, May 16, 2024.

Pashukanis, Evgeny. *Selected Writings on Marxism and Law.* Edited by Piers Beirne and Robert Sharlet, translated by Peter B. Maggs. London: Academic Press, 1980.

Passavant, Paul. *Policing Protest.* Durham: Duke University Press, 2021.

Paye, Jean-Claude. "Sovereignty and the State of Emergency." *Monthly Review*, January 1, 2017.

Pereira, Anthony W. "Understanding Right-Wing Populism (or the Extreme Right)." *LASA Forum* 54, no. 4 (Fall 2023).

Perelman, Michael. 2000. *The Invention of Capitalism: Classical Political Economy and the Secret History of Primitive Accumulation.* Durham: Duke University Press.

Polanyi, Karl. *Great Transformation: The Political and Economic Origins of Our Time.* Boston: Beacon, 2001.

Poole, Thomas. "Judicial Review at the Margins: Law, Power, and Prerogative." *University of Toronto Law Journal* 60, no. 1 (2010).

Poole, Thomas. *Reason of State: Law, Prerogative and Empire.* Cambridge: Cambridge University Press, 2015.

Prados-de-la-Escosura, Leandro. "A History of Economic Freedom." *World Economic Forum*, November 26, 2015.

Prozorov, Sergei. "A Farewell to Homo Sacer? Sovereign Power and Bare Life in Agamben's Coronavirus Commentary." *Law Critique* 34 (2023): 63–80.

Ramos, Gabriela. "Ethics of AI and Democracy: UNESCO Recommendation's Insights." *Turkish Policy Quarterly* 20, no. 4 (2021).

Rancière, Jacques. *Disagreement: Politics and Philosophy.* Minneapolis: University of Minnesota Press, 1999.

Rancière, Jacques. *Dissensus: On Politics and Aesthetics.* London: Bloomsbury, 2010.

Rancière, Jacques. *Hatred of Democracy.* London: Verso, 2013.

Rancière, Jacques. "Ten Theses on Politics." *Theory & Event* 5, no. 3 (2001).

Rancière, Jacques. "Who Is the Subject of the Rights of Man?" *South Atlantic Quarterly* 103, nos. 2–3 (Spring/Summer 2004): 297–310.

Ravecca, Paulo. *The Politics of Political Science*. London: Routledge, 2019.

Ravecca, Paulo, Emiliano Robaina, and Facundo Zannier. "Reading the Far-Right beyond Self-Righteousness: Neoliberalism, Democratic Deficit, and Javier Milei's Global Leadership." *Lua Nova* (forthcoming).

Ravecca, Paulo, Marcela Schenck, Bruno Fonseca, and Diego Forteza. "What Are They Doing *Right*? Tweeting Right-Wing Intersectionality in Latin America." *Globalizations* 20, no. 1 (2022): 38–59.

Regilme, S. S. "Constitutional Order in Oligarchic Democracies: Neoliberal Rights versus Socio-Economic Rights." *Law, Culture and the Humanities* 19, no. 1 (2023).

Rejali, Darius. *Torture and Democracy*. Princeton: Princeton University Press, 2007.

Resmini, Fabio. "The Long Coup in Ecuador." *NACLA*, November 18, 2019.

Reyes, Antonio. "Strategies of Legitimization in Political Discourse: From Words to Actions." *Discourse & Society* 22, no. 6 (2011): 781–807.

Richardson, Neal P. "Export-Oriented Populism: Commodities and Coalitions in Argentina." *Studies in Comparative International Development* 44 (2009): 228–55.

Rigakos, George. "Marxist Legal Theory: Security." *Critical Legal Studies* (2020). https://criticallegalthinking.com/2020/06/09/marxist-legal-theory-security/

Riofrancos, Thea. *Resource Radicals: From Petro-Nationalism to Post-Extractivism in Ecuador*. Durham: Duke University Press, 2020.

Roa Avendaño, Tatiana, and Jessica Toloza. "Dynamics of a Songful Resistance." *The Commoner* 13 (Winter 2008–9).

Roberts, Christopher. "The Age of Emergency." *Washington University Global Studies Law Review* 20 (2021): 99.

Robin, Corey. "Nietzsche, Hayek, and the Meaning of Conservatism." *Jacobin*, June 26, 2013.

Robin, Corey. *The Reactionary Mind: Conservatism from Edmund Burke to Sarah Palin*. Oxford: Oxford University Press, 2011.

Rodgers, Christopher, and Duncan Mackay. "Creating 'New' Commons for the Twenty-First Century: Innovative Legal Models for 'Green Space.'" *Journal of Environmental Planning and Management* 61, nos. 5–6 (2017): 1051–69.

Rodilosso, Ermelinda. "Filter Bubbles and the Unfeeling: How AI for Social Media Can Foster Extremism and Polarization." *Philosophy & Technology* 37, no. 2 (2024): 1–21.

Rodrik, Dani. "Goodbye Washington Consensus, Hello Washington Confusion? A Review of the World Bank's *Economic Growth in the 1990s: Learning from a Decade of Reform*." *Journal of Economic Literature* 44 (2006): 973–87.

Rosenblum, Nancy L. "Constitutional Reason of State: The Fear Factor." In *Dissent in Dangerous Times*, edited by Austin Sarat. Ann Arbor: University of Michigan Press, 2010.

Ross, Daniel. *Violent Democracy*. Cambridge: Cambridge University Press, 2004.

Rossello, Diego. "Fleshing Out Political Theology: Santner's *The Royal Remains*." *Theory & Event* 14, no. 4 (2011): 1.

Rossello, Diego. *La teoría política en el antropoceno: Animalidad, soberanía, dignidad*. Valencia: Tirant Humanidades Valencia, 2024.

Roth, Kenneth. "The Great Civil Society Choke-Out." *Foreign Policy*, January 27, 2016.

Rousseau, Jean-Jacques. *The Social Contract; and the First and Second Discourses*. Edited and translated by Susan Dunn. New Haven: Yale University Press, 2002.

Rozitchner, León. "Terror and Grace." *Journal of Latin American Cultural Studies* 21, no. 1 (2012): 147–57.

Rueschemeyer, Dietrich, Evelyne Huber Stephens, and John D. Stephens. *Capitalist Development and Democracy.* Chicago: University of Chicago Press, 1992.

Runciman, David. *The Confidence Trap: A History of Democracy in Crisis from World War I to the Present.* Princeton: Princeton University Press, 2013.

Saad-Filho, A. "From COVID-19 to the End of Neoliberalism." *Critical Sociology* 46, nos. 4–5 (2020): 477–85.

Sabuktay, Aysegul. "Locating Extra-Legal Activities of the Modern State in Legal-Political Theory: Weber, Habermas, Kelsen, Schmitt, and Turk." *Crime, Law and Social Change* 51 (2015).

Salvage Collective. *The Tragedy of the Worker.* London: Verso, 2021.

Santner, Eric L. *The Royal Remains: The People's Two Bodies and the Endgames of Sovereignty.* Chicago: University of Chicago Press, 2011.

Sapir, Gideon. *The Israeli Constitution: From Evolution to Revolution.* Oxford: Oxford University Press, 2018.

Scarry, Elaine. *Thinking in an Emergency.* New York: Norton, 2012.

Scheidel, Arnim, Alevgul H. Sorman, Sofia Avila, Daniela Del Bene, and Jonas Ott. "Renewables Grabbing." In *Routledge Handbook of Global Land and Resource Grabbing*, edited by Andreas Neef, Chanrith Ngin, Tsegaye Moreda Shegro, and Sharlene Mollett. London: Routledge, 2023.

Schenck, Marcela, "Doblar hasta quebrar. Una mirada sobre los extremismos de derecha en América Latina," *Estado de situación de las democracias en América Latina y el Caribe*, edited by René Ramírez Gallegos. Buenos Aires: CLACSO, 2024.

Scheppele, Kim. "Symposium: Emergency Powers and the Constitution: Comment: Small Emergencies." *Georgia Law Review* 40 (2006).

Scheppele, Kim Lane. "The International Standardization of National Security Law." *Journal of National Security Law & Policy* 4 (2010). https://jnslp.com/wp-content/up loads/2010/12/06_Scheppele_vol4no2.pdf

Scheppele, Kim Lane. "Underreaction in a Time of Emergency: America as a Nearly Failed State." *VerfBlog*, April 4, 2020.

Scheuerman, William E. "States of Emergency." In *The Oxford Handbook of Carl Schmitt*, edited by Jens Meierhenrich and Oliver Simons. Oxford: Oxford University Press, 2014.

Schmitt, Carl. *Political Theology: Four Chapters on the Concept of Sovereignty.* Chicago: University of Chicago Press, 2005.

Schott, Richard. "Qualified Immunity: How It Protects Law Enforcement Officers." *FBI Law Enforcement Bulletin*, September 2012.

Schrader, Stuart. *Badges without Borders.* Berkeley: University of California Press, 2019.

Schulz-Forberg, Hagen. "Embedded Early Neoliberalism: Transnational Origins of the Agenda of Liberalism Reconsidered." In *Nine Lives of Neoliberalism*, edited by Dieter Plehwe, Quinn Slobodian, and Philip Mirowski. London: Verso, 2020.

Schwenk, Katya. "Wall Street Is Buying Up Entire Neighborhoods." *Jacobin*, May 15, 2024.

Searle, John. "Derechos humanos." *UNED: Revista de Derecho Político*, no. 86 (January–April 2013).

Searle, John. *Making the Social World*. Oxford: Oxford University Press, 2010.

Seri, Guillermina. "'The Dream of State Power': Accumulation, Coercion, Police." *Social Justice* 47, nos. 3–4 (2020).

Seri, Guillermina. *Seguridad: Crime, Police Power, and Democracy in Argentina*. London: Bloomsbury, 2012.

Seri, Guillermina, and Mary Rose Kubal. "How Policy Fields Are Born: The Rise of Democratic Security in Argentina." *Journal of Latin American Studies* 51, no. 1 (2019): 137–51.

Seri, Guillermina, and Jinee Lokaneeta. "Police as State: Governing Citizenship through Violence." In *Police Abuse in Contemporary Democracies*, edited by Michelle D. Bonner, Guillermina Seri, Mary Rose Kubal, and Michael Kempa. Basingstoke, UK: Palgrave Macmillan, 2018.

Servigne, Pablo, Raphaël Stevens, and Gauthier Chapelle. *Another End of the World Is Possible*. Cambridge: Polity Press, 2021.

Sharp, Gene. *From Dictatorship to Democracy: A Conceptual Framework for Liberation*. New York: New Press, 2012.

Sharp, Gene. *The Politics of Nonviolent Action*.

Sheeran, Scott P. "Reconceptualizing States of Emergency under International Human Rights Law: Theory, Legal Doctrine, and Politics." *Michigan Journal of International Law* 34, no. 3 (2013).

Sieyes, Emmanuel Joseph. "Reasoned Exposition of the Rights of Man and Citizen." In *Emmanuel Joseph Sieyès: The Essential Political Writings*, edited by Oliver W. Lembcke and Florian Weber. Leiden: Brill, 2014.

Sikkink, Kathryn. *The Justice Cascade: How Human Rights Prosecutions Are Changing World Politics*. New York: Norton, 2011.

Sikkink, Kathryn. "Latin American Countries as Norm Protagonists of the Idea of International Human Rights." *Global Governance* 20, no. 3 (2014): 389–404.

Sikkink, Kathryn. "Transnational Politics, International Relations Theory, and Human Rights." *PS: Political Science & Politics* 31, no. 3 (1998).

Sikkink, Kathryn, and Booth Walling. *International Human Rights Regimes*. Cambridge: Cambridge University Press, 1998.

Sitrin, Marina. "Definitions of Horizontalism and Autonomy." *NACLA Report on the Americas* 47, no. 3 (Fall 2014).

Sitrin, Marina. *Horizontalism: Voices of Popular Power in Argentina*. Edinburgh: AK Press, 2006.

Sly, Maria Jose Haro. "The Argentine Portion of the Soy Commodity Chain." *Palgrave Communications* 3, no. 1 (2017): 1–11.

Smith, Adam. *An Inquiry into the Nature and Causes of the Wealth of Nations: Volume 1*. Indianapolis: Liberty Classics, 1979.

Snyder, Edward C. "The Dirty Legal War: Human Rights and the Rule of Law in Chile, 1973–1995." *Tulsa Journal of Comparative and International Law* 2, no. 2 (1994). https://digitalcommons.law.utulsa.edu/tjcil/vol2/iss2/5

Sousa Santos, Boaventura de. *Derecho y emancipación*. Quito: Corte Constitucional para el Período de Transición, 2012.

Standing, Guy. "The Precariat." *Contexts* 13, no. 4 (2014).

Stedman Jones, Daniel. *Masters of the Universe: Hayek, Friedman, and the Birth of Neoliberal Politics*. Princeton: Princeton University Press, 2013.

Stokes, Susan C. *Mandates and Democracy: Neoliberalism by Surprise in Latin America*. Cambridge: Cambridge University Press, 2001.

Stritzel, Holger, and Juha A. Vuori. "Security." In *Concepts in World Politics*, edited by Felix Berenskoetter, 41–56. London: Sage, 2016.

Sutton, Barbara. *Bulletproof Fashion: Security, Emotions, and the Fortress Body*. London: Routledge, 2023.

Svampa, Maristella. "El 'Consenso de los Commodities' y lenguajes de valoración en América Latina." *Nueva Sociedad* 244 (2013).

Tanguay-Renaud, François. "The Intelligibility of Extra-Legal State Action: A General Lesson for Debates on Public Emergencies and Legality." *Osgoode CLPE Research Paper* 47, no. 6 (2010).

Tarrow, Sidney. "Charles Tilly and the Practice of Contentious Politics." *Social Movement Studies* 7, no. 3.

Taylor, Keeanga-Yamahtta. *From #BlackLivesMatter to Black Liberation*. Chicago: Haymarket Books, 2016.

Taylor, Marcus. "An Historical-Materialist Critique of Neoliberalism in Chile." *Historical Materialism* 10, no. 2 (2002): 45–75.

Thucydides. *The Peloponnesian War*. Oxford: Oxford University Press, 2009.

Tilly, Charles. *Regimes and Repertoires*. Chicago: University of Chicago Press, 2006.

Tilly, Charles, and Sidney Tarrow. *Contentious Politics*. Oxford: Oxford University Press, 2015.

Toles O'Laughlin, Tamara. "The Fight to Stop the Climate Crisis Is Local." *Common Dreams*, October 2, 2019.

Torbisco Casals, Neus. "Covid-19 and States of Emergency." *Global Challenges*, June 2020.

Tosa, Hiroyuki. "Anarchical Governance: Neoliberal Governmentality in Resonance with the State of Exception." *International Political Sociology* 3 (2009).

Tufekci, Zeynep. *Twitter and Tear Gas*. New Haven: Yale University Press, 2017.

Ucelli, Juliet. "Janus and My Ode to Capital." *Against the Current*, no. 196 (September–October 2018).

Valcárcel, Amaya, and Vera Samudio. "Colombia: Durable Solutions for the Forcibly Displaced." *Forced Migration Review* 56 (2017): 28–29. www.fmreview.org/

Valdés, Pablo Cuevas, and Teresa Rojas Martini. "The Neoliberal Chilean Process Four Decades after the Coup." *Social Justice* 40, no. 4 (2013): 25–37.

Valdivia, Gabriela. "The Sacrificial Zones of 'Progressive' Extraction in Andean Latin America." *Latin American Research Review* 50, no. 3 (2015): 245–53.

Valguarnera, Filippo. "Legal Ideology and the Commons: Why Are Jurists Falling Behind?" *Philosophy and Society* 29, no. 2 (2018).

Van Dijk, Teun. "Discourse and Manipulation." *Discourse & Society* 17, no. 3 (2006): .

Vásquez Hurtado, David, Carlos Mejía Suárez, and Carlos Gardeazabal Bravo. "Politics in the Streets: Colombian People's Resistance to the State of Exception." *Critical Legal Thinking*, September 13, 2022.

Viroli, Maurizio. *The Liberty of Servants: Berlusconi's Italy*. Princeton: Princeton University Press, 2012.

Viroli, Maurizio. "The Origin and the Meaning of the Reason of State." In *History of Concepts: Comparative Perspectives*, edited by Iain Hampsher-Monk, Karin Tilmans, and Frank van Vree. Amsterdam: Amsterdam University Press, 1998.

Vitale, Alex S. *The End of Policing*. London: Verso, 2017.

Waever, Ole. "Securitization and Desecuritization." In *On Security*, edited by Ronnie Lipschutz. New York: Columbia University Press, 1985.

Wainwright, Joel, and Geoff Mann. *Climate Leviathan: A Political Theory of Our Planetary Future*. London: Verso, 2020.

Waldstein, David. "In Chile's National Stadium, Dark Past Shadows Copa América Matches." *New York Times*, June 17, 2015.

Walker, Greg. "Henry VIII and the Invention of the Royal Courts." *History Today*, February 1997.

Weinberg, Bill. "Bolivia's New Water Wars." *NACLA Report on the Americas* 43, no. 5 (2016): 19–24.

Wenar, Leif. "Rights." In *The Stanford Encyclopedia of Philosophy*, edited by Edward N. Zalta. 2020.

Weyland, Kurt. "Populism in the Age of Neoliberalism." In *Populism in Latin America*, edited by Michael L. Coniff. Tuscaloosa: University of Alabama Press, 2012.

Whyte, Jessica. "Is Revolution Desirable? Michel Foucault on Revolution, Neoliberalism and Rights." In *Re-reading Foucault: On Law, Power and Rights*, edited by Ben Golder, 207–28. Oxford: Oxford University Press, 2013.

Whyte, Jessica. *The Morals of the Market: Human Rights and the Rise of Neoliberalism*. London: Verso, 2019.

Wilde, Matt. "Contested Spaces: The Communal Councils and Participatory Democracy in Chávez's Venezuela." *Latin American Perspectives* 44, no. 1 (2017).

Williamson, John. "What Washington Means by Policy Reform." In *Latin American Readjustment: How Much Has Happened*, edited by John Williamson. Washington, DC: Institute for International Economics, 1989.

Wilson, James Q. "Dilemmas of Police Administration." *Public Administration Review* (September–October 1968).

Winn, Peter. *Victims of the Chilean Miracle: Workers and Neoliberalism in the Pinochet Era, 1973–2002*. Durham: Duke University Press, 2004.

Wolin, Sheldon. *Politics and Vision*. Princeton: Princeton University Press, 1960.

World Bank. "Economic Growth in the 1990s: Learning from a Decade of Reform." *Journal of Economic Literature* 44 (December 2006).

Wright, Claire. *Emergency Politics in the Third Wave of Democracy*. Lanham, MD: Lexington Books, 2015.

Wright, Claire. "Going beyond the Roman Dictator: A Comprehensive Approach to Emergency Rule, with Evidence from Latin America." *Democratization* 19, no. 4 (2011): 713–34.

Wright, Susan, Oren Gross, and Fionnuala Ní Aoláin. *Emergency Politics in the Third Wave of Democracy*. Cambridge: Cambridge University Press, 2006.

Yllanes Ramos, Fernando. "The Social Rights Enshrined in the Mexican Constitution of 1917." *International Labour Review* 96, no. 6 (1967): 590–608.

Zamora, Daniel. Introduction to *Foucault and Neoliberalism*, edited by Daniel Zamora and Michael C. Behrent. Cambridge: Polity, 2016.

Zuboff, Shoshana. *The Age of Surveillance Capitalism*. New York: Public Affairs, 2019.

Index

abandonment, 7, 65, 106, 121, 122, 166

abuses, xi, xii, 9–10, 12, 35–36, 44; under emergencies, 47, 50; seeking redress, 30; state, xii, 7, 9–10, 12, 30, 35, 36, 41, 88, 120, 121, 127, 134, 137, 188

Abu Ghraib, 108

acclamation, 100, 115

American Civil Liberties Union (ACLU), 115

African American, 8, 77, 136–37

Agamben, Giorgio: acclamation, 100; anomie, 63; appearance, 84; bare life, 30, 65, 166; biopolitical hierarchies, 30; camps, 60; destituent power, 150, 168; detainees, 59; emergency, 36, 62; exception, 47, 58; glorification, 75, 85; inclusive exclusion, 65; police, 75; rights, 66, 167; security, 68–69, 72, 93; spectacle, 95, 98; sovereign power, 166; unalienable rights, 160

algorithms, 96–97, 101, 113–14, 185

Allende, Salvador, 1

"America First," 82

Amnesty International, 8, 43, 128, 150, 171

anti-immigration campaigns, 57

Antifa, 112

antiterrorist laws, 43, 60, 148–49

arcana imperii, 102

Arendt, Hannah: authority, 83; council system, 150; Isonomia, 157; political action, 117, 141; reason of state, 18, 39; rights of man, 165; rule of law, 178

Argentina: 2001 protests, 118; antiterrorist legislation, 148; camps, 47; environmental conflicts, 135; failed neoliberal experiment, 129; killings by police, 77; land and environmental defenders, 148–49; Milei, 189; military dictatorship, xi, 6, 47, 119, 171; Operation Condor, 49; protests, 125, 149; state of emergency, 119; neoliberal laboratory, 192

arrests, 7, 25, 78, 136, 145, 148

artificial intelligence (AI), 37, 70, 78, 95, 100, 113, 196

austerity, 5, 6–7, 24, 25, 28–30, 35–36, 43, 121, 128, 132, 165, 171, 192–93, 199, 201

automation, 70, 98, 114–15, 147

authoritarian, 5, 8, 9, 21, 36, 45, 68, 116, 191, 196, 201

autocratization, 8, 36

bare life, 30, 65, 166

Benjamin, Walter, 116, 117

Berlusconi, Silvio, 98–100

big data, 101

biomarkers, 70

Black Lives Matter, 37, 50, 136–37, 140

Bolivia: environmental conflicts, 135, 139; Operation Condor, 49; protests, 120, 129, 134, 152; animal and environmental rights, 187; shock therapy, 25; state of emergency, 28; suma qamaña, 162; "water wars," 28

borderless threats, 57

Botero, Giovanni, 14, 15, 17, 84

Brazil: military dictatorship, 4; environmental conflicts, 135; Operation Condor, 49; shock therapy, 25